PLANTS, ANIMALS, PEOPLE, ALIENS

PLANTS, ANIMALS, PEOPLE, ALIENS

An Aristotelian-Thomist Perspective on Life in the Universe

MARIE I. GEORGE

The Catholic University of America Press
Washington, D.C.

The paper used in this publication meets the minimum requirements of American National Standards for Information Science—Permanence of Paper for Printed Library Materials, ANSI Z39.48-1992.

Cataloging-in-Publication Data is available from the Library of Congress

ISBN: 978-0-8132-3956-0
eISBN: 978-0-8132-3957-6

Text set in Minion Pro and Bodoni URW
Book design by Burt&Burt

For Warren Murray

Mentor of many
an Aristotelian-Thomist

Contents

Part III: The Human Animal: Language

Part IV: The Differnce Between Plants and Animals

Part V: Intelligent Life Beyond Earth

Acknowledgements

I would like to first thank my parents, Breda and Richard George, who afforded me numerous opportunities to learn about nature, including visits to tide pools, botanical gardens, and science museums, plus attendance at summer classes at the zoo. My father was also the first person to introduce me to philosophy.

I also would like to express my gratitude to my teachers, beginning with my tutors at Thomas Aquinas College, and especially my senior thesis director, the late Marcus Berquist, who patiently guided me through a thesis on Aristotle's definition of sensation. I would next like to thank my teachers at Université Laval: Warren Murray, Yvan Pelletier, and Louis Brunet. Warren Murray has provided me with numerous helpful suggestions and criticisms over the years. Lastly, I would like to thank my biology professors at Queen's College, especially the late Paul Mundinger (animal behavior), Timothy Short (plant physiology), Jon Sperling (botany), and Andrew Greller (botany).

I would like to thank the biologists who so kindly shared their thoughts and their research: Kim Bard, Daniel J. Povinelli, and Jennifer Vonk.

I would like to thank Carol Day (Thomas Aquinas College) for reading over large sections of the manuscript, Pierre-Luc Boudreault (Thomas Aquinas College) for his comments on the appendix on substance, Steven Jensen (University of St. Thomas, Houston) for explaining to me what "immanent activity" means, and Christopher Decaen (Thomas Aquinas College) for his insights and for matching my sense of wonder in the many discussions we've had. I would also like to thank the anonymous reviewers for their extensive, helpful feedback.

I am grateful to St. John's University (Queens, NY) for providing me with a research leave to work on this volume.

Lastly, I am grateful for the permission to reproduce the following essays in whole or in part. "The Biologist's Need for Philosophy as Seen Through a Comparison of Aristotle's Views on Living Things with Those of Modern Biologists," chapter 7 in *Science and Faith Within Reason*, ed. Jaume Navarro (Ashgate, 2011), 125–44; "Neuroscience and the Human Soul," *The Aquinas Review* 23 (2019–20): 123–52; "Thomas Aquinas Meets Nim Chimpsky: On the Debate about Human Nature and the Nature of Other Animals," *The Aquinas Review* 10 (2003): 1–50; "Humans and Apes: On Whether Language Usage, Knowledge of Others' Beliefs, and Knowledge of Others' Emotions Indicate That They Differ When It Comes to Rationality," in *Reading the Cosmos: Nature, Science, and Wisdom*, ed. Giuseppe Butera (American Maritain Association Press, distributed by The Catholic University of America Press, 2012), 163–91; "Does Might Make Right in the Animal Kingdom, or Do Some Animals Act on Moral Grounds," in *Facts are Stubborn Things: Thomistic Perspectives in the Philosophies of Nature and Science*, ed. Matthew K. Minerd (American Maritain Association Press, 2021), 199–224; "Does Knowing What Things Are Require Language (As a System of Physical or Imaginable Signs)?," *American Catholic Philosophical Quarterly* 95, no. 1 (2021): 357–78; "On the Meaning of 'Immanent Activity' According to Aquinas," *The Thomist* 78, no. 3 (2014): 537–55; "A Defense of the Distinction between Plants and Animals," *Proceedings of the American Catholic Philosophical Association* 93 (2019): 349–66; "A Defense of the Distinction Between Plants and Animals," *The Aquinas Review* 26, no. 2 (2023): 69–108; "Aquinas on Intelligent Extra-Terrestrial Life," *The Thomist* 65, no. 2 (2001): 239–58; "ET Meets Jesus Christ: A Hostile Encounter between Science and Religion?," *Logos* 10, no. 2 (2007): 69–94; and "Would St. Thomas Aquinas Baptize an Extraterrestrial?, Revisited," *New Blackfriars* 99, no. 1082 (2019): 1–16.

Abbreviations

De Pot.	*Quaestiones Disputatae de Potentia*
De Sensu	*In Aristotelis Libros: De Sensu et Sensato Commentarium*
De Spir. Creat.	*Quaestio Disputata de Spiritualibus Creaturis*
De Vert.	*Quaestiones Disputatae de Virtutibus*
De Verit.	*Quaestiones Disputatae de Veritate*
In DA	*In Aristotelis Librum De Anima Commentarium*
In Ethic.	*In Decem Libros Ethicorum Aristotelis ad Nicomachum Expositio*
In Meta.	*In Duodecim Libros Metaphysicorum Aristotelis Expositio*
Q. DA	*Quaestio Disputata de Anima*
SCG	*Summa contra Gentiles*
Sent.	*Scriptum Super Sententiis*
ST	*Summa Theologiae*

"We should approach our investigation into each of the animals unabashedly, as in each and every being of this kind there is nature and beauty."

—Aristotle, *Parts of Animals*

"God produces things for the sake of communicating his goodness to creatures, and through them to represent his goodness. And because it cannot be adequately represented by one creature, he produces many and diverse creatures, so that what is lacking in one for the purpose of representing divine goodness is filled up by others."

—Aquinas, *Summa Theologiae*

Introduction

The past few decades have seen a resurgence in scholarly and popular interest in the Aristotelian-Thomistic philosophical tradition across a range of topics, both theological and philosophical. Contrary to the perception of many scientists and even philosophers of science, who think of Aristotelian natural philosophy as something that has been replaced by modern physics, the Aristotelian-Thomistic (AT) revival has had much to say about natural things, including living things.[1] A neo-Aristotelian viewpoint does not stand in simple opposition to modern biology, as a remnant of an older worldview, but rather provides a philosophical framework through which we can make sense of the data furnished by modern studies of living things. Aristotelian-Thomism, by adding Aristotle's insights to those of the thinker who is arguably the best commentator on Aristotle, namely, the medieval philosopher and theologian, Thomas Aquinas, provides an even wider view of the phenomena in question. Contrary to those who would simplistically view science as eliminating the need for philosophy or theology, this book aims to demonstrate the perennial fruitfulness of the AT approach.

This book, which is a collection of essays, is not a systematic treatise covering all of the fundamental questions concerning the nature of living things. Nor is the book a substitute for careful study of the particular works of Aristotle and Aquinas that bear on living things. Both kinds of studies can be found in other books. What this book uniquely offers are three things. First, it addresses fascinating questions about living things that have received relatively little attention by AT authors, such as whether animals know whether other animals are happy or sad and whether plants sense, and it

1 Nancey Murphy is one among many who maintain that the Thomistic understanding of the soul has been undermined by modern physics. See Warren S. Brown, Nancey Murphy, and H. Newton Malony, eds., *Whatever Happened to the Soul?* (Fortress, 1998), 31: "The rejection of hylomorphism represented by the development of modern physics meant the rejection of animal and plant souls, understood as the substantial forms of their bodies."

treats subjects on which the existing AT literature appears to need correction, such as with respect to the nature of immanent activity.

Secondly, the book demonstrates the vitality of AT thought by its engagement with contemporary science. It defends key AT tenets in the face of questions raised by scientific findings, for example, by providing arguments against the view that the performance of certain animals on relational match-to-sample tasks shows that they have abstract knowledge of what a relation is. It also strives to show how AT distinctions drawn from common experience can shed light on scientific research, including on animal language studies and theory of mind experiments. While the book does not attempt to prove that its answers are superior to what is found in other schools of thought in contemporary philosophy of biology (which are largely left aside),[2] it does endeavor to show that the AT tradition has resources for articulating solutions worthy of consideration. And it certainly aims to show the superiority of the AT tradition to a popular "scientism" that would dismiss out of hand philosophical questions such as the nature of the soul.

Lastly, in its final section, the book offers some original ideas on questions that pertain to the philosophy of science and religion, namely: What is the likelihood that intelligent extraterrestrials exist? And would their existence call Christian belief into question? Unlike other parts of the book, which address questions solely from the point of view of reason, this part incorporates arguments drawn from the Christian faith, while also advancing some philosophical and scientific arguments.

A word now about the general approach to questions concerning living things that is employed in this volume. At the basis of this approach is a certain understanding of the relationship between philosophy and science. Authentic philosophy is based on common experience, that is, experience that is commonly shared by all human adults with intact mental faculties and bears on the common or general features of reality. An example of something known from common experience is "some things move." Everyone knows this because at least a part of oneself has to move if one is alive. Motion is a general feature of all natural things, in contrast to specific motions, such as

2 Some of these schools include emergentism, new biological mechanism, or process philosophy of biology. I do not often address adherents of these schools in these pages, although, of course, I hope any readers familiar with their tenets can find some appreciation for the AT insights included herein.

rusting or moving in elliptical orbits, which only belong to certain natural things.

Science, on the other hand, is based on experience that only some people have, as it is gained either by doing controlled experiments or by making systematic observations, such as Jane Goodall's observations of chimpanzees in the wild. It bears on detail, such as how fast objects move in free fall or how chimpanzees locomote.

Knowledge gained through more specific experience does not supersede the knowledge gained through more general experience. For example, the discovery via scientific observation of how chimpanzees move does not replace the general knowledge that some animals move. In addition, what is known through common experience is more certain than what is known through scientific observation because it bears on what is more general. An observer of chimpanzee locomotion might make a mistake about it due to generalizing from too small a sample, but it is impossible to be mistaken about whether some animals are able to move from place to place.

The problem with common experience, however, is that although the knowledge it yields is certain, it is also vague. No one doubts that motion exists, but it is not easy to know exactly what it is. Answering questions of this sort generally requires considerations that are rather abstract. Therein lies one of the main difficulties that philosophers experience in getting answers.

Science faces a different challenge in getting answers, rooted in the different kind of experience it starts from. Again, the experience that science starts from bears on detail, something about which it is easier to make a mistake than about generalities. This is partly why science needs to make use of the "educated guess," the hypothesis. The hypothetico-deductive method, however, suffers from an inherent logical weakness: if a hypothesis is true, then the consequences deduced from it, for example x, y, and z, should occur. But if x, y, and z do in fact occur (and the experiments in question are replicated), that does not prove that the hypothesis is true. This is why science is said to be "always subject to revision," at least to the extent that it utilizes this method, a reality illustrated by Newtonian physics being superseded by general relativity. Philosophy, by contrast, proceeds for the most part by way of categorical syllogisms.

The differences between philosophy and science outlined above lead to the conclusion that philosophy, and especially natural philosophy, provides both a framework and a complement to science. It provides a framework, as it treats more general questions concerning natural things, while science treats more detailed questions that fall under those general questions. Natural philosophy thus can keep science from going astray, as is the case, for example, when claims are made that neuroscience has shown that there is no such thing as the soul.

Science, on the other hand, can at times prevent philosophy from going astray, as happens when philosophers draw conclusions that exceed what can be known through common experience. Aristotle's conviction that there were only four elements—earth, air, fire, and water—is an example of venturing beyond what common experience can show us.

Philosophy treats what is more universal and science what is less universal, but the more universal and the less universal are not separated by a sharp line but are relative to one another. The more universal descends to the more particular by gradations (e.g., being, living being, animal, insect, ant, fire ant, *Solenopsis invicta*). And so, it is not surprising that errors are made as to the kind of experience required to answer a given question, and for this reason philosophy and science can serve as correctives to one another.

Natural philosophy is a complement to science, and science to philosophy, insofar as they treat the same things but at different levels of generality. For example, natural philosophy will examine the various life activities of organisms in a very general way, understanding nutrition as an activity by which the organism transforms food into its very substance, whereas science will examine the precise composition of the food and exactly how it is broken down and reconstituted as parts of the organism. Scientists often engage in philosophical reflections in cases where such are prerequisite to devising experiments appropriate for discovering the detailed knowledge that the scientists seek. For example, some of the scientists who research theory of mind in animals seek to define mind and theory of mind before devising experiments to determine whether specific animals have specific theory of mind capabilities.

In principle, then, there should be a harmonious relationship between natural philosophy and science, as the two share a common goal, namely, understanding natural things, even though the two disciplines differ in their methodology, as is required by the generality or specificity with which they consider them. Nowadays, as I mentioned at the outset, AT natural philosophy and science are too often pitted against each other, not only by scientists but even at times by AT natural philosophers. As we will see, however, more often than not, it is not science as such, but philosophical interpretations of scientific findings that generate conflict with the perennial philosophy.

The book is divided into five sections. The first section is entitled: "Philosophy as a Framework for and Complement to Biology." In the opening chapter, I show how Aristotelian-Thomistic thought can aid and complement the study of biology, doing so by comparing Aristotle's approach to living things with that of modern biologists. In the second chapter, I defend the AT understanding of the human soul in the face of objections drawn from neuroscience. In the third chapter, I consider whether the Aristotelian division of living things at the most universal level into plants, animals, and human beings is the most natural division or whether contemporary biology offers a more natural one. In the sections that follow, I examine the subdivisions of living things—plant, animal, and human being—in more detail.

The second section is devoted to investigating similarities and differences between human and nonhuman animals, especially in response to the claim that there is no essential difference between the two. I consider whether animals have language, whether they know what others know and how others feel, and whether they are moral agents.

Having argued in the second section that the only earthly beings that possess language are human beings, in the third section, I advance the understanding of what it means to be human by addressing a specific question about the nature of language, namely, whether thought is prior to language or language to thought.

In the fourth section, I consider the nature of plants. The main question I address is whether plants are animals. That is, I consider the view that all living things, oaks and daisies included, are sentient, in which case they would fall in the category "animal." Some may be surprised to learn that a number of scientists maintain that plants sense. It is quite fascinating to examine this claim.

In the fifth and final section, I consider life beyond earth, specifically the possibility of intelligent life on other planets. I also consider whether the discovery of such life forms would be prejudicial to Christian beliefs, such as belief in the Incarnation and Redemption. While the first two chapters in this section offer philosophical and scientific arguments alongside theological ones, the final chapter, on whether Aquinas would baptize an extraterrestrial, is entirely theological.

There are of course many major questions concerning living things that I do not address in this volume. Some of the more important ones are whether some unicellular organisms are sentient, what is the relationship between systems theory and the soul, how are we to understand the virtual presence of elements in living things, and in what sense is an animal a self. Then there are also certain prerequisite philosophical notions that I do not examine, probably the most important of which is the nature of substance.[3] Nevertheless, I offer this set of essays to my readers confident that there is plenty of "substance" to the topics and arguments contained therein. If the reader comes away not fully satisfied but eager for more engagement with the AT tradition and modern science, I will be pleased with that result.

3 The appendix offers a brief explanation of substance. Two other important concepts that are not explained are potency and act. I refer the reader to Mariusz Tabaczek, *Emergence: Towards a New Metaphysics and Philosophy of Science* (Notre Dame University Press, 2019), 275–77. See also Edward Feser, *Scholastic Metaphysics*: A Contemporary Introduction (Editiones Scholasticae, 2014), 38–41.

PART I

PHILOSOPHY AS A FRAMEWORK FOR AND COMPLEMENT TO BIOLOGY

1

The Biologist's Need for Philosophy as Seen Through a Comparison of Aristotle's Views on Living Things with Those of Modern Biologists

Introduction

While there are some differences in the species we have today and those extant in Aristotle's day, what it is to be a living thing has not changed. Yet the way the Father of Biology spoke about living things and the way that modern day biologists do are widely different. Aristotle opens his treatise *On the Soul* by asserting that the soul is something that is known with the greatest certitude, and that investigating it "seems likely to make a substantial contribution to the whole body of truth, and particularly to the study of nature; for the soul is in a sense the principle of animal life."[1] In sharp contrast is Richard Dawkins's gleeful affirmation

1 Aristotle, *On the Soul*, in *The Basic Works of Aristotle*, ed. Richard McKeon, trans. J. A. Smith (Random House, 1968), 402a1–7.

that science either has "killed the soul or is in the process of doing so."[2] Biology textbooks generally do not display the same hostile attitude toward the notion "soul;" they typically do not even mention it. Whether hostile or indifferent to the notion, biologists today certainly do not regard an inquiry into the soul as "making a substantial contribution" to understanding the biosphere.

Aristotle distinguished three main life forms (plants, animals, humans) and four grades of life (animals being of two sorts, immobile and mobile). He saw the grades of life to be arranged in a hierarchy of perfection, with humans being the superior life form.[3] Biologists nowadays often tell us to the contrary that no type of living thing is better than another. Each species has its own set of adaptations to its local environment allowing it to survive, and that is all.[4] Many biologists are especially eager to deny that humans belong in a group by themselves. For example, Steven Jay Gould insists:

> The only honest alternative is to admit the strict continuity in kind between ourselves and chimpanzees. And what do we lose thereby? Only an antiquated concept of soul to gain a more humble, even exalting vision of our oneness with nature.[5]

And Aristotle and modern biologists disagree on many other issues as well, for example, on questions regarding classification. Such radical differences in viewpoints on such fundamental questions about living things make us wonder whether the two groups are talking about the same sort of being. Has one or have both overlooked basic features of living things? Has the method that either has adopted blinded them to seeing living things for what they are? Are there ideological biases that cause them to overlook or explain away certain features of organisms?

In this chapter I will investigate the modern scientific understanding of what a living thing is, and the effect this understanding has on how biologists nowadays conduct research. I will do the former primarily by contrasting the modern biologists' understanding of living things with that of Aristotle. The

2 Richard Dawkins and Steven Pinker, "Is Science Killing the Soul?" (Guardian–Dillons Debate, February 10, 1999), www.edge.org/documents/archive/edge53.html, 6.

3 See Aristotle, *Politics*, bk. 1, chap. 8.

4 See, for example, the popular college-level biology textbook, William K. Purves, et al., *Life: The Science of Biology* (Sinauer, 1998), 6.

5 Stephen Jay Gould, *Ever Since Darwin: Reflections in Natural History* (Norton, 1977), 50.

principal points of comparison will concern their respective views on what it means to be alive; whether the notion of soul is expendable; whether purpose or finality is to be found in the living realm; whether there is hierarchy in the biosphere; and whether human beings are a life form differing in kind from other animals. I will then also consider what effect modern biologists' understanding of living things has on the way they do research. In principle, a person's general understanding of what a thing is should guide that person in choosing a method that will allow a deeper understanding of that thing; a mistaken understanding of one's subject matter can result in the adoption of inappropriate methods of study, whereas a correct understanding contributes greatly toward the development of fruitful methodologies.[6] Throughout, I will make a case that biology suffers when biologists lack an educational acquaintance with certain philosophical investigations concerning life, nature, reality as a whole, and how we know things.

Does Considering Aristotle's Concept of the Soul Add Anything to Our Understanding of Living Things?

Aristotle begins his treatise on the soul fully confident that there is such a thing, and indeed asserts that the study thereof is characterized by remarkable certitude.[7] People cannot help noticing that they are not just bodies, but that they have feelings and thoughts as well as control over certain parts of their bodies. Moreover, as Aristotle later notes, living things in general are plainly different from nonliving ones in that they move on their own, and there must be some cause for the difference. People have traditionally called the cause of the various life activities (growing, seeing, thinking, etc.) "the soul." So Aristotle calls it that too, while being perfectly aware that people's understanding of what exactly the soul is differs, and that there is a need to work out a more accurate understanding of what it is—something that he

6 Aristotle talks about how a misunderstanding as to the nature of one's subject matter leads to the use of incorrect methodology in the *Nicomachean Ethics*. He points out that determining the ultimate good of human beings is not something that can be determined with the same precision as the conclusions of mathematics are determined, due to the inherent variability of the lives of human individuals. To seek mathematical precision in ethics would be a flawed approach, as it would not suit the subject matter. See *Nicomachean Ethics*, bk. 1, chap. 3, 1094b12–28.

7 See Aristotle, *On the Soul*, 402a1–4.

regards as a formidable task.[8] Although he is plainly familiar with some of the various religious conceptions of the soul, he does not assume that any of them are true.[9]

Aristotle investigates the nature of the soul by considering the "two characteristic marks [that] have above all others been recognized as distinguishing that which has soul in it from that which has not—movement and sensation."[10] The dog sees someone putting food in its dish and walks over to get some. It's alive. It is plain from what Aristotle says later on that by movement he means "self-motion," for nonliving natural things plainly move, but not in any sense on their own.

Biologists typically regard living things as machines, rather than as beings that are ensouled.[11] Why is this so? Doubtlessly, there is the historical influence of Descartes who posited that humans have a spiritual soul, but that plants and animals are not essentially different than machines, but simply have smaller parts (they are made up of microscopic cells). This neat, if simplistic, division leaves it to science to experiment on and measure different features of the body, and to religion to deal with the spiritual. Descartes's division was also, at least in part, motivated by the discovery of apparent inadequacies in Aristotle's notion of living things moving on their own. Many life activities, such as the circulation of the blood, were yielding in Descartes's day to a mechanistic form of explanation. Accordingly, Descartes would say that "it is no less natural for a clock constructed with this or that set of wheels to tell the time than it is for a tree which was grown from this or that seed to produce the appropriate fruit."[12]

8 See *On the Soul*, 402a10–28.

9 See *On the Soul*, 407b22 and 410b28.

10 *On the Soul*, 403b23–27. Here Aristotle opposes motion and sensation. By motion he is referring to whole or part of the living thing changing place on its own; an example of the latter is the movement of our diaphragm when we breathe. Self-motion can also be understood in a broader sense, one that includes sensation; see chapter 3.

11 See Yoshimi Kowade, "On the Nature and Subjectivity of Living Things," *Biosemiotics* 2 (April 29, 2009): 205: "The perennial question, 'what is life?,' now has an answer, accepted widely by most molecular biologists as well as many others, which asserts that living things are machines, each superbly constructed as an assembly of molecular machines. This view is considered to be supported by contemporary biology, which has been highly successful both in basic research and practical applications, especially due to the power of molecular biology."

12 *Principles of Philosophy*, in *Descartes: Selected Philosophical Writings by René Descartes*, ed. John Cottingham, Robert Stoothoff, and Dugald Murdoch (Cambridge University Press, 1988), 1:209 (at VIIIa, 326).

Without doubt, trying to understand the different activities of living things in terms of the material parts that make these activities possible has been a wildly successful project; this approach has also led to the understanding of many human diseases and has facilitated the development of treatments for them. Certainly, these discoveries were not made by reflecting on the nature of the soul. It is one thing, though, to acknowledge that the reductionist method has furthered our understanding of the life processes of living things; it is another to assume that the success of this method has answered this question: Are living things essentially machines or are there fundamental differences between the two?

Does Aristotle have an answer to the scientist who argues that nutrition in plants is no more a self-motion than the motions executed by machines are? An electric clock needs to be plugged in and its hands set in order for it to henceforth tell the correct time on its own. Similarly, photosynthesis requires that photons strike the chlorophyll pigments that are found in the two photosystems in order for the plant to make sugar from H_2O and CO_2. Both machine and plant need to be started up by an outside agent.

Photosynthesis is part of the greater process whereby the plant transforms materials other than itself into itself. Photosynthesis leads to the production of sugar, which provides both energy for building up new parts of the plant and in some cases a chemical skeleton that will be modified to form parts of the plant. Without photosynthesis the plant could not generate new cells. Machines, on the other hand, while sharing in common with plants the need to be started up, do not make new parts for themselves.

If somehow one could invent a machine that would make replacement parts for itself, there would still be the difference that a machine is not an "itself" in the sense of being a substance. Although Aristotle never explicitly contrasts living things with machines,[13] he faults his predecessors for crudely materialist propensities that overlook a fundamental point about living things, namely, that when a living thing dies, "none of its parts remains the same, except only in shape, just like the animals in the story that were turned into stone."[14] When a machine breaks down, it can no longer move in a way that allows it to perform its human-assigned function. When a living

13 Aristotle does in certain places talk about "automata," e.g., in *On the Generation of Animals*, 734b10 and 741b9.

14 Aristotle, *Parts of Animals*, trans. A. L. Peck and E. S. Forster (Harvard University Press, 1968), bk. 1, chap. 1, 641a21.

thing dies, it can no longer move in the ways it used to in view of preserving its life and reproducing. But in addition, when a living thing dies, not only do its parts cease to move in the said ways, but they also cease to be what they were. Granted at death not all organic parts instantaneously lose their ability to function, still without some special intervention such as transplanting them, they do so in a relatively short period of time. The broken machine's nonbroken parts are not affected in a like way.

When Aristotle speaks of nutrition and growth as self-motion, it would be a mistake to think that he was attributing to plants the kind of self-motion that characterizes a being that has free will, that is, one that has motions that are determined by itself and not by external or internal factors that it has no control over. While plant and machine both require being moved from the outside in order to then move on their own, again the difference between the two is that the plant is a substance, a unified whole. The machine is only one thing to the extent that we so arrange its parts to serve a purpose. The parts have no essential relation to one another. Thus, even if a machine could make itself new parts, these parts would be made by some motion or change other than a substantial change of some material into the machine's substance, because the machine is not one substance, that is, it is not a single thing; rather it is a collection of things.[15] We see that when a machine breaks it goes from being a collection of parts to a collection of parts with one or more broken or misadjusted parts, whereas when a living thing dies it goes from being one thing (one squirrel, one daisy) to many different things, different chemicals.

We see then that Aristotle's teachings about the soul start from general considerations about the nature of living things, namely, their self-motion and unity. Although a consideration of these things pertains properly to philosophy and requires more sustained investigation than has been engaged in so far, nevertheless it befits biologists to partake in this consideration, at least up to a point, because they should have some idea why their object of study falls in the category of "natural thing," that is, a thing that, unlike a machine, has an intrinsic principle of motion and rest. They should recognize that the whole-part relationship in organisms and in machines is very different. The

15 In order to fully understand the argument being made here one needs to understand what Aristotle means by "substance" and by "substantial change." The latter will be discussed in chapter 3 and the former is discussed in the appendix. See also Aristotle, *Metaphysics*, bks. 7 and 8 on substance, and *Physics*, 190b1–4 and 191a7–12 on substantial change.

whole machine is a collection of independently existing parts arranged in a certain manner, whereas the whole organism is one thing that has parts, parts that depend on the whole for their identity and existence.[16] The failure to engage in these philosophical considerations leads biologists to adopt the widespread view that "living things are machines."[17]

Notions of the Soul That Aristotle Rejects Are Often the Only Notions of Soul That Biologists Are Familiar With

The mistaken assimilation of living thing to machine is one reason why some biologists reject the notion of soul. Another reason is that often the only concepts of soul that they are familiar with are vitalist and Cartesian ones, both of which Aristotle rejects.

Vitalism takes two main forms. One would have the soul to be some subtle elemental substance or a force emanating from it, while the other coincides with the Cartesian position that would have it to be an immaterial thing that is added to a body. The version of vitalism in which living things contain some special gas or the like—ironically derived from the mechanistic conception of living things that modern biologists typically espouse and that Aristotle rejects—was proposed by quite a few ancient thinkers.[18] Aristotle refutes this notion using multiple arguments; for example, he points out that no element could account for living things moving in a variety of ways, since

16 In regard to the "new mechanism," developed by Carl Craver and others, see Tabaczek, *Emergence*, 29: "Arguing that components of biological mechanisms can be widely distributed and escape precise localization, and that their operations cannot be limited to the Cartesian machine-like push-pull dynamics, new mechanists seem to line up with the proponents of nonreductionism in scientific explanation. At the same time, however, they do not want to abandon a physicalist worldview, which seems to be dogma for all natural sciences." As we shall see, the attempt of the new mechanists to distance itself from the crude mechanism of Descartes fails because ultimately, it, like the mechanism of Descartes, bases itself on the notion that organisms are specific arrangements of separately existing interacting parts. See Carl F. Craver and William Bechtel, "Top-Down Causation Without Top-Down Causes," *Biology and Philosophy* 22 (2007): 548: "Mechanisms are organized collections of entities and activities." See also Tabaczek, *Emergence*, 30–31 for a critique of specific new mechanist theories.

17 Kowade, "On the Nature and Subjectivity of Living Things," 205.

18 See *On the Soul*, 405a8–28.

every element moves in a determinate way. A heavy element explains why an animal falls down, but not why it gets up.[19]

Aristotle also rejects the view that we nowadays associate with Descartes, namely, that the soul is an immaterial substance that is added to a physical substance, the body. For Aristotle, souls are not separate substances from the bodies they animate but relate to each other as form to matter. For this reason, he maintains that "we can wholly dismiss as unnecessary the question whether the soul and the body are one: it is as meaningless as to ask whether the wax and the shape given to it by the stamp are one, or generally the matter of a thing and that of which it is the matter."[20]

This does not mean, however, that Aristotle rejects in advance the possibility that some type of soul be separ*able* from the body.[21] (For a soul to be a separable form, it would have to be immaterial.)

The Cartesian view is roundly criticized by scientists on the grounds that if it were true that the mind (which Descartes often equates with soul) is a separate substance from the body, then it would not be the case that damage to the body would affect one's mental state. Aristotle's view is immune to this criticism. Aristotle regards thinking thoughts (i.e., considering universal concepts) to be one activity and imagining images another activity. However, he also maintains that thinking depends upon imagining and that imagining requires an organ (the brain or parts thereof).[22] Thus, Aristotle has no problem accounting for why brain damage, be it temporary or permanent, affects thinking.

Aristotle and Dawkins are then in agreement when it comes to rejecting the vitalist and Cartesian notions of soul. Where the two part company is on the question of whether some kind of soul is immaterial. Aristotle, unlike Dawkins, seriously entertains this possibility, and he regards the human soul with its capacity for abstract thought as plausibly being such.[23] Dawkins's proclivity for materialist explanations hinders him from objectively treating the question.

19 See *On the Soul*, 406b20–26.

20 *On the Soul*, 412b4–9.

21 *On the Soul*, 403a3–8.

22 See *On the Soul*, 432a3–14.

23 See *On the Soul*, 403a11 and 413a5.

Adopting materialism, which is a philosophical view, cannot be justified on the grounds that it is a prerequisite for doing science. To understand science's task to be the consideration of the material aspects of natural things does not require one to assume that everything about every type of living thing is material. The method one adopts does not determine what does or does not exist in reality. For example, if one uses a light telescope in order to detect bodies in space, this does not determine whether or not there are other bodies that exist in space that are undetectable by that method. Thus, embracing methodological reductionism in the pursuit of science does not entail a commitment to ontological reductionism. Such a commitment to materialism is simply an ideology, one that blinds the biologist to whatever nonscientific evidence there may be that some kind of living thing is composed of an immaterial soul and an organized body.

Modern biologists often think that in rejecting the notions of soul as some material or immaterial substance added to the body that no notion of soul worthy of consideration has been left standing. Yet Aristotle himself rejects the same notions but is proposing another that merits consideration, given that it avoids the mistakes associated with these other views. We will consider this view later on, namely, that the soul is the substantial form of the living body. Even if Aristotle's more precise account of soul is incorrect, biologists would obtain a better grasp of the sort of thing that a living thing is by engaging in the considerations that led up it. Biologists need to realize that there are aspects of living things, in particular their unity and self-motion, that can only be understood by reflecting on common experience rather than through the detailed experience gained by doing experiments. They should be aware that positing a soul, at least in the first instance, is no more than acknowledging that the self-motion and unity distinctive of living things requires a cause. They would also do well to follow Aristotle in remaining open-minded as to whether living things manifest activities that transcend matter.

The Soul and Consciousness

We have discussed above what modern biologists are liable to think about the soul as a principle of self-motion and their preference for understanding living things as machines. The second main note of a living thing is sense perception. Here biologists are somewhat more open to the notion of the soul.

When scientists speak about consciousness and other activities like it, they often draw back from reducing them simply to the material parts and interactions upon which these activities depend. Biologists typically place perception, consciousness, and emotion in the special category of "emergent properties."[24] Even Dawkins admits that science cannot currently explain consciousness,[25] and for this reason science has not as yet "killed the soul." However, not all scientists show Dawkins's reticence about rejecting the soul. For example, George Paxinos maintains: "As a neuroscientist and psychologist, I have no use for the soul. On the contrary, all functions attributable to this kind of soul can be explained by the workings of the brain."[26]

The question to ask regarding emergent properties is as follows: Are they simply collective properties or are they properties that are not fully explainable in terms of the material parts involved and their interactions? Many collective wholes manifest properties that go beyond what any individual part could do: A group can move a piece of furniture that an individual cannot; a bicycle can serve as a means of transportation while a pedal cannot; a lone individual cannot play football. However, the things that the collective whole can do that the individual parts or members cannot are able nonetheless to be traced back to the interaction of the parts. Some biologists favor the view that consciousness, emotion, etc. are collective properties: "Biologists could never discover the existence of human emotions by studying single nerve cells, even though they may be able to eventually explain those emotions in terms of interactions among many nerve cells."[27]

The optimism that an understanding of perception, consciousness, emotion, etc. will be reached in terms of understanding how many cells work together is ill founded. For example, if it were possible to present a deaf person with a complete biological account of all the parts involved in hearing

24 See Purves et al., *Life*, 14, "Each level of biological organization has properties, called emergent properties, that are not found at lower levels. For example, cells and multicellular organisms have processes and characteristics that are not shown by the molecules of which they are composed. . . . Emergent properties do not violate principles that operate at lower levels of organization. However, emergent properties usually cannot be detected or even suspected by studying the lower levels."

25 See Dawkins and Pinker, "Is Science Killing the Soul?," 7.

26 George Paxinos, "Why Psychology Lost Its Soul: Everything Comes from the Brain," The Conversation, September 22, 2016, https://theconversation.com/why-psychology-lost-its-soul-everything-comes-from-the-brain-54828.

27 Purves et al., *Life*, 14.

along with the way these parts interact when people hear, the deaf person would still not understand what hearing was. The closest one could get to conveying what hearing was to a deaf person would not be in the scientific terms of biology, but in terms of everyday experience. One could tell the person that just as seeing is awareness of colors and tasting is awareness of flavors, so too there is another form of awareness that bears on some other type of sensible quality.

Similarly, a description of the physical changes occurring in a person who feels fear, no matter how detailed, would not provide a complete account of fear.[28] Ordinarily we feel fear when we are aware of a future evil that is difficult to avoid. Although the feeling of fear is not independent of a certain bodily state, it cannot be fully explained in terms of that state. If we asked a person, "Why are you afraid?," and got as a response that the hormone epinephrine was acting upon her heart cells, etc., we would not be satisfied. Fear is ordinarily fear of something (just as sadness is sadness about something). It's not like growing taller. Any number of questions can be asked about fear that have no reference to physical factors, for example, Can fear itself be feared? Is having some deficiency a cause of fear? Emotion is not the same sort of thing as surface tension, which we can understand once we better understand water molecules.

As we will see in chapter 2, understanding the soul to be the substantial form of the body provides an explanation for emergent properties. Though Aristotle's concept of soul does not explain why specific parts and chemical substances allow for this sort of perception or emotion any more than the reductionist account does, it does, however, point to the need to investigate the psychic or mental aspects of perception and emotion, and not just their physical substrate. Aristotle says the true natural scientist is not going to understand anger solely as "a boiling of the blood or warm substance around the heart,"[29] but also as "returning pain for pain, or something like that."[30]

The failure to recognize that animal behavior involves more than the sort of physical changes found in nonliving things had a negative impact on how research on animals was carried out. Ethology, the study of animal

28 Here is another way of seeing that emotions are not reducible to the material factors involved when experiencing them: For a person who had never experienced sexual attraction, describing the physiological changes involved would not make the person know what it was.

29 *On the Soul*, 403a33.

30 *On the Soul*, 403a30.

behavior, was slow to develop because many of its early practitioners worked on the general assumption that animals were devoid of consciousness, emotion, or any sort of mental state. James Watson, one of the founders of behaviorism, insisted that all behavior was to be explained in terms of stimulus and response, and maintained that, "the behaviorist, who has been trained always as an experimentalist, holds . . . that belief in the existence of consciousness goes back to the ancient days of superstition and magic."[31]

Biology would have done better to have followed Aristotle in recognizing that animals possess mental abilities and what nowadays are more commonly called mental states. The first things Aristotle investigates in regard to animals are each of the external senses (sight, hearing, etc.); sense perception in general; and then consciousness, imagination, emotion, and so forth—all those properties of animals for which a mechanistic account is plainly incomplete.

It is not that Aristotle thinks that the material aspects of these life activities are unimportant. Indeed in his initial discussion of the different external senses, he speaks quite a bit about the physical causes involved, including the role of light in vision, the physical requirements for sound production, and the physiological requirements for an animal to have a voice.[32] However, instead of continuing in the direction of examining the material parts in more detail, which is the sort of thing that he does at length in treatises such as the *Parts of Animals*, his first priority is to examine those aspects of sensation that stem from living things having souls, for example, consciousness.[33]

Now one might argue that a biologist need not espouse the Aristotelian notion of soul to recognize that investigating the mental abilities of animals is an important part of coming to understand them. After all, Donald Griffin, author of *Animal Minds* and a major figure urging those studying animal behavior to break away from purely behaviorist approaches, had this to say about the soul:

> I will take it for granted that behavior and consciousness in both animals and men result entirely from events that occur in their central nervous systems. In other words, I will operate on the basis of emergent materialism . . . and assume that there are no immaterial, vitalistic,

31 James B. Watson, *Behaviorism* (W. W. Norton, 1970), 2.

32 See Aristotle, *On the Soul*, 418b4, 419b9–18, and 420b5–421a7.

33 See *Parts of Animals*, 641a28–33.

> or supernatural processes involved in the small fraction of human or animal brain events that result in conscious, subjective thoughts and feelings.[34]

It is hard to see how Griffin's emergent materialism is finally any different than crude reductionism. The emergent properties of animals and humans "result entirely from events that occur in their central nervous systems." They are collective properties at most. As argued above, this view does not do justice to life activities such as sense perception and emotion. So while it is possible for someone to deny the existence of the soul while acknowledging that animals have minds, the denial seems to bring with it its own problems.

Is there some other way that one could acknowledge the existence of minds and mental states while denying that souls exist? This is what some emergence theories, such as nonreductive physicalism, claim to do.[35] Nonreductive physicalists acknowledge that living things have properties that cannot be fully explained by physiology or physical causes in general. They maintain that while a lower level (e.g., the brain and its activities) is necessary for these properties to emerge, it is not sufficient to explain them.[36] At the same time, they hold that everything has a physical explanation, and for them a physical explanation is typically one that is stated in terms of

34 Donald R. Griffin, *Animal Minds* (University of Chicago Press, 1992), 5.

35 I do not intend to distinguish supervenience theories from nonreductive physicalist theories. I am interested in those of the former that overlap with the latter insofar as they maintain that supervenient properties are not causally reducible to the subvenient entities or properties that they supervene on.

36 See Nancey Murphy, "Physicalism Without Reductionism: Toward A Scientifically, Philosophically, and Theologically Sound Portrait of Human Nature," *Zygon* 34, no. 4 (January 2003): 561:

> If we take the hierarchy of levels to include the moral and the social (with its political, economic, and legal dimensions), we can see that a vast array of concepts will appear that most philosophers would agree is not logically reducible to neurobiological variables. These higher levels of reality are not in danger of causal reduction to the biological level. . . . One way of putting this is to say that there are *emergent levels* as we go from the neurobiological to the cognitive, to the interpersonal, to the political, economic, and legal, to the moral, and finally to the spiritual. Although all human behavior supervenes on the biological (genetic and neurobiological), little of it is reducible to biology.

efficient causality, the action of one thing on another causing some motion or change in that other.[37]

The fundamental problem with nonreductive views in regard to emergent properties is that they assume that living things are systems of interacting parts, neurons, molecules, or other things that have their own independent existence.[38] A being that is a collection of things can only have collective properties. As Michael Dodds, OP notes:

> To the extent that emergence denies to the whole any unity beyond the incidental arrangement of its parts, it fails to explain the being of the whole. And without some ground in the being of the whole, emergence can only affirm but not explain the activity that proceeds from the whole. So long as emergence remains unable to account for the being of the whole, its tendency will be to slip back into a kind of reductionism.[39]

If the whole is what simply results from the arrangement and interaction of its parts, the whole cannot have some activity that does not trace back to its parts and their interactions. As we have seen, activities such as seeing and feeling sad cannot be fully explained by interactions of body parts. This gives reason to consider Aristotle's more precise notion of soul

37 Murphy affirms that nonreductive physicalism is a research project with "the plan to explain physicalistically all of the operations once attributed to the mind or soul" in "Physicalism Without Reductionism," 563. On the propensity of nonreductive physicalists to resort to explanations in terms of efficient causality, see Tabaczek, *Emergence*, 76 and 179. Tabaczek's examination of emergence is deeper than mine to the extent that he examines at some length both the Aristotelian and modern understanding of causality.

38 See, for example, Murphy, "Physicalism Without Reductionism," 553: "During the modern period (beginning about 1600) a different understanding has gradually supplanted the Greek—that there exists not a hierarchy of beings but a hierarchy of *complex systems*." For a detailed Thomistic examination of a number of the different nonreductive theories of emergence, see Tabaczek, *Emergence*, chap. 1, "The Central Dogma of Emergence," and chap. 2, "Metaphysical Challenges for Emergence and Downward Causation."

39 Michael Dodds, "Top Down, Bottom Up or Inside Out? Retrieving Aristotelian Causality in Contemporary Science," June 25, 1997, Jacques Maritain Center, Thomistic Institute, https://www3.nd.edu/~afreddos/papers/dodds.htm. See David. J. Chalmers, *The Conscious Mind: In Search of a Fundamental Theory* (Oxford University Press, 1996), 121–22:

> Any account given in purely physical terms will suffer from the same problem. It will ultimately be given in terms of structural and dynamic properties of physical processes, and no matter how sophisticated such an account is, it will yield only more structure and dynamics. . . . The existence of consciousness will always be a further fact, relative to structural and dynamic facts, and so will always be unexplained by a physical account.

as an explanation, as it appeals to formal causality instead of to the efficient causality of separately existing parts upon one another, something we will examine in the next chapter.

The Biologist's Need for Natural Philosophy

Certainly, there are biologists who do not manifest Dawkinesque hostility toward the notion of soul, and who even think they have a soul; few of them, however, see their notion of soul as having anything to do with biology. Yet, as argued above, there are costs attached to dispensing with the notion of soul: First, one either ends up denying the unity and self-motion of organisms or that there must be a cause for these unique properties; secondly, one either ends up denying that consciousness and emotion are not fully explicable by interacting material parts or one ends up proposing causes that cannot adequately account for them. Perhaps the positions Aristotle ultimately adopts on these matters are incorrect. (We will examine them further in chapter 2.) Still, biologists who have not considered the fundamental questions concerning the nature of life that Aristotle examines in determining what the soul is are deficient in their understanding of life.[40] A biologist should be able to articulate the differences between organisms and machines that Aristotle speaks of.[41] In addition, the biologist as biologist would benefit from

40 Biologist Carl R. Woese maintains that biology in recent years has been dominated by a molecular view of the organism and that there is a need to change this; see Woese, "A New Biology for a New Century," *Microbiology and Molecular Biology Reviews* 68, no. 2 (June 2004): 176:

> CHANGING THE OVERVIEW
> Let's stop looking at the organism purely as a molecular machine. The machine metaphor certainly provides insights, but these come at the price of overlooking much of what biology is. Machines are not made of parts that continually turn over, renew. The organism is. Machines are stable and accurate because they are designed and built to be so. The stability of an organism lies in resilience, the homeostatic capacity to reestablish itself. While a machine is a mere collection of parts, some sort of "sense of the whole" inheres in the organism, a quality that becomes particularly apparent in phenomena such as regeneration in amphibians and certain invertebrates and in the homeorhesis exhibited by developing embryos.

41 The opening chapter of college-level textbooks typically have a brief discussion of what distinguishes living things from nonliving things. However, none of them mention the whole-part relationship that Aristotle speaks of (e.g., the eye ceases to be an eye when separated from the body). While the textbooks generally make brief mention of emergent properties, they do

connecting the specific questions about living things that are amenable to scientific inquiry with the more general questions that natural philosophy studies, for as we have seen, the failure to do so can have a negative impact on the study of animal behavior and the study of consciousness.

The need for better connection between the two disciplines is also seen when it comes to determining what aspects of living things should be considered first. Aristotle sees familiarity with natural history, something which provides a more descriptive account of the lives of living things, as prerequisite for a causal investigation of them, and most biologists would agree with him here. Where they generally part company is on what constitutes a proper introduction to causal explanations. Aristotle would have the introductory textbook stress the central importance of addressing questions concerning animal behavior, and would also have it explain why an investigation of animals' cells, macromolecules, and molecules plays a subordinate role in understanding their lives.[42] Although biologists earning their living in a laboratory setting may never have reason to look at a single organism, as students they should not be given the impression that looking at cells or genes is the best manner to obtain knowledge of living things. The biologist's basic formation at an undergraduate level should include a course on animal behavior, which would take up philosophical questions such as whether

not distinguish between weak and strong emergent properties (the latter being irreducible to the interacting parts on which they depend). What little they say about emergent properties suggests that reductionism is an adequate approach to understanding all of them. Here are a few examples. Robert Brooker et al., *Biology*, 5th ed. (McGraw Hill, 2019), 3, tell us: "New properties of life emerge from complex interactions: Our ability to see is an emergent property due to interactions among many types of cells in the eyes and neurons that send signals to the brain." Neil A. Campbell et al., *Biology*, 8th ed. (Pearson Benjamin Cummings, 2014), after noting that "New Properties Emerge at Successive Level of Biological Organism," proceed to talk about reductionism, "which reduces complex systems to simpler components which are more manageable to study. Reductionism is a powerful strategy in biology." Campbell et al., *Biology*, 4. Mentioned earlier was Purves et al., *Life*, 14: "Biologists could never discover the existence of human emotions by studying single nerve cells, even though they may be able to eventually explain those emotions in terms of interactions among many nerve cells." I could give a number of other examples of the inadequate treatment of emergent properties typical of introductory biology textbooks. None of these books makes the distinction between methodological reductionism and ontological reductionism. In all of them, the brief discussion of what it means to be alive is immediately followed by a chapter or section on the chemical basis of life (atoms and molecules), and after that, by a chapter or section on the cell, something that contributes to the formation of the intellectual habit of looking at living things in a mechanistic manner.

42 See Aristotle, *Parts of Animals*, 641a18–33.

animals have minds, what are the proper methods for investigating their mental capacities, what theory of mind is, and so forth. While following such a course might be considered a setback from the point of view of learning lab techniques, which are important for understanding the material aspects of living things, as well as generally being needed for holding a job in biology, it is indispensable from the point of view of understanding what is most essential about living things.[43]

Hierarchy

A common view among biologists is that humans are a species like any other, no better, no worse, because "all organisms that have survived are successfully adapted to their environments."[44] From this standpoint, if any organism can be called superior, it is certain species of bacteria, for they are both more ancient and represented by more individuals.

Aristotle maintains to the contrary that there are different grades of life that represent a hierarchy of perfection. He distinguishes two meanings of the word "perfection." In one sense, one being is more perfect than another insofar as it has more being; in another sense a being is either perfect or imperfect insofar as it has or lacks the parts it is supposed to have to carry on its life. Looking to perfection in the second sense, Aristotle argues that shellfish are not imperfect in the sense of missing something, despite their inability to move about like many other animals, for they reproduce individuals like themselves.[45] The type of perfection and imperfection in question here corresponds to the biologist's notions of fitness and lack thereof.

43 It should be apparent to the reader familiar with Aristotle that there are many nuances in his thought which cannot be brought out in this short chapter, much less be critically evaluated. Aristotle takes more interest in animals than in plants because animals are more obviously alive, but at the same time he regards the life activities of plants, such as nutrition, as more fundamental, and for this reason acknowledges the need to study them first in a general way; see *On the Soul*, 415a18–25.

44 This view traces back to Darwin, who says: "It is absurd to talk of one animal being higher than another." *Notebook B* (1837–38), 74: Transmutation of Species, ed. John van Wyhe, *Darwin Online*, http://darwin-online.org.uk/content/frameset?itemID=CUL-DAR121.-&viewtype=side&pageseq=38. This is a consequence of regarding the diversity of species solely from the point of view of natural selection. Species whose individuals are adapted to their environments survive and those whose individuals are not, do not. The earthworm is adapted to its environment and the chimpanzee to its environment, and from this point of view one is not higher than the other.

45 *On the Soul*, 432b25.

Later on, however, Aristotle speaks of certain animals as being imperfect in another sense, namely, because they lack senses that other animals have.[46] A sense allows a being in some manner to be more than just itself. As Aristotle puts it, "the soul in a certain way is all things."[47] This is readily seen in the case of seeing something and later imagining it. One could not later imagine it if it had not initially in some way come to exist inside one; it has become part of one in some sense. Sense knowledge then extends one's being (granted not one's substantial being); a plant is limited to being a plant, whereas an animal seeing a plant becomes that plant by way of the likeness that comes to be within it. Animals, then, in virtue of possessing sense perception, have more being than plants do, and in this way are more perfect than they are.

One sometimes finds on the part of biologists the assumptions that gradual changes in genetic sequences are what are primarily responsible for the origin of new species, and that this being so, no organism can exhibit a new feature that is radically different from those present in its immediate ancestor.[48] This is an example where a narrow focus on material changes necessary for speciation blinds people to seeing a feature of a living thing for what it is. It may be hard in specific cases to determine whether a given type of organism possesses sense perception or not; nonetheless, it remains

46 See *On the Soul*, 433b32.

47 *On the Soul*, 431b20.

48 The view that evolution is gradual originated with Darwin. See *Origin of the Species*, chap. 6 (Mentor Books, 1964), 180–81. See also *The Descent of Man*, chap. 3 in *The Darwin Compendium* (Barnes & Noble, 2005), 777:

> If no organic being excepting man had possessed any mental power, or if his powers had been of a wholly different nature from those of the lower animals, then we should never have been able to convince ourselves that our high faculties had been gradually developed. But it can be shown that there is no fundamental difference of this kind. We must also admit that there is a much wider interval in mental power between one of the lowest fishes, as a lamprey or lancelet, and one of the higher apes, than between an ape and man; yet this interval is filled up by numberless gradations.

Gradualism in Darwin's own day was challenged by the gaps in the fossil record, and later on by the discovery that mutations can cause significant changes, as well as by the theory of punctuated equilibrium. However, some biologists hold that overall evolution is gradualistic. For a recent defense of Darwinian gradualism, see Mark Pagel et al., "General Statistical Model Shows That Macroevolutionary Patterns and Processes Are Consistent With Darwinian Gradualism," *Nature Communications* 13, no. 1113 (2022), https://www.nature.com/articles/s41467-022-28595-z.

the case that some organisms are aware of certain aspects of reality, and that they are in a sense superior to those that are not.

Aristotle goes on to delineate a life form superior to the animal (taken in the sense of a merely sentient organism). This life form is capable of a further expansion of its being; just as the sensitive soul is open to becoming all sensible things, so too the intellectual soul is open to becoming all intelligible things. The difference between the two types of knowledge lies in their objects: "What actual sensation apprehends is individuals, while what knowledge [episteme] apprehends is universals."[49] Intellectual knowledge surpasses sense knowledge both in the scope of things known and how they are known. We can know the existence of things we cannot sense, such as UV light, and we can ask questions about the existence of things that are immaterial. And while our senses tell us what things look like and feel like and so forth, our intellects are capable of knowing what things are and why they are the way they are.[50] For this reason Aristotle would be in full accord with philosopher Errol Harris, who dryly observes that while mosquitoes have allegedly become adapted to wider differences in climate than have humans, no mosquito is capable of making such an assertion.[51]

The question of whether or not there is a difference between sense and intellect has, of course, been debated by philosophers through the ages. Should biologists be concerned with the answer to this question, especially when philosophers cannot seem to see clearly on the issue? They should, because this answer is needed in order to determine the primary categories of life forms, and knowing these constitutes part of a general understanding of the biosphere. In addition, understanding whether and how sense and intellect differ holds importance for those areas of biology that study animal behavior. If indeed there is a radical difference between the capacity for abstract thought and sense perception, then the researchers who are unaware of this are at a loss when it comes to devising tests for animals that are adequate to show whether or not animals have humanlike intelligence. This problem comes up over and over when primatologists who have taught apes to use symbolic means of communication attempt to determine whether the

49 *On the Soul*, 417b22–23.

50 See Aristotle, *Posterior Analytics*, bk. 1, chap. 31.

51 See Errol Harris, *Cosmos and Anthropos: A Philosophical Interpretation of the Anthropic Cosmological Principle* (Humanity Press International, 1991), 79. See also Aristotle, *On the Soul*, bk. 3, chap. 8.

apes are true language users; language usage is defined in terms of understanding what the words mean, but too often "understanding what the words mean" is inadequately defined. The consequence of this has been that every time an ape passes a given language test, some philosopher comes along and shows why that test is inadequate for establishing true language usage.[52] Experimenters in this area ignore at their peril philosophical discussions concerning the nature of rational understanding.

The Final Cause

It is well known that Aristotle gives the pride of place in biological explanations of organs and behavior to the final cause.[53] The final cause is "'that for the sake of which' a thing is done, e.g. health is the cause of walking about ('Why is he walking about?' we say. 'To be healthy,' and having said that we have assigned the cause)."[54] While biology in the twentieth century went through a phase where some biologists were trying to get rid of explanations in terms of final cause—partly in an effort to be more like what were considered "hard" sciences (physics and chemistry), and partly due to a confusion about the relationship between explanations in terms of different kinds of causes—this phase did not last long.[55] Here biologists did not show their usual reticence in acknowledging the need to engage in philosophical discussion. Ernst Mayr, among others, wrote a number of pieces concerning the role of teleology in understanding living things.[56] Mayr maintains that the "occurrence of goal-directed processes is perhaps the most characteristic feature of the world of living things,"[57] and he rejects the attempts of some

52 That primatologists who attempt to teach apes language typically fail to define language will be apparent from considerations offered in chapter 4, which examines the animal language studies.

53 See Aristotle, *Parts of Animals*, bk. 1, chap. 1, 639b12–17.

54 Aristotle, *Physics*, bk. 2, chap. 5, 194b33–34.

55 See Francisco J. Ayala, "Teleological Explanations," in *Philosophy of Biology*, ed. Michael Ruse (Macmillan, 1989), 191–93. See also Ernst Mayr, *Towards a New Philosophy of Biology* (Harvard University Press, 1988), chap. 3, "The Multiple Meanings of Teleological," 40–41. Note that some biologists distinguish between "proximate causes" and "ultimate causes," and include the final cause among the latter; see John Alcock, *Animal Behavior* (Sinauer, 1998), 4: "Why Questions about Ultimate Causes . . . What is the purpose, the function, of the behavior?"

56 See Mayr, *Towards a New Philosophy of Biology*, 40–41.

57 Mayr, 45.

biologists to reduce the final cause to an end state.[58] The lub-dub sound that the heart makes is not its final cause; circulating the blood is. Common sense and the biologist's natural curiosity also did a lot to retrieve the notion of final cause; biologists on the whole cannot help wondering about cells, organelles, and behaviors whose purpose is not apparent.

Final Causality and Evolution

Where one does still find biologists distancing themselves from the notion of teleology is in evolutionary biology. This is because it seems that in explaining the origin of the species, one has to choose one member of a dichotomy that pits action for an end against chance. Aristotle was in fact the first to propose this dichotomy. He argues that organic parts either come to be by chance or they do so for the sake of something; the fact that such parts invariably arise in the same way eliminates the possibility that they come to be by chance, and so Aristotle concludes that they must come to be for an end.[59] Evolutionary biologists typically explain the origin of the diverse species of animals with their various adaptations in terms of random variation and natural selection, and not in terms of nature acting for an end.

In the *Physics*, Aristotle engages in no further speculation as to whether there is an intelligence responsible for the ordering to an end that he maintains is present in nature. Indeed, throughout the part of his opus that has come down to us he never states in any clear way whether he takes this to indicate a mind behind nature. Of course, thinkers like Thomas Aquinas will build on Aristotle and argue that finality in nature is reason enough to conclude that there is an intelligence behind nature.

58 See Mayr, 45:

> Let us take, for instance the sentence: "the Wood Thrush migrates in the fall into warmer countries *in order to* escape the inclemency of the weather and the food shortages of the northern climes." If we replace the words "in order to" by "and thereby," we leave the important question unanswered as to *why* the Wood Thrush migrates. The teleonomic form of the statement implies that the goal-directed activity is governed by a program.

Note that Mayr does not see his notion of teleonomy as opposed to Aristotle's notion of teleology. See Mayr, 47. The notion of teleonomy adds the notion that some mechanism must be present in order for a goal to be achieved. See Mayr, 49.

59 See Aristotle, *Physics*, 198b23–37.

The evolutionary biologists who regard chance and necessity as the ultimate causes of organs that serve a purpose not surprisingly conclude that positing an intelligence behind nature is superfluous.[60] Whence Dawkins's claim that Darwin made it possible to be an intellectually fulfilled atheist.[61]

It is not the biologist's task, however, to be answering the question of whether there is an intelligence behind the biosphere, granted that observations of the marvelous adaptations of living things naturally brings this question to mind. Unfortunately, many evolutionary biologists, as well as their critics, instead of remaining within the realm of biological explanation, tack onto Darwin's biological theory of evolution a philosophical position about God. For example, William Provine asserts that "nine percent [of Americans polled] accepted the scientific version of biological evolution, namely that evolution has occurred over a long period of time and is a process not guided by God."[62] And Christoph Cardinal Schönborn writes: "Evolution in the sense of common ancestry might be true, but evolution in the neo-Darwinian sense—an unguided, unplanned process of random variation and natural selection—is not."[63] What Schönborn most likely means by neo-Darwinism is a philosophical position that some espouse as if it were a necessary consequence of neo-Darwinian biology. However, affirmations such as this contribute to the confusion concerning which statements about evolution pertain to the biological theory of how species evolved and which statements about evolution lie outside the science of biology, belonging rather to philosophy.[64]

60 See Jacques Monod, *Chance and Necessity*, trans. Austryn Wainhouse (Vintage Books, 1970).

61 Of course, there are other arguments for God's existence besides the argument from design; thus, defeating the design argument would not suffice for establishing that atheism is true.

62 William Provine, "Evolution and the Foundation of Ethics," *MBL Science* 3, no. 1 (Winter 1998): 26.

63 Christoph Schönborn, "Finding Design in Nature," *New York Times*, July 7, 2005.

64 Stephen M. Barr criticizes Cardinal Schönborn for "slip[ping] into the definition of a scientific theory, neo-Darwinism, the words 'unplanned' and 'unguided,' which are fraught with theology" in "The Design of Evolution," *First Things* 156, October 2005, 9–10. Barr goes on to give examples to show that "'random' as used in science does not mean uncaused, unplanned, or inexplicable; it means uncorrelated." Barr, "Design of Evolution," 10. One of the examples he gives is of viewing out-of-state license plates from one's car. The order is random because seeing a plate from one state, e.g., Kentucky, tells one nothing about the next out-of-state plate that one will see. Yet each car comes within one's view for a reason.

Biologists do rightly seek to investigate an issue that is closely related to the question of a Mind behind nature, namely, whether the immediate causes of evolution are for the sake of something or are random. Whether mutation is random or directed is certainly something one can seek to determine through experimentation.[65] The biologist may then be faced with the need for an answer to the philosophical question of whether randomness in nature precludes the presence of action for an end. An incorrect answer to this question would potentially prevent the biologist from seeing the finality that is there.

Let us investigate the question about randomness in order to see in more detail how answers to philosophical questions sometimes have an impact upon biology. Aristotle's chance-finality dichotomy makes it seem that randomness is in nowise reconcilable with action for an end.[66] Yet while the two are mutually exclusive at the same level, since a process is called random because the operative causes are not tending to produce a specific outcome, nonetheless such a process can be a means of achieving a goal at another level. Biology itself provides a beautiful example of how random processes not only can serve an end but can be the most appropriate means to that end. The immune system of an organism produces millions of cells, each with a different antibody specificity. How does it do so? The variable regions of the antibody, which are what confer immunological specificity, result from genes that have been randomly shuffled.[67] If the body only had a fixed set of foreign invaders it had to deal with, an arsenal of a fixed set of types of antibodies would do. However, given that viruses and bacteria evolve, the vastly greater variety of antibodies produced through random gene mixing is the better design. We see then that general reflections on the nature of random processes show that they do not automatically exclude

65 See J. Grey Monroe, et al., "Mutation Bias Reflects Natural Selection in *Arabidopsis thaliana*," *Nature* 602 (2022): 101–5, abstract: "Since the first half of the twentieth century, evolutionary theory has been dominated by the idea that mutations occur randomly with respect to their consequences. Here we test this assumption with large surveys of de novo mutations in the plant *Arabidopsis thaliana*. In contrast to expectations, we find that mutations occur less often in functionally constrained regions of the genome—mutation frequency is reduced by half inside gene bodies and by two-thirds in essential genes."

66 Problems arise in understanding the relationship of randomness to finality when randomness is conflated with chance. Here, however, is not the place to examine the differences between chance and randomness and how the two relate to final causality.

67 See Purves et al., *Life*, 419–20.

finality at another level, but rather that random processes can be the best means to achieve certain goals. Adopting the opposite view constitutes an antiscientific viewpoint to the extent that it prevents biologists from recognizing finality in instances where random processes are a means to realizing a goal.

Plainly, the philosophical positions on randomness and on contingent events in general that biologists adopt affect how they read life's story. Is evolutionary history in some sense progressive and tending toward the production of a being like ourselves or is it no more than a catenation of fortuitous events lacking any direction? Many biologists would agree with Gould's position:

> The pageant of evolution [is] a staggeringly improbable series of events, sensible enough in retrospect and subject to rigorous explanation, but utterly unpredictable and quite unrepeatable. Wind back the tape of life to the early days of the Burgess shale; let it play again from an identical starting point, and the chance becomes vanishingly small that anything like human intelligence would grace the reply.[68]

And a number of biologists take this line of reasoning, which denies that evolution tends toward any goals, a step further:

> From a philosophical perspective, the most important aspect of evolution is the rise of complex creatures from simple ones. This "vertical" dimension of evolution has been co-opted by those who proclaim it as evidence of an unseen creator. Wallace Arthur, National University of Ireland, Galway, attacks that anti-science worldview by building a persuasive picture of how "unaided" evolution produces advanced creatures from simple ones by an essentially accidental process.[69]

The notion that there is a creator responsible for evolutionary processes does not constitute an antiscience worldview as it in nowise interferes with the scientific investigation of the immediate causes responsible for the origin of the various species. It is from our general understanding of the way nature is that reasonable attempts are made to establish the existence of God. Our

68 Stephen Jay Gould, *Wonderful Life: The Burgess Shale and the Nature of History* (Norton, 1989), 14.

69 Blurb for a presentation at the American Museum of Natural History entitled "Creatures of Accident: The Rise of the Animal Kingdom."

knowledge of the existence or nonexistence of God does not serve to ground particular conclusions about the various specific features and behaviors of living things; it is the knowledge that is gained through scientific observation that plays this role.[70]

Again, what is an antiscientific worldview is the mistaken adoption of the philosophical position that the blind causes involved in evolution preclude the possibility that evolution is tending toward a goal or goals.[71] For this causes a potential misreading of the story of life: the biological evidence for evolutionary trends seen as tendencies toward certain goals is dismissed in advance on the grounds that evolution involves random and/or other contingent causes and so can have no goals.

Philosophy, Ally of Biology

Throughout this chapter I have argued that biologists would stand to profit from greater familiarity with natural philosophy, both because they could gain an understanding of living things that complements the understanding obtained through biology, and because their ability to do research in some cases depends on having in hand the correct answers to certain philosophical questions. There are truths about living things that can only be known by reflecting on our more general, nonexperimental, experience of them; this is the only way we are able to understand the unity of living things, their self-motion, the hierarchy of the different life forms (including the place of humans in this hierarchy), and also certain aspects of the mental abilities characteristic of higher living things. Mistakes about these issues not only constitute a failure to achieve a general understanding of life, but they also often have negative repercussions on how biologists carry on the detailed studies of living things that are properly theirs. For example, incorrect answers given to philosophical questions about the nature of consciousness

70 The creationist affirmation that God directly produces each of the diverse species separately is another matter; it constitutes a rejection of the scientific evidence that evolution has occurred.

71 I have made a case that randomness does not necessarily exclude finality at another level; space does not allow me to show that this is also true in the case of other blind causes commonly invoked in evolutionary explanation, namely, chance causes and necessary causes. The need here for further distinctions and arguments, however, illustrates my main point, which is that answers to philosophical questions are sometimes needed in order to answer biological questions.

and intelligence have led some biologists to deny that some animals have minds and others to commit a variety of mistakes in studying animal behavior, such as formulating inadequate tests for whether animals are capable of language. Lack of an educational acquaintance with natural philosophy can also lead biologists to make methodological mistakes of a general nature, such as starting the study of biology by examining the nonliving parts of organisms rather than the behavior of the organisms that are most manifestly alive or rejecting introspection of our mental activities as a starting point for understanding animal behavior.

It is not only philosophical reflections that directly concern living things that the biologist has reason to take interest in. Familiarity with certain very general considerations of natural philosophy, such as those concerning the role of the final cause in explanations of natural phenomena and of the relationship of chance and randomness to final causality can also help students of life avoid errors, such as refusing to give explanations in terms of final causes and of denying the possibility that a given random process may be ordered to a goal at another level.[72]

In addition, biologists also need to be exposed to certain metaphysical questions concerning the nature of reality as a whole and concerning knowledge in general and scientific knowledge in particular. This need is particularly acute in regard to three questions. The first is the question of whether everything that exists is material. To assume this in advance instead of carefully considering all pertinent evidence is plainly to abandon objectivity and to embrace an ideology. Fear of letting a "divine foot in the door" is often the motive for abandoning reason here.[73] The blind espousal of materialism affects one's ability to come to a balanced judgment on important questions, such as those concerning hierarchy and finality in the living realm.

The second question is whether adopting methodological reductionism as the working method for science commits one to ontological reductionism. It is not too difficult to see that a working method allows one to know determinate kinds of things that exist, but it does not determine what does

72 The nature of the different causes is fully investigated by the metaphysician. The natural philosopher is able to grasp the basic distinctions needed for pursuing the discipline without engaging in an exhaustive discussion of causality. Also, to the extent that the notion of randomness pertains both to nature and to mathematics, its full investigation pertains to metaphysics.

73 See Richard Lewontin, "Billions and Billions of Demons," *New York Review of Books*, January 9, 1997, 31, http://www.nybooks.com/articles/1997/01/09/billions-and-billions-of-demons/

or does not exist. Thus, it is one thing to say that one will attempt to explain some life activity in terms of the material parts involved; it is another to assume that such a method affords an entirely adequate way of treating all life activities. The espousal of ontological reductionism as if it were a logical consequence of accepting methodological reductionism as the valid way of doing science has a further ill consequence, namely, it helps fuel the myth that being a scientist is incompatible with being a religious believer.

The third question concerns the relation of biology to other disciplines and especially to the philosophical disciplines and to theology. The study of living things pertaining to natural philosophy is arguably continuous with biology. Still, each answers different sorts of questions about living things, generally using a different method; philosophy clarifies very general concepts concerning living things starting from common experience, whereas biology pursues a more detailed understanding of living things through experiment. Biologists need to be aware of this, and they also need to see that the answers to the more general questions of philosophy in some cases provide a framework for answering questions in biology. Nowadays, biologists especially need to understand the relation of their discipline to the various attempts by natural philosophers to argue from the order in living nature to a Mind behind it. They should be aware that maintaining that there is a Mind behind evolution does not constitute an antiscientific worldview, and why it does not. It is when biologists fail to grasp what sort of questions biology can answer, and what sort of questions fall to other disciplines to answer, that they readily fall into errors such as defining evolution as an "unguided, unplanned process of random variation and natural selection."[74] Errors like these both vitiate the biologist's research and engender unwarranted conflict between science and religion.

I rest my case that biologists who have acquired an educational acquaintance with certain philosophical questions pertaining to natural philosophy and to metaphysics will be both better biologists and better students of life in general. They will also be better equipped than the average biologist to avoid errors when examining philosophical questions concerning the relation of science and religion. Biologists who integrated their study within a broader philosophical framework would thereby come to appreciate what Aristotle means when he suggests that an investigation of the soul stands to make a "substantial contribution to the whole body of truth."

74 Schönborn, "Finding Design in Nature."

2

Neuroscience and the Human Soul

Neuroscience is the part of biology that studies the nervous system. The branches of neuroscience that have the most direct bearing on whether humans have a soul are those concerned with understanding the brain and its relationship to cognition and emotion.

In order to understand what the human soul is, the Thomistic tradition maintains that one must first talk about what the soul is in general and then about what is distinctive about the human soul, namely, that it is the cause of the life activities of thinking abstractly and of making free choices. Many of those who think that the findings of neuroscience challenge the notion that humans have souls do not engage in these considerations; for example, they often conflate soul and mind.[1] Since what these people propose in

1 See neurophilosopher Patricia Smith Churchland, "I Have No Soul (And I'm Okay with That)," *National Post*, August 8, 2013, https://nationalpost.com/opinion/patricia-smith-churchland-i-have-no-soul-and-im-okay-with-that:

> I often think about my brain in terms that are different from those I use when thinking about myself. I think about my brain as *that*, and about myself as *me*. I think about my brain as having neurons, but I think of me as having a memory. But when I reflect on the matter, I realize that my memory is actually all about the neurons in my brain. Lately, in fact, I've come to think about my brain in more intimate terms—as *me*, full stop. Memories exist as modifications to the connectivity of neurons in the brain. Memories come into existence when brain cells—neurons—change how they connect

many cases has more immediate bearing on the faculties of the human soul, intellect and free will, than on the soul itself, I will begin by looking at these faculties, and later consider the soul.

In regard to the intellect, some claim that neuroscience shows that our thoughts have physical causes, and so they maintain that scientists are able to "read people's minds" by identifying the physical causes in question. And as for free will, certain experiments done by neuroscientists appear to show that our choices are determined by our brains and that free will is an illusion. I will elaborate further on these claims, but I'm going to begin by explaining why the Thomistic tradition maintains that the intellect is immaterial—from which it would follow that neuroscience can say nothing about the intellect as such.

A Defense of the Immateriality of the Intellect

There are any number of different meanings of the word "intelligence." An animal that can learn is in some sense intelligent. But the word "intellect" generally names a very specific form of intelligence, one that is different from the sensory knowledge that makes animals capable of learning.

How exactly does intellectual knowledge differ from sense knowledge? The intellect is capable of grasping universal truths, such as physical and chemical laws and various philosophical truths, as well as very simple truths and basic principles, such as that the whole is greater than the part and equals added to equals give equals. In order to understand these truths, we must first form the individual concepts involved, for example, "whole," "part," and "greater."

A number of thinkers maintain that there is no difference between a concept or abstract thought and a sense perception. However, the senses only know particular things: I see and smell this rose, not rose in general. Imagination is a type of sense ability as it too apprehends what is particular. I imagine a specific rose, again, not rose in general. The intellect forms the

to other neurons by sprouting new structure and pruning back old structure. Information about events in my life and about what makes me *me* are stored in patterns of connections between living brain cells. Social skills, the knowledge of how to ride a bicycle and drive a car, memories of childhood—all exist in the way that neurons connect to each other. This understanding of the brain challenges the idea that we possess some character-defining soul that stands apart from our brain and controls the moral aspect of our decisions.

universal concept "rose," which it understands to belong to every particular rose that is, was, or will be (many thinkers confuse intellect or reason[2] with imagination). It is not hard to see that image and idea (or thought) are not the same thing. If you are asked to think of a dog, you do two things: You picture a particular dog and you bring to mind the concept "dog." It is obvious that these two things differ. For example, when asked to think of a dog, you will imagine a dog of a certain size, for example, a large dog such as a German Shepherd. Yet upon being asked whether a small dog such as a Chihuahua is a dog, you will reply "yes." If your concept of dog was the same as the image you initially formed, you could not know that a small dog was a dog.

The difference between the universal and the particular is reflected in the way we speak: We can't say this dog is that dog, but we can say of every particular dog that it is a dog. The concept "dog" abstracts from the features that make a particular dog the particular dog that it is.

A corollary of this is that concepts are not physical things—all physical things have some quantitative dimension. So go back to the example "think of a dog." The dog that you imagine has a size in your imagination—you can imagine a bigger or smaller dog next to the dog you initially imagined. Now, in reality a dog that is three feet high is taller than one that is one foot high, and the image of a three-foot-high dog is greater in height than the image of a dog that is one foot high. But the concept of "three feet" is not a bigger concept than the concept of "one foot." It is a concept of a bigger length, but it itself has no size. If the concept had a specific size, it would be an image of sorts and would not be applicable to everything that has a dimension of three feet.[3]

If we form and consider ideas with our intellect, the intellect cannot be an ability belonging to a merely physical thing. Physical things can act upon other physical things, either imparting new accidents to them, such as

2 Intellect and reason have both a broader and a narrower meaning. They are synonymous with each other when understood to be the capacity for abstract thought. They differ from one another when reason is taken to mean the ability to go from what is known to a conclusion hitherto unknown, as occurs in argumentation, whereas the intellect is taken to mean the ability to apprehend self-evident principles (or to mean the habitual possession of such principles). Unless otherwise indicated, I am using the two words as synonyms.

3 See Aquinas, *SCG*, https://www.corpusthomisticum.org/iopera.html, bk. 2, chaps. 49–51. Quantity is a proper accident of all material substances, and it underlies in one way or the other all the other accidents of material substances, e.g., a quality such as color is found in a surface, and action and passion involve contact, which again requires a surface, etc. The fact that concepts lack any sort of dimensionality shows them to be entirely separate from matter.

warmth or a new location, or causing them to be transformed into another substance, as when a spark causes oxygen and hydrogen to form water. But physical things can't act on another physical thing and thereby turn it into a non-physical thing—there is always some underlying matter involved in physical changes that persists through the change. So neither the brain, nor any body part, can produce an idea. This shows that our intellect must be immaterial.

A complementary argument for the immateriality of the intellect stems from considering the way in which less general concepts fall under a more general concept. In the Platonic dialogue the *Parmenides* (131b), it is suggested that the more general concept is like a tent that covers a number of different things; so, for example, the concept "animal" would cover the concepts of dog and pig and frog, etc. The problem with this view is that only part of the tent covers each thing under the tent. Yet the whole concept "animal" applies to the concepts of dog and pig and frog. Everything that is true of animal is true of dog, pig, etc. and not just part of what is true of animal. So the extension of the concept "animal" cannot be some type of physical extension. In which case, the intellect that forms the concept also cannot be a physical thing.

The Activity of Thinking Depends on the Activity of Imagining

One thing that causes many people to dismiss the notion that thinking is a nonphysical activity is that it seems that if this were true, then thinking thoughts could not be affected by damage to a physical organ, namely, the brain. And strictly speaking it is true that brain damage cannot affect the intellect's ability to form and consider concepts. However, as Aristotle points out, thinking depends on imagining (which in turn is dependent on sensing with one or more of the five senses). Just as cooking dinner depends on having obtained food to cook, but those are two different activities, so too thinking depends on imagining, and imagination is an activity that is carried on using the brain. Just as I can't cook if I have no food, the intellect cannot think without an appropriate image. Why is that?

We cannot form a concept of a tree or a cat without first sensing those things. If what we perceive leaves no lasting impression, we are not going to be able to form a thought. If someone were to ask a person: "What did you see?," and the person were to respond, "I don't know, I don't remember," that person is not going to have thoughts about that thing. So what we sense needs to be retained in our imagination if we are going to form a concept.[4]

Even once we've formed concepts, when thinking those thoughts there is still a need to do so in conjunction with imagining. Why? Well, the natures of material things exist in particular individuals. Thus, we cannot completely and truly conceive the natures of these things without reference to a particular individual, and particulars are apprehended by sense and imagination.[5] Thus, when we want to understand in a clear way what some abstract statement means, we spontaneously relate it back to what is concrete and imaginable. So, for example, the statement "as a thing is, so it acts" comes into sharp focus when we imagine a concrete example, such as a strong person can lift a heavy object while a weak person cannot. And the organ of the imagination is a part or parts of the brain. So again, thinking thoughts is an immaterial activity, but it depends on an activity exercised by using the brain, namely, imagining. This is why, if the parts of the brain required for imagining are affected, thinking thoughts is also affected.

One might object that many times we do not picture anything particular when we think. When most people think, what they most obviously imagine most of the time are words.[6] People generally have a mental verbal stream and/or imagine written words. It still remains the case, however, that if we

4 Imagination here is taken in a broad sense that includes memory.

5 As Aquinas puts it:

> The proper object of the human intellect—which is united to a body—is the whatness or nature existing in a material body (and through the natures of visible things it ascends to a certain knowledge of invisible things). Of the notion of this nature is that it exists in some individual which is not without bodily matter; as it belongs to the notion of the nature of stone that it exist in this stone, and it belongs to the nature of horse that it exists in this horse, and so on for the rest. Whence, the nature of stone, or of any material things whatsoever, cannot be completely and truly known except according as it is known as existing in a particular. We apprehend the particular through sense and imagination. And therefore, it is necessary in order for the intellect to understand its proper object to turn itself to the images in the imagination, so that it may observe the universal nature existing in the particular. *Summa Theologiae*, Instituti Studiorum Medievalium Ottaviensis, ed. (Commissio Piana, 1953), I, q. 84, a. 7.
>
> All translations of Aquinas are my own.

6 Some people use images more than words when they think. One such person is Temple Grandin, who is autistic: "I THINK IN PICTURES. Words are like a second language to me. I translate both spoken and written words into full-color movies, complete with sound, which run like a VCR tape in my head. When somebody speaks to me, his words are instantly translated into a picture. . . . When I was a child and a teenager, I thought everybody thought in pictures." Temple Grandin, *Thinking in Pictures* (Vintage Books, 2016), 3–4.

are to truly and completely understand a material thing, we have to relate it back to more than this—not just to signs, but to something concrete and imaginable. Otherwise, whatever words might be in our minds are finally just words.[7] They would lack a connection with reality. Most of the time, when thinking about speculative matters, we are habitually capable of imagining an appropriate image but simply do not bother to do so.[8] Yet even in those cases imagination seems important to the extent that we imagine words. It is possible to think without words. This can be seen from the fact that sometimes we think of something and cannot remember its name. Words do, however, help us remember our thoughts. If I ask myself what motion is, the words of Aristotle's definition pop up in my mind, seemingly even before I think about exactly what I take these words to mean. It has become second nature for us to think in terms of words, and consequently it is irksome when we can't find the word we are looking for. So it seems that if the part or parts of our brain that have to do with language were damaged that this would at least initially impede thinking, until such time as we became habituated to thinking without words.[9]

There are people who are capable of thinking while being unable to picture things at will (a condition called "aphantasia"). This seems to show that thinking does not always depend on imagining. However, the fact that it is only recently that research has been done on aphantasia and that it is not very well understood gives us reason to hesitate in drawing this conclusion.

7 Aquinas, commenting on Aristotle, notes that young people sometimes toss words around without actually understanding them: "As for wisdom, however, he adds that they do not have conviction about matters sapiential or metaphysical, that is, they do not attain them with their minds, granted they may say things with their mouths . . . for the notions of mathematical things are imaginable, whereas sapiential things are purely intelligible." *In Ethic.*, Raymundi M. Spiazzi, ed. (Marietti, 1964), bk. VI, lec. 7, no. 1210.

8 In the case of thinking about practical matters, not in a speculative mode, but in order to actually do something, we generally use images of things, and generally the more so when it comes to immediate action than in remote planning.

9 Tom Lubbock, who lost much of his ability to name things, claims that his ability to think was not thereby impeded. Note, however, that it is hard to be sure how much language he lost, and it is also hard to be sure whether his claims about his thought being unimpeded are accurate. Lubbock says: "My language to describe things in the world is very small, limited. My thoughts when I look at the world are vast, limitless and normal, same as they ever were. My experience of the world is not made less by lack of language but is essentially unchanged." Quoted in Evelino Fedorenko and Rosemary Varley, "Language and Thought Are Not the Same Thing: Evidence from Neuroimagining and Neurological Patients," *Annals of the New York Academy of Sciences* 1369, no. 1 (April 2016): 132.

In addition, various alternative explanations come to mind. A blind person cannot imagine what a dog looks like but can know what a dog is from touching it, hearing it, and smelling it. So perhaps those with aphantasia have tactile, auditory, or olfactory images that take the place of what in most people would be primarily a visual image.

An alternative explanation is that these individuals have the equivalent of blindsight when it comes to their imagination. People with blindsight, a condition caused by damage to the primary visual cortex, claim to not see anything, and yet when forced to guess what is there, they do so correctly in more cases than would occur by mere chance. Perhaps, similarly, individuals with aphantasia do imagine but are unaware that they are imagining. Note that most of the individuals who are unable to voluntarily imagine things do dream, which presumably is an operation of our imaginative power.

Yet another possible explanation is that the visual images of people with aphantasia are so vague and ephemeral that they do not recognize them as such. Consider how many people cannot imagine the smell of a lemon and yet are capable of recognizing the smell. They must in some way remember it, otherwise every time they would smell a lemon it would be a new smell to them. It is hard to see how the memory of the smell could be possible in the absence of a stored image of the smell.[10] Similarly, then, if people with aphantasia can recognize a dog upon seeing it, one would think that they had some image of its appearance, but one that is so fuzzy and/or fleeting that they do not recognize it.[11]

One might also object that there are things we are capable of understanding that we are unable to imagine, such as ultraviolet and the soul, and so it does not seem possible that thinking about these things depend on imagining. However, while we do not directly imagine such things, what we understand is based on the negation of something that is understood by reference to something imaginable. For example, we cannot imagine something that is immaterial. However, in order to understand what is immaterial, we need to negate that it is material, and we can only understand what is material by reference to a specific, material thing that we can imagine. Similarly, in the case of ultraviolet, we understand it in reference to the spectrum of

10 "Image" refers to anything the imagination produces. In this sense, people with the sense of hearing can produce images of sounds; and some people can produce images of smells and flavors.

11 When I try to imagine color, I am never entirely sure that I have succeeded.

colors that we can imagine, as being another color in that spectrum, one that we cannot see. As for the soul, if we understand it to be a substantial form, we understand substantial form by analogy with accidental form, which is something we can imagine, while at the same time we deny that substantial form is the same thing as accidental form.

Mind Reading

There are all kinds of fascinating studies done by neuroscientists that involve "reading people's minds." What's really happening, however, is that scientists are correlating what people are perceiving or imagining with their brain activity, and then using the correlation to interpret the brain activity into what people are likely to be perceiving or imagining.

For example, scientists have found a way to identify by looking at brain activity which picture among a thousand pictures an individual happens to be looking at. The author of the study, Jack Gallant, presented data that went even further—actually reconstructing what volunteers were seeing from their visual cortex activity, as they viewed a series of movie trailers. For instance, "the program would spit out an outline of a white torso just when a man in a white shirt was shown to the subject."[12] And T. Horikawa et al. have even been able to tell some of the contents of people's dreams from brain scans (verified by waking them).[13] What is being decoded in this case is what these people are imagining.

Another type of mind reading has to do with reading people's intentions. In an experiment carried out by Kathinka Evers and Mariano Sigman, "subjects were given the choice between two tasks to perform: adding or subtracting two numbers, and asked to hold onto their intention during a variable period of delay during which fMRI measurements were taken."[14] Measurements of activity in the prefrontal cortex were found to predict with 71 percent accuracy which operation the subject intended. However, it is not really surprising that this can be done. When we intend to do something, it is

12 Daniel Bor, "The Mechanics of Mind-Reading," *Scientific American*, December 22, 2009, https://www.scientificamerican.com/article/the-mechanics-of-mind-rea/.

13 T. Horikawa et al., "Neural Decoding of Visual Imagery During Sleep," *Science* 3 (May 2013): 639–42.

14 Kathinka Evers and Mariano Sigman, "Possibilities and Limits of Mind-Reading: A Neurophilosophical Perspective," *Consciousness and Cognition* 22, no. 3 (2013): 893.

always specific—we can't add or subtract in general, but rather perform this or that act of adding and subtracting, and our intention to add or subtract necessarily involves an image, and forming an image involves brain activity, something that fMRI can detect.

Those who belong to the Thomistic tradition look upon the aforesaid feats with admiration, not with consternation. Scientists and philosophers involved with this kind of research will talk about "reading thoughts from brain activity"[15] and make claims such as, "We've shown that, with the right technology, these people's thoughts could be decoded and understood by any listener."[16] Thomists recognize that the word "thought" is sometimes loosely used to mean "image in the imagination," rather than abstract thought as produced or considered by the intellect.[17] When we *think* of a dog, we actually perform two mental processes: we picture a dog and we bring to mind the concept "dog." As we noted earlier, people often do not distinguish these two activities and consequently use the word "thought" as though an image and a concept were the same thing.

The word "mind" also has more than one meaning: "mind" can refer to the intellect or to the imagination or to both taken together. If one takes "mind" to mean intellect, the brain is not the organ of the mind, for the intellect has no organ. If one takes "mind" to mean imagination, then the brain (or the parts thereof) is the organ of the mind.[18] There is plenty of evidence

15 Evers and Sigman, "Possibilities and Limits of Mind-Reading," 891.

16 Nima Mesgarani, quoted in James Wood, "Machine That Can Read Your Mind and Convert THOUGHTS into Speech Is Developed by Scientists and Gives Fresh Hope to Stroke Victims," *DailyMail.com,* January 29, 2019, https://www.dailymail.co.uk/sciencetech/article-6644101/Machine-read-mind-convert-THOUGHTS-speech-developed-scientists.html. See also Martha J. Farah and Paul Root Wolpe, "Monitoring and Manipulating the Human Brain: New Neuroscience Technologies and Their Ethical Implications," *The Hastings Center Report* 34, no. 3 (2004): 36: "The brain is the organ of mind. . . . Our sense of privacy and confidentiality of our own thought processes may also be threatened by technologies that can reveal the neural correlates of our innermost thoughts." See also F. Vieira da Cunha and J. B. Relva, "Who's Afraid of the Big Bad Neuroscience?: Neuroscience's Impact on Our Notions of Self and Free Will," in *The Human Sciences After the Decade of the Brain*, ed. Jon Leefmann and Elisabeth Hildt (Elsevier/Academic Press, 2017), 26: "Recent studies have allowed us to discern people's preferences, to relate specific thoughts to [fMRI] images and access mental content."

17 The "thought (e.g., the intention or recognition) is recognizable and identifiable via its cerebral process because of this stereotypical relationship." Evers and Sigman, "Possibilities and Limits of Mind-Reading," 894.

18 "EEG . . . MRI . . . Have opened a door that was previously sealed to entering the minds of others, and to communication without 1st person overt external behavior or speech." See Evers

that higher animals have minds while lacking intellects. It is not wrong to speak of an animal "mind" or to speak of imagination as a "mental" function. Much of the supposed threat of neuroscience to the notion that the intellect is immaterial comes from the failure to understand the difference between the intellect and the imagination.

Maybe at a certain point neuroscientists will be able to decode even our mental verbal stream—our internal verbal monologue. Currently quite a bit of work is being done on this.[19] Just to give one example, Nima Mesgarani and his team had epilepsy patients who were already undergoing brain surgery listen to sentences spoken by different people while the scientists recorded their brain activity. The neural patterns recorded were used to train a decoder that can translate brain activity into intelligible speech. The researchers then asked the patients to listen to speakers reciting numbers between 0 and 9 and recorded the brain signals. The brain signals were then run through the decoder. The sound produced by the decoder in response to those signals was analyzed and cleaned up by a type of AI that mimics the structure of brain cells. The end result was a robotic-sounding voice reciting a sequence of numbers with about 75 percent accuracy. So, scientists were able to know what a person was hearing, starting from their brain waves.[20]

Even if scientists succeed in decoding our mental verbal stream, words signify thoughts, but are not themselves thoughts. So strictly speaking they would not be reading the thoughts we are thinking but would infer our thoughts by detecting the physiological activities required for us to imagine words. Even if you hear people say something, you cannot be entirely sure

---

and Sigman, 888. Also, "reading thoughts from brain activity in healthy individuals: Neurotechnological access to mental contents. Neurotechnology is also used non-clinically to enter and read the contents of the human mind via its cerebral activities." Evers and Sigman, 891.

19 See Alexander G. Huth et al., "Natural Speech Reveals the Semantic Maps That Tile Human Cerebral Cortex," *Nature* 532 (2016): 453–58.

20 Wood, "Machine That Can Read Your Mind," https://www.dailymail.co.uk/sciencetech/article-6644101/Machine-read-mind-convert-THOUGHTS-speech-developed-scientists.html. Researchers in the Knight Laboratory seem even closer to decoding our mental verbal stream. They have developed a way to decode some of the words of subjects who were silently reading; see Stéphanie Martin et al., "Decoding Spectrotemporal Features of Overt and Covert Speech from the Human Cortex," *Frontiers in Neuroengineering*, May 27, 2014. Other similar publications can be found on the website for the Knight Laboratory: https://knightlab.berkeley.edu/publications/. Recently, researchers at the University of California at San Francisco have found a way to translate signals from the brain to the vocal tract into words on a screen; see David A. Moses, et al., "Neuroprosthesis for Decoding Speech in a Paralyzed Person with Anarthria," *New England Journal of Medicine* 385 (2021): 217–27.

what they are understanding by their own words. If perceiving language was the same as perceiving thoughts, then we could not misunderstand what others mean (aside from when we simply do not hear them properly). I remember a case where a student came up to me all excited and said that she now understood a statement I made; but she then went on to explain it incorrectly. The same words meant one thing to her and another thing to me. Misunderstandings such as this happen with a certain frequency.

So if we got to the point where we could decipher the verbal mental streams of minimally conscious persons, we would not be perceiving their thoughts, but rather would be inferring from the neurophysical activities required to imagine specific words what words they are using to express their thoughts.

Another thing to note, to which I will return when I consider the soul near the end of this chapter, is that the scientists are not accessing the individual's conscious experience, but only the neural correlates thereof. They could not know that the neural activity corresponded to the imagining of a word unless the subject told them so.

We have seen so far that the claim that neuroscience poses a challenge to traditional ideas regarding the nonmaterial component of the human mind is unfounded. Neuroscience can pick out the brain activity that correlates[21] with sensing and imagining things, but not with thinking abstractly. Again, a common reason why people think there is some kind of conflict between neuroscience and the notion that the intellect is immaterial is due to their failure to reflect upon the difference between thinking and imagining and the manner in which the former depends upon the latter.

Free Will

We all have direct experience of having free will. For example, I know that I did not have to write this chapter. And you know that you didn't have to choose to read it. Some will claim in the name of neuroscience that this seeming knowledge we have that we don't have to choose what we choose is illusory.

21 Note that the brain activity when one person imagines a dog may differ from that which occurs when another person imagines a dog. Also, one has to be aware that, as with any correlation, it may be the case that when a person imagines a dog, such and such brain activity occurs, but that does not necessarily mean that whenever that brain activity occurs, the person is imagining a dog.

Benjamin Libet's experiments in the 1980s are often cited as having shown that free will is an illusion. In these experiments, the participants were asked to flex their wrist whenever they felt like it and then report the moment they became conscious of their intention to do so—which they kept track of by observing a modified clock where a revolving hand moved faster than normal clock hands. We would expect that we first have a conscious awareness of an intention to act, which activates the motor area of the brain, resulting in a "readiness potential" that results in a signal being sent to the muscles of the wrist or fingers. In the experiment, the participants' "readiness potential" spiked about 550 ms before the actual motion, but the participants' reports of their intention to move preceded the motion only by 200 ms.[22] Conscious awareness of a desire to flex the wrist arose only *after* the brain got ready to send signals to the muscles. So it seems that our brain makes up our minds for us, and we only became consciously aware of our "decision" after the fact. Based on this experiment, and other similar experiments, some people concluded that free will does not play a role in our decisions.

Philosopher Andrew Mele rejects this interpretation of Libet's experiments on the grounds that this test involves an arbitrary action where nothing is at stake and there is no reason to perform the action at one time rather than another. Mele compares it to being in a grocery store and picking out one jar of peanut butter rather than other like jars that are sitting next to it. Picking this one or that one makes no difference.[23] Whereas in the cases we are clearly exercising free choice—what college to go to, whether to marry this person—something is at stake, and it does matter which individual we choose. Even in more everyday choices, such as should I do the dishes or leave them for others, or should I attend this lecture, our decisions have consequences—whereas again it is inconsequential whether we pick the jar on the left or right. So Libet's experiment involving flexing one's wrist really sheds no light on free will.

There are other similar experiments that are subject to Mele's critique. To name one, scientists at UC Davis found that decisions could be predicted based on patterns of brain activity, but the "decision" was to look to the right

22 Adapted from da Cunha and Relva, "Who's Afraid of the Big Bad Neuroscience?," 32.

23 See Alfred R. Mele, *Why Science Hasn't Disproved Free Will* (Oxford University Press, 2014), 14.

or left of a cue symbol when it appeared.[24] Their research in nowise justified one journalist's headline: "Free Will Could Be the Result of 'Background Noise' in the Brain, Study Suggests."[25]

Fr. Anselm Ramelow, OP, gives another argument against the view that Libet's experiment shows that we do not have free will.[26] He points out that the subjects made a free choice when they agreed to follow the directions given them. They freely agreed at the start of the experiment to flex their wrist within thirty seconds, once they felt the urge to do so. An urge is not something one chooses to feel; an urge is something that happens to one. It is possible to have an urge and then become conscious of it (e.g., one can wake up in the middle of the night and then realize one needs to go to the bathroom). Added to this is the fact that once we decide to do something, the execution of our decision is often on autopilot. For example, once I have agreed to meet a colleague at the faculty club at noon, I do not make a separate choice later on when it comes time to head for the faculty club unless something comes up that would give me a reason to reconsider my decision.[27] So one way of looking at Libet's experiment is that from the start one has made the choice to always flex when one feels an urge, and this prior free decision is automatically and unconsciously applied to the specific

24 Jesse J. Bengson et al., "Spontaneous Neural Fluctuations Predict Decisions to Attend," *Journal of Cognitive Neuroscience* 26, no. 11 (November 2014): 2578–84.

25 Antonia Molloy, "Free Will Could Be the Result of Background Noise in the Brain Study Suggests," *Independent*, June 21, 2014, https://www.independent.co.uk/news/science/free-will-could-be-the-result-of-background-noise-in-the-brain-study-suggests-9553678.html.

26 Fr. Anselm Ramelow, "Do We Have Free Will?," Thomistic Institute podcast, https://soundcloud.com/thomisticinstitute/do-we-have-free-will-fr-anselm-ramelow-op.

27 See John McCrone, "A Bifold Model of Freewill," *Journal of Consciousness Studies* 6, nos. 8–9 (1999): 256:

> Neuroscience also has much to say about why many of our actions seem unwilled—that is, not the result of planning but released automatically or spontaneously. The rousing of a global intention creates a dominant context (Baars, 1988) in which any habitual actions compatible with that context will simply be released. So, for example, if our explicit intention is to enter a room, then this implicitly permits the many component acts needed to get us into that room, such as taking steps down a corridor and reaching for a doorknob. The way the basal ganglia learn to slot in such component skills has recently been described in some detail (Graybeil, 1998).

McCrone goes on to apply this to the Libet experiment using the same line of reasoning as Fr. Ramelow. Note that when we do things habitually, we often are unaware of making any conscious decision in a specific instance, e.g., if we are habitually polite, we thank people when they give us a gift or do us a favor, sometimes without conscious reflection—it's automatic.

instances of when one feels the urge. Libet's experiment, then, does not bear on free choice, but on the execution of a previously made choice.

Even if we set aside Mele's and Ramelow's arguments, there would still remain a way of interpreting Libet's experiment in a way that is compatible with free will. Libet's experiment also showed that people can choose to override the urge to flex; their conscious decision to not flex after all in response to the urge precedes a flattening of the readiness potential that had been activated. Consequently, some concluded that our free will takes the form of "free won't." Looked at this way, Libet's experiments don't reveal anything other than what ordinary experience tells us: We often spontaneously have inclinations to do certain things, but we can override them. For example, the smell of coffee outside a coffee shop triggers a desire for a cup of coffee, but one doesn't have to act on this desire. And sometimes for no reason known to ourselves we feel like doing something, and may even take steps toward doing it, but we can still override it and decide to stay on task. Our senses, including the internal senses, such as memory and imagination, provoke various emotions without our choosing to feel those emotions, but what we do in response to those emotions is a matter of choice. So even if we were to not entirely reject Libet's experiments as having no bearing on free will, as Mele and Ramelow do, here is yet another way to understand them, one that does not rule out free will. An urge for something specific arises and we then become aware of it, but it doesn't determine our choice because we can always resist the urge at that point.

Aquinas, by the way, thinks that many people largely follow their feelings. In one particularly pessimistic passage, Aquinas does not reject Aristotle's statement that the bad is found in many and the good in few but takes it to mean that many people pursue sensible goods, as being better known to them, forsaking the good of reason, which is known to few.[28]

So our everyday experience of making free choices has not been eliminated by neuroscience, at least not by the experiments most commonly invoked as showing that free will is an illusion. If we do have free will, then what reason is there to think that it is an immaterial faculty? If it was a faculty that used an organ, then its operation would be determined by physical causes.[29] For example, I see blue because that is the light that is not absorbed

28 See *ST* I, q. 63, a. 9, ad 1.

29 The fact that people with certain kinds of brain damage (e.g., severe traumatic brain injury and Alzheimer's disease) are unable to exercise free will does not show that free will

by the surface I'm looking at, but is the light that reflects off the surface and impinges on my eye. I'm not free to see another color. Now, some think they can save free will while maintaining that it is a physical ability by having recourse to quantum mechanics.[30] Quantum indeterminacy can be illustrated by the notion of the half-life of a radioactive material. A half-life is the time it takes for half of the nuclei in a given radioactive isotope to undergo decay. Although a half-life has a determinate value, what cannot be predicted is which individual nuclei will disintegrate during that period.

However, even if we agree with the interpretation of quantum mechanics that holds that the indeterminacy is inherent in nature and is not simply a matter of our ignorance, this is not going to provide an opening for free will. Why? Well, it does not matter if our decision is caused by determinate causes or indeterminate ones (such as random events taking place in our brain); so long as our decision is not caused by ourselves, we are not free. The only way we can be capable of making free decisions is if part of us is immaterial, for only what is immaterial can escape the action of physical causes.[31]

---

is material. The exercise of free will depends on one's ability to think abstractly, and as was explained in chapter 2, thinking depends on imagining, and the organ of imagination is the brain (or parts thereof). Just as an act of thinking is other than an act of imagining and yet depends upon it, so too an act of free will is other than an act of imagining and yet depends upon it. Thus, if due to some brain pathology, one is unable to imagine or one's images are distorted, one will be unable to exercise free will.

30 See Mario De Caro and Hilary Putnam, "Free Will and Quantum Mechanics," *The Monist* 103 (2020): 415–26. The abstract reads:

> In the last few decades, the relevance of quantum mechanics to the free-will debate has been discussed at length, especially in relation to the prospects of libertarianism (the view according to which humans enjoy an indeterministic kind of free will). Basing his interpretation on Anscombe's seminal work, Putnam argued in 1979 that, given that quantum mechanical indeterminacy is holistic at the macrolevel—i.e., it is not traceable to atomistic events such as quantum jumps of single atoms—it can provide libertarians with the kind of freedom they seek. As shown in this article, however, Putnam ultimately reached the conclusion . . . that his argument was wrong due to problems with the way it appealed to the Uncertainty Principle.

31 See Aquinas, *De Verit.*, vol. 1, Raymundi M. Spiazzi, ed. (Marietti, 1964), q. 24, a. 2:

> Nonrational animals in nowise have free choice. To make this evident, note that since three things concur for our operation, namely, cognition, appetite, and the operation itself, the whole notion of freedom depends on the mode of cognition. For appetite follows cognition, since it is only for the good, which is proposed to it through a cognitive power. . . . And therefore if the judgment of the cognitive power is not in one's power, but is determined by something else, neither will the appetite be in one's power, and consequently neither is the motion or the activity absolutely in one's power. However, a judgment is in the power of the one judging insofar as he is able

People object to this conclusion, saying that "it seems to make our freedom turn on our possession of an ability to defy natural laws, an ability that is hard to explain convincingly, and even harder to show that we have."[32] This objection is based on a materialist assumption. It assumes that everything that happens in the world is a result of exclusively physical causes acting according to natural laws. Is my thinking that this view is false a product of physical causes acting on my brain according to natural laws? No, I reject this view on the basis of reasons, namely, those given earlier concerning the immateriality of abstract thought. Indeed, the very fact that we can argue about free will shows that thought transcends the material world: brains are not convinced by reasons but are simply in one physical state or another due to the physical causes acting on them.[33] If there are then reasons to reject materialism, the conclusion that follows from it, that free will cannot transcend physical causality, is unwarranted.[34]

Another typical objection that is raised against the notion that the freedom of the will is rooted in its immateriality is that this "simply transfers the problems presented by scientific explanations of brain activity to a different and less familiar set of entities."[35] In other words, who is to say that immaterial souls do not produce choices as the result of antecedent spiritual causes?

---

to make a judgment about his own judgment; for we are able to judge what is in our power. To judge its own judgment belongs to reason alone, which can bend back on its own act, and know the relations of the things about which it judges and through which it judges. Whence the root of all freedom is located in reason. Whence in the manner in which something stands in regard to reason, in this manner it stands to free choice. Reason, however, perfectly and fully is found in man; whence in him alone is free choice fully found.

32 Hilary Bok, "The Implications of Advances in Neuroscience for Freedom of the Will," *The Journal of the American Society for Experimental NeuroTherapeutics* 4, no. 3 (July 2007): 556.

33 "Suppose we are convinced by the mechanistic view that we are not intentional, rational agents after all. Of course, the notion of being 'convinced' would be an illusion too. Being convinced means that we are persuaded by evidence or an argument, but a mechanism is not persuaded by anything. A mechanism is simply neurophysically transformed." Stephen J. Morse, "Neuroscience, Free Will, and Criminal Responsibility," in *Free Will and the Brain: Neuroscientific, Philosophical, and Legal Perspectives*, Walter Glannon, ed. (Cambridge University Press, 2015), 271.

34 Given that we commonly think that we have free choice because we can think before we act and that there is reason to think that the intellect is immaterial, it's not surprising that free will would also be an immaterial ability.

35 Bok, "The Implications of Advances in Neuroscience," 557.

First, no evidence is offered for why we should think that it is possible for the action of our immaterial wills to be determined by antecedent spiritual causes. Secondly, Thomas Aquinas provides reasons why this cannot be the case. I can only sketch here what he would say.

If free will and the human soul are indeed immaterial, it follows that the only way they can come into existence is through creation: they cannot come about through change, that is, through the transformation of some existing matter.[36] There is reason to think that God is the only being that can create.[37] If this is true, then God is the only one that has direct control over the will. Free will cannot be taken away from us by a being that is not the cause of the rational nature, any more than any other natural property can be taken from a natural thing, such as conductivity from a metal. So, just as only God can prevent flesh from being burned by fire—no other being can—so too only God can directly affect the freedom of the will. Spiritual causes other than God can at most try to persuade us or can manipulate our imaginations and emotions to make doing such-and-such attractive. They cannot change the will's very nature, which is to move freely. How God acts on our will would take us far beyond the scope of this chapter, but it suffices to say he does not act on free will in a way that annihilates its freedom.[38] I'm not trying to gloss over the difficulty of these considerations. My point here is that it is a mistake to assume that there is no response to the objection

36 Substantial forms that are not self-subsistent do not need to be created, that is, brought into existence from nothing. Natural agents educe such forms from the potency or prime matter of an existing substance or substances. A comparison with accidental change is helpful here. A blob of clay does not have a spherical shape, but when an agent forms the clay into a ball, that agent doesn't make the spherical shape from nothing. It existed in the clay in potency. Similarly, if an agent transforms one substance into another, the agent does not create the substantial form of the new substance. That substantial form existed in potency in the substance that was transformed by the agent. On this point, see *ST* I, q. 45, a. 8.

37 See *ST* I, q. 45, a. 5 and I, q. 90, aa. 2 and 3 for an explanation of why God alone can create.

38 See *ST* I-II, q. 10, a. 4:

> As Dionysius says, it does not belong to divine providence to corrupt the natures of things, but to preserve them. Whence all things move according to their condition, so that from necessary causes the effects follow of necessity according to divine motion, whereas from contingent cause the effects follow contingently. Therefore, since the will is an active principle not determined to one, but standing indifferently to many, God moves it in such a manner that it is not determined to one of necessity, but its motion remains contingent and not necessary, except as to those things to which it naturally moves.

that there could be antecedent spiritual causes that compel our choices and therefore the immateriality of the will does not secure its freedom.

The Soul

In the opening part of this chapter, I chose to focus on how neuroscience is thought by some to overturn the notion that humans have the immaterial faculties of reason and free will. Humans possess these faculties in virtue of their rational soul. So now I need to speak about the human soul and show that arguments drawn from neuroscience do not disprove its existence. But first, I will address what the soul is more generally. The initial philosophical notion of the soul arises from observing that some things are alive and others are not. As was explained in the previous chapter, living things move themselves and nonliving things do not.[39] Living things thus must have something about them that causes them to differ from nonliving ones. That is what the soul is. According to this view, a live pine tree has a soul, as does a live cat. So, the soul is first understood as simply the cause of a being's ability to carry on life activities. But what exactly is it?

The Soul is Not a Harmony

In antiquity, certain thinkers maintained that the soul is a harmony, or in other words, that it is simply the complex, interactive order of the living thing's parts.[40] And there are philosophers and scientists nowadays who defend this position. According to them, the cat's soul is understood to be the respiratory system of the cat interacting with the cardiovascular system interacting with the nervous system, etc. Death is explained solely by the breakdown of essential interactions among these systems. One variant of this view sees the soul to be the totality of ordered interactions at the level of the molecules composing the living thing.[41] Another variant is the view of neuroscientist Bill Newsome:

39 The self-motion of living things is further discussed in chapter 3.

40 See Aristotle, *On the Soul*, chap. 4. Here he refers to "supporters of the view that the soul is a kind of harmony" (407b31). The only one he refers to by name is Empedocles (408a18).

41 Nicanor Austriaco, OP, proposes a version of classical Aristotelian-Thomistic hylomorphism in terms of systems theory. He fails to see that a systems theory approach reduces the soul to a harmony:

> I think that souls or self identity are high level states of organization of the brain. . . . And I think that the critical thing is not the molecules, it's not the carbon and the nitrogen and the hydrogen and the oxygen, those obviously, were critical for our being here in this world in the first place. But what's critical to my identity is not so much those molecules as it is those higher states of organization, that actually make those molecules, in some sense, come alive and come sentient and become purposeful.[42]

Aristotle and Aquinas reject that understanding of soul. Aquinas explains why in his commentary on Aristotle's *De Anima*:

> For the soul cannot be said to be a harmony, according as harmony is found in composite things and things having composition. . . . For the order of the composite parts in the body is quite apparent; for it is easy to know the order of bones to bones, and of nerves to nerves, and of the arm to the hand, and of flesh to bones. But an account (*ratio*) of the order of the parts of the soul is not apparent to us. For we are not able to know through this order [i.e., of the bodily parts] the order that exists among the intellect and the sense and the appetite and things of this sort.[43]

Indeed, not only does studying the body alone tell us nothing about the relationship of sensation, imagination, emotion, intellect, etc. to each other, but it also does not give us the knowledge that is crucial for knowing even one of these faculties. As physicist Erwin Schrödinger notes: "We

---

Systems biology is an emerging field of research that seeks to understand the living whole as a dynamic network of integrated parts. Its goal is to uncover the fundamental design principles of living systems by looking at what system theorists call a system's structure and its dynamics. An analysis of a system's structure identifies all the parts of the system and describes their interactions. In biology, this would involve cataloging all the molecules that go into assembling a living organism and then determining which ones interact with each other. An analysis of a system's dynamics focuses on the behavior of these interacting molecules over time. Nicanor Austriaco, OP, "The Specification of Sex/Gender in the Human Species," *New Blackfriars* 94, no. 1054 (November 2013), 704.

42 Bill Newsome, "Neuroscience, Faith and Free Will," podcast transcript, https://biologos.org/podcast-episodes/bill-newsome-neuroscience-faith-free-will. See Marcelo Gleiser, "Is Neuroscience Rediscovering the Soul?," *NPR* (April 5, 2017), https://www.npr.org/sections/13.7/2017/04/05/522738015/is-neuroscience-rediscovering-the-soul. Gleiser, a physicist and astronomer, suggests that "we consider your soul as the sum total of your neurocognitive essence, your very specific brain signature, the unique neuronal connections, synapses, and flow of neurotransmitters that makes you you."

43 *In DA*. (Italy: Marietti, 1959), bk. 1, lec. 9, no. 139.

may be sure that there is no nervous process whose objective description includes the characteristic 'yellow colour' or 'sweet taste,' just as little as the objective description of an electro-magnetic wave includes either of these characteristics."[44] The neuroscientist would not know that he was tracing physical changes involved in vision if he did not first have the experience of seeing. The experience of seeing cannot be reduced to a series of physical changes among interacting parts because to see is to be aware of color (even if only color on a grey scale). None of the physical parts involved in the visual system have the property of being aware: neurons lack awareness, as do the proteins, etc. that make them up.

Some will claim then that if enough physical parts interact in certain ways, awareness will emerge. They will point to properties such as fluidity, which a single water molecule does not have, but which many together have, or to surface tension, which again a single water molecule does not have, but many together have.[45] These properties, however, are partially contained in the individual molecules. To give a comparison: One person cannot surround another but can be part of a group that does because each person can partially surround someone. Similarly, someone might not be able to lift a heavy object, but together with another person is so able, because each of them is capable of lifting some of the weight. Similarly, each water molecule has the ability to contribute to the formation of a field that accounts for why many together have the property of fluidity; each water molecule also has part of the ability to produce surface tension because each actually is

44 Erwin Schrödinger, *What is Life? With Mind and Matter and Autobiographical Sketches* (Cambridge University Press, 1992), 155.

45 See Terence Horgan, "From Supervenience to Superdupervenience," in *Philosophy of Mind*, ed. David J. Chalmers (Oxford University Press, 2002), 158:

> For at least some kinds of properties we seem to have a fairly good idea about what would count as a materialistically acceptable explanation of why such a property is supervenient on a given configuration of physical properties. Consider, for example, the property of *liquidity*. . . . Explaining why liquidity supervenes on certain microphysical properties is essentially a matter of explaining why any quantity of stuff with these microphysical properties will exhibit those macro-features. . . . A variety of recent so-called naturalizing projects, in philosophy of mind and elsewhere in philosophy, can be regarded as being, in effect attempts to articulate the essential or definitive characteristics of certain higher-order properties (e.g., mental properties) in such a way that these properties, as so characterized, are susceptible to materialistic explanations of their supervenience.

a dipole.[46] In the case of collective properties, nothing of a different kind emerges. We see this in artifacts: no one part of an inkjet printer can print, but one part can move another part that moves the ink on to the paper. It is the same for a bicycle: an isolated part cannot serve as transportation for a person, but it can move and bear weight, and this is what allows it along with other parts to do so.

Sense knowledge, however, is different in kind from the physical motions that are required if it is to occur. One can see this by asking how one could best explain sight to a person who was blind from birth. One approach would be to explain the physiology of the visual system in all its scientific detail. But a second approach would be to say to the blind person: sight is similar to hearing and smelling. You are aware of sounds and you are aware of odors; so you realize that awareness can be of different things. There is another sensible thing called color, and sight is awareness of it. Of course, the blind person will not then know exactly what it means to see, but still gets a better idea of what sight is when it's explained in terms of the subjective experience of sensing than when it's explained in terms of physical interactions.

The same point can also be made in regard to emotion. Certain physiological changes take place when we feel different emotions. However, emotions are not reducible to these changes because ordinarily emotions are about something. When one is sad, one is sad about something, and the same is typically the case of the other emotions as well. If I asked you why you were sad and you told me that there was increased communication between your amygdala and your hippocampus, or something of the sort, I would not be satisfied. Physiological activities simply are; they are not about something. No scientist could identify that a person was angry by monitoring physiological changes in the body, if she did not first know from internal experience that anger is a desire to get even; the desire to get even can be correlated with the physiological changes but is not reducible to them.

For Aristotle and Aquinas, the inability to fully explain sense perception and emotion in terms of the interaction of physical parts is a reason to hold

46 See Andy Coghaln, "Science: What Really Makes Water Wet?," New Scientist (February 15, 1997), https://www.newscientist.com/article/mg15320693-200-science-what-really-makes-water-wet/. See also J. K. Gregory et al., "The Water Dipole Moment in Water Clusters," *Science* 275 (February 7, 1997): 814–17. See also Water Science School, "Surface Tension," June 6, 2019, https://water.usgs.gov/edu/surface-tension.html.

that the soul of the living thing is not the totality of the living thing's physical parts and their coordinated interactions.

Readers may recall that they have seen these arguments before, leveled against the reductionists and the nonreductive physicalists who deny that living things have souls. As a matter of fact, there really is no difference between the views of those who deny the existence of the soul and those who regard it to be the arrangement and/or interactions of body parts. The latter call the arrangement and/or interactions of the body parts that are proposed to explain life activities "the soul," whereas the former see the soul as a misleading and outdated term, adding nothing to the explanation of life activities in terms of body parts and their interactions. Both views are subject to the same criticism. If the whole is what simply results from the arrangement and interaction of its parts, the whole cannot engage in some activity that does not trace back to its parts and their interactions. Both views leave activities such as seeing and feeling sad unexplained.

The Soul, a Substantial Form

Aristotle and Aquinas reject views that would reduce the soul to the harmony of the organism's parts. What do they hold that the soul is? Here we need to try to understand the difficult notion of substantial form. In what follows I'll do my best to explain the notions of substantial change and substantial form, but don't be surprised if they do not immediately make sense to you—these notions need to be repeatedly considered, especially in contrast to their alternatives—but one has to begin somewhere. One of the things that I want to bring out is that nothing I have said commits me to the Cartesian view that we are composed of two substances: an immaterial substance, the soul, and a second substance, a physical body. I'll very briefly sketch out the Aristotelian-Thomistic "hylomorphic" (i.e., "matter-form") alternative, which is sometimes labeled as "dualism," but is a dualism of a very different sort from that of Descartes.[47]

47 See Michael J. Dodds, OP, "Hylomorphism and Human Wholeness: Perspectives on the Mind-Brain Problem," *Theology and Science* 7, no. 2 (2009): 141–62. Dodds provides a helpful account of substantial change, as well as providing arguments for the superiority of the Aristotelian understanding of the soul as substantial form of the body to materialistic and dualistic accounts of the human person. See also Michael J. Dodds, OP, "The Reality of the Soul in an Age of Neuroscience," *Nova et Vetera* 17, no. 3 (Summer 2019): 893–912.

If I have in my hand a piece of blackboard chalk, I have in my hand both a cylinder and calcium carbonate, but I do not have two things in my hand. The cylindrical form is not something separate from the calcium carbonate whose form it is.[48] Form is not matter, but the two together make up one thing.

The notion of *substantial* form is arrived at by Aristotle through an analysis of different kinds of changes. When I get a tan or a potbelly, I remain a human being. These changes are referred to as "accidental changes"; and an accident is something that exists in another as in a subject. So my skin color is an accident; the same goes for my girth. However, when I die, I will turn into a bunch of chemicals. This is a substantial change. Aristotle goes on to draw a parallel between accidental changes and substantial changes. He says just as going from being flat-stomached to being pot-bellied supposes an underlying subject, so too a change from being one substance to being another must suppose something that underlies the change, and he calls this "prime matter"—prime matter is the ability a substance has to become another substance. It accounts for continuity in substantial change. When a squirrel dies it is not as if a number of chemicals mysteriously come to exist where a living body was before. Just as the subject that has undergone an accidental change acquires a new accidental form, so too does prime matter that undergoes a substantial change acquire a new substantial form. A substantial form makes a thing to be one individual thing possessing a certain nature. Nonliving natural things have substantial forms that make them to be one substance rather than another, and they have "prime matter" that is the capacity to be changed into another substance. Oxygen, for example, seems to be a substance.[49] It has the capacity to be transformed into another substance by means of a nuclear reaction, and in addition to this capacity

48 The matter of the piece of chalk is a collection of many contiguous calcium carbonate molecules. It is one, in some sense, by reason of the uniformity and continuity of the constituent molecules.

49 As noted in the appendix on substance, it is hard to determine what the nonliving substances are. Is oxygen a substance or are its parts (protons, etc.) substances or are the parts of its parts substances? This difficulty is not a reason to deny that there nonliving substances. The thing that we are most sure is a substance is ourselves. We know from our internal experience that we are a single human being, not a collection of parts. When we die we turn into other things that are nonliving and that are substances, even if we are not able to identify specifically what substances they are.

for change, it has a substantial form that makes it oxygen and not nitrogen or something else.[50]

Note that neither substantial form nor prime matter are observable or imaginable, unlike a thing's shape or structure (be it static or dynamic) and the matter it is the form of. Aquinas explains this in his commentary on Aristotle's *Physics*:

> It [prime matter] is known by analogy, that is according to a proportion. For we know that wood is something other than the form of a stool or bed because sometimes it exists under one form and sometimes under another. Therefore, when we see that air sometimes becomes water, it is necessary to say that something existing under the form of air, sometimes exists under the form of water; and thus, it is something other than the form of water and other than the form of air, as wood is something other than the form of a stool and other than the form of a bed.[51]

Nowadays we know that air is more than one substance. However, Aquinas's point is still intelligible. As accidental forms (the structure of a stool or a bed) stand to some matter that we can observe, such as wood, so too do substantial forms stand to prime matter that we cannot observe but understand to be the principle of continuity in substantial change. While material substances, whose prime matter is actualized by a substantial form, are plainly observable, the substantial form that actualizes that prime matter cannot be observed, for the substantial form is not a shape or structure—these are accidental forms—but is rather what makes a substance to be one thing possessing a certain nature (The failure to understand this point is at the root of many faulty reformulations of hylomorphism).[52]

So a plant, a worm, a cat, etc., like nonliving substances, each have a substantial form that make them to be the particular kind of substance that they are, and they have prime matter, that is, an underlying capacity to be changed into another substance. Why talk about living things having a particular kind of substantial form, namely, a soul? This goes back to what

50 See Tabaczek, *Emergence*, 230–31, for a discussion of the difficulty of determining what are the nonliving substances.

51 *In Phy.*, bk. 1, lec. 13.

52 Many neo-hylomorphic views fail because they in effect substitute accidental form for substantial form and/or they adopt the view that living things are constituted of separately existing parts, a view that is incompatible with a hylomorphic understanding of organisms. For an analysis of why particular neo-hylomorphic views fail, see Tabaczek, *Emergence*, 217–23.

I was saying earlier: It is because living things manifest activities that go beyond those that nonliving natural things are capable of performing, be it individually or collectively. In other words, we do not think that the fact that a dog when dropped falls downwards requires us to posit that the dog has a soul. In the case of the dog, a reason to posit it has a soul is that the dog is aware of smells, sounds, etc., and sensing is not reducible to the interactions of a group of physical parts, all of which lack awareness. The dog's soul makes the dog to be a substance of a specific sort that is capable of carrying on activities that go beyond what nonliving natural things are capable of, be it individually or collectively.

Now one might maintain that the soul is not posited to explain sensing, feeling emotions, etc. but only to explain why the body decays. There are two reasons to reject this view. First, all natural bodies, living and nonliving, are subject to corruption. We don't maintain that oxygen has a soul because it can be transformed into another element. Secondly, action follows being. If a sighted animal is one living thing because of its soul, then its life activities will depend upon its having a soul, rather than on causes independent from the soul. To say that a dog is a dog because it has a dog soul, but that it does dog-like things such as see due to a set of physical causes independent of its soul, dissociates action from being, what the dog does from what the dog is. The dog's eyes would not be dog eyes without the soul and so plainly would not be functional. As Aquinas explains:

> Now the substantial form is not only the perfection of the whole but also of every part. For since the whole consists of parts, the form of a whole which does not give being to the individual parts of a body is a form which is arrangement and order, such as the form of a house, which is an accidental form. The soul is in fact a substantial form, whence it is necessary that it is the form and act not only of the whole, but of each and every part. And therefore, when the soul recedes, one does not speak of an animal or a human except equivocally, in the manner in which we speak of a painted or stone animal, and the same is true for hand and eye or flesh and bone, as the Philosopher notes. A sign of this is that when the soul recedes, no part of the body has its proper operation, whereas everything that retains its species retains its proper operation.[53]

53 *ST* I, q. 76, a. 8.

As we saw earlier, those espousing various theories of emergence, both reductive and nonreductive, maintain that living things only have the accidental form of arrangement and order. They regard the whole organism to arise from its parts, and so are at a loss explaining how the whole can exhibit some activity that does not trace back to the parts. Aquinas, on the other hand, maintains that living things have a substantial form, which not only makes the whole to be what it is, but also makes the parts to be what they are. Since action follows being, the soul which makes the parts to be what they are is at the root of the life activities performed through them.[54] It explains why dogs can see with their eyes and digest food with their gut.

I would be remiss if I did not mention here a difficulty in understanding Aquinas's hylomorphic view. What Aquinas says about the organs applies even to their constituents, the proteins, etc. that make them up, and further to the constituents of these constituents. Aquinas would maintain that a protein, amino acid, or carbon atom does not have an independent existence in the living body as it does outside of the body. In the body, a carbon atom, an amino acid, etc. is only "virtually" present.[55] While it is obvious that organs quickly undergo decay when the organism dies, it is not obvious that what is identified to be a carbon atom, amino acid, etc. inside the body becomes a different substance when removed from the body.

The basic AT teaching on the virtual presence of the elements in a composite substance, such as a living body, consists of the following three assertions.[56] First, the elements no longer exist in act in the composite; their prime matter is now actualized by the substantial form of the composite.

54 See *SCG*, bk. 3, chap. 97: "For since everything acts insofar as it is in act, for what is in potency, as such, is found devoid of action; everything whatsoever is a being in act through form; it is necessary that the operation of a thing follow from its form. Therefore, it is necessary that where there are diverse forms, that diverse operations are possessed."

55 The way that Aristotle and Aquinas speak at times could be misconstrued as affirming that the elements exist in act in living things; see *In DA*, bk. 3, lec. 1, no. 571: "He [Aristotle] says, therefore, that the organs naturally apt for sensing are to consist of only two of the simple bodies, namely, from air and water, for these are the more passible bodies."

56 See Tabaczek, *Emergence*, 233. The *locus classicus* for virtual presence in Aquinas is *De mixtione elementorum ad magistrum Philippum de Castro*, 17–18:

> Therefore, the powers (*virtutes*) of the substantial forms of simple bodies are preserved in mixed bodies. Therefore, the forms of the elements in the mixed bodies are indeed not in act but in power. And this is what Aristotle says in bk. 1 of *De Generatione* [327b29–31], "Therefore they do not remain, namely, the elements in a mixed body, in act as body and white [remain in act], nor are they corrupted, nor some third thing, nor both: for their virtue is preserved."

Second, when the composite corrupts, it corrupts back into the elements virtually present in it. Third, the elements are not entirely destroyed in the composite but are present by their powers.[57] These powers, however, are generally understood to be modified in some manner by their presence in the composite; for if the powers were identical, this would give credence to the notion that they belong to a substance that exists in act, both inside and outside the body.[58]

I will leave it to other Thomists to further explain and defend the notion of virtual presence.[59] I would like to point out, however, that if the notion

---

(One "third" option is the view of Averroes who held "that the forms of the elements, on account of their imperfection, are intermediaries between accidental forms and substantial forms." [*ST* I. q. 76, a. 4, ad 4]). See also in the *Summa*:

> According to the Philosopher in *De Generatione*, bk. 1 it ought to be said that the forms of the elements do not remain in the mixed body in act, but by power. For the qualities proper to the elements remain, albeit diminished [*remissae*], in which qualities lie the power of the elementary forms. And a quality of this sort, belonging to the mixed body, is the proper disposition for the substantial form of the mixed body, for instance, the form of a stone or the soul of any [living] thing. *ST* I, q. 76, a. 4, ad 4.

57 The fact that parts are distinguishable one from another does not mean that they are different substances. See *ST* I, q. 76, a. 5, ad 3: "The parts of the animal, such as the eye, the hand, flesh, and bone, and things of this sort do not belong to a species, but rather the whole does, and therefore, it cannot be said, strictly speaking, that they are of diverse species but that they are of diverse dispositions." The composition and organization of the eye is different than that of the hand, but the eye and hand do not differ in the manner that two substances differ from one another. It is only the whole animal that is a substance, belonging to some species, e.g., frog or dog. Similarly, one can distinguish a part of the body with the properties of water from a part of the body with the properties of calcium, but the two parts do not exist as two substances.

58 There are Thomists who do not think that Aristotle's teaching on virtual presence means that the powers of the elements in living things are somewhat modified. See Jean-Philippe Murray, "Qu'est-ce que l'âme? Examen de la conception aristotélicienne de cette notion," *Peripatetikos* 12 (2017): 93–94: "The elements that are found in the living thing are not experimentally distinguishable from those present in the inanimate world." According to Murray, "The new form, in addition to being the cause of new properties which the substances that it has replaced do not possess, assures the properties of these substances" (translation mine). See also John Goyette, "St. Thomas and the Unity of Substantial Form," *Nova et Vetera* 7, no. 4 (2009): 788: "If, as the evidence of modern science suggests, a water molecule absorbed by the body remains chemically unchanged, how can we maintain that the water contained in the blood is caused by the substantial form of the whole organism?" Goyette's response is that "higher forms, precisely because they are higher, are able to contain the perfections found in a lower form." Goyette, 788.

59 See Christopher Decaen, "Elemental Virtual Presence in St. Thomas," *The Thomist* 64, no. 2 (April 2000): 271–300. See also Tabaczek, *Emergence*, 19–20 and 229–34. Note that there is a need to integrate Aquinas's teaching on disposition with his teaching on virtual presence. Aquinas says in regard to the view that the soul is a harmony:

of virtual presence seems a high cost to accepting hylomorphism, it nevertheless appears lesser than the cost of affirming that you are no more than a collection of interacting parts inside a membrane, as well as the cost of affirming that the death of an animal is essentially a mere rearrangement of parts.[60]

In light of the teaching on virtual presence, let us revisit the explanation of emergent properties using the example of the dog's seeing. The molecules etc. that make up the visual system of the dog do not exist as independent entities but as parts of the dog existing under the dog's substantial form. The dog's substantial form, its soul, actualizes matter more completely than the substantial forms of the elements actualize it. Aquinas, following Aristotle, compares the substantial forms of things to numbers.[61] The greater number contains the lesser number and more:

> For as the Philosopher says, the forms of things are like numbers, in which the species is diversified through the addition and subtraction of the unit; and the formal differences of things consist in a certain perfection of order. For plant differs in species from stone in this that it adds life, and brute animal from plant in this that it adds sense, and human from brute animal in this that it adds reason.[62]

> It seems that this view is highly probable, for when one is posited something other is posited, and when the former is removed, the latter is removed, for when a harmony recedes from some body the soul recedes, and when the harmony remains, the soul remains. But this does not follow, for a proportion of this sort is not form, as its proponents believed, but is a disposition of matter for form. If one takes the harmony of composition properly as disposition, it correctly follow that so long as the disposition of matter to form remains, the form remains, and when the disposition is destroyed, the form is removed. Nevertheless, it is not the case that the harmony is the form, but a disposition of matter for form. *In DA*, bk. 1, lec. 9, n. 13.

60 Positing a multiplicity of substantial forms is no solution. This view holds that a carbon atom in an organism exists at the same time under its own substantial form and under the substantial form of the organism. That is like saying that a whole piece of clay exists simultaneously with a cubic form and with a spherical form. Aquinas refutes this view in *ST* I, q. 76, a. 4. The sed contra reads: "Of one thing, there is one substantial being. But substantial form gives substantial being. Therefore, of one thing there is only one substantial form. The soul, however, is the substantial form of man. Therefore, it is impossible that in man there exist some other substantial forms than the intellectual soul."

61 See *Metaphysics*, bk. 8, chap. 3, 1043b36–1044a11.

62 *De Pot.* in *Quaestiones Disputatae*, vol. 2, P. Bazzi et al., eds. (Marietti, 1965), q. 10, a. 5. See *Quaestio Disputata de Anima*, un., a. 9.

Accordingly, "the most perfect form gives everything that the more imperfect forms give, and something more."[63] The dog's more perfect substantial form is why it is capable of activities such as seeing, activities that a collection of separate interacting nonliving substances cannot account for.[64]

In the case of humans, not only is the reason to say that dogs have a soul applicable, for we too sense and have emotions, and so forth, but there is reason to say that our soul is of a different kind than that of the dog because we in addition have the ability to think abstractly and to freely choose. In both cases, the souls are not something separate from the body, but are what make the body to be a living body of a specific kind, canine and human. Again, the relationship is similar to the calcium carbonate and the cylindrical shape of a piece of chalk not being separate entities. The soul is a substantial form that makes matter exist as a specific kind of being.

There is a further difference between the human soul and the dog soul, namely, the human soul is separable from the living human individual, that is, it remains in existence after death because it is an immaterial thing. On the Aristotelian-Thomistic view, it is not the whole human individual.[65]

One might still wonder, How does the soul relate to the mind? Again, "mind" can refer to the ability to imagine or to the ability to think. The relation between both these abilities and the soul is somewhat similar to the relationship between the capabilities of a smartphone and the phone's structure. A phone's capabilities include things such as playing music, relaying text messages, doing web searches and so forth. These capabilities depend on a determinate arrangement of the matter that makes up the phone. This arrangement is not the same as the phone's capabilities but is their cause. In a somewhat similar way, the soul is the cause of the human being's various abilities: our ability to imagine, our ability to think abstractly, our ability to see, our ability to transform food into ourselves, and so forth. The soul, however, is a substantial form, and in this way differs from the ordered juxtaposition

63 *De Spir. Creat.*, in Bazzi et al., *Quaestiones Disputatae*.

64 Note that we see even in the case of the accidental forms of artifacts that one form in some way embraces and exceeds another. For example, the smartphone can do what a cell phone does and many more things as well. While this is partly due to differences in their parts, it is also partly due to the organization of those parts, which is far more sophisticated in the smartphone. The spatial organization or arrangement of separate parts and the order of their interactions in time are accidental forms. Accidental forms of this sort are a necessary cause of emergence as found in collective wholes.

65 See *Q. DA*, unicus, a. 1.

of the smartphone's parts.[66] Just as the substantial form of a nonliving natural thing, such as oxygen, is not the same as its properties (e.g., its electronegativity, or atomic mass, or its breathability and combustibility), but stands to them as their common and foundational source, so too the substantial form of living things, the soul, is not the same as the properties of living things, but is their root cause, in a sense "where they all come from," and therefore what they are manifestations of.

So much for this very brief account of the Thomistic understanding of the soul. I hope that this sketch makes it clear that nothing I've said in the earlier part of the chapter about the immateriality of the intellect and free will need be construed as an endorsement of Cartesian dualism, which makes human beings into two separate substances. The human soul in a living person is the substantial form of the living body and not something separate from it. It, however, unlike an animal's soul, is capable of existing separated from the body. I also hope to have shown that the notion of substantial form provides a more adequate explanation of strong emergent properties, such as seeing and feeling angry, than nonreductive physicalist accounts do.

Conclusion

Neuroscience-based arguments against the soul do not face up to the evidence that life activities such as sensation cannot be accounted for solely in terms of material parts and their interactions. Neuroscience-based arguments against the *human* soul are generally directed at giving a materialist account of the life activities of choosing and of thinking abstractly. As we have seen, arguments that are based on Libet's and other similar experiments fail to eliminate free choice. And as we have seen, if free choice exists, it must be an immaterial faculty—in which case neuroscience has nothing to say about it, as such. Similarly, we have seen that the mind reading that neuroscientists are currently capable of, and predictably will be even better capable of in the future, does not involve observing abstract thoughts, but rather detecting neural correlates of images, including those for words. If the reflections on what we do when we think, articulated above, are correct, ideas are immaterial, and so we must conclude that the findings of neuroscience cannot have any bearing on our capacity for abstract thought as such. These

66 A smartphone does not have a substantial form. The phone is an accidental whole consisting of a collection of parts that are positioned in a particular manner.

conclusions by no means denigrate the tremendous power neuroscience has to identify the physiological underpinnings of human activities such as imagining, remembering, feeling emotions, and so forth, knowledge that has amazing potential for developing ways of communicating with minimally conscious persons, preventing memory loss, and treating various emotional conditions such as post-traumatic stress disorder. Philosophy can't do these things. Philosophy, however, can help us reflect on our ordinary experience—which is what I've tried to do here.[67]

67 I wish to thank Christopher Decaen for his helpful comments.

3

The Natural Division of Material Living Things at the Most Universal Level

Carl R. Woese, Otto Kandler, and Mark L. Wheelis claim that the division they propose for living things into the domains of Archaea, Bacteria, and Eukarya is the natural division of living things at the most universal level and they explicitly reject the division into plants and animals, which is the division that Aquinas espouses, albeit adding a third category, human being.[1] My main purpose is to argue that the division Aquinas proposes is more natural than the one Woese et al. propose. I will then add some reflections regarding what Aquinas would think about Woese et al.'s approach and also regarding the utility of Aquinas's method of division for biology. I will close by comparing my analysis to other recent defenses of Aquinas's division.

1 Carl R. Woese et al., "Towards a Natural System of Organisms: Proposal for the Domains of Archaea, Bacteria, and Eucarya," *Proceedings of the National Academy of Sciences, USA* 87 (June 1990): 4576–79.

Aquinas's View on the Natural Division of Material Living Things at the Most Universal Level

According to Aquinas, what distinguishes living things from all other things is that living things move themselves: "Every living thing in some manner moves itself."[2]

Every life activity involves self-motion: nutrition, growth, seeing, imagining, etc. Some life activities are motions in the strict sense, and others only in the broad sense. Motions in the strict sense involve imperfection. For example, the animal walking to the watering hole gets closer and closer to the hole while not being there. And the skin of a person who is tanning gets darker and darker but is not yet fully tanned. Motions in the broad sense are acts of things that are perfect, as is the case of sensing and understanding. The one that senses (for example, sees green) does not do so gradually, as if partly seeing and partly not seeing, but does so immediately.[3] There is a motion in the sense of a change from sensing in potency to sensing in

2 *ST* I, q. 78 a. 1 See also *ST* I, q. 18, a. 1: "Those things strictly speaking are living which move themselves according to some species of motion." See also *In DA*, bk. 2 lec. 5, n. 7: "For this is seen to be proper to living things: they act as moved by themselves." See also *De Pot.*, q. 10, a. 1: "For we say of anything that we find to operate through itself and in itself in any manner that it lives." Note, however, that things that are only able to move themselves but are not in fact doing so are also alive. However, we can only recognize for sure that they are alive when they begin to move on their own. For example, a frozen human embryo is not engaging in any self-motion. It is only when after being unthawed it starts growing that we know that it is alive. Similarly, a dormant seed may contain a live plant embryo or a dead one, but this is only known when it sprouts or fails to sprout.

3 Sent. IV, https://www.corpusthomisticum.org/iopera.html, d. 17, q. 1, a. 5, qc. 3, ad 1:

> For there is motion that is the act of the imperfect, which is a going forth from potency to act; and it is necessary that such motion be successive, as always awaiting something in the future for the perfection of its species, because part of the motion is other in kind from the whole motion . . . as is obvious in alteration from the motion which is to whiteness, part of which motion is to a middle color differing in species, if taken separately. Another motion is the act of the perfect, which is rather called "activity" (operatio), which does not await some completion of its species in the future, e.g., to sense; and such a motion is not successive but sudden.

See also *In DA*, bk. 3, lec. 12, n. 2:

> And because everything in potency, insofar as it is such, is imperfect, therefore that motion [from contrary to contrary] is the act of the imperfect. But this motion is the act of the perfect; for it is the activity of the sense already brought into act through its species. For to sense does not belong to the sense except when it exists in act; and therefore, this motion, simply speaking, is other than a physical motion.

act; however, this operation does not become more perfect over time; for example, one does not see the green of the grass one is gazing at any better at a later moment than from the first moment one saw it. In addition, unlike true motions, which all involve some loss (e.g., the skin loses its whiteness in tanning), sensing and understanding involve perfection without any loss.[4]

It does not seem, however, to be unqualifiedly true that sensing lacks the character of true motion. When one opens one eyes in the dark, one sometimes goes from seeing nothing or next to nothing to gradually discerning the shapes of objects, and this is due to a motion in the strict sense, namely, of one's pupils, which open up more to let in more light. This does not occur, however, when there is adequate light. Similarly, when it comes to seeing a moving shape in the distance, one gradually sees that shape more and more distinctly as it draws closer. This, however, would not occur if the object was in an appropriate range to begin with.[5] That there are elements of motion in the strict sense attached to sensing is finally not surprising given that sensing requires physical interaction between what is able to be sensed and the sense organ, and this in turn requires determinate physical conditions.[6] Intellectual understanding more perfectly fits the description of a motion that is the act of the perfect, as it does not involve an organ. Once the possible intellect is informed by the intelligible species abstracted by the agent intellect, the person immediately understands in act. And the same is true for knowledge of self-evident principles; once one knows what whole and part are, one immediately knows that the whole is greater than the part.

One might object that sensing is not a self-motion because the one sensing does not move itself but is moved by the sensible object. It is true that the sensible object brings the sense into act by acting on the sense organ. However, when the sense is brought into act, the sensing being itself carries on the activity of sensing.[7] The same sort of thing occurs in nonliving things

4 See *In DA*, bk. 2, lec. 11, n. 12 (Marietti, no. 369).

5 There is also something like a motion in seeing in the case where one first sees a whole and then looks more carefully at a part of that whole, for one sees the part more distinctly when one focuses on it than one sees it when looking at the whole as whole. It is not the case, however, that by focusing on the part, its details gradually become more visible.

6 See *Sent.* IV, d. 49, q. 1, a. 2, qc. 3: "Operation is not measured by time except according as it is connected to motion."

7 See *Sent.* I, d. 40, q. 1, a. 1, ad 1:

> There is a certain operation which is not signified as proceeding to some effect, but rather according as something is in it; and in the case something is received in it, that

that passively undergo the action of some agent: Once they are brought into act by it, they are able to act. For example, the water in a pot when heated by a fire is able to heat an egg. The two cases differ, however, in that once the sense is brought into act, it carries on an activity that perfects the subject, namely, knowing something sensible, whereas in the case of nonknowing subjects, their actualization by an outside agent only enables them to carry on activities perfective of other things.[8]

One might also object that green plants, when they photosynthesize, are activated by light, and so are not self-movers. It is true that living things need energy to carry on their life activities. They are not self-movers in an absolute sense. However, they use some of the energy, be it light energy or from the food they eat, to modify themselves, producing new parts of themselves through their internal activity. They are not like clocks or other artifacts which do not use the energy powering them to produce new parts of themselves or increase the size of their existent parts. Even if these artifacts were to do so, it would not constitute a self-motion in the strict sense, as these beings are not substances in the Aristotelian sense, but collections of substances.

If self-motion distinguishes living things from all other things, then the correct way to divide living things into kinds would seem to be based on differences in kind of their self-motions. As Aquinas points out in many places: "An essential division is always through differences which of themselves divide something common; as having feet is of itself divided by biped

reception is called "passion." And the action following the union of what is received and the recipient is called "operation;" for operation is always of what is perfect, as is manifest in sense, for sensing is a certain operation of the one sensing, proceeding not to some effect regarding the sensible [object], but rather according as the sensible species is in it. Whence, to sense, as to the reception itself of the sensible species, is named "passion," and similarly to understand is also a certain passion, as is said in *De Anima*, Bk, 3. But it is called "operation" as to the act following the sense itself perfected through the species, which is said to be the motion of the sense, about which the philosopher speaks, which is the act of the perfect.

8 Some maintain that some of the time when we think we are seeing something we are actually remembering it. Our eyes engage in small, rapid jerking motions (called "saccades") that result in us not looking at things continuously, though we experience our activity of seeing them as continuous. This view does not deny that we ever see anything. Thus, it does not affect my main point, which is that seeing is an activity that is carried on by the organism. See John Grimes, "On the Failure to Detect Changes in Scenes Across Saccades," in *Perception*, ed. K. A. Akins (Oxford University Press, 1996), 108.

and quadruped, but not by white and black."[9] Living things should then be divided according to their different kinds of life activity.

In various works, Aquinas names the divisions of material living things at the most universal level, but he rarely explicitly divides living things, and when he does so it is not his principal concern. He lists plants, animals, and humans in several places; for example, in the *Summa Theologiae* he says: "In the order of things, the living are more perfect than the nonliving, and animals than plants, and humans than brute animals."[10]

Aquinas does divide material living things in some places but not with the same precision with which he divides souls. For example, in the *Commentary on the Sentences*, he says:

> Something is said to be living from the fact that it is able to move itself according to some activity. Whence even plants are said to live from the fact that they move themselves according to growth, and animals, in addition, insofar as they move themselves according to place and insofar as they move themselves according to sensing; in humans, however, in addition, insofar as they move themselves to willing and understanding.[11]

What Aquinas says here is ultimately ordered to show that human beatitude consists in a kind of life, namely, eternal life. While the division he gives is based on living things' life activities, some living things engaging in more than others, he does not make it clear here why certain life activities are singled out as distinguishing one category of living thing from others.

What Aquinas does divide with great precision are living things' souls. This division can serve as the basis for a division of material living things insofar as the soul, as formal principle of the living thing, is the more principal part of its nature.[12] The life activities of living things, while proper to

9 *Sent.* I, d. 37, q. 1, a. 2, ad 2. See also *SCG*, bk. 2, chap. 59.

10 *ST* I, q. 76, a. 3. See also *SCG*, bk. 3, chap. 22: "Elements, therefore, are for the sake of mixed bodies; these indeed are for the sake of living things; among which plants are for the sake of animals, and animals for the sake of humans." See also *Sent.* II, d. 32, q. 2, a 3, *Super Evangelium S. Ioannis*, chap. 1, lec. 3, and Super Iob, chap. 38.

11 *Sent.* IV, d. 49, q. 1, a. 2, qc. 3.

12 The subtitle of this book, *An Aristotelian-Thomist Perspective on Life in the Universe*, is somewhat misleading in that the book only treats those living things that have bodies (i.e., organisms) in keeping with its intention to engage with science. Accordingly, while some of the things said in this chapter about life apply to all living things, the division of living

and revelatory of their natures, are not their natures. Growing, for example, is natural for a plant, but is not the nature of the plant. As Aquinas frequently notes, action follows being: "A proper activity belongs to each thing according as it has being, for everything acts according as it is a being."[13] Organisms have their being as living in virtue of their substantial form, their soul. If one grants that "form is more nature than matter is,"[14] a division of material living things according to their natures corresponds to a division according to the kinds of souls they have.

The different kinds of souls that living things have, however, are known through their different kinds of life activities. So, in the order of knowledge, dividing material living things according to their natures, which is primarily their souls, depends on determining differences in kind as to their life activities.[15] Thus, while it is correct to divide material living things according to the different kinds of life activities, underlying this division, and more fundamental in terms of nature, is a division that is based on differences in the formal cause of the organisms, that is, the soul, from which flow the

---

things in question here is the division of organisms and not of living things in general. Both Aristotle and Aquinas maintain that there are living things that are immaterial. See Arthur Martin Hippler, "Impediments to Aristotle's Life-Sciences," PhD diss. (Boston College, 1993) for a provocative treatment of life in Aristotle's works. Hippler notes: "Most discussions of Aristotle on life and living things fail to address God and the first movers" (151).

13 *In DA*, bk. 2, lec. 5 n. 3: "Activity (operatio) of the soul, however, is the activity of the living thing. Since the proper activity of each thing belongs to it according as it has being, for everything acts insofar as it is a being, it is therefore necessary to consider the activities of soul according as they are found in living things."

14 See *In Phy.*, bk. 2, lec. 2, n. 5: "Further from the reason set forth, he [Aristotle] proceeds to show that form is more nature than matter; for anything is more said [to be something] according as it is in act than according as it is in potency. Whence form, according to which something is natural in act, is more nature than matter, according to which something is natural in potency." See also *In Libros De Caelo et Mundo*, bk. 1, lec. 1, n. 2: "Certain things have body and magnitude, as is the case of plants and animals, of which the more principal part is the soul (whence they more are what they are according to the soul than according to the body)." Thus, while substances are primarily what are categorized into genera and species (see *Q. DA*, unicus, a. 11, ad 14), natural substances are what they are primarily because of their form; see *In Meta.*, Raymundi M. Spiazzi, ed. (Marietti, 1950), bk. 5, lec. 2, n. 2: "For although some material parts are put in a definition, nevertheless what is principal in a definition must be what is on the side of form."

15 See *SCG*, bk. 2, chap. 59: "But in man is found a higher operation pertaining to life than in the animal, namely, understanding (intelligere). Therefore, man will have a higher form of life. But life is through the soul. Therefore, man will have a higher soul by which he lives than the sensitive soul." Here Aquinas argues from the nature of man's life activity, which is better known, to the nature of his soul, which is less known.

powers underlying those activities. But again, the latter is known through the former. At least, such are the views of Aquinas, who draws from Aristotle's natural philosophy. I think these views are defensible but doing so is beyond the scope of this chapter. Moreover, even if one were to reject (or simply ignore) Aquinas's hylomorphic natural philosophy, this would not affect the notion that living things should be divided at the highest level according to differences in kind in their life activities.

How then does Aquinas divide the life activities or activities of soul? There are three places where he does so.[16] I will focus on what he says in the *Disputed Question on the Soul*, as this text is clearer in certain ways than are the other two:

> It is necessary, however, to consider three grades in the actions of the soul. For the action of the soul transcends the action of nature working in inanimate things; and this happens as to two things; namely, as to the manner of acting and as to what is done. It is necessary, however, that as to the manner of acting, every action of the soul transcends the operation or action of inanimate nature; for since an activity of the soul is a life activity, and the living is what moves itself to acting, it is necessary that every operation of soul be according to some intrinsic agent. But as to what is done, not every action transcends the action of inanimate nature.[17]

Living things, in moving themselves, act in a way that goes beyond what inanimate natural things can do. Their self-motions can go beyond what nonliving natural things can do in two ways. In one way, simply by how the living things do what they do, namely, by themselves. In another way, as to what they do as well. Plants are in the former category, since in carrying on the vegetative activities of nutrition, growth, and reproduction, they do not achieve ends different from those that are realized in inanimate nature. As Aquinas explains:

> For it is necessary that a natural being come into existence and also those things that are required for its doing so, be the body inanimate or animate. In inanimate bodies this comes about by an extrinsic agent, in animate bodies from an intrinsic agent; and the powers of the vegetative

16 The other two passages where Aquinas proposes a division of souls are *In DA*, bk. 2, l. 5, n. 4 and *ST* I, q. 78, a. 1. See the note at the end of this section for a brief treatment of them.

17 *Q. DA.* in Bazzi et al., *Quaestiones Disputatae*, unicus, a. 13. See also *In DA*, bk. 2, lec. 5, n. 3–7.

> soul are ordered to activities of this sort. For the generative power is ordered to the end that an individual is produced in existence; the power of growth is ordered to the end that it acquires a suitable size; the power of nutrition is ordered to the end that it is maintained in being. These things, however, inanimate bodies obtain from an extrinsic natural agent alone; on account of which these powers of soul are called "natural."[18]

It is hard to dispute what Aquinas claims here. Nonliving natural things grow by addition or accretion from without, as in the formation of crystals, and they do not maintain themselves in existence by transforming materials into themselves.[19] The generation of nonliving natural things involves an external agent, as when water is produced from oxygen and hydrogen by means of a spark or when heavier elements are formed from lighter ones by fusion in stars. Compounds, as well, come into existence as the result of outside agents acting on other preexistent matter. By contrast, in the case of reproduction, the parent has to perform some internal activity for the new individual to be generated, be it to produce gametes or a new shoot or a part that will fall off and take root or the changes necessary for cell division (as is

18 *Q. DA*, unicus, a. 13.

19 Ilia Guzei, "How are Crystals Formed?," Morgridge Institute for Research, https://morgridge.org/blue-sky/how-are-crystals-formed/:

> Unlike biological systems, crystals do not draw nourishment from within. They grow from the outside by one of three major ways: either from a vapor, from a melt or from a solution. In each case, it's a three-step process. It begins with nucleation, in which a few molecules or atoms approach each other in a suitable orientation to form a stable submicroscopic aggregate. The second stage is growth, which is an orderly addition of further molecules or atoms to the surface of the crystal in a regular manner. And the final step—termination—stops the growth process.

The crystal grows as the result of the ions on its surface attracting other ions. The crystal does not have organs whereby it transforms material taken in from the outside into itself, as is prerequisite for true growth. The crystal gets bigger but unlike the organism is not one thing. In the case of a single natural nonliving substance, as Aquinas notes: "An inanimate natural thing simultaneously receive its species and its due quantity, which is not possible in the case of living things, which must be of a relatively small size in the beginning of their generation, because they are generated from seed." Q. DA unicus, 13, ad 15. Growth is also involved in the reproduction of unicellular organisms (which reproduce by binary fission or by budding). Aquinas points out another difference between the growth of a crystal and the growth of an organism in *De Pot.*, q. 3, a. 11, namely, in the case of living things as opposed to nonliving natural things, "the term for growth is fixed in advance." A crystal will continue to grow so long as the solution is sufficiently saturated and the container big enough. Organisms, by contrast, generally grow to determinate sizes. Even animals like fish, which grow throughout their lives, have the rate of growth of their various parts determined by internal factors.

the case of unicellular organisms). Moreover, the new individual completes its development through its own activities.[20]

The subdivision "plant" includes every kind of organism that only performs life activities that differ from what nonliving natural things can do as to how they do them. This category then includes fungi and at least some bacteria, as well as the more familiar vascular plants (e.g., daisies and oaks) and nonvascular plants (e.g., mosses).[21]

Aquinas then talks about more perfect forms of self-motion. Here it is not just the case that the living thing realizes by its own activity ends that are realized by nonliving natural things, but what it does transcends what nonliving things can achieve:

> There are, however, other higher activities of soul, which transcend the activities of all natural forms also as to what is done, namely, insofar as the soul is apt to be all things according to immaterial being. For the soul, in a certain manner, is all things according as it is sensing and understanding. There must be, however, diverse grades of this kind of immaterial being. For there is one grade according as things are in the soul without their own matter, but nevertheless according to their singularity and individual conditions, which are consequent upon matter. And this grade is sense, which is receptive of the forms of individual things without matter, but nevertheless in a bodily organ. However, the higher and more perfect grade of immateriality is the intellect, which receive forms without any matter at all and abstract from the conditions of matter, and [does so] without a bodily organ.[22]

Aquinas first refers here to a distinction that Aristotle makes concerning sensation. There is a difference between an animal getting hot and feeling

20 Organisms with a parent or parents have to complete themselves by developing their parts through cell division; the parents do not add new parts to them. In unicellular organisms, once the daughter cells are separated, each new cell has to close up its cell membrane.

21 Vascular plants have special cells that serve to transport food, water, and minerals throughout the plant. Nonvascular plants lack such cells.

22 *Q. DA*, unicus, a. 13. See also *In DA*, bk. 2, lec. 5, n. 5:

> There is a difference in being in these two cases. For according to material being, which is constricted by matter, each thing is only what it is, as this rock is not something other than this rock, whereas according to immaterial being, which is more ample and in a certain manner infinite, insofar as it is not bounded by matter, a thing is not only what it is but in a certain manner is other things. Whence all things exist in a certain way in superior immaterial substances, as in universal causes.

hotness. The animal gets hot because its body changes in a physical way. Feeling hotness, however, is not the same thing as getting hot. In fact, the more the body changes physically, the less sensitive it becomes to the hotness it is feeling. Think, for example, of soaking a foot in hot water. As the foot heats up, one starts to lose awareness of how hot the water is. The reception of an accidental form is termed "material" when the being acquiring it comes to possess it in same manner that it exists in the agent acting upon it, for example, water heated by a fire acquires hotness in such a way as to become hot itself. When a being receives an accidental form, such as heat, in such a way as to be aware of heat, that reception is termed "immaterial," meaning not in the manner that matter receives a form, for again to receive a form in a material way would be to become hot.[23] The negation in Aristotle's definition of sensation is a way of getting at the reality that one cannot reduce awareness to physical interactions among parts that lack awareness. Of course, a functioning organ is necessary for sensing and there must be physical interactions between it and what is sensed. However, that is not sufficient to account for awareness. If one were to explain sight to a blind person solely in terms of all the physical interactions involved, the person would have less understanding of what sight is than if one were to explain it in terms of the subjective experience of awareness of a sensible quality different from those the blind person is aware of.

In the case of intellectual understanding, "immaterial" is not only to be taken in the negative sense of not in the manner that matter receives, but in the sense of involving nothing physical whatsoever. Here is not the place to rehearse Aquinas's arguments concerning the immateriality of the intellect that forms and considers abstract concepts. Even if Aquinas was mistaken here, and consequently, there was one fewer main subdivision of organism, this would not show that his principle of division was incorrect.[24]

23 Here are some other examples showing that physical change ("material reception") on the part of the organ renders it less sensitive. When the organ of smell itself has a smell (as when one puts strong smelling ointment, such as Vicks Vaporub™, at the base of one's nose), it prevents one from smelling other things. Also, if one stares at a thing, say a red circle, for a certain length of time, the physical change that occurs at the level of the cones (i.e., the color receptors in the eye) results in the sensory illusion of seeing afterwards a blue-green circle when one looks at a white surface.

24 Here are some brief comments on the two other passages where Aquinas treats the division of souls at length. The earliest of the two, *In DA*, bk. 2, lec. 5, n. 4, is very similar to *Q. DA*, except that Aquinas does not speak in detail about the operation of sensing but only qualifies it as intermediary between the purely immaterial activity of part of the intellectual soul and the

There are some who reject Aquinas's subdivision of "plant," maintaining rather that all living things are sentient.[25] As I will argue in chapter 8, I think the subdivision "plant," understood as nonsentient living things, is defensible. For one, plants lack sense organs. My main thesis, however, is that Aquinas's *principle of division* is the correct one for dividing material living things at the most universal level. If all living things were animals and no more than animals, then the most fundamental divisions of living things would be determined according to their activities of sensing, or more fundamentally according to the sensitive souls that underlie the various kinds of sensorial activities.[26]

Woese et al.'s View on the Natural Division of Living Things at the Most Universal Level

Let us now consider the division of organisms proposed in 1990 by Woese et al. in "Towards a Natural System of Organisms: Proposal for the Domains of Archaea, Bacteria, and Eucarya."[27] This division was widely accepted by

material activities of the vegetative soul, which surpass the activities of natural bodies only as to the higher manner in which they are performed. The second passage is *ST* I, q. 78, a. 1. Here Aquinas articulates the same principle of division presented in *Q. DA*, though somewhat differently: "Diverse souls are distinguished according to the operations of the soul which in diverse ways go beyond the operation of a natural body, for natural body in its totality is subject to the soul and compares to it as matter and instrument." In this passage, Aquinas not only speaks about activities of soul transcending those of inanimate nature, but he also underscores the role of the soul as a final cause to which other natural things are ordered. Aquinas goes on to make the same distinctions as in *Q. DA* and *In DA*, while emphasizing the instrumental nature of matter in the operations of the soul, starting from intellectual activity, where such instrumentality is absent and ending with the vegetative activities where this instrumentality is most present (think of the chemical reactions involved in digestion), with sensing falling between the two.

25 Nicanor Austriaco, OP, in personal communication: "Modern biologists would challenge this account [i.e., that there is a nutritive soul that is other than the sensitive soul] because all living things have to respond and to adapt to their environments to survive, and they do this by sensing different external cues. Thus, all living things must have sensitive souls."

26 See *ST* I, q. 50, a. 4, ad 1: "Therefore, nonrational animals differ in species according to determinant, diverse gradations of the sensitive nature."

27 Carl R. Woese et al., "Towards a Natural System of Organisms," 4576–79. We will see later on the manner in which Woese et al. define archaea, bacteria, and eucarya. Both archaea and bacteria are unicellular organisms that lack a nucleus. Archaea live in extreme environments,

other biologists until recently.[28] Woese et al. begin by explicitly rejecting a division that is very close to the one Aquinas favors:[29]

> Our present view of the basic organization of life is still largely steeped in the ancient notion that all living things are plant or animal in nature. Unfortunately, this comfortable traditional dichotomy does not represent the true state of affairs. Thus, as a prerequisite to developing a proper natural system we have to divest ourselves of deeply ingrained, cherished assumptions, as regards both the fundamental organization of life and the basis for constructing a system of organisms. The system we will develop will be one that is completely restructured at the highest levels.[30]

Woese et al. never address what this ancient division is based on, much less why it is defective. They simply assume that the only sound basis for a natural taxonomy is phylogeny, or in other words, that living things should be divided into kinds at the highest level according to their evolutionary origins: "The only truly scientific foundation of classification is to be found in appreciation of the available facts from a phylogenetic point of view. Only in this way can the natural interrelationships [among organisms] . . .

---

such as thermal vents in the ocean. Eucarya have a nucleus in which their DNA is contained. Eucarya includes organisms as varied as unicellular yeasts and *Homo sapiens*.

28 Woese et al.'s division has been recently challenged by those who propose a two-domain system; see, for example, Kasie Raymann et al., "The Two-Domain Tree of Life Is Linked to a New Root for the Archaea," *Proceedings of the National Academy of Sciences, USA* 112, no. 21 (2015): 6670–75. The reason I focus on Woese et al. is because of the strong claim they make about their division being *the* natural division. The proponents of a two-domain system employ a similar principle of division with the same goal in mind as Woese et al. They look to protein sequences and genes in order to establish phylogenies. Thus, even if Woese et al. are mistaken as to what are the main subdivisions, they still could be correct as to the principle of division they use to establish a natural classification at the highest level.

29 Aquinas would add a third division, "human." One might argue that this subdivision is of no importance to the biologist who treats humans solely insofar as they are animals. However, to understand the final cause of certain human features and behaviors, one needs to refer to our intellect. Humans do not have hands simply because we evolved from an ancestor that had hands. We have hands because without them we could not deploy our practical intelligence, or, at most, only to an exceedingly small extent. Scientists who are deeply committed to evolutionary gradualism typically maintain that we belong to the animal kingdom. See, for example, Frans de Waal, *Mama's Last Hug* (W. W. Norton, 2019), 11: "I will only rarely refer to other species as 'other animals' or 'non-human animals.' For simplicity's sake, I will mostly call them just 'animals,' even though for me, as a biologist, nothing is more self-evident than that we are part of the same kingdom."

30 Woese et al., "Towards A Natural System of Organisms," 4576.

be properly understood."[31] Classification of living things is to be based on ancestry and on ancestry alone. A living thing's ancestry, however, while important for understanding how it came to be as it is and its evolutionary relationship to other living things, is not the living thing's nature.

Woese et al., in keeping with what they regard as the sole goal of classification, base their highest-level division on the molecules that are indicative of the first major divergences in evolution from the original type of cell. They maintain:

> What must be recognized is that the basis for systematics has changed; classical phenotypic criteria are being replaced by molecular criteria. As Zuckerkandl and Pauling (5) have made clear many years ago, it is at the level of molecules (particularly molecular sequences) that one really becomes privy to the workings of the evolutionary process. Molecular sequences can reveal evolutionary relationships in a way and to an extent that classical phenotypic criteria, and even molecular functions, cannot; and what is seen only dimly, if at all, at higher levels of organization can be seen clearly at the level of molecular structures and sequences. Thus, systematics in the future will be based primarily upon the sequences, structure, and relationships of molecules, the classical gross properties of cells and organisms being used largely to confirm and embellish these.[32]

Woese et al. regard ribosomal RNA (rRNA) as a molecule important to consider in the determination of phylogeny. Ribosomal RNAs are essential parts of ribosomes which are organelles responsible for protein synthesis. The RNA polymerase is another molecule they view as helpful for determining phylogeny.[33] The RNA polymerase plays a role in the transcription of DNA into messenger RNA, the latter being necessary for protein synthesis. In general, the determination of phylogenies depends on choosing molecules

31 Woese et al., 4577.

32 Woese et al., 4577.

33 See Woese et al., 4577:

> Molecular characterizations also reveal that the evolutionary differences among eubacteria, archaebacteria, and eukaryotes are of a more profound nature than those that distinguish traditional kingdoms, such as animals and plants. . . . All eubacteria, for example, exhibit nearly the same subunit pattern . . . in their RNA polymerases; however, this pattern bears little relationship to that seen in either the archaebacteria or the eukaryotes. On the other hand, eukaryotes are unique in using three separate RNA polymerase functions.

that are found in all organisms and that evolve slowly.[34] Molecules found in all organisms are going to be involved in "the functions that must have evolved early in the cell's history and are basic to its workings."[35] Based on cytological and molecular criteria, Woese et al. define one of the three domains, namely, the domain of bacteria as: "cells prokaryotic; membrane lipids predominantly diacyl glycerol diesters; ribosomes contain a (eu)bacterial type of rRNA." Their definitions of the two other domains follows a similar pattern.

Woese et al.'s division then is based on differences in molecular parts, such as those that are needed for organisms to carry on the vegetative activities needed to stay alive, and on the organization of the major components of a cell, such as whether the DNA is enclosed in a nucleus or not. The division is not based on differences in kind of the life activities of organisms, much less on the differences in the kind of the souls that are their root source. If the latter is indeed the basis for the most natural division, as was argued above, then Woese et al.'s division is not the most natural division of living things at the highest level. Woese et al. see determining lineages as the proper goal for subdividing organisms at the highest level and regard considering differences in certain molecules as the appropriate means of doing so. Aquinas sees determining differences in nature as the proper way of subdividing organisms at the highest level and regards looking to differences in the activities of the soul as revealing differences in organisms' substantial forms, their souls, as the appropriate means of doing so.[36]

34 See Purves et al., *Life*, 513: "The larger number of similarities [in amino acid sequences], the more recent the presumed common ancestor of the species." In the case of molecules that evolve quickly the rapid changes in sequences make it hard to see similarities. This is why molecules that evolve slowly are chosen when it is a matter of determining phylogeny.

35 Woese et al., "Towards a Natural System of Organisms," 4577.

36 One might wonder whether Woese et al.'s domains could be fit into the most natural division. Given that the principle of division that each employ differs, the two divisions could only coincide by chance. For example, if one person is dividing animals with feet according to the number of feet and another person is dividing them according to color, since the principles of division are not mutually exclusive, there will be potential overlap, e.g., some four-footed animals may be brown, and some two-footed animals may also be brown. And in fact, some of the organisms that Woese would categorize as eukarya fall into the Thomistic category of plant and others into the category of animal; and some of the organisms that Aquinas would categorize as plant would fall into the three different categories that Woese proposes.

Some Thomistic Reflections on Woese's Division and on Classification in General

What Role Does Knowledge of the Organisms' Body Play in Classification?

Woese et al. divide living things into three domains based on differences in their bodily composition, whereas Aquinas divides them into three kinds based on differences in their souls. This might make it seem that Aquinas thinks that understanding organisms in terms of their bodily make-up is entirely misguided, something that is not the case. Rather, he views how one is to understand living things at the most universal level to differ from how one is to understand them at the level of the species. This can be seen from how he divides the part of natural philosophy which treats animate things into its subdivisions in the prooemium to his commentary on Aristotle's *De Sensu et Sensatu*. Aquinas begins by explaining the principle according to which the speculative disciplines are to be divided:

> As the Philosopher says in the third book of the *De Anima*, in the same way that things are separable from matter so too do they stand in regard to the intellect.[37] For anything whatsoever is intelligible insofar as it is separable from matter. Whence those things which according to nature are separated from matter are in themselves intelligible in act; those things which are abstracted by us from material conditions become intelligible in act through the light of our agent intellect.[38]

After applying this principle to divide the speculative sciences into metaphysics, mathematics, and natural philosophy, Aquinas proceeds to divide natural philosophy into its parts in accord with the same principle of division:

> And just as the diverse genera of sciences are distinguished according to this that the things [they treat] are separable from matter in diverse ways, so too in the particular sciences, and chiefly in natural science, the parts of the science are distinguished according to the diverse manner of separation and concretion. And because universals are more separated from matter, therefore in natural science one proceeds from the [more]

37 This is exactly what Aristotle says in *De Anima*, bk. 3, chap. 4, 429b22.

38 *De Sensu*, ed. Raymundi M. Spiazzi, OP (Marietti, 1949), bk. 1, lec. 1, no. 1. See also Charles De Koninck, "Introduction to the Study of the Soul," trans. David Quackenbush, *The Aquinas Review* 23 (2019–20): 29–33.

> universal to the less universal, as the Philosopher teaches in the first book of the *Physics*.[39]

Aquinas goes on to explain the sense in which what is more universal is more separated from matter:

> Whence also natural science begins to teach from those things which are most common to all natural things, which are motion and the principle of motion, and then proceeds through the mode of concretion, or application of common principles, to certain determinate mobiles, of which certain are living bodies: concerning which one also proceeds in a similar mode distinguishing this consideration in three parts. For indeed one first considers the soul in itself, in a certain abstraction, as it were. Secondly, one considers those things which belong to the soul according to a certain concretion, or application to the body, but in a general way. Thirdly, one continues the consideration by applying all these things to individual species of animals and plants, determining what is proper to each species.[40]

Let us flesh out what Aquinas says about the division of natural philosophy and of the part of natural philosophy that treats living things. In the *Physics* Aristotle treats what is common to all natural things, starting

39 *De Sensu*, bk. 1, lec. 1, no. 2. It is puzzling that Aquinas cites *In Phy.*, bk. 1 in support of the thesis that "universals are more separated from matter," as the *In Phy.* seems to affirm that the opposite is true. Our intellects go from the more universal to the less universal because they move from potency to act. We arrive first at a vague understanding of things because our minds start from sense experience from which the intellect is unable to immediately gather a clear understanding of the natures of the things which present themselves to sense. The universals we first arrive at are less perfectly separated from matter to the extent that the genus of a thing is taken on the side of matter; this imperfection accounts for the vagueness of our first knowledge. We know man as animal before we know man as rational animal. Aquinas associates the more universal part of the definition, the genus, with what is material in a thing, although he says explicitly that the genus is not the matter of the thing defined:

> The genus is taken from what is material in a thing, the difference indeed from what is formal. As the genus of man is "animal," which signifies something having a sensitive nature; this certainly stands in a material way to the intellectual nature, from which "rational" is taken, which is the difference of man. For rational indeed signifies something having an intellectual nature. And whence it is that the genus contains the difference in potency, and that the genus and difference stand to one another as matter to form." *In Meta.* bk. 8, lec. 2, n. 7.

40 *De Sensu*, bk. 1, lec. 1, no. 2.

with what is most fundamental, namely, motion.[41] In treating motion, Aristotle speaks about act and potency and about the need for a terminus from which and a terminus to which. What he says applies to all motions while prescinding from what is proper to any specific motion, for example, from iron filings moving toward a magnet or copper turning green. These general considerations, necessary as they are for understanding all motions, are not sufficient for understanding the motions of specific natural things in their specificity. Here one needs to examine the matter involved.

What holds true of understanding natural things also holds true for understanding the specific kind of natural thing that is the living thing. One needs to first understand them in terms of the most fundamental thing they all share in common, namely, the soul, which is their principle of self-motion.[42] However, in order to obtain proper knowledge of the various species of living things, one needs to also look at their matter. Aquinas is insistent on this latter point:

> Therefore, their determinations concerning the soul are insufficient when they try to say only what sort of thing the soul is and neglect to show of what sort the body receptive of the soul is. Here they agree with what Pythagorean myths hold, namely, that any soul may enter any body, for example, that the soul of a fly may enter into an elephant body,

41 See *In Phy.*, bk. 1, lec. 2, n. 7:

> It is supposed in natural science that natural things move, *either all or some*—which is said because there is doubt about certain of them as to whether they move and how they move, e.g., the soul, the center of the earth, the pole of the heavens, and natural forms, and other things of this sort. And that natural things move, is able to be made manifest from induction; for it appears to sense that natural things move. It is necessary, however, to suppose motion in natural science, as it is necessary to suppose nature, in whose definition motion is placed; for nature is the principle of motion, as will be said later on.

42 See De Koninck, "Introduction to the Study of the Soul," section 5, "The Order to Follow in the Study of the Living," 22:

> The word *soul*, in fact, signifies at present nothing other than the principle and cause of the operations that consist in moving oneself and sensing, which are very manifest so far as the fact. This cause is precisely that by which the bodies in which we encounter these activities, and that, for this reason, we call living, differ in the first place from other bodies. The body that has life differs from that which is deprived of it, not by being a body, but by being a *living* body. "For, in saying <a body that has life,> I say two things—namely, that it is a body, and that it is this sort of body, namely, one that has life; one cannot say that the part of the body that has life, and that is called body, is the soul. Indeed, by 'soul' we understand: that by which what has life, lives." De Koninck quotes *In DA*, bk. 2, lec. 1, n. 10.

> although this is not possible, since every body whatsoever, and above all those of animals, have their own form and their own species, and a proper moving [part] and proper moved [part], and the body of a worm differs greatly from the body of a dog, and the body of an elephant from the body of a flea. . . . Thus, therefore, Plato and other philosophers, speaking only about the nature of the soul, have spoken insufficiently, by omitting to determine what body be suitable to what soul, and in what manner and how it exists united to the soul.[43]

To divide living things at the highest level, Aquinas would maintain that we must look to their souls considered in a certain abstraction from the body, as the same kind of life activity can be realized through quite different bodies. For example, life activities of the vegetative soul can be carried on by bacteria and by green plants, whose bodies are vastly different. Of course, the species falling within each of the highest categories (plant, animal, human) are understood to have a body with organs, but the specifics of any given body cannot be part of that division, as this would exclude other organisms that carried on the same kind of life activities but through a different body. To divide living things into species, however, requires knowledge of the bodies of which these organisms' souls are the act.[44]

Note that Aquinas's classification would work for living things on another planet, which is not the case for Woese et al.'s classification. For since phylogeny is what matters for Woese et al., given that the tree of life of organisms on the two planets would be different (assuming life was not seeded on earth from the other planet), Woese et al. could not put organisms on the two planets into the same category, and this would be true even if the organisms had the same ribosomal RNA.

43 *In DA*, bk. 1, lec. 8, n. 25. See *In DA*, bk. 2, lec. 5, n. 16 (Marietti, no. 294): "For since the intellect does not have a corporeal organ, those that possess intellect are not able to be diversified according to the diverse physical make-up (complexionem) of organs, as the species of sensitive beings are diversified according to diverse make-ups (complexiones), by which they are related in diverse ways to the operations of sensation."

44 In the case of determining species of unicellular organisms, a determination of the specific manner in which they perform the vegetative activities may well require the molecular approach that Woese et al. employ, given the simplicity of their bodies.

Would Aquinas See Any Value to Woese et al.'s Division?

Though Aquinas would reject Woese et al.'s position that the division into domains is the most natural way of dividing living things at the highest level, if he were to accept that evolution has occurred, he would recognize that their division is valuable for understanding living things, in two ways. First, it contributes to an understanding of biological evolution. For example, a consideration of ancestry allows us to recognize phenomena such as convergent evolution. An example of convergent evolution is the evolution of cacti and euphorbia. These two groups look very similar and live in similar climates but have different ancestors. The fact that evolutionary causes can result in the production of very similar organisms, despite the difference in ancestry, teaches us something about the nature of living things.

Secondly, looking at a species' ancestry often provides some knowledge concerning the species itself. Aquinas, in his commentary on the *Politics* of Aristotle, speaks of the importance of ascertaining things' origins in order to understand them:

> For the knowledge of a whole, it is necessary to divide what is composite down to what is incomposite, that is, down to the indivisibles which are the smallest parts of the whole (for example, to know what speech is, it is necessary to divide down to the letters, and to know what a natural mixed body is, it is necessary to divide down to the elements).... For in all things, we see that if we examine things according as they arise from their principle, we are best able to contemplate the truth concerning them.[45]

Aquinas would agree that Woese et al.'s division, which reveals how organisms are related in terms of their origins, allows us to know something important about them. If Aquinas were to accept evolution, he would be open to the explanation of some of the parts of organisms in terms of ancestry. Human wisdom teeth, for example, are typically explained by our ancestors needing these teeth to eat coarse, uncooked foods.[46] Nowadays they are not necessary and in many individuals cause more harm than good.

45 *Sententia libri Politicorum*, bk. 1, lec. 1, n. 8.

46 If Aquinas were to accept evolution, he would relate ancestry in some cases to features of organisms that are attributable to the "necessity of matter." Things attributable to the "necessity of matter" are undesired side effects of something that is for an end, e.g., that an iron knife rusts is an undesired side effect of the knife's being made from iron, a metal capable of

The last line in the passage from the commentary on the *Politics* might give one pause as to why Aquinas does not give priority to Woese et al.'s division, given how emphatic he is concerning the importance of understanding a thing in terms of what it originates from.

In response to this concern, Aquinas is not claiming here that one understands everything about a whole by understanding the parts it originated from. Indeed, if one considers his example of how an understanding of speech requires an understanding of letters (or phonemes), it is obvious that knowledge of letters alone is insufficient for understanding speech. Letters are only the material parts of words; the formal part of a word is its meaning, the concept that it signifies.

The same is true of living things and their evolutionary origins. Knowledge of the body parts of the ancestors of the individuals of a descendent species (and the genes that code for these parts) tells us something about the features of the new species, but hardly tells us everything about the new species. For example, it does not even tell us about the inherited features as properly belonging to that species. Why do humans have five fingers and five toes? It appears that our pentadactyl limbs are due to our evolutionary ancestry. However, knowing this alone does not inform us as to what is proper to human pentadactyl limbs, neither when it comes to their precise structure nor as to their function. Whales too have pentadactyl limbs due to an ancestor shared with humans and many other organisms. Here too, knowing the ancestry of whales' fins does not inform us as to what is proper to the whales' pentadactyl limbs. Nor must it be forgotten that these animals would not have limbs at all if it were not for their souls.

Why Woese Should be Receptive Toward the Thomistic Division

It is ironic that Woese, in a 2004 paper, criticizes biologists who have taken the path of metaphysical reductionism:

> Empirical reductionism is in essence methodological; it is simply a mode of analysis, the dissection of a biological entity or system into its

holding an edge. See *ST* I, q. 91, a. 3 and ad 1 and *ST* I-II, q. 85, a. 6. Similarly, certain defects in the members of a given species are due to the fact that their species originated from an earlier species and features useful to individuals belonging to the earlier species are not always beneficial for individuals of species that descended from it.

> constituent parts in order to better understand it. Empirical reductionism makes no assumptions about the fundamental nature, an ultimate understanding, of living things. Fundamentalist reductionism . . . on the other hand, is in essence metaphysical. It is ipso facto a statement about the nature of the world: living systems (like all else) can be completely understood in terms of the properties of their constituent parts. This is a view that flies in the face of what classically trained biologists tended to take for granted, the notion of emergent properties. Whereas emergence seems to be required to explain numerous biological phenomena, fundamentalist reductionism flatly denies its existence: in all cases the whole is no more than the sum of its parts.[47]

In light of what Woese says here, one wonders whether he would reconsider having taken the molecular route rather than looking to emergent properties in formulating his division of livings things. Aquinas's approach to dividing living things at the highest level seems to be precisely what Woese is looking for. While it may be unreasonable to expect biologists to have an understanding of hylomorphism and of the notion of the soul as the substantial form of the body, biologists, as Woese notes, should be familiar with the notion of emergent properties, and this is part of what is needed to understand Aquinas's division when the division is put in terms of life activities.[48] What biologists typically regard as emergent properties of living things— sensing, consciousness, imagining, thinking abstractly, and the like—are the activities that Aquinas identifies as transcending those of inanimate natural bodies as to what is done. Aquinas, of course, rejects the notion that thinking abstractly is an emergent property, because he holds that it is an activity that does not depend on matter.[49] Even on this point, at least some scientists might be convinced that humans are not just one

47 Woese, "A New Biology for a New Century," 174.

48 While Aquinas never uses the expression "emergent properties" he does use similar expressions. He speaks in a number of places of substantial forms as being to a greater or lesser degree "immersed in matter" (*materiae immersa*). Thus, for example, he says: "Whence, it is necessary that the principle by which man understands—which is the intellectual soul—and exceeds the condition of bodily matter, not be entirely taken hold of (*comprehensa*) by matter or immersed (*immersa*) in it, as are other material forms." *SCG*, bk. 2, chap. 68, n. 12. Aquinas also quotes with approval Avicenna's view that the human soul is a "form whose being is not submerged in matter." Sent. II, d. 19, q. 1, a. 1, "non esse forma submersa in materia."

49 *De sensu*, no. 4: "The intellect is the act of no body part, as is proved in *De Anima*, bk. 3: whence it cannot be considered through concretion or application to the body or to some bodily organ."

animal alongside others by starting from an examination of the failure of the attempts to teach nonhuman animals language and then proceeding to a consideration of the transcendent character of abstract thought. Aquinas's identification of organisms that transcend the activities of nonliving natural things only as to the manner in which their ends are realized is readily comprehensible through comparisons, such as how a crystal grows as opposed to how an organism grows.[50]

Aquinas's division of living things would return the wonder to biology that is lost when biologists drift from methodological reductionism into metaphysical reductionism. Even if biologists cannot always answer the question of what basic kind of living thing they have before them, plant or animal, starting with that question focuses attention on the living thing as living, rather than as a collection of molecules. To this end, it would be a good thing if all biologists had to take a course in animal behavior, where they would be exposed to discussions of specific emergent properties of animals, such as mirror self-recognition, toolmaking, and theory of mind experiments. Even when these discussions don't explicitly speak in terms of emergent properties, they are what is being talked about. Doubtlessly the specialization generally required to make a living as a biologist requires the vast majority of students to focus their attention on molecules, but this is not a reason to bypass some study of life where it is more clearly seen.

Conclusion and a Comparison with Other Authors Who Defend Aquinas's View

"Phylogeny is not ontology."[51] Aquinas maintains that while acknowledging a thing's origin is helpful for knowing something about a thing's nature, it is not the same as knowing its nature, and it is on this point that he disagrees with Woese. I am not the first contemporary author to point this out, nor am I the only contemporary author who undertakes a defense of the Aristotelian division that Aquinas adopts. Edward Feser and David Oderberg have

50 Vocabulary poses a minor obstacle for biologists to accept Aquinas's division to the extent that they understand "plant" to refer to members of the kingdom Plantae, from which many vegetative organisms, e.g., mushrooms, are excluded. One solution is to use "vegetative organism" in place of "plant."

51 The quip is from Christopher Decaen; personal communication.

done both these things.[52] However, what I have tried to do, beyond what they have done, is to show why the division of material living things at the most universal level is based on the primary division of souls. I have also endeavored to clarify the precise manner in which Aquinas divides souls, namely, according to the ways in which the motions that they are the cause of differ from those of nonliving natural things.[53] Some activities of soul differ from those of nonliving things only as to how these activities are performed, namely, by an intrinsic rather than extrinsic agent; in growth, for example, the living thing adds to itself. Some activities of soul further differ from those of other natural bodies as to what they accomplish. This is due to the immaterial character of these activities, of which there are two forms—sensing (which is a reception of form not in the manner of matter, though requiring an organ) and intellectual understanding (which is an entirely immaterial activity, involving no organ).

While Aquinas maintains that the essence of life is the capacity for self-motion, by contrast, Oderberg maintains that "the essence of life: [is] immanent causation. . . . That essence, I claim is what Aristotelians and Thomists sometimes call *immanent causation.*"[54] And Feser is in agreement

52 See Edward Feser, *Aristotle's Revenge* (Editiones Scholasticae, 2019), 391–400 for a treatment of classification, especially 400 in regard to the difference between Aristotle and Woese's division. He explicitly agrees with David Oderberg, who says in *Real Essentialism* (Routledge, 2007), 184: "It is one of the themes of this section and section 8.3 that there is an important metaphysical distinction between what things are and where they come from." On this point, we are all in agreement. While both authors provide many other helpful explanations concerning living things and their activities, at times they depart from central Aristotelian-Thomistic teachings. For example, Oderberg says that "cells themselves are organisms, even when existing as parts of other organisms." *Real Essentialism*, 182.

53 Cf. Feser, *Aristotle's Revenge*, 40:

> The Aristotelian tradition draws a distinction between three basic types of living substance. . . . The most basic kind of life is vegetative life, which involve the capacities of a living thing to take in nutrients, to go through a growth cycle, and to reproduce itself. . . . The second kind of life is animal life, which includes the vegetative capacities . . . but in addition involves the capacities of a thing to take in information through specialized sense organs and move around. . . . The third kind of life is the rational kind. . . . This form of life incorporates both the vegetative and animal capacities, and adds to them the intellectual powers of forming abstract concepts, putting them in propositions, and reasoning logically.

54 David Oderberg, "Synthetic Life and the Bruteness of Immanent Causation," in *Aristotle on Method and Metaphysics*, ed. Edward Feser (Palgrave MacMillan, 2013), 213. See Oderberg, *Real Essentialism*, 180: "Life is the natural capacity of an object for self-perfective immanent activity. . . . Living things, unlike non-living things, exercise *immanent* causation: this is a kind of causation that begins *with* the agent and terminates *in* the agent for the sake *of* the agent."

with him. Both misconstrue the meaning of "immanent." For Aristotle, an immanent activity is an activity which is perfective of the agent rather than of some product resulting from it.[55] Immanent activities are divided against transient activities, whose perfection lies in their products and not in the activities themselves.[56] For this reason, Aquinas would disagree with Feser who, following Oderberg, attribute immanent activities to plants:

> The mark of a living or organic substance is that in addition to transeunt causation it exhibits immanent causation, in which the effect remains within the agent and perfects it. An animal's digestion of a meal would be an example insofar as it allows the animal to stay alive and grow (though there are also external or transeunt effects like the excretion of waste products).[57]

55 See *Metaphysics*, bk. 9 where Aristotle is trying to establish that act is the end of potency. This gives him reason to distinguish two types of acts:

> And while in some cases the exercise [of the potency] is the ultimate thing (e.g., in sight the ultimate thing is seeing, and no other product besides this results from sight), but from some things a product follows (e.g., from the art of building there results a house as well as the act of building), yet none the less the act is in the former case the end and in the latter more of an end than the potency is. For the act of building is realized in the thing that is being built, and comes to be, and is, at the same time as the house. Where, then, the result is something apart from the exercise, the actuality is in the thing that is being made, e.g., the act of building is in the thing that is being built and that of weaving in the thing that is being woven, and similarly in all other cases, and in general the movement is in the thing that is being moved; but where there is no product apart from the actuality, the actuality is present in the agents, e.g., the act of seeing is in the seeing subject and that of theorizing in the theorizing subject and the life is in the soul (and therefore well-being also; for it is a certain kind of life).

Metaphysics, bk. 9, chap. 8, 1050a24-b1, in McKeon, *The Basic Works of Aristotle*, trans. W. D. Ross. Aquinas's commentary on this passage is little more than a paraphrase. See also *SCG*, bk. 1, chap. 100.

56 Transient activities are sometimes called "transeunt" and also "transitive" activities.

57 Feser, *Aristotle's Revenge*, 39. See also Oderberg, *Real Essentialism*, 180: "When a person eats food (immanent), she uses transient instrumental causes . . . and there are also transient causal results or effects of the immanent nutritive and eliminative process." See also Feser, 194: "We cannot even understand the kind of adaptation distinctive of living things without a prior grasp of immanence, which is shown in Bedau's use of the term 'flourishing.' Living creatures do things *to* themselves *for* themselves, whereas non-living creatures do not"; Feser, 197: "The argument is that fundamental kinds of causation must derive at least in part from the same kinds. The fundamental kinds are: formal (essences); material (material constitution) efficient (transient); final (immanent)"; and Feser, 197: "Immanent causation is a preferable way of talking about the phenomena of life because teleology and final causation do not of themselves import the notion of *self*-directedness." One finds this error in earlier scholastic writings; for example, Henry J. Koren, uses "immanent" to characterize vegetative activities

Aquinas agrees that plants, unlike nonliving things, take in materials from the outside and through their own activity transform some of these materials into their own substance. However, the *activity* of nutrition is not of itself perfective of the agent. For Aquinas, the activity of nutrition perfects the "new flesh" it produces. This product, the "new flesh," perfects the organism as a whole.

Stated in more precise terms, when an animal ingests food containing proteins, various enzymes in its digestive tract break these proteins down into amino acids. Eventually these amino acids will be constructed into new proteins by cellular components called ribosomes.[58] Signals are added so that the new proteins are transported to their correct destination in the body, be it inside or outside the cell in which the ribosomes that produced them are found. It is plain that the activity of breaking down the ingested protein produces products, and this activity is not perfective of the enzymes responsible for it. It is equally plain that the activities of the ribosomes produce products (proteins) and that the activities themselves do not perfect the ribosomes themselves or the organism as a whole. Nutrition only takes place when new body parts, including proteins, have been properly synthesized (or perhaps it can only be said to be entirely completed when the newly synthesized parts are transported to their proper place in the body). Thus, nutrition does not meet the definition of immanent activity, for in nutrition something is produced outside of the activity itself, and it is this product and not the activity itself which is perfective of the agent.[59]

An example of an immanent activity is seeing, as the activity itself perfects the agent rather than perfecting some product internal or external to the agent. Aquinas does not use the immanent-transient distinction when dividing living things, because it does not suffice to separate plants from

in *An Introduction to the Philosophy of Animate Nature* (Pearson Custom Publishing, n.d., repr., Herder, 1955), 152.

58 Plants also have ribosomes that produce proteins from amino acids. Note that plants and animals synthesize other parts of themselves as well, e.g., lipids. To synthesize is of course to produce something.

59 Strictly speaking, the agent in protein production is the organism, not the ribosome. Just as it is the sighted animal that sees with it eyes, so too it is the organism that produces new parts of itself with its ribosomes. The fact remains, however, that the activity in question produces something, and therefore is not immanent.

nonliving natural things, for all the life activities of plants are transient, as are all the activities of nonliving natural things.[60]

One might argue that the difference between Aquinas on the one hand and Oderberg/Feser on the other is simply a difference of terminology. Even so, it remains the case that Oderberg and Feser appear to have misconstrued the Aristotelian distinction between immanent and transient activities, and they have consequently imposed a new meaning on the word "immanent" when words such as "intrinsic" and "self-moving" suffice to articulate the nature of living things. It is confusing, to say the least, that the same activity, nutrition, should be called both transient and immanent—transient according to Aristotle's notion and immanent according to Oderberg/Feser's notion.

60 For a thorough discussion of the transient nature of the vegetative activities, see Marie I. George, "On the Meaning of 'Immanent Activity' According to Aquinas," *The Thomist* 78, no. 3 (October 2014): 537–55.

Part II

HUMAN AND NONHUMAN ANIMALS: SIMILARITIES AND DIFFERENCES

4

Thomas Aquinas Meets Nim Chimpsky: On the Debate About Human Nature and the Nature of Other Animals[1]

Introduction

Does *human being* constitute a life form distinct from the other animals? On the whole, people throughout most of history have thought so, both common folk who ate meat, and the many philosophers who thought that humans were different from other animals because we can think, whereas they cannot. And then in the nineteenth century Darwin arrived on the scene, and the idea that natural selection acting on random variation resulted in some nonhuman primates producing human offspring that was not all that different than its parents cast a shadow of doubt on the neat line of demarcation between Man and Beast.

1 Nim Chimpsky was the name Herbert Terrace gave to the chimpanzee that he used in his language studies. The name was humorously modeled after that of the well-known linguist, Noam Chomsky.

Later, in the twentieth century, the discovery of toolmaking by animals and the successful teaching of sign language to apes were perceived by many as additional evidence against human uniqueness.[2]

The new, evolutionary understanding of humans had a particularly marked impact upon many Catholic institutions of higher learning in the United States. In the first half of the twentieth century, courses in natural philosophy were standard fare in Catholic colleges. The rationale for this was that an understanding of philosophy was not only desirable for its own sake, but also as an aid to understanding theology. Typically, a "Philosophy of Man" course was offered, and the textbooks or manuals used for it most often took the form of a résumé of sorts of what Thomas Aquinas said on the subject.[3] In some cases, those teaching these courses had received their own instruction from like textbooks rather than from original sources. There were several problems with the instruction based on these textbooks. First, they lacked examples and comparisons that could help the learner acquire new knowledge, and they often lacked dialectic as well, proceeding rather by setting out premises and conclusions.[4] The absence of dialectic reduced wonder about the questions raised, and its absence, accompanied by the lack of examples and other learning aids, rendered the answers given dry, abstract, and hard to follow. Secondly, their content sometimes deviated from the sources they were trying to be faithful to. For example, Vincentio Remer, SJ, maintains that "strictly immanent activities occur in plants."[5] Thirdly, those who did not fully grasp the truths that Aristotle and Aquinas articulate were at a loss to situate recent findings of science, such as toolmaking by animals,

2 The great apes include gorillas, chimpanzees (*Pan troglodytes*), bonobos (*Pan paniscus*; sometimes called pygmy chimps), and orangutans.

3 Here are some of the titles of scholastic manuals or textbooks that treat living things: Joseph Gredt, OSB, *Elementa Philosophiae Aristotelico-Thomisticae* (Herder, 1958); Henry J. Koren, CSSp, *An Introduction to the Philosophy of Animate Nature* (Herder, 1955); Vincentio Remer, SJ, *Summa Philosophiae Scholasticae: Psychologia* (Gregorian University, 1956); Henri Renard, *Philosophy of Man* (Bruce, 1948).

4 Aquinas would disagree with the manualists' way of proceeding. See Marie I. George, "Mind Forming and Manuductio in Aquinas," *The Thomist* 57, no. 2 (April 1993): 201–13.

5 Remer, *Summa Philosophiae Scholasticae: Psychologia*, 37. I argue in chapter 3 that Aristotle would hold that plants do not perform strictly immanent activities. Another example of deviation from traditional Aristotelian-Thomistic teachings is Henry J. Koren's conflation of speculative philosophy with metaphysics. Koren, *An Introduction to the Philosophy of Animate Nature*, 5. Aristotle divides speculative philosophy into natural philosophy, mathematics, and metaphysics; see *Metaphysics*, bk. 6, chap. 1, 1026a18.

within an Aristotelian-Thomistic framework. The inadequate engagement with science, combined with the increasing importance given to science in higher education, led many of those at the head of Catholic institutions in the 1960s and 70s to believe that the resources needed to treat questions raised by science were not to be found in Aquinas's teaching. This was one factor, among others, that led many Catholic institutions to replace a Thomistic course on human nature with a survey course of what various philosophers have thought about it, when they did not simply eliminate as a requirement a course on human nature, Thomistic or otherwise.[6]

What are some of the results of the ape studies that led to the apparent downfall of the traditional understanding of human nature? In one case, two chimpanzees learned to communicate to each other what tool was needed in order to obtain food. The chimpanzees were separated by glass with a window for communication. On one side food would be put in a container that could only be opened with a specific tool. The chimpanzee on that side had to figure out which tool was needed and had to type the symbol (lexigram) for that tool so that the chimpanzee on the other side that had access to the tools, upon seeing the symbol (lexigram) typed, could then hand over the appropriate tool. Once the chimpanzee gained access to the food, it shared some of the food with the other. In the words of the experimenter: "Such a complex inter-twining of symbols, cooperation, and use of objects is usually seen only in man."[7]

Then there is the chimpanzee, Sarah, who apparently learned what the symbol for the color brown meant, not by having the symbol-token shown to her in the presence of brown-colored objects, but rather by being told via symbol-tokens, in the absence of anything brown, that brown was the color of chocolate (she had already learned the symbols for chocolate and "color of"). Later when commanded via tokens, "Sarah insert brown [in] red dish," she correctly selected and inserted the brown disk from a set of

6 The decline of the view that philosophy was important for studying theology was another reason for Catholic colleges to reduce the number of required philosophy courses. These colleges were often also caught up in a societal trend dismissive of liberal education; consequently, philosophy courses that did not have immediate practical application were destined to be eliminated from college requirements.

7 E. Sue Savage-Rumbaugh, *Ape Language: From Conditioned Response to Symbol* (Columbia University Press, 1988), 195.

four differently colored disks.[8] This seems to show mental activity beyond simple association.

Two Questions about Humans: One Philosophical, the Other Scientific

Aristotle and Aquinas were obviously not aware of cases such as these, nor were they aware of the theory of evolution, which seems to lend support to the notion that there is no radical discontinuity between human and nonhuman animals. Does this mean that the Aristotelian-Thomistic tradition is now at a loss when it comes to answering the question of whether humans differ from other animals? We need to recognize that there is a hidden ambiguity in the question of whether humans are radically different from other animals, and that really there are two questions lurking here, one answerable by philosophy alone, the other requiring scientific inquiry as well. The first question seeks to discover whether human being constitutes one of the fundamental divisions of living thing alongside plant and animal or whether humans fall within the division "animal." If the former proves to be the case, then a subsequent question arises: Are our fellow humans the only representatives of this division of living being, or are there other beings that also belong to this category? In other words, if human-type being is a category, it might include bonobos and intelligent extraterrestrials, in addition to ourselves. I maintain that answering the more general question about whether there is a difference between animals and humans is the philosopher's job, whereas questions about specific organisms (e.g., a chimpanzee) may require scientific investigation in addition.[9] Why I hold this should be clear by the end of this chapter.

8 Duane M. Rumbaugh, "Language Behavior of Apes," in *Speaking of Apes*, ed. Thomas A. Sebeok and Jean Umiker-Sebeok (Plenum Press, 1980), 246.

9 I used to maintain that the general difference between plant and animal can be determined without scientific investigation, whereas whether a specific organism is one or the other may require scientific investigation, such as whether a Venus Fly Trap is a plant or an animal. Now I am more hesitant, as plants manifest directional growth; many plants grow toward light. Are they aware of the light? They do not have eyes like we do or any signs of an analogous organ visible to the naked eye. Still, it seems that we need to understand the cause of their directional growth before we can conclude for sure that they do not have some simpler form of vision. If this is correct, then further investigation is needed in order to determine whether "plant" is a genuine category, which would not be the case if in fact all plants were sentient, for then they would all be animals.

Does human being constitute one of the most fundamental divisions of living thing, alongside plant (characterized by nutrition and growth, while lacking sensation) and animal (characterized by sensation, in addition to nutrition and growth)? The other alternatives are that human beings are simply animals with different sense abilities, such as a better imagination than other animals, or, if we are to look at physical features rather than behavior, humans are simply animals constituted by a combination of parts, be they organs or molecules, that are not found in other animals.

Note that the question just mentioned amounts to asking whether the word "animal" has one meaning or two meanings. It is obvious that humans are animals, in the sense of living things endowed with sensation. What is disputed is whether there only exist animals whose highest ability is to sense or whether there also exist animals that have an ability other than and superior to sensation (reason being the front-runner here). If the latter is the case, then "animal" would mean two things: "sentient living thing" and "sentient living thing devoid of reason"; and "sentient being devoid of reason" and "sentient being possessing reason" would be two separate kinds of living things. If the former is the case, "animal" would refer to sentient beings alone.

Throughout the history of philosophy, virtually all of the philosophers who maintain that there is a radical difference between human beings and other animals hold that the difference lies in our ability to think, something other animals lack.[10] And so I will first investigate what thinking is. Note that answering this question will allow one to readily settle the question of whether thinking is really different in kind from sensing, or whether it is just another type of sensing or a more refined form of some type of it (similar to the eagle's ability to see farther than we do)?[11]

What is Thinking?

The history of philosophy bears witness to the difficulty of determining what thinking is. From the pre-Socratics to our day quite a number of "thinkers" have failed to understand what thinking is and distinguish it from sensing, and thus they have also conflated the ability to think (i.e., the intellect) with

10 See Mortimer Adler, *The Difference of Man and the Difference It Makes* (Holt, Rinehart and Winston, 1967), 54.

11 The word "think" has more than one meaning. Here I am considering whether there is some form of thinking that is different from sensing.

the ability to sense. How are thinking and sensing (and the corresponding abilities of intellect and sense) to be defined and distinguished? As Aristotle pointed out long ago,[12] abilities of the soul are known through their activities, and these are understood in reference to their object. Sight is known from seeing, and seeing is known as perception of color. To understand what the intellect is requires looking at thinking. To understand what thinking is requires considering its object.

What is the object of thinking? In the first instance, it is the nature (or "whatness") of a thing, apprehended in a *universal* manner. By contrast, the object of sensing is particular (or individual) things. One does not see or hear "cat" in general, but *this* cat. By contrast, when thinking about cats, one's concept of cat applies to (and the name signifying this concept can be said of) every cat that ever was, is, and will be.[13] There are doubtlessly many puzzling and difficult questions about the nature of the universal.[14] However, our vague experience of sensing and thinking assures us both that we sense (for example) particular animals, and that when we think about animals, for example, that every animal is a living thing (or no animal is a plant), this refers to a certain nature that can be shared by many, and that is why in affirmative propositions it is best expressed by the singular "every," rather than by "all," which suggests a collection.[15]

A second difference between the objects of thinking and sensing is this: What one grasps through thinking is the *unchanging* natures of things,

12 See Aristotle, *De Anima*, bk. 2, chap. 3, 415a12–23.

13 See Feser, *Scholastic Metaphysics*, 227:

> Concepts are *abstract and universal* in a way no image can be. The concept *triangle* applies to every triangle without exception, but any mental image we can form of a triangle will always be of an isosceles, scalene, or equilateral triangle. . . . The concept *man* applies to every man without exception, but any mental image we form of a man will always be of a tall man or a short one.

14 The nature of the universal deserves treatment in its own right. It suffices for my purpose to understand that there is a difference between knowing this cat is not that cat and knowing that every cat is an animal. The former is knowledge of a particular truth that we acquire by sensing, whereas the latter is a universal truth that we arrive at by thinking. The senses plainly cannot know every cat, whereas the intellect can grasp, at least vaguely, the nature belonging to all cats.

15 See Feser, *Scholastic Metaphysics*, 248: "Universals like *triangularity, redness, humanness,* etc. are not reducible to any particular triangle, red thing, or human being, nor even to any collection of triangles, red things, or human beings. For any particular triangle, red thing, or human being, or even the whole collection of these things, could go out of existence, and yet triangularity, redness, and humanness could come to be instantiated once again."

for example, a cat is always an animal, whereas what one grasps through the senses is subject to change. Muffy is no longer here in the house; Muffy eventually is no more. But "catness" does not cease to be when a cat or even all cats die—and this is what the intellect grasps.

A third characteristic of the object of thinking is that the nature known exists in the intellect in an *immaterial* manner, in contrast with the object of sense which is a particular that exists as a material entity. That the universal nature existing in the intellect is immaterial can be seen in a number of different, but related ways. Consider what makes a material thing the specific material thing that it is. Why is this cat this cat and not that cat? Why is this patch of white not that patch of white? Most radically it is because of matter: The material out of which this cat is constituted is not the same material as that of out which other cats and all other things are constituted; this patch of white is reflected back from different matter than that patch. Now if matter is indeed the ultimate cause of the individuality of sensible objects, in order for the intellect to attain to universal knowledge, it must grasp what is commonly shared by all individuals having a given nature, leaving aside the individual features, which are in a radical way due to matter.[16] If the intellect did not abstract from matter, its knowledge would be of the particular, as is the case of sense perception.[17]

There are other arguments as well, for the immateriality of the intellect. Two of them, which are based on the immaterial nature of concepts, were given in chapter 2.[18]

16 An exception to the form of material individuals being individuated by matter is the rational soul, which is an immaterial substantial form. Nevertheless, the individuation of each rational soul necessary implies a relationship to a unique body. See Aquinas, *SCG*, bk. 2, chap. 75:

> For we acknowledge the possible intellect to be one in species in diverse men and many according to number. . . . Nor nevertheless does it follow that it is a material form depending on the body for its being. For just as it belongs to the human soul according to its species that it be united to such a body according to its species, so this soul differs from that in number only from this, that it has a relationship to a body other in number. And in this manner human souls (and as a consequence the possible intellect, which is a power of soul) are individuated according to bodies, not as though with an individuation caused by bodies.

17 It is not true that if something is an individual, it is material, although this is the case for sensible things. However, if something is material, it is necessarily a "this something."

18 Aristotle gives another argument (the "intus apparens" argument) for the immateriality of the intellect in the *De Anima*, bk. 3, chap. 4, 429a20–30 and Aquinas endorses it. See *In DA*, bk. 3, lec. 7, nos. 677–81. See also *De unitate intellectus*, chap. 1. For a partial defense of

In sum, the one thinking attains to the unchanging universal nature of things, known necessarily in abstraction from matter, whereas the one sensing acquires knowledge of material individuals subject to change.[19] Given that these two activities have objects with opposite properties, it cannot be said that one of them is a form of the other; they are plainly two quite distinct types of knowing. The abilities or faculties from which these activities proceed, sense and intellect, are consequently also distinct.[20]

Now doubtless many questions and objections can be brought up concerning the above abbreviated account of the nature of sensing and thinking. Aquinas alone brings up numerous difficulties, the responses to which often involve subtle distinctions. However, most modern authors do not assess the above discussions and find them wanting—they simply ignore them.[21] To mention one of many examples, Marc Houser, the author of *Wild Minds: What Animals Really Think*, says that the question "Do animals think?," is an "unhelpful question because [it is] vague, relying on general concepts that are often defined on the basis of what humans do."[22]

---

this argument, see Michael Augros, "Aquinas's Proof of the Human Soul's Subsistence," *The Aquinas Review* 27, no. 1 (2024): 1–28.

19 We are speaking of the first and most fundamental act of the intellect, sometimes called simple apprehension (*simplex apprehensio*). This act serves as the basis for composition and division (the formation of affirmative and negative propositions) and ultimately also for reasoning, in which the mind goes from the known to what was hitherto unknown.

20 See Alasdair MacIntyre, *Dependent Rational Animals: Why Human Beings Need the Virtues* (Open Court, 1999). MacIntyre maintains that we:

> Indeed we need to mark the difference between the kind of reason for action that some nonhuman animals have and the kind of reasons that language-using, reflective human beings have. But we need not and should not deny that on occasion such nonhuman animals in some sense have reasons for acting as they do. . . . It is important because any exercise of the power to reflect on our reason for action presupposes that we already have such reasons about which we can reflect prior to our reflection. . . . To acknowledge that there are these animal preconditions for human rationality requires us to think of the relationship of human beings to members of other intelligent species in terms of a scale or a spectrum rather than of a single line of division between "them" and "us" (56–57).

However, the fact that sense experience is a prerequisite for abstract thought in no wise requires us to deny that there is a single line of division between human and nonhuman animals, one that is demarcated by the difference in kind between sense and abstract thought.

21 Mortimer Adler back in the 1960s noted that contemporary authors ignore Aquinas's reasoning regarding the immateriality of the intellect. Adler, *The Difference of Man*, 220.

22 Marc D. Hauser, *Wild Minds: What Animals Really Think* (Henry Holt, 2000), xviii.

Why Some People Confuse Thinking and Sensing

Probably the most common reason why people get led astray and confuse thinking with sensing has to do with the dependence of thinking on imagining. We cannot think without also imagining.[23] Temporary or permanent damage to the imagination resulting from causes such as birth defects, injury, alcohol, or fatigue hinders us or prevents us entirely from thinking. Included among the images accompanying thought are not only visual representations, but representations of things perceived by other senses as well, and especially words (one's internal dialogue voice is produced by one's imagination). Thus, there is a good deal of overlap between the Aristotelian insight that images are needed for thought and the view of many contemporary philosophers regarding the necessity of language for thought. Aristotle, however, unlike a number of these thinkers, acknowledges that images other than words suffice for thinking certain thoughts. Moreover, ultimately words do not make sense if the one using them cannot refer back, either directly or indirectly, to something imaginable—directly in the case of a material thing such as a frog, indirectly in the case of nonsensible things or attributes (for example, understanding something to be "immaterial" involves a negation of what is material, which is only understood in reference to some particular material thing which is imaginable).[24]

From the dependency of thought on imagination some people jump to the conclusion that there is no radical difference between the two, that both are brain functions. This is generally due to their prior commitment to materialism,[25] or to a failure to see that a dependency relationship is not necessarily some sort of identity relationship, or to a combination of the two. Some people correctly recognize that imagining is a brain function affected by drugs and damage to certain parts of the head, etc. And they also recognize that thinking depends upon imagining. And so they conclude that thinking too must be a brain function. However, this is like concluding

23 Aristotle was the first to insist upon the dependency of thought upon imagination. See *De Anima*, bk. 3, chap. 7, 431a14–19.

24 See Thomas Aquinas, *In Librum Boethii de Trinitate*, ed. Bruno Decker (Brill, 1959), q. 2, a. 3.

25 See Griffin, *Animal Minds*, 142: "Taking it for granted that both behavior and conscious thinking result from the functioning of brains or central nervous systems, we may appropriately inquire whether the extensive studies of brain functions have provided any evidence concerning the particular processes that produce conscious thought."

that cooking requires (or is carried on in) a supermarket because cooking depends on getting groceries, which requires a supermarket. A dependency relationship does not necessarily entail partial identity between the things so related. A more appropriate parallel in the case of the imagination and intellect is just as a chef cannot cook a dish when lacking the ingredients to do so, so too the intellect cannot form a concept when lacking the requisite image(s).[26] Again, independent arguments show that the intellect is immaterial, and thus that thinking is not a brain function.

The more common and even cruder error occurs when people perhaps start out by having some vague idea that thinking is different from imagining, but end up conflating the two, on the grounds that since the intellect cannot actually think without an image, thinking must simply be a matter of producing images (in which case it would be a brain function). Again, the difference between the universal nature grasped by the intellect and the particularity of images formed by the imagination is something that virtually no one ever mentions, much less insists upon. And this is not surprising behavior on the part of those who have a prior commitment to the thesis that material causes afford the only legitimate sort of explanation. For acknowledging the difference between the object of imagination and that of intellect leads ineluctably to entertaining the notion that the intellect may be immaterial, in which case thinking could in no wise be a brain function. When one believes that thinking is a brain function, it is easy to go from there to attributing thought to animals, especially to those that have large brains and display flexible and adaptive behavior.

Another reason why people may have difficulty in recognizing the difference between thought and sensation is the ambiguous language used in regard to the latter. The word "think" is a case in point. When one is asked to think of a dog, one both imagines a particular dog and brings to mind the idea "dog." The word "mind" also has multiple significations. It can be used to refer to internal senses (imagination, memory, etc.) or the intellect or both together,[27] and "mental process" can refer to thinking and also imagining/remembering. These analogous words often lead astray those who take them

26 I address the relationship between the intellect and the imagination in a more precise manner in "Philosophers of Mind Would Do Well to Keep Aquinas's Teachings in Mind," forthcoming.

27 From Merriam-Webster's *New Collegiate Dictionary* (1980): "mind 2a: the element or complex of elements in an individual that feels, perceives, thinks, wills, and esp. reasons."

to have a single meaning. If instead of one name, two different names were used these people would be less likely to overlook the difference between the two sorts of cognitive faculties, namely, that imagination and memory are sense powers that perceive individual things, whereas the intellect grasps universals. Similarly, the word "concept" is used by some to name an abstract thought, whereas it is used by others to refer to images and memories as well. Those who use it in the latter sense are more prone to overlook differences between the former and latter. This is why some philosophers, for the sake of clarity, speak of "abstract thought" rather than "thought" and of "thinking abstractly" rather than "thinking."

If what we have said is correct, and intellect is different from sense, then two of the most popular positions regarding the relation of human nature to animal nature have been eliminated. Humans are not simply more intelligent ("smarter") apes in the sense that we have a greater degree of the same kind of ability when it comes to solving problems. Humans have an entirely different manner of solving problems, namely, through abstract thought, and this makes us intelligent in a completely different manner than other animals. As for those who would differentiate human beings by a feature of our brain endowing us with a unique ability, such as our ability to speak grammatically,[28] they have missed a more fundamental difference which is not coded for by some gene or genes, namely, our ability to form universal concepts.

Are Humans the Only Member of the Category "Human Being" ("Rational Animal")?

So far, I have argued that human being is a fundamental division of living thing alongside plants that grow but lack knowledge, and animals that have sense knowledge but not intellectual knowledge. The question now becomes: Are humans the only member of this fundamental division, or not?

28 Noam Chomsky is one of the main advocates of the view that "it is not very surprising that there are striking qualitative differences between humans and other species in 'capacity for language,' given the enormous selectional advantages conferred by language—for humans, in a period of human evolution that is recent in evolutionary terms." Noam Chomsky, "Human Language and Other Semiotic Systems," in Sebeok and Umiker-Sebeok, *Speaking of Apes*, 439. For Chomsky, this special capacity for language has a purely biological explanation (e.g., such as a special center in the human brain). Ray Jackendoff holds the same view; see *Patterns in the Mind*, chap. 4, "Language and the Brain" (Basic Books, 1994).

Interestingly Aquinas, who thinks that this is an appropriate question, offers a number of a priori arguments why humans are the only species in this division. He draws one argument from the side of an immaterial power of the soul, another from the side of the physical constitution of the body, and a final one from the intermediary character of human nature.

> Granted, there is not some kind of living thing that has intellect among mortal living things, other than the human species. For since the intellect does not have a corporeal organ, those that possess intellect are not able to be diversified according to the diverse physical make-up (*complexionem*) of organs, as the species of sensitive beings are diversified according to diverse make-ups (*complexiones*), by which they are related in diverse ways to the operations of sensation.[29]

> For if it [an intellectual substance] were united to another body, either it would be united to a mixed body or to a simple body. It cannot however be united to a mixed body, because it is necessary that that body be of the most balanced make-up according to its genus among the other mixed bodies . . . that body which has the most noble form, as an intellectual substance, would have to be of the most temperate mixture. . . . The most balanced constitution is the constitution of the human body. It is necessary, therefore, that if an intellectual substance is united to some mixed body, it be of the same nature as the human body. The form of this being would be of the same nature as the human soul, if it be an intellectual substance. There would not therefore be a difference according to species between this animal and man.[30]

> That there is only one species of rational animal, while there exist many species of irrational animal, arises from the fact that the rational animal is constituted from this that corporeal nature reaches the highest thing it can attain to, [namely], the nature of spiritual substance which [in turn] attains its lowest [grade]. There is only one highest grade, as well as lowest grade, of one nature.[31]

There is no intrinsic impossibility for another kind of being with an intellect that forms ideas starting from sense experience to be united to a body

29 *In DA*, bk. 2, lec. 5, nos. 293, 294.

30 *SCG*, bk. 2, q. 90.

31 *De Spir. Creat.*, unicus, a. 8, ad 10.

somewhat different than ours and to be reproductively isolated from us.[32] Whether one ought to call it another species in the philosophical sense of species, is another matter (and admittedly a difficult one).

Proceeding on the assumption that one cannot exclude a priori the existence of other human species (or human-type beings), one then might ask if there is at least not some criteria based on common experience or on experience close to common experience that would allow one to quickly eliminate the various animals on earth from the category of humankind.[33] It is not a matter of common experience to come across any given kind of animal, granted most people eventually come across flies and rodents. If we look at the cumulative experience of humankind, our collective experience is that animals do not show any manifest signs of intelligence, such as having a civilization with complex artifacts and works of fine art or speech resembling that of humans. Though in the nineteenth century Darwin offers general arguments in the *Descent of Man* supporting the view that animals' ability to form concepts only differs from ours in degree, it was mainly in the twentieth century that the question of animal intelligence became subject to intense scrutiny, due to certain detailed observations made by scientists. In particular, Jane Goodall observed toolmaking by chimpanzees in the wild,

32 Even Aquinas thinks that there is room for doubt whether there might not be another human-type species. In his argument in *De Spir. Creat.*, unicus, a. 8, ad 10, after he says that "there is only one highest grade, as well as lowest grade, of one nature," he adds, "although it could be said that there were many species of rational animal, if one were to posit that the celestial bodies are animate."

33 John R. Berkman claims that "since George [Marie, the author of this book] clearly believes or presumes that 'intelligent beings' = 'human beings' and 'intelligent' = 'human-like,' all that George is arguing here is that since non-human animals do not act like human beings, therefore non-human animals are not human-like." John Berkman, "Towards a Thomistic Theology of Animality," in *Creaturely Theology*, ed. Celia Deane-Drummond and David Clough (SCM, 2009), 38. This is inaccurate. First, I understand "human-like being" to be one of the fundamental divisions of living things, alongside plant and animal. This division is differentiated from the other two divisions in that the material organisms contained in it have the capacity for abstract thought. Intelligent extraterrestrials, if such exist, would fall in this category. I typically refer to this category as "human," rather than "human-type," since we are the only known member of it. Secondly, I ask whether there is evidence indicating that nonhuman animals have the capacity for abstract thought by examining what this evidence would consist in and by looking to see whether in fact it is present. I am looking for a specific type of intelligence, one that is not sensory, to determine whether certain nonhuman animals belong in the category "human-type being" instead of in the category "animal." I don't assume that in order for an organism to fall into this category that it has to be like us in any way other than possessing the capacity for abstract thought.

and experimenters who attempted to teach language to animals observed seemingly positive results.

How then to test the most likely contenders for humankind? Failure to formulate adequate criteria is another major factor fueling the confusion concerning the difference between the human kingdom and the animal kingdom. Plainly if one does not distinguish thinking from sensing, one is not going to come up with appropriate criteria for whether a being is thinking, and thus is human. Unfortunately, however, even if one does distinguish thinking from sensing in principle, this does not automatically ensure that one will elaborate appropriate criteria for testing for thought. The chief reason why people fail to apply their knowledge properly is that they have an inadequate understanding of what the senses, and especially the internal senses, allow an animal to do. Thus, some seem unaware that some animals can accomplish goals not only through instinct, but also by using their external senses and other internal senses, while others recognize that animals can learn, but underestimate the sorts of learning that the animals' senses allow for.

Inadequate Criteria for Recognizing the Presence of the Capacity for Abstract Thought

Let us look at examples of inadequate criteria stemming from the mistakes just mentioned. Some people who fail to recognize how sense and intellect differ erroneously attribute thought to those animals that are capable of "problem-solving." The same sort of mistaken attribution is also made by those who do distinguish intellect from sense, but at the same time hold that all adaptive behavior is either due to instinct (understood as innate knowledge of an appropriate means to a goal) or to intelligence, in the sense of the capacity for abstract thought. Thus, when animals manifest adaptive behavior that cannot be attributed to instinct, such as solving novel problems, these people are compelled to concede that animals think (and consequently are not really different from humans), or alternately they give forced explanations in which they reduce learned behavior to instinct. Consider, for example, the following passage from Henri Renard's *The Philosophy of Man*:

> In brute animals, therefore, the estimative power, or instinct, is a sort of natural prudence, so that we can note some of the higher animals are able and learn to acquire new behaviors—for example, to avoid danger,

> and to obtain food in such a prudential manner that they seem to be capable of choosing the proper means to an end. Because of these striking facts, some scientists have maintained that the brute animals, like human beings, possess an intellect, or "mind," with the same powers of abstraction and reasoning, even though these powers are quite undeveloped in the present stage. This assertion shows a lack of philosophical insight. While an animal can learn particular facts, it can never abstract a principle and apply it to particular cases. This is evident from the fact that through the ages each species of animal has always operated in the same unchanged manner and has learned no new mode of doing.[34]

Renard starts out by noting that some animals can acquire new behaviors and ends by saying that no species of animal has acquired any new mode of acting, but always operates in the same manner. The problem with this is that scientific observations reveal that both individual animals learn new behaviors and populations within a species learn new behaviors,[35] for example, a Japanese macaque learned to wash the sweet potatoes that scientists had put out for the macaques, and this practice gradually spread through this particular population.[36] Thus, invoking instinct as Renard does here is

34 Renard, *Philosophy of Man*, 110. This Thomistic work is typical of the period.

35 There is a growing body of literature documenting differences in behavior in animal populations that more readily admit of a social learning explanation as opposed to a genetic one, e.g., some chimp groups fish for wood-boring ants, whereas other groups dip for driver ants, even though both species of ants are found within the range of both groups. See Michael Tomasello, "Cultural Transmission in Chimpanzee Tool Use and Signaling?," in *"Language" and Intelligence in Monkeys and Apes*, ed. Sue Taylor Parker and Kathleen Rita Gibson (Cambridge University Press, 1990), 277. It takes young chimps several years before they acquire adult competence at these tasks. Tomasello, "Cultural Transmission," 276–77. There also is evidence of song traditions in birds; see Paul C. Mundinger, "Animal Cultures and a General Theory of Cultural Evolution," *Ethology and Sociobiology* 1, no. 3 (1980): 183–223 and Clive Catchpole, *Vocal Communication in Birds* (University Park Press, 1979), 65–66.

36 See Ann J. Premack, *Why Chimps Can Read* (Harper & Row, 1976), 40:

> About a year after the artificial feeding program started [scientists left sweet potatoes on the beach], a two-year-old female, named Imo by the researchers, carried her sweet potato to the edge of a brook, dipped the potato in the water and washed off the sand particles. Most of the macaques continued to remove the offending sand particles by dry-brushing the potatoes with their hands, but in the ensuing years many of the animals began to wash their potatoes. Gradually potato washing shifted to the nearby sea rather than the brook. The adoption of this new technique was slow. At the end of the first year, only four of the sixty animals followed Imo's example, the younger animals being the first to adopt the new trend. Five years later almost all the younger animals washed their potatoes, while few of the older animals adopted the custom.

not adequate to dismissing scientists' claims about animal intelligence that are based on the fact that animals do learn.

I think that the tendency of certain natural philosophers to skip over learned behavior and focus on instinct is due to a number of reasons. One reason for the instinct-intelligence dichotomy is the fact that the limited observations of animals[37] made by the average individual, combined with what is now a fairly extensive amount of scientific literature on animal behavior, do indicate that much of animal behavior is instinctive or partly instinctive.[38] Secondly, the human tendency to oversimplify makes it easy

37 How much does the average person or philosopher know firsthand about animals? Do people really have such extensive contact with animals that they can say one way or the other that animals do or don't always do the same things in the same way? People who would regularly observe the behavior of certain animals include pet owners and farmers who raise animals. Depending on where one lives, one might have an opportunity to repeatedly observe a kind of animal, e.g., one might see that barn swallows build the same kind of nests, year after year. This experience, however, is inadequate to conclude that the same is true of all birds, much less of all animals. On the other hand, one would expect that scientists observing animals in the wild would witness such differences and inform the general public of them.

38 As the body of observation of animals increased, scientists became aware that some animal behavior is the joint product of instinct and learning. For example, male bower birds instinctively build bowers to attract females; however, there is a period of learning extending over about two years during which the male bower bird perfects his bower-building skills. Griffin, *Animal Minds*, 83. While some species of birds such as doves will produce species-specific songs even when reared in isolation (see James L. Gould, *Ethology: The Mechanism and Evolution of Behavior* [W. W. Norton, 1982], 268), others must hear this song within a crucial period. Some of the latter will learn the songs of other birds if exposed to them during this period (see Alcock, *Animal Behavior*, 47, 48), whereas others pretty much will filter out those of other species, and only learn the song of their own species. Gould, *Ethology*, 268, and Paul C. Mundinger, "Behaviour-Genetic Analysis of Canary Song; Inter-Strain Differences in Sensory Learning, and Epigenetic Rules," *Animal Behaviour* 50 (1995): 1491–1511, and especially 1506. See also de Waal, *Mama's Last Hug*, 276:

> Imagine that a male animal, like a machine, was programmed to react to the sight of a female with automatic sexual arousal, courtship approach, and mounting. Sometimes this might work, but what if the object of attention was fiercely unwilling? What if a jealous dominant male sat nearby? Or imagine a predator coming around the corner at the wrong moment. Clearly, a fully automated response might get our male in trouble. The reason scientists rarely talk about instincts any more is that they are just too inflexible.

Even if one grants this, there is still a difference between behavior the knowledge of which is innate as opposed to learned. Birds build nests of various shapes, depending on the species, and beavers build dams. While these animals do get more experienced at doing so, the knowledge to build these specific structures is inborn. And this is true for many other animal behaviors.

to forget the third option of learning by using the senses.[39] Thirdly, I think that some Thomistic natural philosophers are occasionally made careless by their reliance on Thomas Aquinas. Aquinas does on occasion simplify (and perhaps oversimplify) matters. For example, when discussing whether animals have immortal souls he says:

> There is not found in the soul of brute animals some operation superior to the operation of the sensitive part; for they neither understand nor reason; which appears from this that all animals of the same species do things in a similar way, as if moved by nature and not operating from art; for every swallow makes its nest in a similar way, and every spider makes its web in a similar way.[40]

(There are other passages where Aquinas is much more nuanced, such as when commenting on the opening chapter of the *Metaphysics*.)

Experience as a Third Option for Explaining Certain Animal Behaviors

How then can noninstinctive problem-solving on the part of animals be explained? Reflection on everyday experience shows that problem-solving does not necessarily require intelligence. There are many problems that a person or animal can solve without thinking. For instance, tying one's shoes keeps them more securely on one's feet. How do people learn to tie shoes? Certainly not by studying knot theory which falls in the branch of

39 What Adler says here is illustrative of the either instinct or intelligence dichotomy, which disregards a third possibility, learning through the senses:

> The principle, stated in a way that most directly bears on the difference of man, is as follows: *With respect to any statement about some performance that man and man alone exhibits, . . . an apparently similar performance by another species of animal does not constitute an infirmative negative instance if the latter is instinctive or species-predictable, while the human performance is acquired or learned and voluntarily or intentionally exercised, as evidenced by its nonubiquitous distribution and by its wide range of variability within the human species.*" (Italics in the original text.) Adler, *The Difference of Man*, 117.

Termite-fishing is something chimpanzees learn and how it is done varies according to group. See Stephanie Musgrave, "The Ontogeny of Termite Gathering Among Chimpanzees in the Goualougo Triangle, Republic of Congo," *American Journal Physical Anthropology* 174, no. 2 (February 2021): 187–200.

40 *SCG*, bk. 2, chap. 82.

mathematics called "topology." Most people probably had someone show them how to do it, and maybe this teacher even held their hands and guided them through it. And then most people engaged in trial and error to repeat the appropriate motions. Eventually they become fully familiar with the pattern and acquired the needed hand-eye skill to execute the steps consistently. One might object that this only explains how people learn to solve problems who have been taught. However, the first person to come up with the idea of the bow, learned how to tie it either through trial and error using his senses, or by using his imagination, or through a combination of the two. A little reflection on everyday experience readily turns up other examples of problems that one solves not by thinking abstractly but by using one's senses. One learns how to ride a bicycle by feeling how to pedal and balance, not by studying the principle of the gyroscope. When people fail to recognize that problems can be solved without thinking, the minute they see an animal that is engaging in a behavior which is flexible and adaptive, they conclude that it must be the product of intellect (instinct being rejected as an explanation because instinct is relatively inflexible).

The Thomistic authors who fall into the trap of the instinct-intellect dichotomy should have taken their cue from Aristotle's *Metaphysics* (along with Aquinas's commentary), which speaks about some animals being able to learn and having "some small share in experience."[41] Really, a Thomist ought to be the first to point out that problem-solving can involve different kinds of knowledge. For Aristotle explains the difference between experience (which is a form of sense knowledge) and art (which is a form of intellectual knowledge):

> Now art arises when from many notions gained by experience one universal judgement is formed with regard to like objects. For to have a judgement that when Callias was ill of this disease this did him good, and similarly in the case of Socrates and in many individual cases, is a matter of experience; but to judge that it has done good to all such persons, marked off according to type [eidos], when they were ill of this disease, e.g., to phlegmatic or bilious people when burning with fever—this is a matter of art.[42]

41 *Metaphysics*, bk. 1, chap. 1, 980b27, trans. H. Tredennick (Harvard University Press, 1980).

42 *Metaphysics*, bk. 1, chap. 1, 981a5–13, in McKeon, *The Basic Works of Aristotle.*

There are numerous examples illustrating the difference between experience and art. Very good cooks cook by experience, yet often lack the art of cooking as can be seen from what happens when one asks them for a recipe: a little of this, a little of that instead of the fixed measurements one finds in a recipe book.

The difference between experience and art is made clearer by Aristotle's subsequent comments on why people who have experience are often more successful than those who possess the art without experience. He says this is because action has to do with particulars, which of course is what the senses know. The person who only has abstract knowledge of the general rules of an art may well fail to identify the salient individual characteristics of the things to be used here and now, identification of which is crucial for achieving the desired end. For example, one might know in theory that flour can vary in its moisture content, and that sometimes one has to adjust the addition of liquid, without being able to recognize that this flour being used right now needs more liquid; whereas, the experienced person has a *feel* for this.

When one understands that not all human behavior is either a product of instinct or of intelligence, it is easier to avoid the false dichotomy of either instinct or intelligence in the case of animal behavior.

Let us now consider an example illustrating why those who realize how intellect and sense differ, and who know better than to fall into the false dichotomy of either instinct or intelligence, sometimes end up attributing thought to animals. The general reason is that they fail to realize the things to which the senses extend. For example, some of them posit that "insight learning" is a form of learning that could only be exhibited by a being that could think. Insight learning is a subset of problem-solving defined as solving a problem the first time one encounters it without using trial and error. Some insight learning does require intelligence as, for example, Sir Isaac Newton's sudden insight,[43] triggered by observing the fall of an apple from a tree, that the orbit of the moon around the earth (and orbits of other celestial bodies, in general) could be explained through a combination of inertial movement and gravitational movement. But not all insight learning requires intelligence. Consider, for example, the laboratory-raised raven that,

43 The example of Newton perhaps does not perfectly fit the definition of insight learning, for it is possible that Newton may have previously tried unsuccessfully to solve the problem of lunar (and planetary) orbit in some other way. What is present is the sudden putting together of elements hitherto seen as unrelated to the problem. Perhaps intellectual "insight learning" always presupposes a prehistory of sorts to the insight.

upon being placed on a branch and seeing for the first time a piece of food suspended from the branch on a string, ratchets up the food by pulling on the string and stepping on it repeatedly.[44] The raven achieves its goal by relying, first, on being ability to sense that there is food on the end of the string; and second, on its previous experience of manipulating objects, namely: 1) that pulling on one end of most objects—sticks, worms, whatever it normally picks up—makes the farther end come closer; 2) that a heavy object must not be released or it will fall down; and 3) that both its feet and bill can hold objects. Thus, the raven's previous experience serves as an adequate guide to what it should do with the food on the string, and so there is no need for the raven to think. It only has to assemble in its imagination the different elements of what it needs to do (namely, pull, hold; pull, hold).[45]

Too often people do not have a proper appreciation of the senses. Sense is a form of knowledge that allows an animal to do many things: find prey, find a mate, avoid predators, etc. Oftentimes animals have better senses than we do, and this can unduly impress people as to their mental capacities. For example, some authors speak of birds' "navigational intelligence."[46] Yet there is no evidence that the birds have developed theoretical means for orienting themselves (e.g., it is not reasonable to think that they use mathematics to do so, as the smarter ones are only known to count up to seven). Evidence indicates that they orient themselves using their senses, which in the case of some birds, includes an ability to sense dips in magnetic field. Just because humans have to devise sophisticated technology to do things that animals do, for example, detect sonar, does not mean that the animals' performance is not explicable by the superiority of their senses alone.

44 Donald R. Griffin recounts that Heinrich's ravens first tried to fly by and pull meat off the string, and they also perched themselves on the pole and pulled on the string from time to time, before they finally hit upon ratcheting up the string. Griffin, *Animal Minds*, 104, 105. If this is so, the raven case also does not fit the strict definition of "insight learning." Perhaps some of what looks like insight learning in animals is the result of luck. They may be actually engaging in trial and error, and the first thing they try happens to work.

45 See Griffin, *Animal Minds*, 16: "Millikan (1984, 1989) doubts that bees and birds 'have inner representations in the same sense that we do.' This wording exemplifies a recent trend to shift from denying that animals experience any significant thoughts to a more modest claim that their thoughts are different from ours." Thoughts, however, are not the only "inner representations" that an organism can have; memories and images in the imagination are two other forms of inner representations.

46 See Theodore Xenophon Barber, *The Human Nature of Birds* (St. Martin's Press, 1993), 3.

Ignorance about what the senses allow an animal to do leads to faulty tests for intelligence. When some animals pass these faulty tests, this appears to give credence to the view that there is no hard line between humans and nonhuman animals.

Ambiguous Language as a Source of Confusion in Regard to Animals' Abilities

The ambiguities of language used in regard to criteria for thinking further fuel the confusion concerning whether animals can think. "Problem-solving" is a case in point. The activity these words refer to is defined in terms of its end result without reference to the manner in which that result is achieved. The expression gives occasion to some to confuse solving a problem using intellect with solving a problem using the senses alone.

A similar ambiguity arises in calling animals "intelligent." Any adaptive behavior (i.e., one in which means proportioned to the end are adopted) can be called intelligent. However, this does not mean that the being performing that behavior is intelligent in the sense of being rational. This is most obvious in the case of instinctive behavior where the animal acts intelligently but did not figure out the appropriate means to an end by itself.[47] Animals that can learn act intelligently when they have done so, but like the case of the crow mentioned above, this may result not from thinking, but rather from sensing. One can say that animals possess practical intelligence in the broad sense of intelligence, insofar as they are able to recognize an appropriate means to a goal. One cannot thereby assume that they have intelligence in the narrow sense of intelligence, which requires a universal knowledge of this relationship. Organisms that cannot grasp a universal principle, such as that only things that are smaller than a hole can fit into that hole, are not intelligent in the narrow sense of the word, though they may be intelligent in the broad sense, that is, if in specific circumstances they can determine an appropriate means to an end by use of their senses, for example, matching stick size to hole size.

47 Many of the investigations made by entomologist Jean-Henri Fabre reveal the blindness of instinct.

Many languages, and perhaps all, are deficient in words specific to animal behavior that is neither instinctive nor thought out. For example, one says that the cat "chose" to eat the moist food rather than the dry food. The cat certainly could sense the difference in the foods and was not forced to eat the moist food. However, given that there is reason to think that selecting the moist food was not something that the cat thought out, the cat did not make a choice in the sense that humans make a choice, as when we pass up a choice morsel out of a desire to be a hospitable host. The generic sense of "choose," that is "to take one alternative when another is available," is applicable to both human and nonhuman animals. The specific sense of "choose" that involves reasoning is applicable to humans. But there is no corresponding word in English for the sense of "choose" specific to animals in cases where they take one alternative when another is available but not as a result of either instinct or reasoning.

One could be misled into thinking that Aristotle attributes thought to animals because he says things such as that certain animals are prudent (*phronimos*)[48] and that some are more prudent than others (*phronimotera*),[49] using the same word that he uses to name the human virtue perfecting practical reason. However, at the beginning of the *Metaphysics*, Aristotle distinguishes humans from other animals: "Thus, other animals live by imaginations and memories, and have but a small share of experience, but the human race lives also by art and reasoning."[50] Thus, when he speaks of certain animals as being prudent, he must have something other than a perfection of reason in mind.

Aquinas is aware that people are apt to misconstrue Aristotle's statement about animal prudence, and so in the *Summa Theologiae*, he formulates the following objection: "But prudence belongs to brute animals, whence it is said in the beginning of the *Metaphysics* that there are prudent beings that lack instruction as they are not able to hear sounds, as is the case of bees."[51] Aquinas responds:

> Just as artificial things stand to human art, so too all natural things stand to divine art. And therefore, order appears in those things which move

48 Aristotle, *History of Animals*, bk. 9 (10), 611a16.

49 *Metaphysics*, bk. 1, chap. 1, 980b23.

50 *Metaphysics*, 980b28.

51 *ST* I-II, q. 13, a. 2, arg. 3.

> according to nature, as it does in those which move due to reason, as is said in Physics, bk. II. And thus, it happens that a certain sagacity appears in the actions of brute animals, insofar as they have a natural inclination to certain most orderly proceedings, inasmuch as they are ordered by divine art. And for this reason, certain animals are called prudent or sagacious, though not because there is in them some reason or choice.[52]

"Prudence" can be taken in the broad sense of an ability to determine well the appropriate means to a being's natural ends, which in the case of the animal are survival and reproduction. As Aquinas puts it:

> But it is necessary that what is prudent vary with diverse individuals, on account of which prudence is predicated according to the proportion and relationship to something. For the one who is able to look out well for the particular things that concern himself is said to be prudent, and prudence is conceded to or attributed to such a person. And whence it is that through a certain likeness people call nonrational animals prudent, namely, whenever they are seen to have a certain power of foresight concerning their own lives, though not from reason, which pertains properly to prudence.[53]

Apart from being misled by the ambiguities of language, there are other many other reasons why people think that animals can think. Since many of the errors people make concern the failure to apply appropriate criteria for rationality in regard to toolmaking and language usage, it is worthwhile to show how Thomistic principles provide more adequate accounts of these two activities than those that invoke reason.

52 *ST* I-II, q. 13, a. 2, ad 3. See also *De Verit.*, q. 24, a. 2:

> Brute animals have a certain likeness of reason, insofar as they share a certain natural prudence, according as the lower nature touches in some manner what belongs to the higher nature. Which likeness is according as they have an ordered judgment about some things. But this judgment is from natural estimation, not from putting two and two together (non ex aliqua collatione), since they are ignorant of the reason for their judgment, on account of which their judgment does not extend to all things, as does the judgment of reason, but to certain determinate things.

Note that I do not intend here to take up the relationship between divine art and evolution; see Marie I. George, "On the Occasion of Darwin's Bicentennial: Finally Time to Retire the Fifth Way?," *Proceedings of the American Catholic Philosophical Association* 83 (2009): 209–26.

53 *In Ethic.*, bk. 6, lec. 6, n. 4.

Does Non-Instinctive Toolmaking Show That the Animals That Do So Are Rational?

Toolmaking, a subset of problem-solving, is often mistaken for necessarily being the product of intelligence in the sense of the capacity for abstract thought. A classic example of toolmaking on the part of animals is the chimpanzee's fabrication of a tool used to extricate termites from their nests.[54] Let us examine how some chimpanzees make these tools. The chimpanzee can see where the termites are going in and out, and it sees and feels that its fingers are too big to fit in the passageway of the termite nest and pull the termites out. The chimpanzee can see the diameter of the termite nest hole. It can see twigs (or vines, etc.) in its proximity that have a smaller diameter than the hole. It remembers it wants to get termites. The chimpanzee can then imagine that one of those twigs will fit in the hole and reach the termites inside.[55] The chimpanzee tries to poke one of those twigs in the hole. It sees and feels that the twig is getting caught because of the leaves attached to it. The chimpanzee removes a leaf, and eventually removes enough leaves so that the twig can be inserted the appropriate distance to extricate the termites. The animal has made a tool to solve a problem, but there is no reason to say that it had to think abstractly in order to do so. At every step, what the animal does can be explained by use of its senses, both external senses such as sight and touch, and internal senses such as imagination and memory.

54 See Michael Tomasello, "Cultural Transmission in Chimpanzee Tool Use and Signaling?," in Parker and Gibson, *"Language" and Intelligence in Monkeys and Apes*, 276:

> To be successful at termite fishing, a chimpanzee must
> 1. locate the passageways and scratch a hole to attain access,
> 2. choose a tool that is appropriately firm, yet supple, [twigs, grass, vines, bark, and fronds]
> 3. modify the tool so that it is free of leaves and twigs,
> 4. navigate the tool into the winding passageways to a sufficient depth,
> 5. wiggle/vibrate the tool so that the termites are attracted to bite it, and
> 6. extract the tool without dislodging the termites (Teleki, 1974).

As mentioned earlier, different chimpanzee groups make termite tools somewhat differently.

55 Apes appear to have creative imagination: "His [the bonobo Kanzi's] favorite pretend game centers around imaginary food. He pretends to eat food that is not really there, to feed others imaginary food, to hide such food, to find it, to take it from other individuals." E. Sue Savage-Rumbaugh, et al., *Apes, Language, and the Human Mind* (Oxford University Press, 1998, 59). See also Herbert S. Terrace, *Nim* (Columbia University Press, 1987), 116: "Nim [the chimpanzee] enjoyed pretending to feed his dolls and puppets."

Assuming that the animal thinks is contrary to the principle of parsimony. Other examples of animal toolmaking admit of a similar analysis.[56]

Language Studies with Animals: How They Were Taught

As for language, first note that scientific expertise comes into play in devising specific tests to judge the linguistic abilities of animals.[57] For a long time it was thought that chimpanzees had no ability to communicate with humans using symbols because they could not talk. In one early experiment a chimpanzee was taught to say a couple of words. However, eventually those who studied chimpanzee anatomy realized that the chimpanzee's vocal tract was not suitable for producing humanlike speech. Thus, later scientists developed means of symbolic communication more suited to the chimpanzees' abilities.[58] These means include 1) a simplified version of American Sign Language taught by molding their hands (some experimenters accompanied ASL with spoken English, others kept silent), 2) magnetized plastic chips of different colors and shapes each of which represented a word; the chips

56 Perhaps in some cases animals do not use trial and error. Still the animal uses its senses, as can be seen in the classic example of Köhler's ape who at first did not put together two sticks that could be fitted together to make one long stick so that it could get bananas out of its reach. Later when playing with the sticks, it succeeded in putting them together, and upon doing so recognized the product as a tool that could solve its banana problem. This recognition involves no more than the memory of the problem and the imagination of the stick as being able to bridge the distance to the bananas. See Wolfgang Köhler, *The Mentality of Apes*, trans. Ella Winter (Harcourt, Brace and Company, 1925; repr. Routledge & Kegan Paul, 1973), 125–30.

57 The animals used in the language projects included chimpanzees, bonobos, gorillas, orangutans, dolphins, and parrots.

58 Savage-Rumbaugh, *Ape Language*, 6:

> Although others have tried to teach apes to talk, their efforts were unsuccessful (Hayes and Hayes 1951; Kellogg and Kellogg 1933). However, these approaches all had one thing in common: they attempted to produce vocal sounds which approximated those of human beings. By contrast, the Gardners reasoned that perhaps the chimpanzee was not anatomically equipped to produce human speech [a fact later confirmed by Lieberman and his colleagues (Lieberman, Crelin, and Klatt 1972) in their comparative studies of the human and chimpanzee vocal tract].

The Gardners later note that "when chimpanzees use their voices, they are usually too excited to engage in casual conversation. Their vocal habits, much more than the design of their vocal apparatus, keep them from learning to speak." R. Allen Gardner and Beatrix Gardner, *The Structure of Learning: From Sign Stimuli to Sign Language* (Lawrence Erlbaum Associates, 1998), 296.

were to be placed on a language board; 3) lexigrams. Lexigrams are arbitrary symbols for words. In some cases, the lexigrams were printed on a piece of cardboard and the chimpanzee would point to one or more of them. In other cases, the chimpanzee had a laptop with lexigrams printed on the keys. When the chimpanzee touched a lexigram key, the key would light up, and on the screen an image of the lexigram would appear. In some projects, the lexigram keyboard allowed the chimpanzee to manipulate food vendors and various mechanical devices (e.g., please machine make window open).[59] As for how the apes were taught: Some experimenters trained the apes by operant conditioning,[60] rewarding their performances with things such as food or watching a movie.[61] Others emphasized emotional rewards like praise and approval coming from people the ape had social bonds with.[62] Generally apes come to regard positive interactions with teachers as more desirable

59 Savage-Rumbaugh, *Ape Language*, 7, 8.

60 See, Michael D. Hixson, "Ape Language Research: A Review and Behavioral Perspective," *The Analysis of Verbal Behavior* 15 (1998), 31:

> Savage-Rumbaugh and colleagues believe that Kanzi's language acquisition was spontaneous. . . . The following is a transcript from a video-tape of Kanzi (Savage-Rumbaugh, 1993): Savage-Rumbaugh: "Can you get a wipey out." Kanzi picks up a different object. Savage-Rumbaugh: "Kanzi stop playing with things you want to play with." She grabs the item away from Kanzi. "Just stop. Just stop. Stop." Such interactions clearly demonstrate the role of conditioned punishment (verbal reprimands) and unconditioned punishment (the removal of a desired object). . . . In other scenes, Kanzi appears to get gum for participation, or he gets to take a break. Kanzi received verbal praise for every correct answer. It seems likely that similar events took place with the apes in the other research project discussed in this paper.

The Gardners perhaps are exaggerating about the extent to which researchers in projects other than their own used operant conditioning but are largely correct in their claim that "Terrace (1979) in his studies of Nim, Rumbaugh and his associates (see Gill and Rumbaugh, 1977) in their studies of Lana, and Savage-Rumbaugh (1984) in her studies of Sherman and Austin, all insisted on operant rigor in their laboratories." Gardner and Gardner, *The Structure of Learning*, 302.

61 See Duane M. Rumbaugh et al., "The LANA Project: Origin and Tactics," in *Language Learning by a Chimpanzee: The Lana Project*, ed. Duane M. Rumbaugh (Academic Press, 1977), 89. See also Ernst von Glasersfeld, "The Yerkish Language and Its Automatic Parser," in Rumbaugh, *Language Learning*, 95. See also E. Sue Savage-Rumbaugh, *Kanzi: The Ape at the Brink of the Human Mind* (John Wiley & Sons, 1994), 68–69.

62 The chimpanzee Washoe was instructed chiefly through social rewards. Bettyann Kevles, *Thinking Gorillas: Testing and Teaching the Great Ape* (E. P. Dutton, 1980), 132. The Gardners, who worked with Washoe, affirm that "members of the human foster family served as testers who could get the chimpanzees to communicate information in signs. They could do this without forcing the animals to beg for food. They responded with social approval, which fed forward to more communication. By separating communication from extrinsic reward, they

than food rewards.[63] In one case a bonobo picked up how to use the lexigram keyboard without any sort of reinforcement. The experimenters had been trying to teach Kanzi's mother to use the lexigram keyboard while paying no attention to the young Kanzi, yet the day after his mother was removed and he was exposed to the keyboard he used it more than 120 times the first day in ways indicating he knew what the symbols meant.[64] In another project, a chimpanzee learned signs exclusively from other chimpanzees.[65]

Are the Animal Language Studies Reliable?

Before we proceed further, it should be noted that various ape language studies have been criticized on a number of counts. For instance, a common criticism directed against them is that they involve conscious or unconscious cueing on the part of the observer.[66] Herbert Terrace only realized that about 90 percent of Nim's utterances were not spontaneous but were occasioned by something the trainer had just signed, after he watched video footage of Nim.[67] Another common criticism concerns selective data reporting.

---

widened the range of communication." Gardner and Gardner, *The Structure of Learning*, 342. The chimpanzee Nim was also instructed through social rewards:

> I wanted to socialize a chimpanzee so that he would be just as concerned about his status in the eyes of his caretakers as he would about the food and drink they had the power to dispense. By making our feelings and reactions a source of concern to Nim, I felt that we could motivate him to use sign language, not just to demand things, but also to describe his feelings and to tell us about his views of people and objects; I wanted to see what combinations of signs Nim would produce without special training, that is, with no more encouragement than the praise that a child receives from its parents. Terrace, *Nim*, 31.

63 See, for instance, Savage-Rumbaugh, *Ape Language*, 45.

64 See Savage-Rumbaugh, *Kanzi*, 135, 136.

65 See Roger Fouts, *Next of Kin* (William Morrow, 1997), 244: "Interestingly, [the chimp] Loulis did not pick up any of the seven signs that we used around him. He learned only from [the chimps] Washoe and Ally. Within eighteen months of his adoption, Loulis was using nearly two dozen signs spontaneously. He was the first nonhuman to learn a human language from another nonhuman." See also Fouts, 303: "By the last year of the study, 1985, . . . Loulis had learned fifty-five reliable signs inside his family." However, an analysis of four corpora of sign utterances from 1992–99 discovered that Loulis had only produced four signs. Esteban Rivas, "Recent Use of Signs by Chimpanzees (*Pan Troglodytes*) in Interactions with Humans," *Journal of Comparative Psychology* 119, no. 4 (2005): 413.

66 See Thomas A. Sebeok and Robert Rosenthal, eds., *The Clever Hans Phenomenon: Communication with Horses, Whales, Apes, and People* (New York Academy of Sciences, 1981).

67 See Terrace, *Nim*, 215–19.

Nonsense redundancies in ape utterances are sometimes deleted, making the animal appear to make more sense than it actually does. For instance, Premack notes that: "'You me you out me,' the actual sequence produced by the animal, was recorded as 'You me.' The signing pattern of the ape, characterized by repetition, intrusion, and irregular word order was 'edited.'"[68] And while much is made of meaningful combinations (like "water bird" for swan), the far more numerous nonsense combinations go unmentioned.

Penny Patterson's research with the gorilla, Koko, is widely discredited by those in her field.[69] This excerpt of a transcript of Koko's AOL responses to questions addressed to her illustrates why:

> **Question**: What are the names of your kittens? (and dogs?) **LiveKOKO**: foot **Patterson**: Foot isn't the name of your kitty **Question**: Koko, what's the name of your cat? **LiveKOKO**: no **Patterson**: She just gave some vocalizations there . . . some soft puffing [**chat host**]: I heard that soft puffing! **Patterson**: Now shaking her head no. **Question**: Do you like to chat with other people? **Koko**: fine nipple **Patterson**: Nipple rhymes with people, she doesn't sign people per se, she was trying to do a "sounds like."[70]

Sue Savage-Rumbaugh's reports of the success of her research with Kanzi sometimes exceed what the data indicates.[71] For example, Savage-Rumbaugh did a study in which she concludes that Kanzi's language competency is equal to that of a two-year old child. Yet, as Clive Wynne observes:

68 David Premack, *Gavagai: Or the Future History of the Animal Language Controversy* (The MIT Press, 1986), 32.

69 In a 2010 lecture on language, biologist Robert Sapolsky notes Patterson's failure to publish data, as well as how she would try to cover for Koko's lack of linguistic abilities by saying things like "stop kidding around," when Koko would give incorrect answers; see https://www.youtube.com/watch?v=SIOQgY1tqrU&t=5710s, mins. 1:37–1:42. See also H. S. Terrace et al., "Response: Ape Language," *Science* 211 (January 2, 1981): 87–88. See also Geoffrey K. Pullum, "Koko Is Dead, but the Myth of Her Linguistic Skills Lives On," *The Chronicle of Higher Education*, June 27, 2018. Pullum is the author of hundreds of articles in linguistics and the author or coauthor of a dozen books.

70 Jane C. Hu, "What Do Talking Apes Really Tell Us? The Strange, Disturbing World of Koko the Gorilla and Kanzi the Bonobo," *Slate* (Aug 20, 2014), https://slate.com/technology/2014/08/koko-kanzi-and-ape-language-research-criticism-of-working-conditions-and-animal-care.html.

71 I evaluate several of Savage-Rumbaugh's exaggerated claims about Kanzi at some length in "Descartes's Language Test for Rationality: A Response to Miller," *American Catholic Philosophical Quarterly* 83, no. 1 (Winter 2009): 107–25.

> They commanded Kanzi, "Pour the juice in [sic] the egg." Kanzi picked up the bowl with the egg in it, smelled it, and shook it. Only after they repeated the command three times with various modifications did Kanzi do what they asked him to do. They nonetheless score this as a correct response. Similarly, although Kanzi's first response to the demand "Pour some water on the raisins" was to hold a jug of water over a lettuce, this was coded as correct. Kanzi's first reaction to the request to pour milk into water was to stick a tomato in the water. When asked to chase Liz, he remained seated; when asked again, he touched Liz's leg, and she chased him. His responses in all of these instances were scored correct.[72]

While I do not think that we should disregard the data gathered by the ape language researchers, we do need to be circumspect about the weight we give it.

What is Language?

The obvious thing that must be done if one is to determine if apes are capable of using language is to define "language." Language is generally considered to consist of words and rules according to which words are put together, that is, grammar. Much of early research on apes sought to establish whether they could form grammatical sentences, whereas later research was more focused on whether apes understood the meaning of words. I will focus on words because they are more fundamental, and also because they are more closely related to thought than grammar is, to the extent that grammar involves more the way we imagine things.[73] Consider, for example, how in some languages the country of one's birth is named "motherland" while in others it is named "fatherland," and how some languages use both words. In addition, these words may or may not have gender, and when they do, they are not always the same gender. For example, "fatherland" in English has no gender, whereas "patria" in Latin is a feminine noun, and in German "Vaterland" is a neuter noun. Yet the meaning of these words in all cases is the same.

72 Clive D. L. Wynne, *Do Animals Think?* (Princeton University Press, 2004), 125.

73 Another reason for not focusing on grammar is that it is difficult to determine whether the animal has simply picked up on a pattern or whether it has understood a grammatical rule. In many cases, humans speak grammatically not because they know the rules of grammar but simply as the result of experience. For example, most native speakers of English are unable to explain the correct usage of the definite and indefinite articles, despite using them correctly.

Aristotle defines a word as a vocal sound significant by convention; what the word signifies is an abstract thought or idea. This definition can be broadened to include nonvocal signs, such as are used in sign languages. Ape researchers often do not bother to define what a word is, but there does seem to be a consensus that usage of signs that can be explained through associative memory is not a genuine language usage. The ability to associate a symbol with a real object via mental images in one's imagination, and on this basis supply the correct symbol when presented with that object (or vice versa), is recognized by most as being just that, association.[74] The researchers are looking for conceptual understanding on the part of the apes, but as noted above, they generally do not have a clear idea of what thought is as distinguished from sense knowledge, and this sometimes even when they acknowledge that words express concepts. Consequently, they often come up with criteria that are inadequate for identifying genuine language usage. What are some of these criteria?

Inadequate Criteria for Judging Linguistic Ability

Duane Rumbaugh proposed to test whether the chimpanzees could "use them [the lexigrams] to represent things not present, a process basic to semantics in human parlance."[75] This criterion, however, for genuine language usage can be fulfilled in the absence of thought. Memory and imagination suffice for animals to pursue things that are not visible (or audible, etc.).

74 H. S. Terrace illustrates how the ability to string signs together in a certain sequence may result from conditioning rather than from understanding the meaning of those signs:

> If a pigeon performed a sequence ABXC, where X referred to different incentives, it would seem far-fetched to refer to that sequence as "trainer give grain R-42." That type of performance is easy to obtain. Pigeons were trained to peck the sequence A-->B-->C-->D, where A, B, C, D were different colors, at levels of accuracy comparable to that reported by Premack in the case of "four-word sentences" (Straub, Seidenber, Bever, and Terrace 1979). On each trial, A, B, C, and D were presented simultaneously in different physical arrays. We have yet to try to extend this performance to ABXC problems (where X_1 could refer to one type of grain, X_2 to another, and so on). If a pigeon could learn such a sequence (a not unlikely outcome), one wonders what is to be gained by assigning names to each member of that sequence. Herbert S. Terrace, "Is Problem Solving Language?," in Sebeok and Umiker-Sebeok, *Speaking of Apes*, 394.

75 Duane Rumbaugh, "Reasoning and Language in Chimpanzees," in *Animal Intelligence: Insight into the Animal Mind*, ed. R. J. Hoage and Larry Goldman (Smithsonian Press, 1986), 61.

Dogs certainly appear to imagine the near future. They go inside looking for food in their dish apparently expecting to find it there just like they have in the past (the distant past or future is another matter). Thus, there is nothing particularly amazing that the chimpanzee that has learned to associate a certain chip with a banana presents that chip in hopes of getting a banana. This differs little from the dog that brings its master its leash when it wants to go for a walk.

Another experiment geared to establish whether chimpanzees formulated conceptual categories was to have them separate objects into two different bins, one marked for food and another for tools. Yet the chimpanzees' ability to sort the objects into two classes is readily explained by association of the edibility or nonedibility of the object with the symbol for food or tool.[76] In fact, one cannot help noticing that the experimenters themselves do not even claim that the animals categorized the tools on the basis of their being a means to some end, but on the basis of a characteristic easily recognized through sense perception, namely, nonedibility.[77] In the face of an unknown object (which might be a tool or might be something else: a piece of junk, a sculpture, etc.), would the chimpanzee ask unprompted, "Can that thing be used to accomplish some task?" If it did, then one would have to concede that it can think.

David Premack points out that even if animals can sort things correctly into categories, this doesn't show that they are grasping them conceptually:

> It is not possible, as far as I can see, to construct nonlinguistic examples of the asymmetrical relation between superordinate and subordinate classes. The most that can be demonstrated nonlinguistically is that the animal can sort objects at increasingly abstract levels, for example, place apples with apples, fruit with fruit, even food or edibles with food. But

76 See Hixson, "Ape Language Research," 29:

> Before Sherman and Austin had learned the category names, they were taught to sort the items into piles of tools and food. Sherman and Austin had difficulty learning to do this. Learning was facilitated when they were prompted to engage in item-related behavior before sorting the item. When prompted to sort a food item, they were encouraged to take a small bite of food, and before sorting a tool they demonstrated the use of that tool.

77 See Duane M. Rumbaugh and E. Sue Savage-Rumbaugh, "Language in Comparative Perspective," in *Animal Learning and Cognition*, ed. N. J. Mackintosh (Academic Press, 1994), 318: "Sherman called a *sponge* a food, rather than a tool. This might not have been an error from his perspective, for he literally consumed sponges as he sucked avidly on them when soaked with favorite juices."

> does the animal grasp that while food encompasses fruit, fruit does not encompass food? Unfortunately, the grasp of class inclusion is no more demonstrated by higher-level than by lower-level sorting.[78]

It is one thing to put banana with banana and food with food on the basis of similarity and it is another to understand that "food" is more universal than "banana."

Another task given to the chimpanzees was to put the lexigrams for the different objects in question in the different bins. The claim was that "only if they [the chimpanzees] literally know the meanings of the 17 test lexigrams could they have labeled them correctly as 'food' or 'tool.'"[79] However, this feat can be more economically explained as a two-step associative process. The banana lexigram is associated with a banana; bananas are known to be edible. So the chimpanzee links the banana lexigram with things that are edible, and on that basis puts the lexigram in the appropriate box. Given that many animals can be conditioned to associate one thing with another, it is not surprising that primates can carry the process a step further.[80] Though such a feat is more than one might have expected at first sight from an animal, closer examination shows that there is no need to appeal to an intellect to explain it, for associative memory affords an adequate and more parsimonious explanation.

Another often-cited "linguistic" feat is the parrot Alex's identification of the things shown it as "same" or "different":

78 Premack, *Gavagai*, 112.

79 Rumbaugh and Savage-Rumbaugh, "Language in Comparative Perspective," in Mackintosh, *Animal Learning and Cognition*, 319.

80 The chimp Ally also performed a two-step association. Ally was first trained on spoken English words and their referents, and then to associate English words with ASL signs. In testing he was able to give the correct ASL sign for the original referent. Jane H. Hill, "Apes and Language," in Sebeok and Umiker-Sebeok, *Speaking of Apes*, 339. Sarah's performance, mentioned at the beginning of the chapter, may be an instance of a two-step association. Sarah, when told via symbols that brown is the color of chocolate, associates in her imagination those symbols with chocolate and a feature of chocolate (namely, its color), and on this basis goes on to form a new association, namely, the hitherto unknown symbol with chocolate's color, brown. This process is facilitated by Sarah's previous experience of answering "What color?" questions where she already knew the symbols for the colors of the objects in question. (See the section on disjunctive reasoning for an alternate explanation.) In a similar manner, Sarah could identify "apple is red" to be the same as "red color of apple," and not as "apple is round," as the first two phrases evoked the same image in her imagination. See Premack, *Gavagai*, 22–23 for a description of Sarah's performance.

> Alex was shown two objects (which might be either familiar or things he had never seen before) and required to say what was the same or different about them (Pepperberg 1987b, 1988, 1991). They differed in color, shape, or material, and Alex usually gave the correct response—"color," "shape," or "matter" . . . (paper, wood, cork, or rawhide). His responses to "What's same?" or "What's different?" were 82–85 percent correct when there were three options—color, shape, or material—so that a chance score would be only 33 percent correct.[81]

How can this feat be explained? The senses certainly can detect that two objects are the same or different in color. Thus, there is no reason to think that by showing a parrot pairs of things that are same or different in color one cannot get the bird to eventually associate the words "same" and "different" with the corresponding pairs. Similarly, the senses recognize sameness and difference of shape, and a bird could learn to associate these terms to things that it sees does or does not match as to shape. Admittedly it takes more attention on the bird's part for it to identify what is same or what is different when it is presented with more than one variable at the same time. However, if the original associations are firmly fixed in the bird's memory, it remains the case that it can see (e.g.) that only one of two objects is wood, whereas both objects are green. Alex's success at this task thus yields to a more economical analysis than one invoking thought. This shows that the test put to Alex proves to be inadequate for distinguishing thinking beings from sensing ones.[82]

Apparent Knowledge of the Relation between Relations as Proof of Animals' Rationality

Another ability that some animals display that leads some to affirm that these animals are rational is their performance on relational match-to-sample tests, as this appears to show that animals are capable of grasping the relation

81 Griffin, *Animal Minds*, 172. David Premack taught the chimp Sarah to use chips to identify whether things were the same or different by essentially associative means. Terrace, *Nim*, 16.

82 See E. Sue-Savage Rumbaugh, Duane M. Rumbaugh, and William M. Field, "Language as a Window on Rationality," in Hurley and Nudds, *Rational Animals?* (Oxford University Press, 2006), 519: "The parrot [Alex] acquired productive symbol use, but does not respond to commands to give items or to engage in behaviors on objects, so in this sense has not acquired comprehension."

between relations, something which is abstract. Animals that can match A to sample A when given a choice of A and B cannot always match BB to sample AA when given the choice of BB and EF, and similarly they cannot always match GH to sample CD when given the choice of GH and JJ. The latter kind of matching is called relational matching to sample, RMTS.[83] (Note that in experiments each letter generally refers to discrete objects, such as cups, or to pictures, either of things, such as bananas, or patterns drawn inside rectangles.[84])

In the case of chimpanzees that succeed at relational match-to-sample tasks, Jennifer Vonk maintains:

> Such conceptual matching problems could not be solved by attending solely to corresponding physical features, because the sample and alternative objects were not perceptually similar. Instead, the abstract relation between the objects must be represented for performance to be successful.[85]

There is, however, another way of explaining the chimpanzees' performance, one that does not appeal to the apprehension of an abstract relationship. What the animals may be doing is pattern recognition, and pattern recognition does not require abstract thought. In the example given above, AA is a simple pattern of two successive identical characters. BB manifests the same pattern, whereas EF does not.

Even some monkeys are good at pattern recognition. Baboons have been trained "to discriminate English words from nonsense combinations of letters that resembled real words," with a success rate of about 75 percent

83 See Timothy M. Flemming et al., "What Meaning Means for Same and Different: Analogical Reasoning in Humans (*Homo sapiens*), Chimpanzees (*Pan troglodytes*), and Rhesus Monkeys (*Macaca mulatta*)," *Journal of Comparative Psychology* 122, no. 2 (May 2008): 177. Rhesus monkeys learned to match to sample when the sample was a single item, but persistently failed "in the judgment of relations-between-relations in the RMTS [Relational Match to Sample] task (a nonperceptually based matching strategy)."

84 See Roger K. R. Thompson et al., "Language-Naive Chimpanzees (*Pan troglodytes*) Judge Relations Between Relations in a Conceptual Matching-to-Sample Task," *Journal of Experimental Psychology: Animal Behavior Processes* 23, no. 1 (January 1997): 31: "Hence an AA sample might consist of a pair of physically identical cups and BB to a pair of identical shoes. CD and EF might refer to pairs of nonidentical objects consisting, respectively, of a bottle top paired with a clothespin and a pen paired with a padlock."

85 Jennifer Vonk, "Gorilla (*Gorilla gorilla gorilla*) and Orangutan (*Pongo abelii*) Understanding of First- and Second-Order Relations," *Animal Cognition* 6 (July 2003): 78.

(e.g., VAST from VIRT).[86] Experiential knowledge is sufficient to explain this. Experiential knowledge allows one to identify concrete cases correctly without having formed a universal rule. People, for example, who have been exposed from infancy to others using the definite and indefinite articles correctly in English, eventually do so themselves, without being able to articulate the general rules for their usage. There are rules for word construction as well, for example, "rt" may be found at the end of words, but never at the beginning, and the opposite is true for "tr." Baboons, after being exposed to many samples, acquire the experience necessary to recognize these patterns. There is no need for them to refer to a universal rule as to where the different letter combinations appear in order to be successful.

Further support for the notion that chimpanzees need not form abstract concepts to match similar patterns is that machine learning makes it possible for an unknowing computer to pick out words from nonwords after being trained on samples of both.[87]

Consequently, I disagree with Flemming et al. who maintain:

> In an analogy, a relationship must be established between the first two elements in the series (i.e., the base relation). Then, and only then, can one continue to the second set of elements (i.e., the target relation) and see the same relation instantiated in the base. . . . If one matches two abstract relations, one has in essence recognized the analogical equivalence of relations.[88]

The assumption is that one needs to apprehend abstractly the relation of sameness (or difference) in the first pair. This overlooks the possibility that one simply notices a pattern in the sample and then sees that this pair is like another pair with a similar pattern and different from a second pair lacking that pattern. One need not have explicit knowledge of what the pattern is, for example, one thing followed by a second thing that looks the same. A pattern is a direct object of perception, just as individual objects are. AA does not look like BB if one focuses on the individual letters (or items), but the

86 See Jonathan Grainger et al., "Orthographic Processing in Baboons (Papio papio)," *Science* 336 (April 13, 2012): 245–48.

87 Genady Ya. Grabarnik, professor of Mathematics and Computer Science, St. John's University, personal communication.

88 Flemming et al., "What Meaning Means for Same and Different," 176. See also Flemming et al., 184: "Analogy completion assumes (and relies on) conceptual knowledge of *same* and *different*."

two pairs look similar if one focuses on the pattern that they both exhibit.[89] For example, a shirt with polka dots looks similar to one with diamonds, assuming the dots and diamonds are similarly spaced. If one was asked to match the best one could a shirt with polka dots, with the choices being one with diamonds and the other with a combination of triangles and squares (again, assuming similar spacing), one would pick the one with diamonds because it looks more similar.

A complementary explanation in terms of entropy detection was offered by Penn et al. in 2008 and was reiterated by Glorioso et al. in 2017.[90] Perceptual entropy is understood here to be "the amount of inter-item variability in an array."[91] If the items in an array do not differ from each other there is zero perceptual entropy. As Penn et al. observe, success in relational match-to-sample tests can be explained by the subjects learning to match the perceptual entropy of one array to that of another instead of their "matching the higher-order role-based analogical relation of *same/different*. . . . In other words, one sees that the items in a given array vary or do not vary and one matches that to whether the items one sees in another array vary or not."[92] In support of this explanation, baboons are able to do relational match-to-sample tasks when the arrays contained sixteen items but when the arrays were reduced to two items their performance "fell to chance on *different* trials, whereas their performance on *same* trials remained the same."[93] This is what one would expect if the animals' choice is based on estimating entropy. One has to understand here that the choices that the baboons were given

89 See Premack, *Gavagai*, 118–19:

> An example is LL GG XY ? AA BB CD, where the letters stand for common household items with which Sarah was highly familiar. The answer to this question is "same." . . . A small rearrangement of the elements, for example, LL GG XY ? XY BB CD, produces the questions for which the answer is "different." . . . It took considerable trial and error to find the limiting conditions under which she could pass tests of this kind [at a 79% level].

It is not surprising that longer series of discrete patterns would be harder to recognize as being the same or different.

90 Derek C. Penn et al., "Darwin's Mistake: Explaining the Discontinuity Between Human and Nonhuman Minds," *Behavioral and Brain Sciences* 31, no. 2 (2008): 109–30; G. C. Glorioso et al., "Still No Solution to Non-Verbal Measures of Analogical Reasoning: Reply to Walker and Gopnik," *Cognition* 214 (2017), 104288.

91 Glorioso et al., "Still No Solution," 1.

92 Penn et al., "Darwin's Mistake," 154.

93 Penn et al., 112.

always contained sixteen items, regardless of the number of the sample items they were presented with. A two-item same sample has zero entropy and is readily matched to the zero entropy sixteen-item display. Whereas a two-item different sample has an entropy of one, which is closer in entropy to the sixteen-item display with zero entropy than the sixteen-item display with an entropy of four.[94] Thus, entropy assessment explains why different samples with a small number of items resulted in chance performance on the part of the baboons.

Animals such as chimpanzees, gorillas, and orangutans are able to do two-item RMTS tasks. However, as Penn et al. observe: "At best, the RMTS task demonstrates that non-human animals can select the choice display that has the same degree of between-item variability as the sample display. But the task says nothing about nonhuman animals' ability to evaluate the non-perceptual relational similarity between those relations."[95]

The entropy explanation and the pattern-recognition explanation are both explanations in terms of perception and not in terms of the concepts of same and different. I think they more or less boil down to the same thing. Given sample AB and choices CD and EE, the entropy explanation says that the animal notices some entropy (variation) in the sample and in the first choice but none in the second choice. The pattern-recognition explanation says that the animal notices no repetition in the sample and no repetition in the first choice, but repetition in the second.

Yet another possible perceptual strategy suggests itself in the case of a 1997 study done by Thompson et al. The authors claim to have shown that chimpanzees are able to conceptually recognize the relationship between relations in this study.[96] The chimpanzees in question had previously learned to use tokens to designate pairs of items that were either the same or different. If the items were the same, they were to choose a heart-shaped token; if they were different, they were to choose a diamond-shaped token. In the 1997 experiment, the chimpanzees were presented with a sample consisting of two items that were either the same or different (e.g., AA or EF) and

94 See Joël Fagot et al., "Discriminating the Relation Between Relations: The Role of Entropy in Abstract Conceptualization by Baboons (*Papio papio*) and Humans (*Homo sapiens*)," *Journal of Experimental Psychology: Animal Behavior Processes* 27, no. 4 (October 2001): 322.

95 Fagot et al., "Discriminating the Relation Between Relations," 322.

96 See Thompson et al., "Language-Naive Chimpanzees (*Pan troglodytes*) Judge Relations Between Relations," 31 (abstract) and 35.

they then had to match that sample to one of the two pairs that they were presented with (e.g., in the case of AA to BB rather than CD and in the case of EF to CD rather than BB). The chimpanzees were not differentially rewarded for correct answers; regardless of their answer, they got a food reward. The animals performed at a level of 75 percent or higher. There is no need, though, to invoke conceptual thought to explain their performance. One way to explain it perceptually is that when they saw the sample pair, due to their previous training, they imagined either a heart or a diamond and the same for when they were presented with the two choice pairs. Based on what they imagined, they could match the appropriate pairs. For example, given AA, they imagine heart and then given CD and BB, they imagine diamond and heart, respectively, and are thus able to recognize at the level of imagination heart as matching heart.[97] Alternately, they may have been using pattern recognition or entropy detection, as was explained earlier. In any case, there is no evidence that conceptual thought is needed to explain the chimpanzees' performance.

To test for conceptual knowledge of a relationship between relations, one needs to pose to the animal problems that are not immediately tied to perception, and even then, some of these problems are apt to be solved by means of associative memory, for example, duck is to water as monkey is to tree (as opposed to banana). We can't ask an animal why it selects what it selects, unlike children who could tell us: "That's where those animals live." The more a relation is remote from sense experience, the better it is for testing conceptual knowledge of sameness of relationship. An example would be a numerical relation, such as 3:7 with the choices being 9:21 or 8:25.

In the literature, the only example of an animal that succeeded on a test for the recognition of relationships between relations where a sensory judgment of entropy or pattern cannot suffice is the chimpanzee, Sarah. Sarah was presented with two pairs of objects (e.g., an apple peel together with a peeled apple and an orange peel together with an orange seed), after which she had to choose a token for same or different. Her success rate for the most demanding of these tasks was 60 percent (18/30).[98] However, we don't know why Sarah matched things the way she did. It is an assumption that

97 See Nancy A. Salay, "Accepting the Povinelli-Henley Challenge," *Animal Behavior and Cognition* 9, no. 2 (2022): 250.

98 See Douglas Gillan et al., "Reasoning in the Chimpanzee: I. Analogical Reasoning," *Journal of Experimental Psychology: Animal Behavior Processes* 7, no. 1 (January 1981): Table A-5, 15–16.

she matched them the way we would according to understanding similarity and difference between the relations. Maybe instead she was using perceptual strategies that happened to yield the same responses. For example, maybe Sarah paired apple peel with orange peel and peeled apple and orange seed, and then chose different because a peeled apple looks very different than an orange seed. Thus, though the results of this experiment are intriguing, the experiment does not show that Sarah was able to conceptually recognize the relationship between relations. An additional reason for skepticism regarding claims of Sarah's conceptual abilities is pointed out by Penn et al.: "Sarah's performance on these analogies has never been replicated by Sarah herself or by any other nonhuman animal."[99]

Apparent Ability to Engage in Disjunctive Reasoning as Proof of Animals' Rationality

Another ability that animals appear to possess that leads some people to affirm that they are rational is disjunctive reasoning. Aquinas, long ago, entertained the possibility that some animals are capable of disjunctive reasoning in an objection he raises when discussing whether animals have free choice:

> A dog chasing a stag, upon coming to a place where the path divides into three, explores with its sense of smell whether the stag went the first way or the second way, and if it discovers that it did not go those two ways, being thus assured, it embarks on the third way without exploring it first, as if using a disjunctive syllogism by which it could conclude that the stag went that way, since it did not go the two other ways and there are not more [than three].[100]

Aquinas denies that animals are capable of reasoning in this manner. He maintains that animals lack reason on the grounds that "all individuals of the same nature act in a similar way,"[101] and he explains why animals act in the sagacious ways that they do in terms of the natural inclinations instilled in them by divine art. I disagree in part with Aquinas's response. As mentioned earlier, individual animals of the same species sometimes act differently due

99 Penn et al., "Darwin's Mistake," 114.

100 *ST* I-II, q. 13, a. 2, arg. 3.

101 *ST* I-II, q. 13, a. 2, ad 3.

to learning. In addition, there is a solution that is more directly tailored to the objection.

Experiments have been done in which dogs are given a command to fetch an item whose name they are unfamiliar with from a group of items composed of things whose names they are familiar with. They will often fetch the correct item.[102] This behavior does not prove, however, that they are capable of disjunctive reasoning, as it can be explained by the fact that dogs avoid bringing back incorrect objects, as this will not earn them a reward (a treat, opportunity to play, or praise). To put it in terms of an example, if a dog can correctly retrieve a ball and a frisbee, then when it is told to fetch the leash when faced with a ball, frisbee, and leash, it knows not to bring back the ball or frisbee and so brings back the remaining object.

Pepperberg et al. argue that experiments with the parrot, Griffin, show that the parrot is engaging in disjunctive reasoning.[103] However, the parrot's behavior can also be explained by the avoidance of nonrewarded behaviors, namely, it avoids picking empty cups. Here is an example of one of the experiments: four cups are placed in a row, and they are separated into pairs by a larger space that is between the pairs. A screen is first put over one pair and a treat is hidden in one of the two cups; the screen prevents the parrot from seeing in which cup the treat is hidden. A screen is then put over the second pair and a treat is hidden in one of the two cups. The screens are then removed, and the first cup is lifted to show that it is empty. The parrot picked the remaining cup in the first pair 94 percent of the time rather than the first cup or either of the cups in the second pair. In order to accomplish this feat, it suffices that the parrot remember that a treat was hidden in the first pair and to avoid the cup that was shown to be empty. Since it is not shown that either of the cups in the second pair is empty, there is no reason for it to pick a cup from that pair.

The same explanation may apply to the case of Sarah mentioned toward the beginning of this chapter. Sarah seemingly learned what the symbol for the color brown meant when told that brown was the color of chocolate. Perhaps, though, when Sarah was asked via symbols to insert the brown

102 See Juliane Kaminski et al., "Word Learning in a Domestic Dog: Evidence for 'Fast Mapping,'" *Science* 306, no. 5677 (June 11, 2004): 1682–83.

103 Irene M. Pepperberg, Suzanne Gray, Shilpa Mody, and Susan Carey, "Logical Reasoning by a Grey Parrot (*Psittacus erithacus*)? A Case Study of the Disjunctive Syllogism," *Behaviour* 156, no. 5 (2018): 1–37.

token into the red dish, she performed this feat by avoiding inserting tokens she had already associated with other color names.

A Definitive Test for Abstract Thought: Giving a Justification for One's Opinion

The fact that all the tests mentioned above are inadequate for showing that the animals in question are capable of abstract thought because they do not exclude alternate explanations of the animals' performance, namely, the use of their senses, does not show that the animals in fact are using their senses alone. It only renders this likely, as an explanation that invokes the senses alone is more parsimonious than one that invokes both the senses and the intellect, and the simpler explanation is the more likely one, so long as it does adequately explain the effect. What then would constitute a definitive test whereby one could distinguish an organism that did think from one that only used its senses?[104]

Grasping universal concepts is ordered to understanding propositions, and beings capable of understanding universal propositions are able to put those propositions together to draw conclusions about things hitherto unknown. If animals grasp universal concepts, then they should also be able to reason. Thus, they should be able to adopt a position on an issue and give a reason for their position. Yet for all their linguistic training, no ape has ever done so. Apes can learn to associate cause and effect in concrete cases (e.g., which tool is capable of accomplishing what[105]) and in principle

104 One can understand the ape researchers' frustration when they complain that every time their apes succeed in meeting the supposed sure test for true linguistic ability, someone else come up with a new definitive criterion which must be met if the apes' performance is to count as true language usage. Savage-Rumbaugh, et al., *Apes, Language, and the Human Mind*, 117. Many of the early criteria were in fact insufficient, oftentimes because of a failure to recognize to what extent memory and experience can mimic thought.

105 See Herbert S. Terrace, "Is Problem-Solving Language?," in Sebeok and Umiker-Sebeok, *Speaking of Apes*, 390:

> The trainer presented the subject with a pair of objects in two different states, for example, a whole apple and a piece of an apple. The task was to place between the two objects the instrument that was responsible for causing it to change from one state to the other. . . . On transfer tests, novel pairs of objects were presented, for example, a sponge marked with a crayon and an unmarked sponge. The choice on this trial might consist of a container of water and a crayon. Sarah, Peony, and Elizabeth performed at typical levels of accuracy on the tests (75 to 95% correct).

could use language to express such a relation. No researcher, however, ever thought it reasonable to try to teach the apes science or philosophy. The apes are incapable of grasping what constitutes an explanation, for example, how the hypothetico-deductive method works, or that we know in an unqualified sense when "we know the cause on which the fact depends, as the cause of that fact, and that the fact cannot be other than it is,"[106] or even more simply, what it means to base a position on evidence.

A Definitive Test for Abstract Thought: The Conversation Test

Certainly, if a being could meet the criterion articulated above, it could think, and only a being that can think can do so. However, it is perhaps a little much to expect ordinary people (whom we know to possess an intellect) to carry on a full-blown scientific or philosophical discussion, that is, a discussion that is narrowly focused on a question in which the participants support their statements with reasons. (As any philosophy teacher will tell you, it is hard to get certain students beyond making simple assertions of the "I feel" sort.) A better test then from the point of view of neither including animals that do not think nor excluding some of those that do is to see whether animals can carry on what is commonly called a "conversation" (which is not to deny that a philosophical or scientific discussion is one form of conversation). The specific sort of conversation that I think provides a good test for intellect is defined by two things: (1) by the interrelated character of the statements made about one subject (broadly construed); and (2) by a desire to share and acquire knowledge that is not ordered toward obtaining

---

See also Premack, *Gavagai*, 106:

> We show apes and young children videotapes in which an individual (an actor) appears to be struggling to obtain food that is inaccessible. The videotapes are accompanied by photographic alternatives depicting different modes of solving the problem, for example, by stepping up onto a chair (when food is out of reach on the vertical) or reaching out with a stick (when it is out of reach on the horizontal) and so forth. . . . Sarah, our most talented ape, and children older than about three and a half consistently choose solutions (Premack and Woodruff 1978). Younger children and apes younger than Sarah do not. Rather than solutions, they tend to choose photographs resembling some salient item in the videotape, for example, a yellow bird because it is yellow like the bananas in the videotape.

106 Aristotle, *Posterior Analytics*, bk. I, chap. 2, 71b10–12; translation adapted from G. R. G. Mure's translation in McKeon, *The Basic Works of Aristotle*.

something. Conversations of this sort involve affirmations and negations and often questions as well. A typical conversation runs like this:

> A: I saw this crazy woman in the supermarket today. She was stacking coffee cans in the middle of the aisle.
>
> B: Well, how do you know that she didn't work there?
>
> A: Well, she was mixing up all the different brands in the stack. Besides, the manager came over to ask her what she thought she was doing.

This conversation could take any number of directions from here. One person might tell another crazy-person story. Or the two might speculate on the causes of the woman's behavior. Or they might start talking about the importance of sensitizing people to the problems of mental illness. Granted that sometimes the ties in conversation prove to be more imaginary (stream of consciousness) than rational, still, people often recognize that they are moving from one topic to another, as one can see from expressions such as "changing the subject" or "went off on a tangent."

Now one might object, as does John Berkman, that the above fictive conversation presupposes a "rather well-developed linguistic ability," and so is not a fair test for rationality.[107] However, it is not hard to find simpler conversations. Betty Vass recounts one:

> When my daughter was a chatty three-year-old, she looked at my stomach and asked: "Why is your tummy so big?" . . . I told her I don't actually have a big stomach. . . . "Yes it is," she assured me and continued to take things further: "Did you eat too much?" "Yes, darling, I must have."[108]

In addition, as I argue in chapter 6, apes that have been trained to use symbols do not even ask questions ordered to gaining knowledge for its own sake, something any rational being that could use symbols would naturally do, for acquiring ideas is the natural perfection of that being's intellect.

Interestingly, many ape researchers apply the criteria for the conversation test I proposed above, and a fair number acknowledge that apes are unable to converse. For instance, Duane Rumbaugh has this to say about the chimpanzee Lana's putative conversations:

107 See Berkman, "Towards a Thomistic Theology of Animality," 37.

108 Beck Vass, "Mummy, Why Is Your Tummy Fat?," *New Zealand Herald*, June 5, 2017, http://www.nzherald.co.nz/lifestyle/news/article.cfm?c_id=6&objectid=11870317

> Conversations with Lana have been examined in detail. It seems clear that Lana has been prone to converse whenever she must do so in order to receive something exceptional or whenever something not in accordance with the routine delivery of food and drinks has occurred—in short, when some practical problem arises for her. She has never in conversation commented extensively on this or that as children and adults are inclined when their attention or motivation shifts unpredictably. For Lana, language is an adaptive behavior of considerable instrumental value for achieving specific goals not achieved otherwise. To date, at least, she has not used expressive language to expand her horizons except to ask for the name of something which she then requested by the name given.[109]

Some researchers will insist that their apes converse, but the exchanges are not of the sort that would indicate rationality, for example:

> Tatu [a chimpanzee]: Time.
>
> Probe 2 [Human]: What time?
>
> Tatu: Food Time Food.[110]

Tatu remains on the topic of time, but her signing is clearly ordered toward getting food.[111]

109 Rumbaugh, "Language Behavior of Apes," in Sebeok and Umiker-Sebeok, *Speaking of Apes*, 249–50. See also R. Allen Gardner and Beatrix T. Gardner, "Teaching Sign Language to a Chimpanzee," *Science* 165, no. 3894 (1969): 665: "We wanted Washoe not only to ask for objects but to answer questions about them and also to ask us questions. We wanted to develop behavior that could be described as conversation."

110 Mark D. Bodamer and R. Allen Gardner, "How Cross-Fostered Chimpanzees (*Pan troglodytes*) Initiate and Maintain Conversations," *Journal of Comparative Psychology* 16, no. 1 (2002): 14–15.

111 Researchers that claim that animals can converse generally have a different understanding of the sort of conversation that serves as a test for rationality. For example, Duane Rumbaugh and Timothy V. Gill maintain that "conversation is primarily a goal-oriented, problem-solving activity," and thus it is not surprising that he is of the view that "Lana had been partner with me in a number of linguistic exchanges that can be called conversations; each was directed toward solving a particular problem that confronted Lana." Duane Rumbaugh and Timothy V. Gill, "Lana's Acquisition of Language Skills," in Rumbaugh, *Language Learning by a Chimpanzee*, 174. Rumbaugh and Gill recount one such conversation:

> Tim presented himself outside Lana's room with another Coke. Lana's first response was the stock sentence Please machine give Coke period, which was correct but not appropriate since the machine had no Coke to vend. Next she said Please Lana drink Coke this room period. Perhaps she intended to say out-of room instead of this room,

As a number of authors points out, given that the apes' mean length of utterance[112] is 1.5-2.2 morphemes,[113] and that the longer strings of signs often contain redundancies (e.g., banana Nim banana Nim[114]), it is not too surprising that they can't carry on a conversation.[115] It is pretty hard to elaborate on

---

but she did not. Tim said No. Lana came back with the original composition, ?Lana drink this out-of room period to which Tim responded with a question for clarification ?Drink what period. Lana answered, Lana drink Coke out-of room period. Tim said Yes, the door was opened, the Coke was shared; and Lana's first conversation, one she had both initiated and successfully negotiated, had been recorded. Rumbaugh, *Language Learning*, 173–74.

H. Lyn White Miles claims that Chantek meets the criteria for conversation due to the spontaneity of his utterances and the relatively low rate of interrupting his caretakers. "The Cognitive Foundations for Reference in a Signing Orangutan" in Parker and Gibson, *"Language" and Intelligence in Monkeys and Apes*, 518. However, given that the mean length of Chantek's communications was two words it is hard to see how Chantek can elaborate on a subject. Roger Fouts claimed that his chimps had conversations among themselves. However, what he reports as a conversation are utterances such as "come hug," and "go there." *Next of Kin*, 299–303. J. Quentin Hartmann would have us believe that chimpanzees are carrying on conversations in his article "Timing of Turn Initiations in Signed Conversations with Cross-Fostered Chimpanzees (*Pan troglodytes*)," *International Journal of Comparative Psychology* 24 (2011): 177–209. The only conversation Hartmann reported is the following: "Chimpanzee: Toothbrush. Human: No. Toothbrush. Chimpanzee: Chase. Human: Chase. Who? Chimpanzee: Chase. Human: Chase." Hartman, 207–9.

112 Mean length of utterance (MLU) is determined by the number of morphemes, which does not always correspond to the number of words. A morpheme is the smallest unit of language that has meaning; this includes grammatical information. For example, "flying" is two morphemes, "fly" and "ing." "Give orange" is also two morphemes. Thus, the number of words used may be fewer than the MLU. To my best knowledge, while some argue that apes can learn grammar in the form of word order, they make no claims that apes use grammatical morphemes. Thus, in their case, the number of morphemes corresponds to the number of words.

113 Nim's MLU was 2.0 (see Terrace, *Nim*, 184), and Koko's was 2.2 according to the graph in Penny Patterson and Eugene Linden, *The Education of Koko* (Henry Holt, 1988), 85, and 2.7 as stated by Patterson and Linden in *The Education of Koko*, 114. After seven years of language training Chantek's MLU "remained approximately 2.0 . . . MLU based on gestural inflected modulations was slightly higher." H. Lyn White Miles, "The Cognitive Foundations for Reference in a Signing Orangutan," 518.

114 Terrace, *Nim*, 213. Nim's longest utterance was: "give orange me give eat orange me eat orange give me eat orange give me you." Terrace, 184.

115 A number of authors point out that ASL utterances may be longer than the actual number of signs used in them. Roger Fouts notes that "Like Hebrew and some other spoken languages, ASL does not have the copula, the forms of 'to be' that link a subject and predicate. As a result, 'you are happy' translates into ASL as the more compact YOU HAPPY." Fouts, *Next of Kin*, 76. A number of authors mention that human speakers of ASL commonly modulate signs in a way that add complexity to a sentence, without adding length. Patterson notes what seems a plausible modulation of a sign on the part of an ape: "Koko sometimes varies the motion of a sign to indicate a specific actor. When she moves the sip sign away from her mouth toward

something when one can't put enough different words together to be adding new information.

It should be noted that it is difficult to find transcripts of what the animals sign. Clive Wynne's claim that "the ape language supporters guard the transcripts of their apes' utterances better than the biological weapons labs guard their anthrax,"[116] is an exaggeration, but I agree that there are not many transcripts that are readily available, in addition to which some of those that are give a distorted picture of the animal's ability due to editing and inaccurate reporting (see note at the beginning of this section).[117]

Conversations of the sort that serve as a test for rationality depend on the ability to make declarative statements for the purpose of conveying knowledge. Researchers, on the whole, maintain that utterances that might be construed as declarative statements are few and far between. The vast majority acknowledge that the animals' signing consists mostly of requests. Leeds and Jensvold are an exception, as they maintain that the five chimpanzees

---

me, Koko is actually saying 'You sip.'" Patterson and Linden, *The Education of Koko*, 117. Other words in sign language are often understood from the context and/or from cues such as eye movement; this is the case, for example, of subject and indirect object in a command/request such as "more tickle." Nevertheless, Patterson admits that Koko's MLU of 2.7 is low compared to the MLU of children. Patterson and Linden, 116. The average MLU for a three-year-old is 3.16 and for a five-year-old is 5.63. J. F. Miller and R. S. Chapman, "The Relation Between Age and Mean Length of Utterance in Morphemes," *Journal of Speech and Hearing Research* 24, no. 2 (1981): 154–61. The range of the average MLU for an adult is between 9 and 12.

116 See Wynne, *Do Animals Think?*, 121: "When Terrace analyzed Washoe's utterances from video-tape, the Gardners threatened to sue for breach of copyright."

117 See Mark A. Krause and Michael J. Beran, "Words Matter: Reflections on Language Projects with Chimpanzees and Their Implications," *American Journal of Primatology* 82, no. 10 (2020): e23187. The authors claim that specific articles contain "rich data sets" of the apes' utterances. It is true that one of these articles contains a dozen very short exchanges and another about twenty. In both cases, however, the exchanges are sustained by human prompts, e.g., "Tatu: COFFEE TATU DRINK/ Probe 2: YES COFFEE YES/ Tatu: DRINK TATU/." A third article presents only one exchange. A fourth article does contain a fairly lengthy list of utterances and compares them to those of young children. Beatrix T. Gardner and R. Allen Gardner, "Development of Phrases in the Early Utterances of Children and Cross-Fostered Chimpanzees," *Evolution* 13, nos. 3–4 (1998): 161–88. The authors begin by telling us that "records of human linguistic development also consist of samples that represent only a fraction of daily output because complete records are impractical, except in the earliest months when a child begins to speak. In the same way, the signed output of cross-fostered chimpanzees throughout the day soon grew to the point where complete records were impractical. Consequently, the output of the cross-fosterlings, like the output of human children is only represented by samples." Gardner and Gardner, "Development of Phrases," 162. For many of the samples, the context is either that of the chimpanzee responding to a "Wh" question posed by a human or the context is not given.

whose signing they evaluated, more often used signs to describe than to request (19 percent vs. 12.5 percent).[118] However, they did not distinguish chimpanzees' spontaneous utterances from answers the chimpanzees gave to questions posed to them. A study by Lyn et al. looked at over one hundred thousand utterances by two bonobos and one chimpanzee and evaluated only the spontaneous ones (which were 73.8 percent of the total number). It concluded that: "The majority of the apes' utterances were requests, as has been reported elsewhere (Savage-Rumbaugh et al., 1986)."[119]

My experience is that it is hard to find anything that might reasonably be construed as a declarative sentence in the ape literature. Most of the combinations are requests for food, tickling, etc. For example, if one looks at an appendix of Total Spontaneous Utterances Across a Three-Month Period (for the chimps Sherman and Austin) what strikes one is the lack of any nonimitative, unambiguously declarative statements.[120] Most of the time in the transcripts that are available, the animal's supposed comments are single words, for example, "flower" or "ice."

The brevity of the apes' utterances adds difficulty to interpreting what they mean. Given that their utterances are generally one or two signs long, and oftentimes the context is not noted, it is hard to gauge whether utterances such as "banana cold"[121] is indeed a descriptive statement, and also

118 Charles Austin Leeds and Mary Lee Jensvold, "The Communicative Functions of Five Signing Chimpanzees (*Pan troglodytes*)," *Pragmatics and Cognition* 21, no. 1 (2013): 235.

119 See Heidi Lyn et al., "Nonhuman Primates Do Declare! A Comparison of Declarative Symbol and Gesture Use in Two Children, Two Bonobos, and a Chimpanzee," *Language and Communication*, 31 (2011): 63–74.

> Several of these papers describe declarative use of symbols by apes (Savage-Rumbaugh, 1986; Savage-Rumbaugh et al., 1986), reporting that declaratives were a relatively low percentage of all ape utterances (approximately 10%). In contrast, in a similar study of early language in children, Greenfield and Smith report that children at the one-word stage use declaratives in as many as 80% of their utterances (Greenfield and Smith, 1976). Lyn et al., "Nonhuman Primates Do Declare!," 65.

See also Esteban Rivas, "Recent Use of Signs by Chimpanzees," *Journal of Comparative Psychology* 119, no. 4 (2005): 404–19. Rivas, who examines four corpora of utterances from 1992 to 1999 consisting of 3,448 sign utterances, comments: "The Gardners and Fouts have often rejected the characterization of chimpanzee signing as being mostly request oriented.... The current data, however, do not support their position." Rivas, 414.

120 Savage-Rumbaugh, *Ape Language*, 286–98.

121 Savage-Rumbaugh, *Ape Language*, 286. This is an utterance of Sherman the chimp. The table indicates that this sign combination may be one that had on an earlier occasion been signed by the ape in imitation of the trainer.

whether it was proffered spontaneously or simply in imitation of its trainer. One of the few putatively declarative spontaneous utterances I could find in the literature is the orangutan Chantek's utterance: "Jeannie Chantek chase" (signed in the kitchen with Kristine).[122] Is Chantek reporting a past event to Kristine or did Chantek mix up the sign for Kristine with the sign for Jeannie and want Kristine to play chase or is there some other reason that Chantek signed this? On this, and on other rare occasions when I've come across a reported exchange that has some resemblance to a conversation, one inevitably has to read into what the ape is signing to make its "discourse" intelligible. Admittedly, we do the same thing with the utterances of young children. Granted that doting parents have tendency to read into their child's babbling more than is there, still the conviction that young children are at least in some cases really trying to communicate what we take them to be wanting to communicate finds some support in the fact that they do communicate these things when their linguistic abilities grow.[123] The same justification cannot be given in the case of apes, as their linguistic abilities plateau; unlike children, they do not go on to make declarative utterances with increased frequency, nor do they make increasingly complex utterances. This is the basis for Noam Chomsky's observation:

> The Gardners argue further that their chimpanzees use symbols in a manner comparable to that of very young children, from which they conclude that the chimpanzees are exhibiting the first stages of "language development" exactly as children are. Again, the argument is fallacious. As has often been remarked, we know that the children are exhibiting "incipient human language behavior" only because of the later stages achieved.[124]

122 H. Lyn White Miles, "The Cognitive Foundations for Reference in a Signing Orangutan," 520–23.

123 Even very young children put forth a running commentary on some activity that they are engaging in. For example, as E. Sue Savage-Rumbaugh notes: "By the time Laura [a child] was 19 months old, she was uttering phrases such as 'Pretty nestor cup,' 'Laura spill milk,' 'Cold milk,' 'All gone,' 'Mama straw blow,' 'Pour juice,' and 'Laura do,' all in contexts where her only previous utterances had been 'Ba.'" *Ape Language*, 25. The natural desire to share knowledge with others is part of what drives conversation.

124 Chomsky, "Human Language and Other Semiotic Systems," in Sebeok and Umiker-Sebeok, *Speaking of Apes*, 437.

Explanations for Apes' Declarative Utterances

Habit and perhaps the desire to play or a combination thereof provide plausible explanations for some of the signing that apes engage in that does not appear to have an immediate utilitarian goal. The apes are regularly asked by their teachers: "What is that?" and are rewarded for giving correct answers.[125] They eventually form a habit of responding to such questions. It is not surprising then that they may name something before they are asked, for example, "that flower," or give the answer to a commonly asked question before it is asked, such as "banana cold." What is done in keeping with a habit is as a general rule pleasurable.[126] It is also possible that given that apes are playful, they may perceive signing as a kind of game.[127]

Note that even when apes were not taught to use symbols by being rewarded with treats for doing so, they were given social reinforcement, praise, tickling, etc. Savage-Rumbaugh observes that the bonobos that did not have a strong attachment to the experimenters from a very early age did not develop the ability to communicate by using lexigrams.[128] Given this is the case, it is not surprising that great apes can be trained by rewarding them with verbal praise alone (as is true of dogs).[129]

125 David Premack reports that the chimpanzee, Elizabeth, after being rewarded for making complete sentences regardless of whether they accurately described something present, "went on to produce some 54 acts of simple play, 15 of which she 'described.' . . . Directly following two of the acts of washing, . . . she 'described' the act, writing 'Elizabeth apple wash.'" Premack, *Gavagai*, 18–19. Although an ape composing a sentence exhibits a more complex behavior than does a dog shaking hands, the two are similar in that both were initially trained by being given treats and eventually went on to perform the behavior without treats.

126 The following is reasonably attributed to habit: "When a training task was begun, instead of waiting for the teacher to ask that certain items be given or labeled, the chimpanzees began naming items spontaneously and then showing the named item to the teacher." Savage-Rumbaugh, et al., *Apes, Language, and the Human Mind*, 326.

127 See Terrace, "Is Problem-Solving Language?," in Sebeok and Umiker Sebeok, *Speaking of Apes*, 404: "Moreover, on more than one occasion, apparently bored by excessive drill, she [Sarah, the chimpanzee] stole all the words before her—retired to the floor where her position was less vulnerable—and wrote out and then answered all the questions taught her." See de Waal, *Mama's Last Hug*, 83: "They're [i.e., the chimps] eager to spend an hour of what they see as fun and games and what we see as cognitive testing. We don't even have to reward them for their performance."

128 See Savage-Rumbaugh, et al., *Apes, Language, and the Human Mind*, 210–11.

129 Hixson criticizes the Gardners for seeing treats as the only way of conditioning animals to display specific behaviors:

Habit also provides a reasonable explanation for apes' self-signing. Herbert Terrace recounts that "[Nim] was often observed to sign to himself, for whatever intrinsic pleasure that produced, while flipping through a book or magazine with his back to the teacher."[130] Roger Fouts recounts that the chimp Dar would sign "coffee" to himself when looking through the window he saw a person drinking coffee.[131] The apes do not express an opinion but simply identify objects. This behavior is most readily explained by the habit they have of naming things, something they have grown used to doing to please the humans they interact with.

In conclusion, the isolated questions and statements that are not requests can be explained through habit, and/or the desire to play, and/or the desire for emotionally gratifying social interaction with their teacher, or by chance. Since there are no accounts of an animal that on a regular basis engaged in exchanges with teachers consisting of questions that are unambiguously ordered to the acquisition of knowledge for its own sake and/or statements ordered to augmenting the teacher's knowledge, it is more reasonable to attribute these isolated questions and statements to causes other than a desire to engage in an exchange of knowledge for the sole purpose of augmenting both one's own and the other's understanding of reality.[132]

> The Gardners also seem to believe that reinforcement is equivalent to the delivery of an edible contingent upon some behavior. For example, during the testing of the vocabulary items they claim that rewards were no longer delivered, but they later say, 'Whether [the observers] . . . were aware of it or not, they often revealed their approval or disapproval of a cross-fosterling's performance by smiling and frowning and by nodding or shaking their heads as well as signing such things [as] GOOD GIRL or SMART BOY' (Gardner and Gardner, 1989b, 188). Whether the Gardners are aware of it or not, such verbal stimuli can come to function as reinforcers or punishers even if the chimpanzees could not eat or drink the words.
>
> Hixson, "Ape Language Research," 28.

130 Terrace, *Nim*, 209. See Leeds and Jensvold, "The Communicative Functions of Five Signing Chimpanzees," 237: "Bodamer et al. (1994) examined the communicative functions of the chimpanzees' private signs. The chimpanzees produced referential utterances, which is describing object or events, most frequently."

131 See Fouts, *Next of Kin*, 303.

132 Susan Goldin-Meadow concludes her article on deaf children who were unable to learn spoken language and who were not exposed to sign language with the following observation:

> Indeed, even when raised without access to conventional language but in the company of other people, human children spontaneously use their hands to communicate. And the hand gestures they invent are used not only to make requests but, more strikingly, to share their thoughts with others. Although many animals have complex social lives and intricate systems of communication, no other animal society has a

A Definitive Test for Abstract Thought: Use of Words Naming Non-Sensible Things

A third criterion for thought is the following: If an animal possesses more than sense knowledge, it should be able to use words that name nonsensible things in meaningful sentences, words such as "God," "soul," "integrity," "rights." Find me an animal that can argue for or even ask about the extension of human rights to animals, and I will be the first to see that they are accorded it.

Conclusion

I have argued that the confusion about human nature and the nature of other animals is twofold. First there is a problem in recognizing that thinking abstractly is different from sensing, and thus that "humanlike being" is a third major life form, alongside plants and animals. To explain the reason why a third subdivision must be recognized is the philosopher's task. Then there is the problem of seeing which organisms fit into which subdivisions. It is the philosopher's task to discern general criteria by which one can distinguish an animal that only senses from one that can also think. It is the scientist's task to adapt these criteria to the organisms in question and devise tests specific to their capabilities. Philosophers in the Thomistic tradition have not always done their part in articulating adequate general criteria (e.g., Henri Renard). The main reason for their failure to do so is due to a poor understanding of the power of the senses, especially of the internal senses, the end result of which is that they underestimate what an animal can do using its senses alone. Showing that animals' apparently intelligent behavior can be explained in terms of its senses does not, however, entirely eliminate the possibility that animals can and do think abstractly. A much stronger case can be made by checking whether animals do the things that a thinking being would naturally do. These things include engaging in a conversation about one topic for the sake of knowledge and using words that name nonsensible realities. Now, the extensive research that has been done on the species of animals most

communication system that is used just to share ideas—to tell stories, to talk to oneself, to talk about talk. The need to interact with others in a symbolic way appears to be a basic human trait, one that is difficult to inculcate in other animals and equally difficult to repress in human children." Susan Goldin-Meadow, "Meeting Other Minds Through Gesture," in *Roots of Human Sociality: Culture, Cognition and Interaction*, ed. N. J. Enfield and Stephen C. Levinson (Berg, 2006), 371.

likely to be intelligent in the narrow sense of the term has shown them to be wanting on these scores. Thus, not only do the linguistic and toolmaking feats most commonly cited provide no compelling reason to say that animals are intelligent, but the absence of behavior natural to intelligent beings gives reason to say that animals are not intelligent. In conclusion then, it is certain that humanlike being represents another subdivision of living thing, and it is virtually certain (barring a discovery in some hitherto unexplored region) that we are the only species in that subdivision—at least on earth.

Epilogue I: A Brief Note on Language Studies with Cetaceans

There has not been as much research done with cetaceans as with great apes, as lacking hands, they cannot be taught sign language, nor can they as readily press keys on a keyboard, though underwater keyboards allowing dolphins to request being rubbed or being given rings and the like were eventually invented.[133]

The field of dolphin-language research experienced a setback in the 1960s when the work of one of the early researchers, John Lilly, was discredited.[134] A later researcher, Louis M. Herman, was a reputed leader in the field from 1969 until 2016. Herman, recognizing the difficulties of training dolphins to use signs productively, focused primarily on sign comprehension,[135] though he did also devise a way for dolphins to answer yes or no to questions concerning whether an object was present or absent in their pool.[136] Herman taught his dolphins to respond to a variety of commands. He used gestures with some subjects and whistle-like sounds with others.[137] Some

133 See Adam A. Pack, "Language Research: Dolphins," in *Encyclopedia of Animal Cognition and Behavior*, ed. Jennifer Vonk and Todd K. Shackelford, https://doi.org/10.1007/978-3-319-47829-6_1628-1.

134 See Thomas A. Sebeok, "Looking in the Destination for What Should Have Been Sought in the Sources," in Sebeok and Umiker-Sebeok, *Speaking of Apes*, 422 and Martin Gardner, *Science: Good, Bad and Bogus* (Prometheus Books, 1981), 391. Lilly's language research on dolphins took place mainly in the 1950s and 60s.

135 See Louis M. Herman and Robert K. Uyeyama, "The Dolphin's Grammatical Competency: Comments on Kako (1990)," *Animal Learning & Behavior* 27, no. 1 (1999): 18–23.

136 Pack, "Language Research: Dolphins," 6–7.

137 Note that when it comes to fetching items, there are border collies that have learned to fetch far more items than dolphins. That the dolphins learned to fetch fewer items may be

examples of the commands the dolphins learned to respond to are "BOTTOM+PIPE+TAIL+TOUCH" (touch tail flukes to the pipe lying on the pool floor) and "FRISBEE+FETCH+BASKET" (bring Frisbee to basket).[138]

Herman's studies provide evidence that dolphins recognize word order, for example, that of subject-verb-direct object.[139] The dolphins' total overall scores on tests in which they were asked things such as to put a ring on a ball (or a ball on a ring) was around 66 percent.[140] While Herman's studies show that dolphins are capable of associating symbols with objects and actions, and also the order of symbols as dictating actions, they do not provide any evidence that the dolphins are capable of abstract thought.

As for whales, researchers examining their communication find that their song sequences vary from group to group within species, but researchers generally reject the notion that the vocalizations are composed of words.[141] The whales' songs are thought to indicate which population the signaler belongs to, to identify the individual itself, and to indicate reproductive fitness. Whales also produce contact calls to keep in touch with one another.

Epilogue II: The Demise of Language Research with Animals

Research on whether animals could be taught language began in the 1960s and continued to the end of the 1990s. Although currently there are some research projects that involve animals that have been trained to use symbolic forms of communication, the efforts of these projects are not primarily focused on teaching the animals language.[142]

---

due solely to the fact that efforts were not made to teach them large vocabularies. It could be the case, though, that their associative memory does not exceed that of dogs.

138 Pack, "Language Research: Dolphins," 3.

139 A lot of the discussion surrounding Herman's work concerns whether his dolphins have learned grammar. Premack argues that they have not; see *Gavagai*, 15–27. For a good secondhand account of the debate, see Griffin, *Animal Minds*, 215–16.

140 See Louis M. Herman, "Cognition and Language Competencies of Bottlenosed Dolphins," in *Dolphin Cognition and Behavior: A Comparative Approach*, ed. R. J. Schusterman, J. Thomas, and F. G. Woods (Psychology Press, 1986), 221–51.

141 See Jacob Andreas et al., "Toward Understanding the Communication in Sperm Whales," *Science* 25, no. 6 (May 13, 2022): 104393, 10.1016/j.isci.2022.104393.

142 The Gorilla Foundation website posts one 1990 research paper on language studies with animals, but no new research publications (https://www.koko.org/communication/) and

There are three reasons for the decline of such studies. One reason is that the funding for such research dried up. Irene Pepperberg attributes this to a conference hosted by the New York Academy of Sciences in 1980. The conference, organized by "Thomas Sebeok, a noted researcher in zoosemotics, and Robert Rosenthal, who studied nonverbal communication and how expectancies influenced conclusions," aimed to debunk the animal language studies, ascribing their putative success to things such as cuing and overinterpretation.[143] According to Pepperberg, the media coverage given to this conference resulted in government agencies cutting off funding for these studies.

A concurrent reason for the decline in ape language studies is that many researchers themselves realized that the ongoing research was not resulting in new discoveries. Researchers learned that apes are capable of learning to associate arbitrary signs with certain things and that they use these signs primarily to get things they want. Once the researchers more or less determined the limits of the animals' symbolic capabilities, they were no longer motivated to seek funding to continue their studies.[144]

---

the Ape Initiative website does not display any research publications on the topic (https://www.apeinitiative.org/science). Language research may be currently going on at the Iowa Primate Learning Center: "Iowa Primate Learning Sanctuary, formerly known as the Great Ape Trust . . . is home to a colony of six bonobos involved in noninvasive interdisciplinary studies of their cognitive and communicative capabilities" (https://www.4apes.com/members/groups/gorilla/61-great-ape-trust-of-iowa). However, there was no reference to specific language studies or projects on the site as of April 2023.

143 Irene M. Pepperberg, "Animal Language Studies: What Happened?," *Psychonomic Bulletin Review* 24 (2017): 183.

144 Tetsuro Matsuzawa, of the renowned Primate Research Institute of Kyoto University (which was recently closed), says in a 2018 video, as if it were noncontroversial, that chimpanzees do not have language (https://www.youtube.com/watch?v=ktkjUjcZid0). There remain relatively few language researchers who still try to make a case that certain animals are genuine language users. There is Penny Patterson who is known for her biased interpretations of the signing of Koko. There is also Sue Savage-Rumbaugh who maintains, "They learned our language." Sue Savage-Rumbaugh et al., *Apes, Language, and the Human Mind* (Oxford University Press, 1998), 213. And then there are Mark A. Krause and Michael J. Beran, "Words Matter: Reflections on Language Projects with Chimpanzees and Their Implications," *American Journal of Primatology* 82, no. 10 (October 2020), https://doi.org/10.1002/ajp.23187. Krause and Beran define "word" in a way that would include a sign associated with a memory or image of a thing: "A signed, spoken, or written symbol that has an ascribable meaning, and is used as a convention among users to communicate about a specific entity." Krause and Beran, "Words Matter," 5. Thus, it is not surprising that they maintain that some apes have language. Most other researchers, even when they do not define language, are looking for understanding that goes beyond associative memory.

The third reason for the decline of language research with animals was the pressure from animal activist groups that maintain that it is unethical to keep animals in captivity to satisfy human curiosity.[145] Some activists go so far as to maintain that apes should be given rights like those of humans, such as the right to liberty. Consequently, researchers had to live with a certain degree of public opprobrium, as well as being more or less obliged to spend time responding to the activists' objections.[146]

Regardless of whether we agree with the view of the animal activists, the bottom line is that teaching symbolic forms of communication to animals did not benefit them in the way that teaching sign language benefitted Helen Keller. Helen had ideas (abstract concepts), albeit few and vague. Once Helen grasped that what her teacher was drawing on her hand constituted a sign for water, she went on to ask for the names of thirty things. Eventually, she started asking questions about things that she now had names for, and she began to converse. Language unlocked Helen's intellectual capacity. If the same had been true in the case of the various animals in the language research studies, it would have been unethical to have ended those studies. Ultimately, the language studies did little, if anything, to improve the animals' lives. It mainly provided them with a novel way of requesting things.

It is not surprising that the language studies revealed an absence of language in nonhuman animals. As Noam Chomsky points out:

> It also seems reasonable to suppose that possession of the language faculty conferred extraordinary selectional advantages, and must be a primary factor in the remarkable biological success of the human species, that is, its proliferation. It would be something of a biological miracle if we were to discover that some other species had a similar capacity but had never thought to put it to use, despite the remarkable advantages it would confer, until instructed by humans to do so—rather as if we were to discover in some remote area a species of bird that had the capacity of flight but had never thought to fly.[147]

145 See Pepperberg, "Animal Language Studies," 181–85. See also Jane C. Hu, "What Do Talking Apes Really Tell Us."

146 Nowadays, if one looks at the website of any center that does research on animals, one always finds a statement about the care provided to the animals, as well as a statement justifying the use of animals in research. It is not uncommon for such centers to be damaged by activists who sometimes also release the animals.

147 Chomsky, "Human Language and Other Semiotic Systems," in Sebeok and Umiker-Sebeok, *Speaking of Apes*, 433.

There are studies of animal communication systems in the wild that are currently being carried on.[148] However, the failure of the language projects is reason to think that these studies are not going to show that animals have language. For once one has grasped the concept of language (i.e., that arbitrary signs signify ideas of things), one is able to learn another language. For example, Helen Keller initially learned words through finger spelling but eventually also learned braille. If the animals in the language studies had their own language, they would have been able to learn the language humans proposed to them. Instead, they only learned to associate symbols with things, as is evidenced by their failure to seek conceptual knowledge by asking questions about the world.

There are also recent analyses of data from the original language projects. I have cited a number of them earlier. I fail to see that they add anything to the observations previously made by the researchers who gathered the data.[149]

148 See, for example, Thore J. Bergman et al., "The Speech-Like Properties of Nonhuman Primate Vocalizations," *Animal Behaviour* 151 (2019): 229–37, and Kate Arnold and Klaus Zuberbühler, "Meaningful Call Combinations in a Nonhuman Primate," *Current Biology* 18, no. 5 (2008) R202–3.

149 See Lyn et al., "Nonhuman Primates Do Declare!," 63–74. See also Rivas, "Recent Use of Signs by Chimpanzees." In this 2015 article, Rivas looks at four corpora of utterances from 1992 to 1999 consisting of 3,448 sign utterances. He observes that the utterances consist mainly of requests with some self-signing and spontaneous naming. He also mentions "wild card" signs that the animals appear to produce to get humans to speed up responding to their requests, such as signing their own names.

5

Theory of Mind in Animals

What is meant by "theory of mind?" A rough idea can be gathered from the following example. If you saw me give a paper on theory of mind, you would know that I see and that I take great interest in my topic. Can an animal know that another animal sees and that another animal experiences interest in something? If they do, they are said to possess "a theory of mind."

One of the earliest, if not the earliest, definitions of "theory of mind" was proposed in 1978 by Premack and Woodruff:

> An individual has a theory of mind if he imputes mental states to himself and others. A system of inferences of this kind is properly viewed as a theory because such states are not directly observable, and the system can be used to make predictions about the behavior of others. As to the mental states the chimpanzee may infer, consider those inferred by our own species, for example, *purpose* or *intention*, as well as *knowledge*, *belief*, *thinking*, *doubt*, *guessing*, *pretending*, *liking*, and so forth.[1]

1 David Premack and Guy Woodruff, "Does the Chimpanzee Have a Theory of Mind?," *Behavioral and Brain Sciences* 1, no. 4 (1978): 515.

I think that Cecilia Heyes is correct when she says that there is no proprietary definition of theory of mind.[2] However, I will use Premack and Woodruff's definition as a point of reference.

Theory of mind investigations often skip over a point which is important for discussions of the similarities and differences between humans and other animals. It is natural to think that "theory" in "theory of mind" implies the view that knowledge of others' mental states involves reason. A theory is a guess as to the cause of a phenomenon, from which one then deduces certain consequences, and goes on to observe whether those consequences obtain.[3] It is not clear that the only way for animals to make predictions about the behavior of other animals based on knowledge of others' unobservable mental states is by formulating a theory that others have minds and/or mental states.[4] I will argue later on that this need not be the case.

There are two questions that need to be addressed before considering theory of mind research. First, what is a mental state? And second, is there reason to think that every kind of mental state is known in the same way?

Intentions, thoughts, perceptions, emotions, beliefs, and pretending are some of the things that are commonly taken to be mental states. But should

2 See Cecilia Heyes, "Animal Mindreading: What's the Problem," *Psychonomic Bulletin & Review* 22, no. 2 (April 2015): 317:

> There is no proprietary definition of what it is to engage in mindreading or to have a theory of mind. The term "theory of mind" embodies a broad claim about the nature of our (adult human) understanding of mental states—that it is theoretical or comprises a "system of inferences" (Premack and Woodruff 1978)—but the type and content of these inferences has been a topic of philosophical debate for centuries, and even the broad claim has been challenged by simulationists, past and present (Goldman 2006). Consequently, researchers who want to find out whether animals are capable of mindreading have considerable freedom in how they define animal mindreading.

3 Krachun et al. adopt G. G. Gallop, Jr.'s view that great apes and humans have introspective awareness of their own experiences and mental states, and this serves as a basis for making inferences about the behavior and mental states of others (called "the theory of mind"). Carla Krachun et al., "Mirror Self-Recognition and Its Relationship to Social Cognition in Chimpanzees," *Animal Cognition* 22 (2019): 1173.

4 The fact that animals have expectations about things does not compel us to posit that they have formed a theory about the way things work, as there are other ways to account for such expectations, such as innate knowledge (instinct) and experiential knowledge (i.e., they expect things to happen in accord with how they remember things to have happened in the past). Thus, although Daniel J. Povinelli's book *Folk Physics for Apes* (Oxford University Press, 2000) is subtitled: *The Chimpanzee's Theory of How the World Works*, Povinelli acknowledges in the closing chapter that "much of the chimpanzee's knowledge about the world will not be ensconced as 'principles' at all, but instead may be encoded as generalized action sequences . . . perhaps instantiated in visual imagery."

these things be referred to as "states"? Part of the problem lies in determining the different meanings of the word "state." Aristotle would have placed some of these things, for example, perceptions and emotions, in the category of affection (Gr. *pathe*; L. *passio animae*).[5] Does some meaning of "state" correspond to affection? Is there some reason to prefer one of these terms to the other? I do not intend to attempt to solve these difficult questions, as beneficial as doing so would be for understanding mental *state* attribution.

As for "mental" in "mental state," here too the word is ambiguous. "Mental" is related to the word "mind," and a mind is an ability to know. Yet if it is the case that the intellect and the senses are radically different knowing powers, "mind" and "mental" in the case of humans mean two quite different things. Thus, for example, keeping something in mind is a different kind of mental activity than using one's mind to draw a conclusion from premises. The former is an act of the memory and the latter an act of the intellect. In addition, if one concedes that emotion is not a cognitive ability, calling it a "mental state" must mean something other than what is meant when this expression is applied to cognitive abilities.

Lastly, theory of mind is often equated with mental state *attribution*. As we will see, there is reason to question this way of speaking about it.

A question arises as to whether a sense perception in the absence of consciousness, that is, awareness that one senses, should be considered a mental state. Aquinas maintains that an interior sense that he calls the "common sense" is needed in order to be aware of one's acts of perception:

> Neither vision nor taste is able to discern white from sweet because it is necessary that what discriminates between two things knows both. Whence it is necessary that this judgment of discretion belong to a common sense to which all apprehensions of the senses are referred to as to a common term; the stretching forth (*intentiones*) of the senses are also perceived by this sense, as when someone sees that he sees. For this cannot come about through the proper sense which only knows the form of the sensible (attribute) by which it is changed, in which change vision

5 See, for example, *Categories*, 10a 6–10: "Those, however, which arise from causes easily rendered ineffective are called affections, not qualities. Suppose that a man is irritable when vexed: he is not even spoken of as a bad-tempered man, when in such circumstances he loses his temper somewhat, but rather is said to be affected. Such conditions are therefore termed, not qualities, but affections." Note that the word "condition" in the last sentence is not found in the Greek. *Categories*, trans. Harold P. Cooke (Harvard University Press, 1973), 71.

> is brought about, and from which change follows another change in the common sense, which perceives seeing.[6]

The question then arises of whether there could be an organism that possessed sense perception but lacked consciousness. It is the case that we are often not consciously aware that we are seeing, as for instance, when we are walking in an area familiar to us without paying any particular attention to anything on our route; yet we could, nonetheless, become aware that we are seeing. Could a being see and yet be unable to ever be aware that it sees? If this is possible, sight would then seem to be scarcely more than the sort of unknowing reaction that goes on in a plant in response to light. In any case, in this chapter, I am going to consider as a mental state something that both involves knowledge and is in principle something one can be conscious of. All mental states share in common having a component that is accessible to the individual, while not being directly observable by others.

Note that consciousness is to be distinguished from self-consciousness. Self-consciousness presupposes consciousness and goes beyond it by reflecting on it. Consciousness consists in the act of knowing that one is sensing or feeling an emotion.[7] Self-consciousness consists in the act of knowing that bears on the knowledge of consciousness, for example, I know that I should be seeing the things that I know myself to be currently seeing (as when watching children on the playground). Self-consciousness is at the basis of questions such as, "Should I be as sad as I know myself to be?" It is what allows one to investigate the kind of self or person one is and to examine one's conscience.[8]

6 Aquinas, *ST*, I, q. 78 a. 4, ad 2. It is puzzling that Aquinas sometimes speaks as if the external senses know their own act. For example, in Quodlibet VIII, q. 9, a. 1, he says: "For it is the case that a power bears on some object before it bears upon its own act: the act of some potency is understood prior to a reflection upon its act. For the act terminates at the object, and so every potency bears on its object prior to on its own act; as sight sees color before it may see that it sees color." See also *De Verit.*, q. 10 a. 9.

7 For a penetrating account of consciousness, see Michael Stock, "Sense Consciousness According to St. Thomas," *The Thomist* 21, no. 4 (October 1958): 415–86.

8 Aquinas holds that animals are conscious beings. They can know that they sense by means of the common sense. Aquinas maintains, however, that only rational animals possess self-consciousness. This is because only rational animals have immaterial faculties and only what is immaterial is capable of self-reflection. Aquinas establishes the latter by pointing out that a material thing has parts that lie outside one another; consequently, if that thing bends back on itself, every part cannot be joined to every part, and thus the whole cannot grasp itself as a whole. Immaterial things do not have part outside part and consequently are capable of

In what follows, I intend to do four things. First, I will discuss theory of mind claims concerning animals and false beliefs. Second, I will examine whether individuals of some species of animal know other animals' emotions, and if so, how this may be explained. Third, I will examine whether individuals of some species know other animals' acts of sense perception, and if so, how this may be explained. Lastly, I reconsider whether animals know others' beliefs, understood as others' acts of remembering or imagining. One of my main theses is that theory of mind in animals in regard to emotion and perception need not involve conscious attribution of mental states but may be adequately accounted for by experience-based recognition.

Theory of Mind and Tests for False Belief

A Classic Theory of Mind Test Fails to Show What It Purports to Show

Some of the classic tests for theory of mind focus on the notion of false beliefs: Is an ape able to mentally represent the false belief of another ape, or in other words, can it know that the other is thinking something that it itself knows is not so? What is the rationale for theory of mind researchers' preoccupation with testing for *false* beliefs? It is sometimes claimed that one does not have a notion of belief until one can recognize that beliefs can be true or false. While I think this is true for a complete notion of belief, it seems that some notion of belief is already present in a child who can understand a question such as, "Who do you think is coming today?" The child need not understand that her answer may be right or wrong in order to answer the question. One can, however, more decisively tell that an individual distinguishes what is mental from what is real by seeing whether he evidences knowledge of discrepancies between the two when such occur.[9]

---

wholly turning back upon themselves. Since the intellect is an immaterial faculty, it is able to reflect on itself. See Aquinas, *De Causis*, lec. 7.

9 See Henry M. Wellman et al., "Meta-Analysis of Theory-of-Mind Development: The Truth About False Belief," *Child Development* 72, no. 3 (2001): 655:

> From the earliest research, however, a central focus has been on children's understanding of belief, especially false belief. Why? Mental-state understanding requires realizing that such states may reflect reality and may be manifest in overt behavior, but are nonetheless internal and mental, and thus distinct from real-world events, situation, or behaviors. A child's understanding that a person has a false belief—one

The experimenters who devise theory of mind tests for false belief generally do not distinguish different senses of "belief." Aristotle denies that animals have beliefs in the sense of a conviction arrived at as the result of reasoning. He says: "No animal has belief [*pistis*], but many have imagination [*phantasia*]."[10] The reason he gives for this view is that "again, every opinion is accompanied by belief, belief by conviction, and conviction by rational discourse; but although some brute animals have imagination, they have no reasoning power [*logos*]."[11] For Aristotle, a dog that saw a squirrel run up a tree can imagine that squirrel is still in the tree but does not have a belief that the squirrel is in the tree in the sense of knowledge that has been reasoned to. Perhaps, the ancient Greek word "*pistis*" in Aristotle's day had a more restricted meaning than the English word "belief," or perhaps Aristotle is using it with a stipulative meaning. In English it can both be said that one has the belief, based on experience, that turning the knob to the left of the faucet will give hot water and also that one has the belief, based on reasoned arguments, that Aristotle's definition of the soul is correct. Aristotle regards "*pistis*" to apply only to the latter.[12]

Accordingly, Aristotle acknowledges that a dog can think that the squirrel is in the tree in one sense of "think," but not in another sense:

> These two then, appetite and mind, are clearly capable of causing movement if, that is, one regards imagination as some sort of thinking process (*noēsis*); for men often follow their imaginations contrary to knowledge, and in living creatures other than man there is neither thinking (*noēsis*) nor calculation, but only imagination.[13]

---

whose content contradicts reality—provides compelling evidence for appreciating this distinction between mind and world. See, e.g., Dennett, 1979.

10 Aristotle, *On the Soul*, 428a20, trans. W. S. Hett in the Loeb edition, modified. Note that "phantasia" in Aristotle often corresponds to the inner senses in conjunction with each other and not only to the imagination in isolation. A cat that has gotten violently ill upon eating a shrew for the first time, upon seeing another animal similar in appearance, will imagine that eating it will make it sick, due to remembering what previously occurred.

11 *On the Soul*, 428a22–25.

12 Alasdair MacIntyre in *Dependent Rational Animals* fails to distinguish these two senses of belief; see chap. 4, "Can Animals Without Language Have Beliefs?," 29–41.

13 Aristotle, *On the Soul*, 433a10–13. Aquinas comments: "These two things are seen to be movers, namely, appetite and intellect; nevertheless, in such a way that imagination is included under intellect, as it has something like the intellect, insofar as it moves [one] to sensible things that are absent, as does intellect, for it [*phantasia*] too is a principle of motion." *In DA*, bk. 3, lec. 15, no. 819 (Marietti edition).

Aristotle distinguishes thinking abstractly from thinking in the sense of imagining, while acknowledging that the two are similar insofar as they are causes of motion. Aristotle would deny that the dog can think that the squirrel is in the tree in the sense of having reasoned to this but would acknowledge the dog can think that the squirrel is up the tree in the sense of imagining it was there.

Aquinas would add that the dog may have beliefs in the form of sense-based estimation that the squirrel may move within reach and/or a sensory judgment that it is worth waiting to see if it does so.[14]

If it is correct to deny that animals are capable of abstract thought, then the only kind of beliefs they have consist of what they remember or imagine or estimate (as to utility or harm). False belief tests, then, can only discover whether a given animal knows that another animal is incorrectly imagining or remembering or estimating something to be the case.

A classic false belief test[15] involves an experimenter, an ape, and a human subject. The three are together in a room and the experimenter, in the sight of all, places an object such as an apple under a cone. The human subject leaves the room. The experimenter then takes the apple and hides it elsewhere in the room. The subject comes back. The ape is asked where the subject will look for the apple. If it answers, "Under the cone," rather than in the new location, it has passed the test for theory of mind. But is this test adequate?

14 Aquinas adopts from the Arab philosophers a fourfold division of the internal senses. It includes the estimative sense by which animals recognize, in the present, singular things as being beneficial or harmful to them. See *ST* I, q. 78, a. 4. This estimation does not proceed from knowledge of an abstract principle but is either innate (instinct) or is based on experience. Aristotle does not speak of this internal sense, but only of the other three: the common sense, imagination, and memory. Aquinas relates the imagination and the estimative in the following manner:

> The motion of sensuality tends towards to things: to things which are delightful to the exterior senses . . . and to those things are known only according to the estimative [sense] as harmful or suitable to the body. . . . The estimative properly stands to it [sensuality] as practical reason to the will, which is also mover; simple imagination, however, and the powers preceding [it] stand to it [sensuality] more remotely, just as speculative reason does to the will. *Sent.* II, d. 24, q. 2, a. 1 and ad 2.

15 This sort of test goes by the name of the Sally Anne test and was originally formulated by Heinz Wimmer and Josef Perner in their paper, "Beliefs About Beliefs: Representation and Constraining Function of Wrong Beliefs in Young Children's Understanding of Deception," *Cognition* 13 (1983): 103–28.

Apparently when very young children take this test, they give the wrong answer, responding that the subject will look for the apple in its new location. Very young children apparently cannot dissociate what they know from what others know *or* what is the case from what is thought by others to be the case. There is a question, though, as to why an ape or child has to understand that the subject is deceived in order to answer that the subject will look for the apple under the cone. I would assume that if the apple was still under the cone, the ape or child would give the same answer when asked, "Where will the person look for the apple?" Thus, this test does not establish whether an individual is aware of the false beliefs of others.

In addition, it is questionable whether this test even shows that an individual is aware that others have beliefs at all. An ape can remember that the subject fixed his eyes on the cone being put over the apple, or at the very least that the subject was present when the apple was covered, and the ape may well remember that subjects that fix their eyes on something positioned in a given place will look for it in that same place.[16] If this is so, the ape would not have to attribute any mental state to the subject to respond that he will look for the apple under the cone.

Children who pass false belief tests often do not explain the other's behavior in terms of beliefs. As Kristin Andrews notes: "If we turn to the verbal explanations 4-year-old children give after passing the Maxi [=Sally Anne] test, they typically refer to the situation, not to belief, with responses such as, 'He looked for the chocolate there because that's where he left it.'"[17]

I think, then, that this test for whether individuals know that other individuals have false beliefs is faulty for two reasons. First, the question posed is not explicitly about the other's false belief. Secondly, the test set-up does not allow one to distinguish whether a correct answer is based on prior experience of certain kinds of behavior being commonly linked together rather than on any knowledge of mental states. It might be that a child or ape goes from giving the wrong answer to the right one by arriving at an

16 It is true that animals show surprise when something they expect to happen, doesn't happen. However, this does not amount to universal knowledge that beliefs may be true or false. To gain this knowledge would require one to consciously reflect that this particular discrepancy between what one thought and what actually was reveals that the realm of thought and the realm of real being are not the same, even though there may be a correspondence between them.

17 Kristin Andrews, "Chimpanzee Mind Reading: Don't Stop Believing," *Philosophy Compass* 12, no. 1 (2016): 5.

understanding of others' mental states. But it might also be that the child or ape makes this transition by having learned through experience that in such circumstances the subject does not go to the object's current location, but rather to where the object and subject were initially together.

Do Apes Know Others as Knowers or Only as Actors?

Consider another theory of mind experiment, this time involving a "baiter," a "finder," and a chimpanzee.[18] The baiter places some food item in a closet which he then locks. He next places the key on a hook near the closet and leaves. Now the finder comes in, takes the key, unlocks the closet and gives the chimpanzee the food item. Every once in a while, the baiter does not put the key in its usual place but hides it somewhere. The finder who now enters is ignorant of where the key is. The chimpanzee, at first, does not try to inform him as to the key's whereabouts. When the finder looks and fails to find the key in the usual place, only then does the chimpanzee try to indicate where it is presently hidden. It is not hard to come up with an explanation of the chimpanzee's behavior that does not ascribe a theory of mind to the chimpanzee: The chimpanzee knows the sequence of events, perceives a blockage in the sequence, and recalls that that the finder must use the key to get the food. There is no reason to conclude that the chimpanzee knows the mental state (i.e., the ignorance) of the finder.

A further twist was added to the experiment. A stranger occasionally came in after the baiter left and moved the key. The chimpanzee often regarded the stranger with some hostility, spitting on occasion. When the finder returned, the chimpanzee now informed the finder of the whereabouts of the key even before the finder showed himself unable to open the closet. This would seem to indicate that the chimpanzee realized after all that the finder was ignorant and needed to be informed.

It is very natural for us to interpret the chimpanzee's directing the finder to the key as being an intentional effort to inform an individual whom it recognizes to be ignorant. However, an alternate explanation is that through experience a chimpanzee knows that if a person or other chimpanzee fixes its eyes on something, the person or chimpanzee may perform some act toward it at some later time; conversely, if a person or chimpanzee does not

18 This experiment is recounted by Juan Carlos Gómez in *Apes, Monkeys, Children, and the Growth of Mind* (Harvard University Press, 2004), 229–31.

fix its eyes on something, it is unlikely to act toward it at some later time. This account works both for this experiment and for the experiment with the cone recounted earlier. In the baiter-finder experiment, the chimpanzee knows that a key located in an area where the finder had not fixed his eyes would not be sought there by the finder. In the cone experiment, the chimpanzee knows that a person seeks a thing in the place where he earlier fixed his eyes.

I agree that such accounts sound forced to us for we humans habitually attribute mental states to other people. But as Daniel Povinelli points out, attributing mental states to others is generally dependent on observing their overt behavior.[19] In the baiter-finder experiment, to know that the finder was ignorant of the displaced key would require one to remember that the finder had not been present or fixed his gaze upon the key when it was placed in its new location. So as far as determining a course of action goes, it makes no difference whether a being directly associates the absence of the fixing of gaze with the inability to locate an object or if a being knows that the absence of the fixing of gaze means that the person does not know where the object is and consequently will not be able to readily locate it. We think to ourselves: *"X was not present when the key or food was placed where it is now, and so X didn't see it, and therefore doesn't know where it is, and thus is unlikely to go after it,"* whereas a chimpanzee may simply know: *"X was not present when the key or food was placed where it is now and is therefore not likely to go after it."*[20]

In other words, testing whether apes are aware of mental states of others involves creating a scenario in which there is something observable from which mental states can be inferred. However, the physical situation the apes observe can in principle always be directly linked through experience with a given course of action or inaction: X fixes eyes on desirable food item; X goes to eat that item—both these things are observable. And the same is true when X does not fix eyes on food item and subsequently does not go to eat that item. So there seems no way for experiments in which one observable behavior could be potentially linked to another to determine whether apes

19 See Daniel J. Povinelli and Christopher G. Prince, "When Self Met Other," in *Self-Awareness: Its Nature and Development*, ed. Michel Ferrari and Robert J. Sternberg (Guilford Press, 1998), 33–107.

20 This example is adapted from Daniel J. Povinelli and Jennifer Vonk, "Chimpanzee Minds: Suspiciously Human?," in *Trends in Cognitive Sciences* 7, no. 4 (2003): 159.

know others as knowers and not simply as actors. Of course, the more parsimonious explanation is to say that they know others only as actors.

I am going to leave off investigation whether animals have knowledge of others' false beliefs to turn to a more tractable problem, namely, whether they know other animals' emotions.

Do Animals Know Others' Emotions?

I initially found Povinelli's minimalist account of apes' performance on false belief tests in terms of behavior alone persuasive. However, I doubted whether it provided an adequate explanation in the case of the mental states of seeing (and sensing in general) and emotion. Is it just our anthropomorphic biases that strongly incline us to think that certain animals know the knowledge states and emotional states of other animals? Do we really want to say that a dog doesn't know that we see it or know when we are sad? If we admitted that the dog knows that we see it and knows that we are sad, would this mean we would have to acknowledge the dog to be essentially the same sort of animal as ourselves? I will first consider whether animals know others' emotions and then whether they know that others sense.

Evidence That Animals Are Aware of Their Own Emotions

I understand emotion to be an inclination involving body and soul toward or away from something known through sense to be good or bad, respectively. Animals are attracted to or repelled by some of the various things that they sense, prior to moving toward or away from them. For example, an animal that is not full, upon smelling food, feels a desire for it. Depending on the circumstances, it may then move or not move toward it.

Before talking about animals, we need to reflect on what we know best about knowledge of emotion, that is, what we know about our own knowledge of emotion. One cannot know that another person is feeling a given emotion unless one has experienced that emotion oneself. Consider, for example, how children are oblivious to manifestations of sexual attraction between adults, because they have as yet to experience such an attraction themselves. Similarly, Temple Grandin, an animal behaviorist and individual with autism, in the absence of ever feeling infatuated with someone, was unable to understand how her roommate felt about one of their teachers.[21] Same for the other emotions: for example, one can only know what anger is when one has experienced it oneself. When one has, then one can go on to realize that when another being similar to oneself is showing external signs of being angry and is in the sort of situation that provokes anger, that individual is *feeling* angry. Assuming that animals are conscious, they know when they themselves are angry. They can also observe another animal *acting* angrily. But it is hard to see how in the absence of reason they can know that another animal is having the internal experience of *feeling* angry.[22] We humans distinguish external changes that express emotion from external changes that do not. We distinguish the look of pain that crosses a person's face from the gesture of reaching for the aspirin bottle. Are animals capable of doing so? Or for them are all such external changes known simply as harbingers of future actions and never as indicating internal feeling?

The first question to ask is whether animals know their own emotions, as knowledge of the internal component of others' emotions cannot be known by observing others but depends on self-knowledge of one's own emotions.

Experience shows that it is possible to be unaware of one's emotions. As Antonio Damasio observes:

> There is, however, no evidence that we are conscious of *all* our feelings, and much to suggest that we are not. For example, we often realize quite suddenly, in a given situation, that we feel anxious or uncomfortable, pleased or relaxed, and it is apparent that the particular state of feeling we know then has not begun on the moment of knowing but rather some time before.[23]

However, organisms that feel the most visceral of the emotions, namely, pain, must sometimes be aware of it. We speak of the feeling of pain, but it is not a feeling in the sense of a perception, as is the case of feeling that

21 See Grandin, *Thinking in Pictures*, 97: "My first inkling that my emotions were different came in high school, when my roommate swooned over the science teacher. Whatever it was that she was feeling, I knew that I didn't feel that way toward anyone."

22 Perhaps animals could know the emotions of other animals instinctually, but such an instinct could not be triggered independent of the animals' knowledge of their own emotions, for emotions cannot be known in the absence of the subjective experience of what they are like.

23 Antonio Damasio, *The Feeling of What Happens* (Harcourt, 1999), 36.

something is hard or hot. Pain is not something in the thing that causes pain, as are its texture, temperature, etc., which are qualities in a thing that are perceived through the sense of touch. Pain is a response in us to something in things that is harmful to our body. It is possible to be in pain without being aware of it. Most people have had the experience of being in pain and losing awareness of it when they become absorbed in something that holds their interest. However, there would be no point to feeling pain if one were never aware of it, as the purpose of pain is to motivate one to eliminate or escape its cause.

Similarly, if animals did not know the feeling of pleasure to be something desirable, then there would be no reason for them to preferentially pursue things that caused pleasure, such as treats offered by a trainer. As for anger, it would be strange to think that a chimpanzee throwing a temper tantrum was unaware of feeling angry.

In general, emotion motivates action. If emotions were always unconscious then why name them differently than other intermediary physiological processes leading from perception to action, for example, from seeing a predator to running from it. Why talk about fear if the animal is never aware that it feels afraid?[24]

There is also some secondary evidence that animals are aware of their emotions. Apes that have been taught to use a symbolic form of communication use signs that for us signify emotions or something related to emotion: "funny," "hurt," "cry," "mad," and "scare."[25] It is particularly chimpanzees' use of "hurt" and "scare" that supports the notion that they recognize their emotions. According to Fouts and Mellgren, "Washoe used her signs to inform her caregivers she had the flu by signing HURT, indicating her stomach

24 There is a condition called alexithymia which consists in a lack of awareness of one's emotions and the inability to name them. If everyone, however, who was afraid was unaware of being afraid, there would be no utility in feeling afraid and there would seem to be no reason to speak of fear as an emotion rather than as part of a motor response to perceived stimuli. Note that some animals appear to identify emotions such as pain and fear, evidence that they do not have alexithymia.

25 See R. Allen Gardner et al., eds., *Teaching Sign Language to Chimpanzees* (State University of New York Press, 1989). The Gardners report chimpanzees signing "funny" (Gardner et al., *Teaching Sign Language*, 93) and "hurt" (Gardner et al., 131, 209). See also George Johnson, "Chimp Talk Debate: Is It Really Language?," *New York Times*, June 6, 1995, Section C1: "PANBANISHA, a Bonobo . . . repeatedly pressed three symbols—'Fight,' 'Mad,' 'Austin'—in various combinations." See Jeffrey Masson, *When Elephants Weep* (Delta, 1996), 233, re: angry.

pain."[26] Savage-Rumbaugh et al. reports that the chimpanzee "Sherman would scream as though he had seen something that had scared him and comment 'scare' at the keyboard,"[27] and on some of these occasions people spotted something that could frighten a chimpanzee. While it is possible that "scare" is used by the chimpanzee solely as a signal to get help or for some other reason, it seems to me more plausible that it in some way associates the sign with the feeling of fear. On one occasion Sherman "rushed inside to announce to people and to [the chimp] Austin 'scare outdoors' when he saw a partially anesthetized ape moaning as it was transported past the building."[28] Admittedly, it is not clear what the chimpanzee intends to indicate. Is there something scary outdoors or is there a scared ape outdoors or is it scared by what it sees outdoors? Still, it seems reasonable to think that the chimpanzee is using the word to express fear or something that causes fear. Savage-Rumbaugh also reports that the bonobo Kanzi could understand the sentence, "Can you go scare Matata with the snake."[29]

Could an animal arrive at an awareness of others' emotions starting from its awareness of its own emotions? It is unfortunate that reports of the usage of signs for "hurt" and "scared" by great apes are extremely limited. It is not clear from any transcripts that I have come across that any ape used them unambiguously in regard to both itself and others. If this had been the case, it would provide some evidence that animals do know others' emotions.

I will come back to the question of whether in the case of emotion there is reason to think that animals are doing more than monitoring others' facial expressions, vocalizations, and the like.[30] Now I intend to investigate whether reason is needed in order for an organism to recognize another's emotions. Again, it seems this must be the case, as the internal dimension of the emotion is hidden and unobservable to others. I will approach this

26 R. S. Fouts and R. L. Mellgren, quoted by Leeds and Jensvold in "The Communicative Functions of Five Signing Chimpanzees," 240.

27 E. Sue Savage-Rumbaugh et al., "Spontaneous Symbol Acquisition and Communicative Use by Pygmy Chimpanzees," *Journal of Experimental Psychology: General* 115, no. 3 (1986): 218.

28 E. Sue Savage-Rumbaugh et al., "Apes with Language," *Critical Quarterly* 38, no. 3 (1996): 53.

29 Savage-Rumbaugh, *Kanzi*, 246.

30 See Frans de Waal, *The Age of Empathy: Nature's Lessons for a Kinder Society* (Three Rivers Press, 2009), 81: "We often focus on the face, but obviously the entire body expresses emotions. As shown by Belgian neuroscientist Beatrice de Gelder, we react as rapidly to body posture as we do to facial expressions. We effortlessly read bodies, such as a fearful pose (reason to run, hands warding off danger) or an angry one (chest out, taking a step forward)."

question by first asking the general question of how animals recognize and, in some manner, categorize different kinds of things. Understanding how they categorize things in general is liable to shed some light on whether their cognitive ability extends to recognizing others' beliefs, emotions, and perceptions.

How Do Animals Categorize Things?

Animals plainly have some way of identifying things of different kinds. A sheep runs from a wolf, but not from a fly. Birds generally fly away when anything large moves in the near vicinity but can get used to passing traffic. Pigeons in studies learn to pick out pictures of kingfishers from pictures of other birds, and pictures of animals from nonanimals.[31] Orangutans match things that fall into intermediate categories, such as "bird" and "reptile." When given a picture of a reptile, for example, a snake, they will match it with a picture of another reptile, for example, an alligator, when given a choice between a picture of an alligator and a picture of an owl.[32] Alex the parrot was able to pick out what was the same and what was different in the case of color, shape, and material; for example, he would be shown two wooden blocks of different colors and could respond correctly to the questions, "What is the same?" and "What is different?" The border collie, Chaser, could fetch over one thousand different items.

I have argued in the previous chapter that the language studies show that animals lack abstract concepts and thus cannot categorize things in function of such. How then do they do so? We obviously cannot get into their minds. However, we can make some reasonable guesses as to the sort of thing that is going on by reflecting on our own subuniversal knowledge and by examining the experiments with animals that are geared to determining how they categorize things.

A subrational way we have of knowing things is by experience, which Aristotle delineates in the following manner:

31 See Stephen Budiansky, *If a Lion Could Talk* (The Free Press, 1998), 86.

32 See Jennifer Vonk, "Matching Based on Biological Categories in Orangutans (*Pongo abelii*) and a Gorilla (*Gorilla gorilla gorilla*)," *PeerJ* 1, no. 1 (2013): e158. See also Masayuki Tanaka, "Discrimination and Categorization of Photographs of Natural Objects by Chimpanzees (*Pan troglodytes*)," *Animal Cognition* 4 (2001): 201–11.

> For to have a judgement that when Callias was ill of this disease this did him good, and similarly in the case of Socrates and in many individual cases, is a matter of experience; but to judge that it has done good to all persons of a certain constitution marked off according to type, when they were ill of this disease, e.g., to phlegmatic or bilious people when burning with fever—this is a matter of art.[33]

The person of experience is on the verge of arriving at universal knowledge but has not yet done so. Experience is constituted by memories of similar things that are grouped together due to their similarity, although the mind as yet has failed to seize on exactly what way they are similar.[34] For example, people can successfully fish or repair cars or speak their mother tongue without being able to explain to others how they do so.[35] So perhaps a squirrel that has become somewhat tame has a mental catalogue of various humans, and upon seeing an individual that is similar to the ones in this mental catalogue, identifies this individual as the sort of being that might feed it.

Another way of recognizing something as belonging to a kind without recourse to universal concepts is by matching it to an idealized model that is stored in one's imagination or memory. Not every human kidney

33 Aristotle, *Metaphysics*, bk. 1, chap. 1, 981a7–10. I have modified somewhat the translation of W. D. Ross. Aristotle also speaks of experience in the *Posterior Analytics*, bk. 2, chap. 19, 100a4–9. This text, however, is more difficult to parse out.

34 See Daniel Povinelli, "Can Comparative Psychology Crack its Toughest Nut?," *Animal Behavior and Cognition* 7, no. 4 (2020): 591:

> I do not write *abstract* whimsically. Any robust theory of action understanding—human or otherwise—must handle the *many-to-one* mapping of sensory inputs onto mental representations that can cope with the superficial differences of particular situations. Thus, as Candy lifts her coconut to smash her mango, she is bringing to bear the full weight of her abstracted set of concepts and operations that allow her to get to the heart of the matter. A novel dry drupe does not fool her. Simply put, after Candy learns to crack open a pecan, she is not left speechless confronting a walnut.

Candy's performance can be explained by experience; there is no need to invoke abstract thought. A walnut resembles a pecan, and on this basis, Candy attempts to crack it open in a way similar to what has worked in the past. Candy does not have an abstract concept of "nut," such as allows us to ask: "Is a nut a fruit or a seed or something else"?

35 A clear example where people had experience but lacked the art occurred when I was fishing with two Cambodian friends. In about half an hour each of them had caught about twenty fish. I had caught two. I asked them repeatedly what the secret was, and at a certain point they became offended that I did not believe them when they told me that there was no secret. They were unable to state what the correct technique was.

looks exactly the same. However, one can learn to recognize a kidney by remembering an idealized drawing of a kidney in a biology book. Perhaps animals' instinctive recognition of enemies is a matter of matching a sensed particular to an innate model of this sort. And perhaps learned recognition of friends and foes is due to the unconscious formation of an idealization based on individual instances that the animal has observed. The idealized model explanation, however, does not seem capable of explaining how an animal could recognize higher categories such as color or shape. It is not possible to form an idealized representation of shape that would allow one to recognize a specific shape as a shape.

Stephen Budiansky, who discusses the above subrational means of recognizing kinds, proposes a third way:

> A competing theory holds that animals form groups by maintaining stripped-down lists of rules governing "family resemblance." Not every feature on the list would need to be present in every case; a pigeon might categorize an object as a tree if it contains several of these characteristics, or some established weighted average among them, which the pigeon has shaped and refined as it encounters new examples. These characteristics might include greenness, leaves, branching limbs, and an overall shape that rises vertically from the ground.[36]

It is not entirely clear to me whether this third way is finally all that different from the other two. Instead of having a collection of images of trees to which the animal unconsciously matches a specific tree as being more similar to individuals in that collection than to individuals in another collection, or instead of having an idealized trunk with green leaves on top, Budiansky is proposing that the animal has a list of rules that it applies ("greenness, leaves, branching limbs, and an overall shape that rises vertically from the ground"). How, though, are these characteristics grouped together in the animal's mind? It seems that it would be either by way of a collection of memories of things sharing these traits or as a single idealization.[37]

36 Budiansky, *If a Lion Could Talk,* 87.

37 Note that while humans imagine primarily in visual terms, there is reason to think that other animals imagine in other sensory modes, e.g., given that smell plays a much greater role in the lives of many animals, one would reasonably expect this to be reflected in how they imagine things. Thus, while I am giving examples in visual terms, I do not mean that animals' representations are necessarily visual.

On the other hand, one might maintain that Budiansky's explanation in terms of a rule is distinguishable from the other two explanations. In one experiment, chimpanzees were given the task of sorting the lexigrams or symbol tokens for various foods and tools into the appropriate container.[38] It seems likely that they did so on the following basis: a token with (e.g.) the symbol for banana has become through habituation associated in their memories with a banana and the banana is associated in their memories with the property of being edible. Anything with the property of being edible is put into the "food" container. Any token of an object lacking that property is put into the "tool" container. So here it does seem likely that rather than matching the image associated with a given lexigram to images of other foods, apes instead categorize foods on the basis of a characteristic, edibility. Similarly, perhaps the pigeons that are able to distinguish animals from nonanimals do so on the basis of a single characteristic, e.g., perhaps they perceive things that have eyes as being similar to one another, and different from things that do not have eyes. The latter case does also seem amenable to the two other types of explanation, e.g., it seems possible that the pigeons pick out living things in function of a vague idealized image of "a thing with eyes."

As for the orangutans seemingly grasping categories such as "reptile" and "bird," it is possible they correctly match things that fall in these categories by noticing a similarity, such as having scales, between samples that they remember and one of the two choices that they are offered. It may also be the case that their performance is due to them noticing differences between the sample and one of the choices rather than the similarities. In one test, given a snake picture as a sample, perhaps the orangutan readily eliminates the owl because it doesn't have smooth skin. In the next test, given an alligator picture as a sample, perhaps the orangutan readily eliminates the puffin which is in flight. So perhaps they do not even look to a feature that makes one reptile similar to another in appearance.

Even if we cannot figure out which, if any, of the above explanations actually corresponds to what is going on in an animal's mind when it categorizes something, we can nonetheless see that in principle some operation of the internal senses (imagination, memory) can account for an animal's doing so. Thus, while abstract thought is not the explanation for

38 See Duane M. Rumbaugh and E. Sue Savage-Rumbaugh, "Language in Comparative Perspective," in Mackintosh, *Animal Learning and Cognition*, 318–19.

how animals categorize things (for as the language studies show, they lack abstract thought), the senses offer an adequate explanation of how they are able to do so.

Can Animals Recognize Others' Emotions by Using Sense Experience?

Having established that some form of identification of kinds is possible on the basis of sense knowledge alone, now the question is whether it is reasonable to think that some form of sense knowledge can allow an animal to know the emotions of another animal. If it can, then the claim that animals know the emotions of other animals is not tantamount to saying that animals possess reason.

Before investigating the case of nonhuman animals, let us first consider human knowledge of others' emotions. It might seem that knowledge of others' emotions requires reason because the inner aspect of others' emotions cannot be perceived by the senses and so seemingly has to be inferred (this is the view of Premack, mentioned earlier).

De Waal distinguishes emotions from feelings, understanding feelings to be a conscious or subjective experience of one's emotions. I agree with him when he notes that we are sometimes not conscious of our emotions. However, I part ways with him when he expresses skepticism as to knowing others' feelings on the grounds that they are private: "If I ask you how you felt about your father's death, you may tell me that you were 'sad,' but does this really allow me to grasp your feelings? I can't get inside you. Who says your sadness is like my sadness?"[39]

People did not invent the word "emotion" and the words for specific emotions, such "sadness," "anger," etc. to name observable physical changes that occur in specific kinds of situations in detachment from any subjective feeling. Though we observe the bloodshot eyes and slurred speech of a drunken person or the change in skin color of a person who has been out in the sun or the tears coming from the eyes of someone peeling onions, we would never call these things emotions because they are not connected to a subjective feeling.

We know from our experience of our own emotions, for example, our sadness, that it differs somewhat under different circumstances, such as our

39 De Waal, *Mama's Last Hug*, 127.

hormonal state, the amount of sleep we have had, and how bad we deem the thing provoking our sadness, and so forth. It is possible for us to realize that we have never known the depths of sadness experienced by a person who has been the victim of a tragedy. We may also recognize that some people are more sensitive and are thus more prone to sadness than others, and also that what people regard as bad, and thus provocative of sadness, differs. However, it is reasonable to think that others' feelings of sadness are similar to ours and are different from feelings of anger or disgust because human individuals are similar in physical make-up and this emotion is observed to drive similar actions in different individuals. Ironically, de Waal makes this point in response to the view that we cannot know that horses feel thirsty:

> But this is a highly unreasonable position given how similarly the emotions manifest themselves in animal and human bodies and how alike all mammalian brains are down to the details of neurotransmitters, neural organization, blood supply, and so on. It would be like saying that both horses and humans seem to get thirsty on a hot day, but in horses, we should call it "water need" because it is unclear that they feel anything. This then raises the question of how a horse decides it needs to drink if not for signs of dehydration inside its own body. The horse's body detects internal changes and sends information to its hypothalamus, which monitors the sodium concentration in its blood. If this level rises above a certain limit, the blood gets too salty, and its brain induces a strong desire for water. Desires work by being felt.[40]

De Waal goes on to note that the detection system in the horse is the same as in us, and he concludes from this that it is unreasonable to think that thirsty horses feel differently from thirsty people. The same conclusion can be drawn a fortiori about thirst in me and thirst in other humans. Your subjective experience of thirst, though not precisely the same as mine, is reasonably thought to be the same sort of thing. And a similar case can be made for other emotions such as sadness and anger, granted they involve more both physiologically and cognitively than does thirst. The greater complexity of these emotions means that the subjective experience of them will come in many more shades (often mirrored to some extent by language; think of all the words there are for fear) and there will be greater variety in the actions they drive, which makes it much easier for us to misunderstand how others

40 De Waal, *Mama's Last Hug*, 128.

really feel than is the case for thirst. However, it is not a reason to think we have no knowledge of others' subjective feelings but only assess external expressions (e.g., crying), sometimes along with the situations provoking them (e.g., the loss of the person's dog).

The situation is somewhat similar to how we know that other people see the same colors we do. We know in fact that this is not always the case. Some people are color-blind and people with cataracts see colors differently before and after cataract surgery, and there are other clear exceptions as well resulting from various pathologies. Even people whose eyes, optic nerve, visual cortex, etc. are healthy are not going to see colors exactly the same, as the various parts of each individual's visual system are not identical, but their color vision will be very close, given how slight the variations in physiology are. For this reason, most people pass tests for color blindness. People's emotions are subject to greater variation due to the greater number of factors that have an impact on them, such as hormones, sleep, stress level, etc. but to think that we never have any idea how others feel is to treat them as aliens rather than as individuals with whom we share a human physiological make-up.[41] Probably most of us, and perhaps all of us, have had the experience of someone who asks us whether we feel a certain way about such-and-such, and this query being spot-on about how we feel. The facts that we don't know precisely how the other feels because we are not the other and that we can make mistakes about others' feelings are not reasons to deny that we do generally correctly identify the basic emotion that they are feeling and sometimes correctly understand their emotion in more detail.[42]

If it is safe to say that we often know at least approximately how others feel, a question remains as to whether we know this by inferring it. For example, do we reason to the conclusion that this person is sad starting from the general premise that "people who cry in response to something they

41 De Waal, who thinks we can't know how others feel, acknowledges that in people's feelings, the

> body is heavily implicated, though. While we are describing how we feel, we use visceral language, place our hand over our heart or stomach, ball our fists, clasp our head, or clutch ourselves as if we're falling apart. Crying, for example, is much more than a sound. We have trouble breathing, our heartbeat becomes irregular, our diaphragm is weighed down, we have a lump in our throat, our face becomes a puddle. De Waal, *Mama's Last Hug*, 257.

42 It is worth noting that we can refine our understanding of others' emotions by asking them how they feel. And we are able to evaluate their answers in light of our estimation of how honest and/or self-aware they are, while being aware that we may be mistaken about this.

apprehend as being bad are people who are sad," and then applying it to a specific case—"this person is crying in response to something they apprehend as being bad, namely, the loss of their dog," thereby concluding that "this person is sad"? While I think we can do that, we often do not, but instead we gauge another's emotion by relying on our experiential knowledge of emotion. Often when we look at a person's face, we immediately gauge that he or she is in a bad mood or anxious without being able to tell exactly what has made us aware of it, and so are plainly not arriving at how they feel by way of deduction. Also, individuals who know each other well are generally better able to judge each other's emotions; this is clearly due to experience and not to more accurate reasoning. The misjudgments we make at one time or another in regard to others' emotions also indicate that we do not always apply our abstract knowledge of emotion to particular cases. We often fail to think that maybe the others' emotional expression is not true to their actual feelings or that the expression they are displaying does not necessarily correspond to the way we would feel if we displayed that expression. As Aristotle says in regard to action: "Experience seems in no respect inferior to art, and men of experience succeed even better than those who have theory without experience."[43] From what has been said above, we see that the same can be said for the identification of others' emotions.

This opens up the possibility that an animal can recognize another's felt emotion experientially, that is, by means of unconsciously matching the other's display of emotion to a memory of its own emotions. For example, a chimpanzee sees another chimp screeching, mouth wide open, teeth bared, at an aggressor, something that matches its own memory of being angry and screeching, mouth wide open, teeth bared, at an aggressor, with the end result that it recognizes that the angry chimp feels angry.

One might object that the chimp that sees another chimp displaying a mouth wide open, teeth bared, directed toward an aggressor may simply register its facial expression. However, a chimpanzee's fear grimace is intimately connected to the animal's fear, as is the dog's yelp to its feeling of pain. They are unlike facial expressions, such as tongue rolling, which have no connection with any emotion. The chimpanzee's fear grimace, the dog's yelp, and the like are for these animals part of the emotion they feel. Thus, when these expressions of emotion are displayed by others, the animal that

43 Aristotle, *Metaphysics*, bk. 1, chap. 1, 981a15.

has felt like emotion is not going to be able to perceive them without them evoking knowledge of the emotion itself.[44]

To clarify the relationship between expression and emotion: The expression of an emotion simply refers to the part of the emotion that consists in a physiological change, primarily insofar as this change is observable by others, as opposed to being subjectively experienced. When I am embarrassed, you see that my face has turned red, whereas I feel that my face is flushed. My face feeling flushed is part of the emotion of embarrassment. There is virtually universal agreement that emotions are embodied entities. As Aristotle argued long ago:

> It therefore seems the affections of soul involve the body—passion, gentleness, fear, pity, courage, joy, loving, hating; in all these there is the concurrent affection of the body. In support of this we may point to the fact that, while sometimes on the occasion of violent and striking occurrences there is no excitement or fear felt, on others faint and feeble stimulations produce these emotions, viz. when the body is already in a state of tension resembling its condition when we are angry. Here is still a clearer case: in the absence of any external cause of terror we find ourselves experiencing the feelings of a man in terror. From all this it is obvious that the affections of the soul have accounts which refer to matter.[45]

One finds a similar view articulated by modern thinkers as well. For example, de Waal defines emotion, in part, as follows: "An emotion . . . is marked by specific changes in body and mind—brain, hormones, muscles, viscera, heart, alertness, etc."[46] When these changes are observable by others,

44 It is possible in the case of an emotion that one has not felt that one may be able to perceive the expression of it as friendly or unfriendly, either instinctually or through learning. However, once one has experienced that emotion, the other's expression is apt to trigger knowledge of the individual's emotion and not simply of whether the individual is friendly or unfriendly. Note also, in the case of knowledge of an emotion as being about something, there also has to be a perception of similarity of context. One animal can know that another animal is afraid without knowing what it is afraid of, but if that animal is going to know what the other is afraid of, it has to sense the thing provoking the fear in addition to the other's expression. Knowledge of context is also important for emotions that are expressed similarly, e.g., crying, which may be an expression of sadness or of joy.

45 Aristotle, *On the Soul*, bk. 1, chap. 1, 403a16–24, translation of J. A. Smith in McKeon, *The Basic Works of Aristotle*, modified somewhat.

46 De Waal, *Mama's Last Hug*, 85.

we refer to them as "expressions of emotion." Insofar as these changes are experienced in us, they are not so much expressions of emotion as parts of the emotion. Both the perspiring we feel which can be felt or smelled by others and the butterflies in our stomach we feel which cannot be perceived by others are parts of the emotion we experience.

It is especially clear in the case of certain emotions that the physiological changes are part of the emotion itself because we generally do not experience these changes apart from feeling the emotion.[47] One example of this is blushing when embarrassed. While it is true that one's face can be flushed for a variety of reasons, and the feeling is similar to blushing, the feeling is also somewhat different. Similarly, while people perspire when they are hot, in the absence of heat, healthy people do not perspire except when anxious. Yet another physiological change that is generally only experienced when feeling emotion is crying, granted people also cry due to eye irritants such as volatiles from onions. Actors that appear to cry on cue generally only succeed because they think of something that is sad. In addition, our facial expression impacts on how we feel. For example, when we smile voluntarily it has the effect of making us feel happier.[48]

The very nature of emotion, with external expression corresponding to part of the internal feeling, affects the way emotion is known. Humans often do not recognize facial expression apart from recognizing the emotion expressed. Think of how children do not notice the expression of a person who is romantically interested in someone else in the room. The child can see the look on that person's face, but it has no meaning for the child. And while we do have words for facial expressions, such as smile and grimace,

47 See de Waal, *Mama's Last Hug*, 67–68:

> Scientists strenuously objected to Darwin's use of the term expression as too suggestive, as implying that the face conveys what is going on inside. . . . Many psychologists didn't like references to hidden processes. . . . They preferred to stick to observable behavior, and regarded facial display as little flags of different colors that we wave in order to alert those around us to our future behavior. . . . If facial expression were mere flags, we should have no trouble choosing which ones to wave and which to leave folded. Every facial configuration would be as easy to summon as a fake smile. But in fact, we have far less control over our faces than over the rest of our bodies. Like the chimpanzees, we sometimes hide a smile behind a hand (or a book, or a newspaper) because we're simply unable to suppress it.

48 See Nicholas A. Coles et al., "A Meta-Analysis of the Facial Feedback Literature: Effects of Facial Feedback on Emotional Experience Are Small and Variable," *Psychological Bulletin* 145, no. 6 (2019): 610–51.

we are equally likely to describe a face with those expressions as happy or pained. Sometimes we can't even describe the facial expression, voice intonation, etc. by which we recognize that someone has a specific feeling, for example, anxiety when being interviewed. Our perception of expressions of emotion tunes us into the emotion itself; for example, we immediately know that he feels sexual attraction toward her by the way he is looking at her. Consequently, the scientists who sought to obtain objective descriptions of human facial expressions had to invent a way of overcoming our tendency to connect a face's appearance to a specific emotion. The Facial Action Coding System, which identifies the minimal units of facial movement according to the underlying musculature, offers the advantage that "by orienting attention towards individual facial movements, researchers are encouraged to view the face objectively and not be biased by the humans' natural tendency to focus on overall expression configuration (Wallbott and Ricci-Bitti, 1993; Calder et al., 2000). Thus, the face can be described, or coded, objectively using minimal units of measurement without interference from its holistic emotional quality."[49]

People are certainly able to eventually identify expressions of emotion separately from the emotions themselves. However, this does not appear to be what they initially do in the case of emotions that they themselves have experienced. In addition, it requires further experience to recognize that certain emotional expressions can be faked and do not correspond to the person's interior feeling. Prior to learning that, when another's expression corresponds to one's own emotional experience, one will unconsciously match one's own experience of emotion to the other's expression of emotion, rather than perceiving the latter merely as a certain configuration of face or a certain tone of voice, etc. And this will often be the case even when one has learned that people can put on an act and that others' expression of emotion may differ from one's own.

Note that in order to recognize others' emotions when they are expressed visibly, primarily by facial changes, though in some cases also by bodily stance, one needs to be able to relate what one sees to what one knows about the appearance of one's own body through proprioception. Most visible expressions of emotion fall in the category of "invisible" (or "opaque")

49 Lisa A. Parr and Bridget M. Waller, "Understanding Chimpanzee Facial Expression: Insights into the Evolution of Communication," *Social Cognitive and Affective Neuroscience* 1, no. 3 (December 2006): 222–23.

gestures, that is, they are things concerning one's own body that one cannot see, such as how one's face looks when one smiles or cries or sticks out one's tongue. In such cases, in order for an animal, be it human or nonhuman, to recognize others' emotions, it has to be aware through proprioception of its own facial expression (and perhaps also its posture) when it is feeling an emotion, and it has to remember it, and it has to be able to unconsciously match this memory with what it sees on another's face (or in their stance, etc.). If one was not able to recognize one's own angry expression as similar to the angry expression it sees on another's face, then the sight of the other's angry expression could not trigger a recognition of the other's anger.

Do Some Animals Recognize Others' Emotions by Using Sense Experience?

We have seen that experiential knowledge can in principle extend to knowledge of others' emotions. What reasons do we have to think that animals do or do not in fact possess such knowledge?

One reason to reject the notion that animals have knowledge of others' emotions would be if their behavior did not accord with what can be expected on the part of an animal that knows another's emotion. This seems to be the case, for example, when animals experience emotional contagion.[50] An animal can become afraid upon seeing other animals afraid without showing any signs that it is aware of the others' feelings of fear, similar to a baby crying when it hears other babies cry, without displaying any knowledge of the other babies' distress.

A reason to doubt that some animals know others' emotions would be if the animals' apparently emotion-sensitive behavior can be explained more parsimoniously in terms of an emotion-blind instinctive response that has been selected for rather than in terms of a cognitive ability that enables the animal to acquire experiential knowledge of others' emotions; and/or if it can be explained as a learned response based solely on the reading of behavior/expressions rather than on additional knowledge that depends on such reading.

Or maybe some combination of contagion and expression reading can better account for animals' behavior than emotion reading.

50 See Ana Pérez-Manrique and Antoni Gomila, "Emotional Contagion in Non-Human Animals: A Review," *WIREs Cognitive Science* 13, no. 1 (2021): e1560.

We know how an organism that knows others' emotions behaves starting from our own knowledge of others' emotions. One kind of behavior we expect from emotion readers is that they will use this knowledge to predict others' behavior. For example, if an animal knows that another animal is in an aggressive mood, it can predict that that animal might harm it if approached. However, the more parsimonious expression-reading hypothesis equally well explains such predictions, for example, an animal can recognize that a certain expression on another animal's face means that it is liable to attack it.

Another kind of behavior to be expected from emotion readers is that they use their knowledge of others' emotions to judge whether the thing toward which these emotions are directed is fearful, disgusting, desirable, or something else. Both chimpanzees and dogs approach or avoid things toward which humans display happiness or fear, respectively.[51] However, here too the expression-reading hypothesis presents itself as the simpler option. Instead of the animal knowing that the other animal (or human) is pleased or distressed by what it is looking at, it can simply take the other animal's facial expression as a cue to avoid or approach that thing. Certain facial expressions correlate with the presence of something beneficial and others with something harmful.

Yet another kind of behavior to be expected from emotion readers is one that addresses the emotional state of another individual. This would include reassuring fearful individuals, consoling sad individuals, and appeasing/calming angry ones.

Studies on appeasement of victorious aggressors do not provide evidence that the appeasing parties are trying to alleviate the aggressors' angry feelings. Pallante et al., in their study of macaques, conclude that while a macaque's appeasement appears to calm the aggressor, appeasing behavior is best interpreted as strategic behavior that benefits the bystander by preventing the aggressor from redirecting its aggression toward it, which then, as a by-product, benefits the group by promoting its stability.[52] Romero et al. conclude in their study of appeasement in chimpanzees that it is not motivated by concern for the aggressive party's feelings but is a political

51 See C. L. Russell et al.,"Social Referencing by Young Chimpanzees (*Pan troglodytes*)," *Journal of Comparative Psychology* 111, no. 2 (1997): 185–93, and Isabella Merola et al.,"Dogs' Social Referencing Towards Owners and Strangers," *PLoS ONE* 7, no. 10 (2012), e47653.

52 Virginia Pallante et al.,"Calming an Aggressor Through Spontaneous Post-Conflict Triadic Contacts: Appeasement in *Macaca tonkeana*," *Aggressive Behavior* 44, no. 4 (2018): 406–15.

strategy "to reduce the spread of aggression or to demonstrate support for the aggressor or existing alliances to others."[53] Perhaps other studies will reveal empathic concern on the animals' part. In any case, human appeasement of angry parties is often motivated by a desire to prevent further aggression, and not by concern for the aggressor's feelings, and so appeasement is not the best place to look for whether an animal is concerned about others' emotions.

Consoling behavior: evidence that it is present in animals

A more promising avenue is consoling behavior, which has as its immediate goal alleviating an individual's emotional distress. A typical example of this kind of behavior in humans is speaking softly to a sad person while gently touching him or her. While the vast majority of animal species do not exhibit consoling behavior, there are a number of species that do, including chimpanzees, bonobos, mountain gorillas, western lowland gorillas, Tonkean macaques, ravens, and elephants.[54] Some researchers decline to speak of animals as consoling recipients of aggression, preferring to refer to such behavior as "third-party affiliation" and/or define consoling behavior in purely behavioral terms, so as to avoid attributing any specific intention to the animals performing it.[55] I will examine here whether such reticence is warranted.

Frans de Waal was one of the first to observe what appears to be a specific type of consoling behavior among chimps. After a combat between chimps, a bystander that was uninvolved in the fight will sometimes comfort

53 Teresa Romero et al., "Post-Conflict Affiliation by Chimpanzees with Aggressors: Other-Oriented Versus Selfish Political Strategy," *PLoS ONE* 6, no. 7 (July 2011), e22173, 5.

54 See M. R. Lindegaard et al., "Consolation in the Aftermath of Robberies Resembles Post-Aggression Consolation in Chimpanzees," *PLoS ONE* 12, no. 5 (May 31, 2017): e0177725, 2. See also Joshua M. Plotnik and Frans B. M. de Waal, "Asian Elephants (*Elephas maximus*) Reassure Others in Distress," *PeerJ*, 10.7717/peerj.278 (2014).

55 Manrique et al. specifically exclude a consideration of the underlying motives of sympathetic concern in their study on empathy: "Herein we do not consider the underlying motives of behaviour in characterizing these phenomena. Instead, we operationalize sympathetic concern and personal distress in terms of the type of reaction and response triggered by the perception of others' distress and its main effects." Ana Pérez-Manrique and Antoni Gomila, "The Comparative Study of Empathy: Sympathetic Concern and Empathic Perspective-Taking in Non-Human Animals," *Biological Review, Cambridge Philosophical Society* 93, no. 1 (February 2018): 250.

the loser, for example, "gently put[ting] an arm around his or her shoulders."[56] De Waal testifies to having seen thousands of such behaviors.

In addition, animals have been observed to exhibit consoling behavior toward humans. Preston and de Waal recount that:

> In home tests of empathy with children, the family pet often responded with consolation to the adult feigning distress (Zahn-Waxler et al. 1984). Lucy, a chimpanzee raised by a human family is anecdotally described as exhibiting efforts to break up conflicts, running to comfort the wife when ill, exhibiting "protectiveness toward her, bringing her food, sharing her own food, or . . . attempting to comfort by stroking and grooming her (Temerlin 1975, p. 165)."[57]

Many dog owners would vouch for what is being said here.

Animals' emotional well-being is important for their survival. We see this in the case of certain domestic animals. Dogs and cats display behaviors similar to human grieving when they lose their human or animal companion. They may lose their appetite, lose weight, be listless, and/or show a loss of interest in physical activity, and even die.[58] If the well-being of individuals in a group depends on the overall well-being of the group or on the well-being of specific "friends" of theirs within the group, it would be advantageous for those individuals to be able to recognize the emotional state of other group members so as to be able to identify those in need of some form of consolation.

56 Frans de Waal, *Primates and Philosophers* (Princeton University Press, 2006), 33. See also de Waal, *The Age of Empathy*, 90: "I have seen literally thousands of consolations—that's how common the behavior is. We have a massive database, compiled over many years, to tell us what happens after spontaneous fights among chimpanzees. Consolation is the most typical outcome."

57 Preston and de Waal, "Empathy: Its Ultimate and Proximate Bases," *Behavioral and Brain Sciences* 25, no. 1 (2002): 17.

58 See Alexandra Anastasio, "Do Dogs Grieve the Loss of Their Human Owners?," American Kennel Club, updated November 2023, https://www.akc.org/expert-advice/lifestyle/do-dogs-grieve/. See also de Waal, *The Age of Empathy*, 10:

> And then there was our Siamese Cat, Sarah, who had been adopted as a kitten by our big tomcat, Diego, who would lick and clean her, let her knead his tummy as if she were nursing, and sleep with her. For about a decade they were best buddies, until Diego died of old age. Even though Sarah was younger and in perfect health, she stopped eating and died two months after Diego for no reason that the veterinarian could determine.

Consoling behavior: Would it be beneficial to consolers to know others' emotions?

The question that remains is: Are the animals who console others aware of the others' emotions or are they simply responding in an emotion-blind way to others' visual/vocal expression of emotion? One question that arises here is whether an animal would be better off were it to know that another animal felt a certain way. If not, it diminishes the likelihood that such an ability would be selected for. It is sometimes suggested that knowledge of others' emotions makes for better social interaction, but a question remains as to how.

In the case of humans, it is beneficial for us to know other people's emotions in order to gauge their future actions. However, it is also useful for us to be able to recognize that people are altering the expression of their emotions; it allows us to be tactful and considerate, as well as to avoid being duped. Humans learn to alter the expression of their emotions partly due to constraints coming from what is considered socially acceptable, and partly due to advantages that can be derived in specific situations from misleading others as to our true feelings. With experience we become aware of the potential discrepancy between expressions of emotion and what a person is actually feeling. We also eventually learn what it means for someone to hurt our feelings, that we can hurt others' feelings, and that we should show concern for others' feelings. We grow to expect that others will make an effort to read our feelings and take them into account, and we sometimes rebuke people by telling them, "You don't know how I feel."

Understanding the moral imperatives related to others' emotional lives depends on reason and thus is beyond the animal's ken. However, an animal could in principle acquire experiential knowledge that another was hiding its emotion. There are accounts of animals appearing to hide their own expressions of emotion, either by simply turning away so that the other cannot see them or by putting a hand in front of their face.[59] In one case, a chimpanzee was observed to manipulate its lips several times so as to remove its fear grin before turning to face another chimpanzee.[60] If in addition to self-experience of this sort, an animal also had experience of a discrepancy

59 See Mariska E. Kret et al., "Emotional Expressions in Human and Non-Human Great Apes," *Neuroscience & Behavioral Reviews* 115 (August 2020): 383.

60 See Casey Kirkpatrick, "Tactical Deception and the Great Apes: Insight into the Question of Theory of Mind," *Totem* 15 (2006–7): 32.

between another animal's expression and behavior, for example, of an animal that had a friendly expression on its face but then went on to bite it, it seems the former animal could become wary of being duped. If this were to occur, the question would still arise as to whether it is wary that the other is masking aggressive feelings or simply masking an expression that would portend potential attack. So, we are back to the question of whether it would be more beneficial for animals to recognize how another feels in place of merely responding to the other's facial and other emotional expressions.

Looking again at humans, all things being equal, the more we know how a person feels, the more motivated we are to address whatever is provoking the others' feelings. People who have undergone similar sufferings are more apt to show compassion to those who are experiencing like sufferings than those who have not (granted the latter can make an effort to put themselves in the others' shoes, thereby eliciting similar compassion).[61] This fact, however, does not give us reason to favor the emotion-reading hypothesis over the expression-reading hypothesis in the case of animals because there is no way of comparing the motivation of an expression-only reader to that of an emotion reader.

One might argue that there is benefit to the animal knowing others' emotions by pointing to the situation of people with autism who are limited in their ability to recognize others' emotions. Temple Grandin says, "Since I don't have any social intuitions, I rely on pure logic, like an expert computer

61 There is a well-known experiment in which two rhesus monkeys are in neighboring cages and can see each other. One monkey has a chain that it can pull which results in food being delivered to it. Pulling the chain also administers a shock to the monkey in the other cage. Monkeys will forgo pulling the chain for varying periods of time, and thus also forgo eating, in order to avoid shocking the other monkey. Those rhesus monkeys that had themselves been on the receiving end of shocks were more likely to refrain from pulling the chain than those that had not. This seems to indicate that knowing in a distinct way how the other feels is more motivating than simply viewing the others' generic signs of pain. However, perhaps the monkeys with the experience of having been shocked are simply more motivated by a desire to avoid creating a situation reminiscent of their own past sufferings. See J. H. Masserman et al., "'Altruistic' Behavior in Rhesus Monkeys," *American Journal of Psychiatry* 121 (December 1964): 584–85. See also J. J. Lavery and P. J. Foley, "Altruism or Arousal in the Rat?," *Science* 140, no. 3563 (April 1963): 172, abstract: "If rats are exposed successively to white noise, then to recorded rat squeals, or alternatively to squeals first and then white noise, and if, in both situations, they are allowed to shut off the auditory stimulation by applying pressure on a bar, they will touch the bar more frequently when exposed to white noise." While this does not show that the rats responding to other rats' squeals are not acting altruistically, it does show that there is an alternative explanation for their behavior.

programmer, to guide my behavior."[62] This approach to social relationships is clearly less successful as an approach than one that is based on recognizing others' emotions.[63] It would seem then that an animal that knew how others felt would engage in more socially appropriate behavior than one that only monitored external cues. On the other hand, animal social interactions are far less complex than human social interactions, and so perhaps it would suffice for animals to monitor external cues.

I acknowledge that it is doubtful whether it would benefit animals to know others' emotions since expression-monitoring alone may well suffice to meet animals' needs. On the other hand, we have no reason to rule out the possibility that it may be beneficial. Thus, it is worth considering apparent consoling behavior in animals to see whether there are signs that it is genuine, that is, whether it is really directed to mitigating the sadness the animal perceives in another animal.

Does consoling behavior console?

Koski and Sterck question the notion of consolation in chimpanzees on the grounds that in their study, the purportedly consoled chimpanzees were not consoled, that is, either their distress was not alleviated, or they were not even distressed to begin with.[64] However, research by Fraser et al. found that consoling behavior does reduce stress in consoled chimpanzees.[65] I do not

62 Grandin, *Thinking in Pictures*, 108.

63 See Oliver Sacks, "An Anthropologist on Mars," *New Yorker*, December 27, 1993:

> In one plant she [Temple Grandin] designed, she said, there has been repeated breakdowns of the machinery, but these occurred only when a particular man, John, was in the room. She "correlated" these incidents and inferred at last that John must be sabotaging the equipment. "I had to learn to be suspicious, I had to learn it cognitively. I could put two and two together, but I couldn't see the jealous look on his face."

64 Sonja E. Koski and Elisabeth H. M. Sterck, "Triadic Postconflict Affiliation in Captive Chimpanzees: Does Consolation Console?," *Animal Behaviour* 73, no. 1 (2007): 133: "We tested whether consolation alleviates postconflict stress in captive chimpanzees, *Pan troglodytes*. . . . We collected 643 postconflict–matched control pairs on aggressees and 576 on aggressors. Consolation occurred equally frequently with aggressees and aggressors. However, we found no evidence that consolation alleviated stress, regardless of the identity of the consoler. In addition, consolation was also directed to conflict participants with no evident postconflict stress."

65 See Orlaith N. Fraser et al., "Stress Reduction Through Consolation in Chimpanzees," https://www.pnas.org/doi/10.1073/pnas.0804141105, *PNAS* 105, no. 25 (June 24, 2008): 8557–62. "A total of 234 PC–MC [postconflict–matched control observational] pairs was collected on 22 recipients of aggression involving 129 distinct aggressor–recipient dyads."

know how to account for the discrepancy. I am going to assume here that at least sometimes consoling behavior does console.

Arguments pro and con as to the genuineness of consoling behavior

Romero et al. offer reasons in favor of empathic awareness of others' emotions as being at the root of chimpanzees' consoling behavior. First, the behavior itself is very similar to human behavior: "The reactions of chimpanzees to distressed others resemble those of humans in both social context and morphology (e.g., touching, hugging, kissing)."[66] This along with our close genetic relationship to chimpanzees is reason to think that chimpanzees and humans alike may be motivated by concern for others' feelings.

In addition, the predictions that are made on the basis of the hypothesis that empathy underlies chimpanzee consoling behavior turn out to obtain: "It occurred disproportionately between socially close individuals and was more typical of females. Consolation also tended to be reciprocated, suggesting that it is an integrated part of mutually beneficial relationships."[67] In addition, "consolation was more often directed at victims who had not reconciled their conflict than at those who had. . . . As predicted if empathy is the main motivation, the increased rate of consolation in the absence of reconciliation may be a response to greater distress."[68]

One might ask, though, whether the expression-reading hypothesis might account for such behavior equally well. Other animal behaviors, such as emitting alarm calls, depend on kin being in the proximity, and there are other examples of reciprocal altruism, for example, in regard to grooming. It is also not surprising that consolation is more often exhibited by females, as one would expect them to be better expression readers, given that they care for the young. And if the expressions of dejection of unreconciled animals are more marked, one would expect more acts of consolation would be directed toward them than toward the reconciled losers of a fight. As for similarity of behaviors with humans who console, similarity may arise from different causes; for example, the linguistic performance of young

66 Teresa Romero et al., "Consolation as Possible Expression of Sympathetic Concern Among Chimpanzees," *PNAS* 107, no. 27 (July 6, 2010): 12110.

67 Romero et al., "Consolation as Possible Expression of Sympathetic Concern," 12110.

68 Romero et al., 12112.

chimpanzees resembles that of young humans, but the chimpanzees never acquire language.

Romero et al. acknowledge that when chimpanzees console others there may be an element of wanting to eliminate a situation stressful to themselves. They note that "the first expressions of consolation in humans, around 1 y of age, have elements of both providing and receiving comfort, and that both elements may be also present in chimpanzee consolation."[69] The authors argue, though, that if a chimpanzee's expression of emotion is causing distress to another, that other should simply move away from the victim instead of approaching it to console it.

One might counter that natural selection in the form of group selection could favor comforting the victim as a means of relieving the consoler's stress, as this would in addition benefit the victim by reducing its stress.

However, there are reasons to question this solution. The first is that consolers do not always display stress. An instance of this is recounted by de Waal: "One young chimpanzee hugged, kissed, and groomed his favourite caregiver when she displayed fear at a novel toy. This infant chimpanzee did not exhibit any fear, recognized the fear displayed in the caregiver, and exhibited an empathetic response."[70] It is possible that the chimpanzee experienced some low level of contagious fear or distress. De Waal's observation did not involve monitoring physiological changes in animals that are associated with increased stress, as some recent studies have done. That being said, there are other situations in which the animal observing another's expression does not catch the same emotion, for example, a subordinate does not become aggressive upon seeing a superior's expression of aggression, and nor does the superior take on its subordinate's expression of fear. So, it is quite possible that de Waal's observation was accurate.

More tellingly, in cases where contagion is present, if approaching the victim has been selected for as a means of alleviating the consoler's own distress, then the more distressed the consoler is, the more likely it should be that it approaches the victim, at least up to a point. However, the pattern that consoling behavior follows is rather that its "performance is best at a moderate level of arousal and decreases with an increase or a decrease in this

69 Romero et al., 12113.

70 Preston and de Waal, "Empathy: Its Ultimate and Proximate Bases," 26.

level of stress."[71] This pattern is best explained by positing that the consoler's primary aim is to alleviate the other's distress. When the animal only feels slight distress upon other's distress, it is insufficiently motivated to console, as it does not regard the other as in any real need of consolation. When the animal feels extreme distress upon another's distress, it becomes too absorbed by its own emotion to direct actions toward others. Accordingly, one would expect that the consolers who are better able to manage their own distress will be those who are more likely to console than those who are poor at managing their own distress. As Roth-Hananiaa et al. note, this is the case in children:

> An important variable affecting whether empathic arousal will lead to concern for the other or to self-focused distress is the individual's ability to regulate negative emotional arousal. Studies with children have shown that the ability to self-regulate negative emotions effectively leads to greater empathic concern (sympathy) to others' distress, whereas poor regulatory capacities reduce the likelihood of sympathy and increase self-distress reactions.[72]

Consoling behavior increases with the ability to not be distressed by others' distress, contrary to what is to be expected on the hypothesis that it is driven by a desire to relieve the consoler's stress. This is not to deny that consolers may have mixed motives; we know that from our own experience of consoling others. However, when consoling behavior in individuals increases with self-regulation over time and when the individuals that display better self-regulation console more often, this is a strong indication that the behavior is at least partly motivated by a concern for the other's distress.

In a study done by Clay and de Waal with bonobos, it turned out that the bonobos that were better at regulating their own emotions (as determined by their speed of recovery from self-distress) were the individuals that more frequently consoled others: "Consistent with the ER [emotional regulation] framework, a Spearman correlation revealed a solid relationship across individuals between faster recovery as a victim and offering consolation to others

71 Emily M. Sanford et al., "Timmy's in the Well: Empathy and Prosocial Helping in Dogs," *Learning & Behavior* 46 (2018): 383.

72 Ronit Roth-Hananiaa et al., "Empathy Development from 8 to 16 Months: Early Signs of Concern for Others," *Infant Behavior & Development* 34, no. 3 (2011): 448.

as a bystander."[73] The authors themselves acknowledge that their study was based on a relatively small number of individuals (thirty-six), pointing to the need for further research. That being said, their results follow the same pattern seen in human children.

While the above renders it unlikely that the bonobo consolers were acting primarily to alleviate their own distress, a question remains as to whether their behavior is elicited solely by others' expressions of emotion, or whether they are like children whose behavior by a certain age is also elicited by their knowledge of others' feelings. I will come back to this question later on.

Two other signs that consoling behavior is genuine

Two other signs that an animal is displaying genuine consolation (signs that are used in testing humans) are that it seeks to know the cause of the distress and it displays facial expressions of concern.

Most of the time when chimpanzees exhibit consoling behavior, it is because they have observed the distressed party to have lost a fight, so the cause of the distressed party's distress is known to the consolers. Anecdotally, one chimpanzee appeared to seek the cause of why its owner was crying. Nadia Kohts recounts that when she cried her home-raised chimpanzee "tenderly takes my chin in its palm, lightly touches my face with his finger, as though trying to understand what is happening, and turns around, clenching his toes into firm fists."[74] Admittedly this is Kohts's subjective judgment about her chimpanzee's behavior.

It is unfortunate that great apes apparently do not exhibit affective expressions of apparent concern for victims, as do humans, who make "a sympathetic face in which eyebrows are drawn down and brow drawn up over the nose."[75] At least none are mentioned by distinguished observers, such as de Waal. Though great apes and humans have similar facial musculature, humans have more expressive faces and display more emotions than great apes do.[76] Even some humans, however, display emotion facially to a

73 Zanna Clay and Frans B. M. de Waal, "Development of Socio-emotional Competence in Bonobos," *PNAS* 110, no. 45 (November 5, 2013): 18123.

74 De Waal, *The Age of Empathy*, 86.

75 Roth-Hananiaa et al., "Empathy Development from 8 to 16 Months," 451.

76 See Kret et al., "Emotional Expressions in Human and Non-Human Great Apes," 379. See also Anne M. Burrows, "The Facial Expression Musculature in Primates and Its Evolutionary

very limited extent, so I do not take the absence of concerned expressions on the part of apes to be a strong sign that they lack concern for others' feelings.

Evidence other than consoling behavior indicating that some animals are aware of others' emotion

If we look for evidence of animals' awareness of others' emotion outside of the context of consolation, there is a study in which chimpanzees were required

> to categorize emotional video scenes presented on a computer monitor by matching them to conspecific facial expressions with similar emotional valence, so that matching was based on emotional similarity instead of perceptual features (Parr, 2001). Without previous training, chimpanzees spontaneously matched positive or negative video scenes to conspecific facial expressions according to their shared emotional valence, suggesting an ability to discriminate facial expressions on the basis of their underlying emotional states.[77]

For example, the chimpanzees, after being shown a video featuring darts, choose the picture of a chimpanzee with a fear grimace rather than of one with a play face. In other words, the chimpanzee, upon seeing an item that causes it fear, matches it with the face of a chimpanzee expressing fear.[78] One could, however, maintain that these chimpanzees had prior experience of witnessing other animals' expressions in similar situations and so they pick the picture displaying the appropriate facial expression in function of this experience, and not because they recognize others' emotions. One wonders whether this could be controlled for. If an animal that had experienced

Significance," *BioEssays* 30, no. 3 (March 2008): 220. See also de Waal, *Mama's Last Hug*, 55–56, in regard to blushing and frowning in concentration.

77 Filippo Aureli and Andrew Whiten, "Emotions and Behavioral Flexibility," in *Primate Psychology*, ed. Dario Maestripieri (Harvard University Press, 2003), 311.

78 See Lisa A. Parr, "Cognitive and Physiological Markers of Emotional Awareness in Chimpanzees (*Pan troglodytes*)," *Animal Cognition* 4, nos. 3–4 (2001): 227:

> It may be that temperature decreases in response to the DART scenes reflected the subjects' own fear when exposed to these highly aversive stimuli, or an empathic fear in seeing conspecifics being injected with needles (INJ). There is no doubt that chimpanzees respond aversively to these stimuli when they themselves, or their cagemates, are approached by the veterinarians for their annual medical survey. Further studies are needed to determine whether these results are indeed indicative of empathic processes.

being darted itself but never seen another animal darted would pick out the picture in which the conspecific had a fearful expression, it seems one could eliminate that it was simply doing so on the basis of associating the event of being darted with a specific facial expression. Unfortunately, it could be the case that the animal would pick the picture of the conspecific with the fearful expression due to generalizing that that is the expression it sees on others' faces when those others are exposed to any kind of threat.

Evidence at the level of the brain that consoling behavior is genuine

I will return now to the question of whether the behavior of bonobo consolers is elicited solely by others' expressions of emotion, or whether they are like children, whose behavior by a certain age is also elicited by the others' feelings. Some weak evidence that the bonobos are not responding to expression alone lies in similarities between their brains and ours in the parts related to emotional cognition in us. This evidence is weak because we do not fully understand the cerebral organization and activity needed for humans to perceive others' emotion.[79] Consequently, even if an animal's brain manifested similar organization and activity, we could not be sure that it was not missing some crucial component for recognition of others' emotions. Still, similarities at the level of the brain between what is known to be requisite in humans for the recognition of others' emotions and what is found in a given species of animal's brains does suggest that the latter serves the same function that it does in humans; and this suggestive evidence becomes increasingly compelling as more and more counterparts in the animal brain are discovered.[80]

Rilling et al. compared chimpanzee and bonobo brains, using as a point of reference what is understood to be needed for empathy in humans:

> Psychopathy, a disorder marked by lack of empathy, is associated with reduced size and function of the amygdala (Gordon et al., 2004; Yang et al., 2009), as well as reduced functional connectivity between the

79 It is sometimes suggested that mirror neurons are involved in emotion recognition, though in the literature they are more often associated with action recognition. See de Waal, *Mama's Last Hug*, 95: "Mirror neurons probably help primates imitate others, such as when they open a box the way a trained model does, when they synchronize with each other when pressing buttons, and when in the wild they remove the seeds from a fruit the way their mother does."

80 Note that discrepancies between the human brain and another mammalian brain would not allow one to rule out that the mammal in question was able to know others' emotions.

> amygdala and ventromedial prefrontal cortex (VMPFC) (Marsh et al., 2008). These results and others have led to the hypothesis that the pathway from the amygdala to the VMPFC is involved in perceiving distress in others and in learning to avoid behaviors that provoke such distress (Blair, 2008). Our results show that bonobos have more gray matter in the dorsal amygdala and a larger pathway linking the amygdala with VMPFC compared with chimpanzees.[81]

Rilling et al. add further evidence of relevant brain similarities. They observe that high testosterone levels in humans have a negative effect on the pathway from the amygdala to the VMPFC, and that bonobo males are lower in testosterone than chimpanzee males. They also point to the fact that the anterior insula is strongly implicated in empathy in humans and that bonobos have more grey matter there than chimpanzees "specifically within the ventral region that is consistently associated with social-emotional processing."[82] They conclude: "Thus, the neurobiological characteristics that differentiate chimpanzees from bonobos bear a striking similarity to those that differentiate patients with empathy deficits from normal controls."[83] The similarities between bonobo brains and human brains that are revealed by Rilling et al.'s comparison, weigh, if only very slightly, in favor of bonobos knowing others' emotions.

It may be the case that Rilling et al.'s characterization of chimpanzees as empathy-deficient is exaggerated. For one, the point they make about testosterone does not apply to chimpanzee females and they, rather than the males, are the ones that engage in the majority of consoling. Also, Kim and Kret mention some similarities to human processing of emotion that are found in chimpanzees, for example, "brain lateralization when processing emotional expressions . . . and specific event-related potential (ERP) waveforms elicited by affective pictures."[84] This provides some weak evidence that chimpanzees too know others' emotions. There may well be other similarities between human and animal brain activity vis-à-vis emotion recognition in

81 James K. Rilling et al., "Differences Between Chimpanzees and Bonobos in Neural Systems Supporting Social Cognition," *Social Cognitive and Affective Neuroscience* 7, no. 4 (2012): 374.

82 Rilling et al., "Differences Between Chimpanzees and Bonobos in Neural Systems," 375.

83 Rilling et al., 375.

84 Yena Kim and Mariska Kret, "The Emotional Expressions and Emotion Perception in Nonhuman Primates," in the *Oxford Handbook of Emotional Development*, ed. Daniel Dukes (Oxford University Press, 2022), 136.

the current literature that I am unaware of, and we can hope that the list of similarities will grow as more research on both humans and other animals is done.

Perhaps the following experiment would help determine whether great apes only discriminate expressions of emotion and not the emotions of others as well. First, the brain activity of human individuals in two situations would be monitored, one in which the individuals are to identify facial expressions but are only given nonemotion-related words to do so (e.g., sides of mouth curved up vs. down) and the other in which the individuals are to identify facial expressions in terms of the emotion expressed (e.g., happy vs. sad). Assuming that the brain activity is different in each case, one would test great ape individuals by showing them pictures of conspecifics with distinctive emotional expressions and then compare their brain activities to the those of humans in the two conditions. If their brain activity resembled that of humans in both conditions, that would be evidence that they recognize emotion in addition to facial expression, whereas if their brain activity only resembled that of humans identifying facial expressions in physical terms, that would cast doubt on whether they recognized the emotions as well.

Visual-proprioceptive matching supports the notion that animals know others' emotions

There are two other things that point to knowledge of others' emotions by great apes, the first of which is their ability to do visual-proprioceptive matching. As was explained earlier, in order for an animal to be able to recognize others' emotions when they are expressed visibly, it has to be able to relate what it sees to what it knows about the appearance of its own body through proprioception. If an animal is to recognize others' emotion, it has to first be aware through proprioception of its own facial expression when it is feeling that emotion, and it has to remember it, and it has to be able to unconsciously match this memory with what it sees on another's face. If an animal cannot recognize its own sad expression as similar to the sad expression it sees on another animal, then the sight of the sad expression of another animal could not trigger in it a recognition of the other's sadness.

Animals that are capable of imitating others' expressions are able to connect what they see with what they feel in their own bodies. There appear to be different forms of imitative ability in living things. Neonatal imitation is often presented as extending to a very limited number of invisible or opaque gestures and is thought to not be under voluntary control, though some question this and perhaps it varies in different organisms.[85] Unconscious rapid imitation of facial expressions and bodily movement is also present in adult animals of a number of species.[86] Mature imitation extends to a wide variety of opaque gestures and is voluntary. I will leave it to scientists to sort out whether these forms of imitation are really different, and if so, how they are related, and then, if different, which one or ones are crucial for recognizing others' emotions through vision. It suffices for my purposes to know that great apes display neonatal imitation,[87] mature imitation,[88] and unconscious facial mimicry,[89] and so are able to connect what they see to how their body appears as known through proprioception.[90] The possession of this ability does not prove that great apes have the ability to recognize other's emotions. However, it increases the likelihood that they are able to do so, as this ability is a necessary condition for doing so.

85 See Kim A. Bard, "Neonatal Imitation in Chimpanzees (*Pan troglodytes*) Tested with Two Paradigms," *Animal Cognition* 10 (2007): 233–34:

> Neonatal imitation in human infants was brought to scientific attention almost 30 years ago (Meltzoff and Moore 1977; Maratos 1982), and remains a popular and still controversial topic. . . . Some argue that only some behaviors are imitated, e.g., tongue protrusions (Anisfeld 1996), however, the majority of labs find evidence for neonatal imitation of multiple behaviors. Not every newborn that arrives in the lab exhibits imitation. . . . The function of neonatal imitation is also debated: some argue that neonatal imitation is a developmental precursor for later imitative abilities; some argue that neonatal imitation serves its function only in the perinatal period, as a "transient ontogenetic adaptation" (Bjorklund 1987, p 89) as the ability declines after 2 months of age.

See also Janine Oostenbroek et al., "Comprehensive Longitudinal Study Challenges the Existence of Neonatal Imitation in Humans," *Current Biology* 26, no. 10 (2016): 1334–38.

86 See Elaine Hatfield et al., "Primitive Emotional Contagion," in *Emotion and Social Behavior*, ed. M. S. Clark (Sage Publications, 1992), 158–59.

87 See Bard, "Neonatal Imitation in Chimpanzees," 233–42.

88 Lara Carrasco et al., "New Evidence on Imitation in an Enculturated Chimpanzee (*Pan troglodytes*)," *Journal of Comparative Psychology* 123, no. 4 (2009): 385–90.

89 See Kret, et al., "Emotional Expressions in Human and Non-Human Great Apes," 391: "Play-wrestling chimpanzees can show both rapid facial mimicry (of the play face, response within 1 s from the triggering play face) and delayed facial mimicry (response from 1 to 5 s from the triggering stimulus) suggestive of some intentionality (Palagi et al., 2018). In gorillas, only rapid facial mimicry was observed."

90 Most great apes are able to recognize that they are being imitated and display mirror self-recognition, both of which depend upon the ability to match what is seen to what is known about one's own body through proprioception.

Infant-mother imitative interactions as weak support for animals' knowledge of others' emotions

A second thing that points toward knowledge of others' emotions by great apes are infant-mother interactions that are apt to facilitate the knowledge of certain emotions. The ideal situation for how an individual could learn to know others' emotions that are displayed visually seems to be that where an infant's emotion is mirrored back to it by its mother. The infant then can come to associate the mother's expression, which it knows itself to have on its face, with the emotion it itself is feeling. As Jonsson et al. put it:

> Malatesta (1980) found mothers responded with imitation to their infants' expressions of categorical affects, as if the mothers were waiting for recognizable emotional displays and then responding by accentuating the infant's emotional displays with an expression change of their own. The theoretical importance of imitation has also been underlined by Malatesta and Izard (1984) who maintain that expressions imitated by the parent permit the infant to view simultaneously and feel an affect, thereby aiding the discrimination of emotions.[91]

Also, the infant's imitation of its mother's expressions can lead it to feeling the same emotion that she is feeling, which may eventually become the basis for recognizing the other's emotion upon witnessing its expression.[92] Contagion can take place without the one contracting the other's emotion knowing how the other feels. However, contagion could provide a foothold for learning to recognize others' emotions, since the individual feeling the emotion contracted simultaneously senses the expression of emotion of the one whom it contracted it from.

91 Carl-Otto Jonsson et al., "How Do Mothers Signal Shared Feeling-States to Their Infants? An Investigation of Affect Attunement and Imitation During the First Year of Life," *Scandinavian Journal of Psychology* 42, no. 4 (September 2001): 378.

92 See Carme Isern-Mas and Antoni Gomila, "Making Sense of Emotional Contagion," *Humana.Mente Journal of Philosophical Studies* 35 (2019): 72–73:

> Despite the importance of emotional contagion, we still lack a satisfactory account of how it works. The principal theory is mimicry theory (Hatfield et al., 1992, 1993, 2009). According to mimicry theory, emotional contagion is mediated by an automatic process of mimicry of the expressive movements perceived which induces the same emotional state in the viewer. Yet emotional contagion is not always a context-independent response, and it is not always mediated by motor mimicry.

One would predict then that animals that know others' emotions when visibly expressed would, in infancy, engage in facial imitation (mother-child or child-mother or both). In the case of humans, even in those cultures where the caregiving of infants does not privilege face-to-face exchanges between mother and infant, some such exchanges with the mother and with others do occur. In rhesus macaques, facial communicative exchanges occur in mother-infant dyads, and neonatal imitation is included among these interactions.[93] In the case of chimpanzees as well, infants engage in eye contact with their mother and are known to display neonatal imitation of humans in experimental settings.[94] I grant that this does not establish that there is affect mirroring going in the macaques and chimpanzees, as these interactions may simply serve some emotion-blind communicative purpose.[95] Still, future research may weigh in favor of some affect mirroring.[96]

93 See Pier Francesco Ferrari et al., "Reciprocal Face-to-Face Communication Between Rhesus Macaque Mothers and Their Newborn Infants," *Current Biology* 19, no. 20 (2009): 1770–71:

> Human mothers interact emotionally with their newborns through exaggerated facial expressions, speech, mutual gaze, and body contact, a capacity that has long been considered uniquely human. Current developmental psychological theories propose that this pattern of mother infant exchange promotes the regulation of infant emotions and serves as a precursor of more complex forms of social exchange including perspective taking and empathy. Here we report that in rhesus macaques, mother-infant pairs also communicate intersubjectively via complex forms of emotional exchanges including exaggerated lipsmacking, sustained mutual gaze, mouth-mouth contacts, and neonatal imitation.

94 See Kim A. Bard and Takeshi Kishimoto, "Early Communicative Gestures in Human and Chimpanzee 1-Year-Olds Observed Across Diverse Socioecological Settings," *Learning & Behavior* 55, no. 1 (2023): 24. This study compared thirty human infants (twelve to fourteen months old) with twenty-one chimpanzee infants of the same age and discovered that the chimpanzee infants held eye contact for two or more seconds almost five times more frequently than did the human infants. See also Bard, "Neonatal Imitation in Chimpanzees," 233–42.

95 People imitate chimpanzees in the zoo and the chimpanzees imitate people, not for the purpose of emotion recognition but simply to establish a connection between one another. See Tomas Persson et al., "Spontaneous Cross-species Imitation in Interactions Between Chimpanzees and Zoo Visitors," *Primates* 59, no. 1 (2018): 19, abstract: "In this observational study, we documented interactions between chimpanzees and zoo visitors and found that the two species imitated each other at a similar rate, corresponding to almost 10% of all produced actions. Imitation appeared to accomplish a social-communicative function, as cross-species interactions that contained imitative actions lasted significantly longer than interactions without imitation."

96 See Zanna Clay et al., "Comparative Perspectives of Empathy Development: Insights from Chimpanzees and Bonobos," in Dukes, *Oxford Handbook*, 284: "The rich and highly

Conclusion in regard to animals' knowledge of others' emotions

Combing through the various studies and observations of animals relevant to the question of whether they know others' emotions has turned up scant evidence, and all of it is either doubtful or circumstantial. The animals that seem most likely to know others' emotions are bonobos and chimpanzees. In the case of the bonobo, the correspondence between their emotion regulation and consoling behavior points to their consoling behavior being genuinely other-directed rather than simply being a means of alleviating the consoler's contracted distress. However, this correspondence was found in a single study with a small sample size. Secondly, there are a number of similarities at the level of the brain between what is currently known to be needed for human knowledge of others' emotions and what is found in bonobo brains. However, this makes it only slightly more likely that the bonobos know others' emotions and are not simply responding to others' expression, as we do not fully understand the cerebral activity needed for human recognition of others' emotions. Thirdly, bonobos are able to identify the expression they see on another's face with the same expression on their own face, as known through proprioception, an ability needed to know others' emotions from their facial expressions. While this is a necessary condition, it is not sufficient condition for knowledge of others' emotions when facially expressed. As for infant-mother facial interactions involving imitation in the case of bonobos, despite an assiduous search through the literature, I could not find any information about them. However, I would be surprised if they do not occur, given that bonobo infants engage in imitation with playmates,[97] and also that macaques and chimpanzee mother-infant dyads engage in it. Such exchanges do not as such establish that affect mirroring is going on, but they do open the door to the possibility.

As for chimpanzees, the case that at least some individuals know others' emotion is similar to that of the bonobos. It is less strong in that there has been no study relating their consoling behavior to self-regulation and it is

interactive nature of affect mirroring in humans may represent a key divergence point from other species which could explain species differences in human empathy development. Such a hypothesis is theoretically important but remains untested, as no systematic data have yet been collected on great apes. Investigating evidence for affect mirroring in great apes is thus a topic ripe for future research."

97 Bonobo infants are known to engage in both rapid and delayed facial mimicry during play interactions with playmates. See Marta Bertini et al., "Playful Interactions and Facial Mimicry in Infant Bonobos (*Pan paniscus*)," *Ethology, Ecology & Evolution* 34, no. 3 (May 2022): 344–59.

stronger in that infant-mother facial interactions involving imitation are known to occur.[98]

Again, it is a pity that there is no record of apes capable of symbolic communication that name both their own and others' emotions, as this would have been strong evidence in favor of them knowing others' emotions.

It is worth noting that while my investigation has turned up little evidence in favor of some animals knowing others' emotions, it has turned up even less evidence weighing against the notion that some animals know others' emotions. To my mind, the only thing weighing against it is that there doesn't seem to be any clear-cut need for animals to know others' emotions in addition to being able to recognize and respond correctly to others' expressions of emotion.[99] Still, it is not impossible that such knowledge on the part of social species would help them better negotiate social situations, as is the case with humans.

Do Animals Know Others' Acts of Perception: That Others See, Hear, Etc.?

Like the case of emotion, whether animals know that others see, hear, smell, etc. depends on whether they themselves are aware of their own seeing, hearing, smelling, etc. Later on, I will provide evidence that chimpanzees know that they see when I discuss an experiment executed by Kano et al. that was designed to determine whether chimpanzees know that others see.

As for tests that seek to establish whether animals know that others see, many of the early ones gave negative results. For example, chimpanzees, to get food that was out of their reach, would gesture indiscriminately to people

98 While there is a fair amount of literature on dogs, I find the support it gives for the view that dogs know others' emotions is even more tenuous than in the case of the great apes, which is why I haven't considered it here.

99 I think, looking from an evolutionary perspective, that the ability to know that others see and feel various emotions most likely arose in nonhuman animals; otherwise, it is hard to see the body of our immediate ancestor as being suitably disposed for the reception of the rational soul. Self-reflective consciousness presupposes consciousness (understood as knowing that one sees, feels emotion, etc.). With the advent of reason comes self-reflective consciousness and also the ability to recognize that other humans have minds, along with the ability to surmise what is going on in other people's minds. It would be strange that the capacity for experiential knowledge of others' emotions and acts of sense perception would only suddenly arise with the advent of reason, given that experiential knowledge of these things depends on sensory abilities.

with and without blindfolds on or with or without buckets over their heads (and this even after they have been familiarized with wearing the buckets themselves).[100] Subsequently, Hare et al. designed an experiment that tapped into the natural competitiveness of conspecific individuals for food:

> In each experiment a subordinate and a dominant individual competed for food, which was placed in various ways on the subordinate's side of two opaque barriers. In some conditions dominants had not seen the food hidden, or food they had seen hidden was moved elsewhere when they were not watching (whereas in control conditions they saw the food being hidden or moved). At the same time, subordinates always saw the entire baiting procedure and could monitor the visual access of their dominant competitor as well. If subordinates were sensitive to what dominants did or did not see during baiting, they should have preferentially approached and retrieved the food that dominants had not seen hidden or moved. This is what they did in experiment 1 when dominants were either uninformed or misinformed about the food's location.[101]

As we will see below, however, one cannot conclude from this experiment that chimpanzees necessarily know that others see, as there is an alternative explanation that can account for their performance.

Many of the more recent tests that seek to establish whether animals know that others see are variations on the goggles experiment proposed by Cecilia Heyes, in which an animal uses its own experience of seeing to know what others see or do not see.[102] One of the most convincing versions of the goggles experiment, devised and executed by Kano et al., separated chimpanzees into two groups.[103] Members of one group were allowed to experience a barrier that allowed them to see through it, while members of the other group were allowed to experience a barrier that did not allow them to see through it. Both barriers looked identical from afar; the see-through barrier did not

100 See Daniel Povinelli and Jennifer Vonk, "We Don't Need a Microscope to Explore the Chimpanzee's Mind," in Hurley and Nudds, *Rational Animals?*, 390 and 399.

101 Brian Hare et al., "Do Chimpanzees Know What Conspecifics Know?," *Animal Behaviour* 61 (2001): 139, abstract.

102 See Cecilia M. Heyes, "Theory of Mind in Nonhuman Primates," *Behavioral and Brain Sciences* 21, no. 1 (1998): 101–48.

103 See Fumihiro Kano et al., "Great Apes Use Self-Experience to Anticipate an Agent's Action in a False-Belief Test," *PNAS* 116, no. 42 (2019): 20904–9. A video of part of the experiment can be found at: https://www.youtube.com/watch?v=oPPloZynLNg&feature=emb_imp_woyt.

appear to be such from afar. Once the chimpanzees had become familiar with a given barrier, they were tested. A chimpanzee and a human, visible to one another on opposite sides of a cage, watch while an object is hidden under one of the two boxes that are in the cage. The human then moves to one side behind the barrier; the human's legs are visible to the chimpanzee. A third party then enters the cage, and after first moving the object from one box to the other, removes the object from the cage. The human then moves from behind the barrier and slowly pulls a tray to retrieve the boxes with what is under them. If the chimpanzees are using their self-experience of the barriers, those that experienced the see-through barriers would not expect the human to look at either box; and indeed, tracking of the chimpanzees' eye movements indicates that the chimpanzees do not preferentially look toward one box more than the other. The chimpanzees that experienced the opaque barriers, on the other hand, did look preferentially to the box where the human had seen the object placed under, which is what is predicted by the hypothesis that they know that the human, while behind the barrier, did not see that the object had been moved.[104]

Though this appears to provide compelling evidence that chimpanzees know that others see, an alternative explanation is available in terms of "line of sight." "Line of sight" is the spatial dimension of gaze that extends from the animal's eyes in a given direction. An animal knows that other animals (humans included) will act toward things that are in their line of sight or have been in their line of sight and not toward things where their line of sight is obstructed. The animal (human) behind the see-through barrier had a clear line of sight and so will not seek the removed object. The animal (human) behind the opaque barrier had an obstructed line of sight and so will seek the removed object where it was last situated under its line of sight. Seeing is not dissociable from line of sight, as one only judges that someone sees something when one recognizes that that individual has a clear line of sight.[105] Thus, it seems that there is no way of knowing that animals recognize

104 Note that Karin-D'Arcy and Povinelli were unsuccessful in their attempt to replicate Hare et al.'s experiment. See M. Rosalyn Karin-D'Arcy and Daniel J. Povinelli, "Do Chimpanzees Know What Each Other See? A Closer Look," *International Journal of Comparative Psychology* 15, no. 1 (2002): 21–54.

105 Robert Lurz explains at length that the results of goggle-type experiments and other similar experiments do not require us to posit that the animal subject knows that another sees. Robert Lurz, "If Chimpanzees Are Mindreaders, Could Behavioral Science Tell? Toward a Solution of a Logical Problem," *Philosophical Psychology* 22, no. 3 (2009): 305–28. He observes:

that another animal sees and not simply that it has an unobstructed line of sight.

Robert Lurz et al. performed an experiment devised to eliminate the line-of-sight explanation using a mirror.[106] The human could see the chimpanzee that was behind it in the mirror, but the human's line-of-sight was not from his eyes to the chimpanzee, as the human's back was turned to the chimpanzee. Thus, the chimpanzees, on the basis of observing that the human's line-of-sight was away from it, should not gesture to that human. The chimpanzees were presented with five conditions: 1) human facing them; 2) human facing away whose reflection was visible to them in a mirror; 3) human facing away whose reflection was not visible to them, as the mirror had been turned around; 4) human with back to them but a picture of that human in place of the mirror; 5) mirror only. Though the chimpanzees preferentially gestured to humans who were facing them, they did gesture more often toward humans who could see them in the mirror, as opposed to gesturing to humans who could not see them in the mirror because the mirror was turned around, and as opposed to gesturing to a picture of the human. The weakness in this experiment, as Lurz et al. note, is that there is a line of sight between the reflection of the human eye in the mirror and the chimpanzee.[107] The fact that the chimpanzees didn't gesture toward a picture that looked similar to what they would see in the mirror was to be expected. Chimpanzees typically do not gesture to pictures in hopes of getting treats. The chimpanzees were familiar with mirrors and so could distinguish a mirror image from a picture.

> A principal part of the observable basis for thinking that another subject sees an object is that there is a certain observable relation between the object and the subject's open eyes, a relation that Heyes . . . calls "eye-object line," Penn and Povinelli . . . call "uninterrupted visual access," and I, following others . . . shall call "direct line of sight." Whatever this observable relation is called, the idea is that in order to judge that another subject sees an object, one must base one's judgment on the observational belief or fact that there is "an unobstructed, notional, straight line between [the subject's open] eyes" and the object seen (Heyes, 1988, p. 113).

Consequently, there is no way to tell whether an animal is simply observing another's direct line of sight or whether they also know that the other sees. Ty Henley and Daniel J. Povinelli critique Kano et al.'s study along the same line in "Seeing Through <seeing through>: An Analysis of Kano et al. (2019)," *Animal Behavior and Cognition* 7, no. 4 (2020): 658–60.

106 Robert Lurz et al., "Chimpanzees Gesture to Humans in Mirrors: Using Reflection to Dissociate Seeing from Line of Gaze," *Animal Behaviour* 135 (January 2018): 239–49.

107 Lurz et al., "Chimpanzees Gesture to Humans in Mirrors," 247.

In 2006, Povinelli and Vonk suggested a way of getting around the problem posed by the seeming impossibility of dissociating seeing from gaze and line-of-sight monitoring:

> In particular, we have proposed pursuing a class of behavioural tasks which have, among their possible outcomes, behaviours that can be generated only by mapping self-experience onto the experience of others (Povinelli and Vonk 2003). Although not motivated by precisely the same theoretical concerns, Gallup (1988) proposed using such a class of tasks to assay whether other species might be capable of using their own mental states to model the experience of others. For example he suggested allowing organisms to receive extensive first-person experience wearing sound-dampening ear muffs and to then determine if they would alter the volume of their vocalizations when attempting to gain the attention of another individual wearing them.[108]

It seems there should be a way of devising an experiment involving hearing similar to the one with the transparent and opaque barriers. However, one might object that this will not work any better than the barrier experiment because being within earshot corresponds to line-of-sight and so the animal need only judge that the other is within earshot and not that it is hearing. Povinelli would agree with this objection, as he currently maintains that knowledge of others' mental states always requires observing their behavior and that there is no way of determining that an animal knows the former in addition to the latter.[109]

Lurz has proposed experiments that involve self-experience of barriers that cause color or size shifts, so as to eliminate line-of-sight explanations.[110] I will not go into the details here. While such experiments may well get around the theoretical problem of determining that the animal's knowledge extended beyond behavior reading, it is unlikely that they would give positive results, given the known cognitive limitations of the animals, such as the inability of most to recognize what size-altering barriers do.[111] So it seems

108 Povinelli and Vonk, "We Don't Need a Microscope," 397.

109 See Daniel Povinelli, "Can Comparative Psychology Crack Its Toughest Nut?," 589–652. I wonder, though, if the differences between earshot and line of sight might not allow for the right kind of experiment targeting hearing, given that earshot in some cases is judged by sight.

110 Robert Lurz, "If Chimpanzees Are Mindreaders," 314–18.

111 See Elske van der Vaart and Charlotte K. Hemelrijk, "'Theory of Mind' in Animals: Ways to Make Progress," *Synthese* 191 (2014): 344, concerning the unlikelihood that competitive

that we are at an impasse when it comes to determining whether animals know that other animals see.

We may ask here: What would the benefit be to the animal to know that other animals see or sense using some other sense? What another animal sees is connected with what it later will remember and act toward. However, it is hard to see any advantage over knowing that others see as opposed to learning behavioral rules concerning gaze and action. The only advantage I can think of is that knowing what another sees or does not see can allow one to better orient that other to seeing something, as is done, for example, by pointing. However, animals, at least in the wild, rarely, if ever, point.[112] Captive great apes, however, do regularly make pointing gestures when interacting with humans.[113] They don't, however, point to things when interacting with other apes. I haven't seen any reports of apes physically reorienting a conspecific so that it can see something. Some rhesus macaque mothers, however, "actively searched for the infant's gaze, sometimes holding its head and gently pulling it towards her face."[114] Are these mothers trying to get their infant to look at them or are they simply wanting to look their infants in the eye? I have not come across any unambiguous evidence of animals orienting others so that they can see something.

Going back to the question of whether animals know that they themselves see, the experiment recounted above designed by Kano et al. provides evidence that they do. Recall that the first step in the experiment was to give the chimpanzee experience with a novel barrier through which one could or

---

seeing-as paradigms yield positive results. The authors conclude: "It seems irrefutable that existing experiments cannot conclusively distinguish mind-readers from behavior-readers. However, it seems like any experiments that *would* be able to do so are so complex that no subject will pass them; therefore, it seems like this question is best left alone" (350).

112 See David A. Leavens et al., "Understanding the Point of Chimpanzee Pointing: Epigenesis and Ecological Validity," *Current Directions in Psychological Science* 14, no. 4 (2005): 185–86:

> Strikingly, however, there are few reports of pointing by wild apes. As noted by Povinelli et al. (2003): "Despite intensive observations of the spontaneous interactions of free-ranging chimpanzees, there is no evidence that these animals . . . gesture with the arm and/or index finger toward other objects, animals, or events in space" (p. 41). Indeed, the only detailed description of pointing by wild apes is an observation of a bonobo pointing twice to human observers who were hiding in some shrubbery (Veà & Sabater-Pi, 1998). Thus, it seems that apes almost never point in their natural habitats.

113 See Marta Halina et al., "The Goal of Ape Pointing," *PLoS ONE* 13, no. 4 (2018): 1.

114 Ferrari et al., "Reciprocal Face-to-Face Communication Between Rhesus Macaque Mothers and Their Newborn Infants," 1768.

could not see. The self-experience with the novel barriers is necessary for the chimpanzees to recognize that when the object was moved, the human had or did not have an unobstructed line of sight. What does this self-experience consist of? Is it primarily of a line of sight (either clear or obstructed)? No. Individuals' recognition that there is an unobstructed line of sight between their eyes and the object depends on them knowing that they see the object. When an object moves behind a barrier, they only know that their line of sight is obstructed because they cannot see the object anymore. Thus, while viewing others one can only know that they see because one perceives that they have an unobstructed line of sight, in one's own case the situation is reversed. Without knowing that one sees something, one cannot know that one's line of sight to that object is unobstructed.

The evidence just given aside, we would expect that animals we know to have memory, imagination, and the estimative sense would also possess the seemingly more fundamental inner sense, the common sense. One could respond that maybe the common sense in them allows them to distinguish between sensible qualities, for example, color from sound, but it does not allow them to be aware that they are seeing and hearing. This, though, would mean that they know color without knowing it as visible (i.e., something seen by them) and that they know sound without knowing it as audible (something heard by them), in which case, as regards sensible qualities, there would seem to be no difference between an animal and a machine.

Setting aside for the moment the question of whether animals in fact know the acts of perception of other animals, let us consider how this might be explained. What I propose is that the animals, rather than consciously imputing or attributing the mental states of seeing, hearing, etc. to others (as we do when, for example, when we ask ourselves what is that person seeing who is looking intently in a certain direction), simply recognize these states by means of unconscious matching with their own memories of like states in similar contexts. This is the same explanation that I offered in regard to how animals could know other animals' emotions. Just as certain animals are aware of and remember their own emotions and unconsciously match the emotional display of another to these memories, so too animals who are aware of their own acts of seeing can remember those acts and unconsciously match to them the physical display in context of another animal, for example, fixing its eyes on a food item. They do not have an abstract concept of seeing as a subjective experience that may or may not correspond to reality nor are they able to understand the difference between the internal activity of being aware and the external activity of looking, but they can recognize specific acts of seeing in an experiential way.

The above explanation obviously does not establish that animals know other animals' acts of perception. Note, however, that there is a similarity between what would be needed for them to know other animals' emotions and what would be needed for them to know other animals' acts of perception. In the case of both emotion and perceptions, the animal has self-experience to serve as a basis for recognizing other animals' emotions and acts of perception. And in the case of both, the animal can observe the expression and/or behavior of other animals in situations familiar to themselves. The cues in the case of perception are generally more subtle than in the case of emotion, for example, a grimace on one's own face or another's face is more obvious than one's gaze or another's gaze. This would render it generally more difficult for an animal to recognize that another sees than that another is angry or afraid. Other than that, however, what is cognitively necessary for doing the latter is similar to what is cognitively necessary for doing the former. If the evidence that some animals know others' emotions had proved to be more decisive, I would have regarded that animals know other animals' acts of perception as the more plausible view. However, given the tenuousness of the evidence in favor of animals knowing others' emotions, which is a more embodied psychic state than others' acts of perception, I remain agnostic on this point.

Do Animals Know Others' Acts of Perception: Remembering and Imagining?

One might wonder whether animals' experiential knowledge can extend to recognizing that others know in the sense of remember. First, we need to consider whether there is evidence that the animals are aware of their own acts of remembering.

Certain animals appear to know whether they do or do not remember something. In an experiment performed by Beran et al. with chimpanzees, the chimpanzees moved to a reward-delivery site based on their confidence in their responses on a computerized memory task. "Crucially, if the chimpanzees did not move to the reward-delivery site before food was dispensed, the reward was lost and could not be recovered. Chimpanzees were significantly more likely to move to the dispenser on trials they had completed correctly than on those they had completed incorrectly, and these movements occurred before any external feedback about the outcome of their responses."[115] And another experiment done by Kornell et al. also indicated that rhesus monkeys are aware of whether they are correctly remembering something.[116]

One might argue that the awareness of their memories takes the form of a feeling that the animal does not identify with remembering. I would agree that animals do not have an abstract concept of memory. However, I think that they experientially differentiate the feeling they get of being presently unsure about a state of things that they perceived in the past from feelings that are emotions, such as anger or pain, as these feelings are quite different.[117]

In addition to having awareness of their memories, animals have experience of looking at things and subsequently remembering where they are. With this as a basis, can they recognize that if others look at things, not only do these others see the things, but also will remember where they are?

Consider this case: If animal A watches animal B watching a treat being hidden behind one of two occluders, after which B's view of the occluders is briefly blocked, does animal A both know that once animal B's line of vision is restored, B both sees the occluders and remembers which of them

115 Michael J. Beran et al., "Go When You Know: Chimpanzees' Confidence Movements Reflect Their Responses in a Computerized Memory Task," *Cognition* 142 (September 2015): 236.

116 Nate Kornell et al., "Transfer of Metacognitive Skills and Hint Seeking in Monkeys," *Psychological Science* 18, no. 1 (2007): 64:

> Rhesus macaques were given the opportunity to choose between two types of trials on a delayed-matching-to-sample task after the sample was presented but before the actual test could be administered (Hampton, 2001). One option was to wait for the test, at which time the subject could earn a desirable reward if it responded correctly, or earn nothing if it made an error. The second option was to end the trial and settle for a less desirable, but certain, reward. Subjects were also given forced-choice trials, on which they could not avoid the test phase. Accuracy was significantly higher for trials on which subjects opted to take the test than for forced-choice trials, a result suggesting that subjects declined to take the test when their memory of the sample was relatively weak.

117 Peter Harrison maintains that "the evidence brought forward to demonstrate that animals feel pain is far from conclusive," in "Do Animals Feel Pain?," *Philosophy* 66, no. 255 (1991): 25–40. I do not think we need a full physiological understanding of how pain occurs to know that the yelp a dog makes when one steps on its tail means that it is in pain. What would be the point of veterinarians anesthetizing animals when they operate on them if the animals do not feel pain?

has a treat hidden behind it?[118] It is hard to see how an animal could know the more interior act of knowing that is remembering, especially since the trigger for this recognition is the same as the trigger for recognition that the other sees. Certainly, behavior monitoring is available as an explanation for why A expects B to seek the treat under the correct cup, but one wonders whether more than that is going on.

One can ask similar questions about imagination in reported cases of deception by apes. In one case, a mother ape, desirous of getting another ape to stop trying to touch her baby, peered intently off in the distance, as though it was seeing something there. Consequently, the other ape started looking in the same direction, which gave an opening to mother to take off in the other direction.[119] Byrne and Whiten recount a similar incident where a male chacma baboon that was on the point of being attacked by other baboons looked in the distance with the result that the other baboons stopped and looked in the same direction, when, in fact, there was nothing to be seen there.[120] Can ape A know that ape B will imagine that there is something to look at if ape A stares in a given direction? De Waal reports that captive chimpanzees sometimes

> quickly collect a mouthful of water from a faucet in their cage when they see a stranger approaching, then wait with a perfect poker face until they can let the intruder have it. Some are such experts that they trick even people who are thoroughly mindful of the possibility. The ape will stroll around in his cage as if occupied with something else, only to swing around at the right moment when he hears his victim behind him.[121]

There are other examples of animals engaging in deception that can be found in the literature.[122] Again, I am not sure what the best explanation is for

118 Experiments show that they act as if they know what a competitor saw and remembers. See, for example, Hare et al., "Do Chimpanzees Know What Conspecifics Know?," 139, abstract.

119 This observation, made by Frans X. Plooij, is recounted by Dale Peterson, "Those Lying Apes," *Psychology Today*, December 13, 2011, https://www.psychologytoday.com/us/blog/the-moral-lives-animals/201112/those-lying-apes.

120 Andrew Whiten and W. R. Byrne, "Tactical Deception in Primates," *Behavioral and Brain Sciences* 11, no. 2 (1988): 237.

121 Frans de Waal, *Good Natured: The Origins of Right and Wrong in Humans and Other Animals* (Harvard University Press, 1996), 7.

122 One amusing example of apparent deceit is stone-caching by the chimpanzee, Santino, who hurls them at unsuspecting visitors. Hours before visitors arrive, Santino caches some

these kinds of behavior. I see no way to rule out that the animals have learned through observation that if they act in a certain way, the other animal, in response, will or won't act in a certain way. Then, that problem aside, it is not clear to me whether experience can in principle extend to knowledge of others' acts of imagining and remembering.

Theory of Mind as Attributing or Imputing Mental States to Others

Often discussions of theory of mind speak of it in terms of attributing or imputing mental states to others. There is a difference, however, between active mind reading and passive recognition of mental states, be these one's own or another's. For example, we may simply have the feeling that we are forgetting something or that one of our memories may not be entirely accurate; or we can decide to investigate why we think that we are forgetting something or why we doubt the accuracy of a given memory. Similarly, we may simply recognize a person's emotion for what it is, or we can try to get into the person's head to better understand how that person is feeling.[123]

Active mind reading requires reason. Intentionally examining the accuracy of a memory involves the application of some general criterion of judgment, such as the concordance or lack thereof with others' memories. Making a conscious effort to get into someone else's mind supposes that one understands the other to have a mind and that one has knowledge of the sorts of things that go on in a mind. Here is an example to illustrate how having concepts about the mind and its workings allows one to actively impute mental states. I learned that a friend, who was having difficulty deciding between two graduate schools, finally opted for one that had some glaring negatives. Based on a general understanding of how people feel after they make such decisions, I inferred that she would be feeling anxious. And based on a general understanding of how anxious people are typically best motivated, I inferred that to help her start school in a positive frame of mind,

---

stones, while also placing some stones in plain sight between the caches. See Mathias Osvath, "Spontaneous Planning for Future Stone Throwing by a Male Chimpanzee," *Current Biology* 19, no. 5 (2009): R190–91.

123 Élisabeth Pacherie, among others, distinguishes different levels of knowing others' emotions. See "L'empathie et ses degrés" in *L'empathie*, ed. Alain Berthoz and Gérard Jorland (Editions Odile Jacob, 2004), 149–81.

I should emphasize the positive aspects of her decision and skip over or downplay the negatives when speaking to her.

Here are some other examples: There is a difference between simply recognizing that a classmate is bored and surmising why that person is bored. (Is it because she already understands what is being presented or it is the teacher's manner of presentation or is it a subject she regards as inherently uninteresting?) There is a difference between recognizing that a woman is distressed because her husband was hospitalized and understanding more fully how she feels by figuring out all that this means for her (how she feels about her husband and what are the consequences of his hospitalization for her and the like). There is a difference between seeing that a person is angry and trying to determine whether she should be angry or as angry as she is. Sometimes we humans spontaneously identify the emotion others are feeling, and sometimes we also try to view things from the other's mental perspective to more fully understand how they are feeling. In the former case, there is passive recognition of the others' emotions and in the latter case, there is active attribution of feelings to others in light of our understanding of how people's minds work. This same distinction can be made in regard to other mental states as well.

Experiential knowledge again is subrational knowledge according to which the individual recognizes what to do in specific instances by way of unconscious matching with similar experiences, rather than by the application of a universal principle. It is a matter of recognition, not of active attribution of a universal concept.[124] I maintain that grasping universals is beyond animals' abilities, for reasons I will not reiterate here. However,

124 Aquinas, who maintains that nonhuman animals do not possess reason, does not see anything problematic about maintaining that the more perfect animals know each other's emotions: *De sensu*, tr. 1, lec. 2, n. 13:

> But hearing makes known to us only the differences of sounds, which are not found in all bodies, nor are they expressive of many differences that are found in these few things. Hearing does, however, reveal to animals the differences of voice. For voice is a sound put forth from the mouth of living things with a certain imagination, as is said in bk. 2 of the *De Anima*; and therefore the voice of the animal, insofar as it is such, naturally signifies the interior passion of the animal, as the barking of dogs signifies their anger; and in this manner more perfect animals know from one another's voices their interior passions, which knowledge is nevertheless absent in imperfect animals. In this manner, therefore, hearing only knows per se the difference of sounds, e.g., low and high (or other things of the sort) and differences of voice, according as they are indicative of diverse passions; and in this manner the knowledge of hearing does not extend to knowing per se so many differences of things as vision does.

experience-based recognition is in principle within animals' abilities. Thus, rather than investigating whether animals attribute or impute the mental state of emotion to others, we should seek to determine whether they recognize others' emotions. The same should be said in the case of any other mental state that animals may have experiential knowledge of.

Conclusion

I have attempted to contribute to understanding whether animals have a theory of mind by addressing Hare et al.'s complaint that when it comes to determining what animals know about other animals, "the problem is that in many theoretical discussions of these issues, only two alternatives are presented: chimpanzees either have a 'theory of mind' like that of humans (i.e. they engage in mental state attribution) or they simply learn by blind behaviouristic conditioning."[125] I address this problem by offering a third explanation of animals' putative theory of mind behaviors, one that is an alternative to reasoning and to behavior monitoring. This explanation takes its inspiration from our knowledge that we humans, in addition to possessing abstract knowledge about things, have a subrational type of knowledge—experiential knowledge (described long ago by Aristotle). I have shown that experience can extend to the mental state of emotion due to its embodied character. The facial expression of a scared individual immediately clues one into the fact that that individual is frightened, as the facial expression is part of the emotion, and the same for other automatic expressions of emotion (e.g., certain vocalizations).[126] Experiential knowledge can also extend to others' mental states such as seeing and hearing to the extent that they too are embodied. "Theory of mind," then, takes more than one form. While rational beings relying on reason are able to actively impute or attribute mental states to others, animals, rational or other, relying on experience alone, are only capable of recognizing others' mental states of emotion and sense perception.

I had hoped also to contribute to the discussion of whether some animals have a theory of mind by establishing that they know others' emotions.

125 Hare et al., "Do Chimpanzees Know What Conspecifics Know?," 149.

126 When one sees a human head peering over a fence, one immediately recognizes that there is a person behind the fence. Seeing the part leads to recognition of the whole. The same is generally true of emotion. Perceiving a part (the expression) generally leads immediately to recognition of the whole emotion, assuming one has previously experienced that emotion oneself.

This seemed to be the best place to look for theory of mind in animals to the extent that emotion is the most embodied mental state. However, despite an assiduous review of the literature, I cannot claim success. Our closest relatives, bonobos and chimpanzees, display consoling behavior, something that is relatively uncommon in the animal kingdom, and their consoling behavior fits the pattern of human empathic behavior in virtually every detail, including, in the case of the bonobos, the correlation between greater emotional regulation in individuals with the greater likelihood that they console. Also present in bonobos and chimpanzees are similarities at the level of the brain with what is needed in humans for understanding others' emotions (more so in the case of bonobos). In addition, both chimpanzees and bonobos are capable of visual-proprioceptive matching, something that is needed to recognize others' emotions from their facial expressions. Lastly, chimpanzees engage in mother-infant facial interactions that include imitation, something that is apt to facilitate learning about others' emotions. While all these things point to chimpanzees and bonobos knowing others' emotions, I acknowledge that the evidence mentioned is circumstantial.

6

Does Might Make Right in the Animal Kingdom, or Do Some Animals Act on Moral Grounds?

Introduction

Literature on animal behavior is replete with observations of seemingly moral behavior on the part of animals. Female gorilla Binti picked up an unconscious toddler who had fallen into the gorilla enclosure and put him by the caretaker's door.[1] Chimpanzees retrieve objects for humans striving to reach them, without being offered any reward, and even when they have to expend a certain amount of physical effort to do so.[2] Capuchin monkeys display inequity aversion: when they see another capuchin get a tastier food item for performing the same task, they get angry and

1 See Marc D. Hauser and Victor Juhasz, "Morals, Apes, and Us: Can Animals Learn to Share, Cooperate, Punish, and Show Empathy?," *Discover* 21, no. 2 (2000), http://discovermagazine.com/2000/feb/featmorals.

2 See Felix Warneken and Michael Tomasello, "Altruistic Helping in Human Infants and Young Chimpanzees," *Science* 311, no. 5765 (March 3, 2006): 1301–3.

sometimes even start throwing away the food item that they have received.[3] Chimpanzees punish the misdeeds of others. In one experiment, when a chimp has its food stolen from it by another chimp, it will punish the thief by pulling a rope that collapses the table the food is on, even though this puts the food out of reach not only of the thief, but of itself as well.[4] Apes display extraordinary affection toward humans who have helped them in the past, suggestive of gratitude.[5]

I argue that, despite these similarities to moral behavior, the animals' behavior lacks the crucial element of being performed in keeping with moral principles. Humans act and evaluate the moral goodness or badness of their actions by looking to universal principles, such as the Golden Rule. I argue that nonhuman animals are incapable of principled behavior because they lack reason, as can be seen by analyzing the language studies done with apes.

Animal Altruism?

Altruism is commonly defined as benefiting another at a cost to oneself without looking for the favor to be reciprocated or rewarded. It is generally considered supererogatory behavior, that is, morally praiseworthy behavior that goes beyond what justice requires.

Upon witnessing seemingly altruistic acts on the part of certain animals, scientists began to investigate whether they were truly altruistic. They realized that in certain cases the self-sacrificing behavior, such as emitting a warning call that calls attention to oneself while allowing others to escape, can be explained by natural selection rather than by a rational decision. For example, Belding ground squirrels are observed to emit warning calls more frequently when close kin are near, and females emit such calls more

3 See Peter G. Roma et al., "Capuchin Monkeys, Inequity Aversion, and the Frustration Effect," *Journal of Comparative Psychology* 120, no. 1 (2006): 67–73.

4 See Keith Jensen et al., "Chimpanzees Are Vengeful but Not Spiteful," *Proceedings of the National Academy of Science* 104, no. 32: 13046–50.

5 See de Waal, *The Age of Empathy*, 177–78:

> I have known apes who've been grateful for years. One was a female whom I had patiently taught to bottle-feed an adopted infant. Previously, she had lost several offspring due to insufficient lactation. . . . In the ensuing years, this female raised her own infants this way as well. Decades later, she was still thrilled if I stopped by the zoo where she lived. She'd groom me with enthusiastic tooth-clacking, showing that I was a hero to her. Animal keepers, most of whom were unaware of our history, couldn't believe the fuss she was making over me.

often than males do—males disperse from the colony in which they are born and so are not as likely to have close kin near them. Such behavior is apt to increase the number of one's genes that are passed on, for close kin share one's genes (a sibling or a parent, half of one's genes; a cousin, one-eighth of one's genes). In other cases, the apparent altruism turns out to be conditional, and thus, not true altruism. Red-winged blackbird males help protect the neighboring male's nest, so long as the neighboring male reciprocates.[6]

Kin altruism and reciprocal altruism, however, do not account for every case of apparent altruism. For in some cases the individual helped is not kin nor is any reciprocity sought, such as when apes retrieve items for humans and dolphins protect humans from sharks.[7] And there are many other similar behaviors that could be named here.

"Wild Justice:" The Utility of Acting Fairly and Punishing Those That Don't

Cooperative behavior, which is one form of helping behavior, often proves to be beneficial to the individual animal practicing it. As Frans de Waal points out, an individual might be successful in hunting squirrels, but together with others can share in the kill of a much larger animal. Thus, cooperative tendencies can increase individuals' fitness.

As de Waal further notes, cooperation is destined to be short-lived in the absence of something like fairness. If individuals that expend more effort do not gain more than those who do not, this will have a negative impact on their reproductive success. At least some social animals are capable of monitoring whether they receive more or less than others do vis-à-vis the effort each expends. De Waal recounts an experiment involving pairs of capuchin monkeys which required them to pull a tray together in order to get a food reward. In one case, one of the monkeys "collected her reward so quickly that she released the tray before Bias [the other monkey] had a chance to get hers. . . . Bias threw a tantrum."[8] And so the other monkey

6 See Robert Olendorf et al., "Cooperative Nest Defence in Red-Winged Blackbirds: Reciprocal Altruism, Kinship or By-Product Mutualism?," *Proceedings of the Royal Society B: Biological Sciences* 271, no. 1535 (January 22, 2004): 177–82.

7 See "Dolphins Rescuing Humans," Dolphins-World (April 26, 2017), http://www.dolphins-world.com/dolphins-rescuing-humans/.

8 De Waal, *The Age of Empathy*, 171.

helped Bias pull the tray out again, even though its own food cup was now empty. As mentioned earlier, capuchins also display "inequity aversion," that is, they react negatively when they are given a lesser reward than another for doing the same task. And chimpanzees in some cases will reject their superior reward when they see that the other chimpanzee received an inferior reward.[9] Some animals also appear to note favors and repay them, though not in kind. De Waal recounts:

> We analyzed no less than seven thousand approaches to food owners to see which ones met with success. During the mornings before every feeding session, we had recorded spontaneous grooming. We then compared the flow of both "currencies": food and grooming. If the top male, Socko, had groomed May, for example, his chances of getting a few branches from her in the afternoon were greatly improved. We found this effect all over the colony.[10]

Interestingly, individuals that are not close seem to take note of favors and specifically reward them more than animals that are "friends" do. The interaction of the latter is not on a strict tit-for-tat basis.[11] This behavior resembles human behavior. We differentiate true friends from useful acquaintances and see this as a reason to expect different things from each.

Many other examples could be added to the above of one animal monitoring how it is being treated and then acting in keeping with what justice requires. So the question is: Are these animals capable of moral action?

Reason is Needed for Moral Agency

The question of whether justice and altruism is to be found in animals boils down to the question of whether some animals are rational. I am going to assume here the commonsensical views of Aristotle and Aquinas that moral agents are ones that are capable of free choice, where choice is understood to

9 See Sarah Brosnan et al., "Mechanisms Underlying Responses to Inequitable Outcomes in Chimpanzees, *Pan troglodytes*," *Animal Behavior* 79, no. 6 (2010): 1229–37.

10 De Waal, *The Age of Empathy*, 174–75. Female baboons appear to grant access to their infants (something other females desire) in exchange for being groomed. De Waal, 176.

11 See de Waal, 174–75.

be a deliberate desire for things it is in one's power to gain, and deliberation is understood to involve a reasoning process.[12]

The reasoning involved in moral matters consists in formulating one or more practical syllogisms, one of the premises of which is universal (and thus knowable by reason alone) and the other of which is particular (and is known through perception), for example: "Things that belong to others are things that should be returned. This basketball is a thing that belongs to another. This basketball is a thing that should be returned." Of course, further assessment may be needed to account for circumstances that fall under other and sometimes higher principles.[13] And while the application of negative moral principles requires no more than a syllogism, as negative principles or precepts hold always and everywhere[14] (adultery is intrinsically evil, and so no specific act of adultery can ever be good), matters are not so simple in the case of affirmative precepts, as the rightness of the acts they command are contingent upon the circumstances,[15] and in some cases such principles may even be lacking. Aquinas provides an example of the latter: "If, however, one of the two [asking for financial help] is closer to one and the other needier, there is no universal rule for determining whom one ought to help more (for there are diverse grades of neediness and of nearness), but this requires prudence."[16] Note, however, that in saying that such cases require prudence, Aquinas is not affirming that prudence is possible without moral principles, but only that moral principles alone do not suffice for making a determination in every specific case. Indeed, in the example given, it is because one sees a conflict between two moral principles—namely, that one's first responsibility is to those who are closest to one, and that those who are

12 We often associate deliberation with a lengthy process of weighing pros and cons. However, deliberation can be quick, as when we pay for our groceries rather than taking them out of the store without paying for them. By a certain age, one immediately applies "do not steal" to particular cases without any need for pondering, as the application is so obvious.

13 One should not return a gun to a person who is threatening sedition, as one's obligation to protect the common good trumps one's obligation to return a private individual's belongings. See *ST* I-II, q. 94, a. 4.

14 See *ST* II-II, q. 33, a. 2.

15 See *ST* II-II, q. 33, a. 2.

16 *ST* II-II, q. 31, a. 3, ad 1. According to Aquinas, prudence "appl[ies] universal principles to particular conclusions about things to be done" (*ST* II-II, q. 47, a. 6) where the "things to be done" do not pertain to a limited area, such as warfare, but to living well without qualification (see *ST* II-II, q. 47, a. 2). Since prudence is a virtue, it enables the one who possesses it to do this well (see *ST* II-II, q. 47, a. 13).

in greatest need are to be given priority over those whose need is slight—that there is a need to have recourse to the experiential knowledge of singulars, which is part of prudence.[17] In sum, moral agency, good or bad, presupposes the grasp of moral principles that need to be applied in making a decision as to what to do in a specific case.

Though people continually act with moral principles in mind, it is in those cases that we speak of acting on "the principle of the thing" that best exemplify the nature of moral decision-making. We use the latter expression when people engage in an action because they think it is the right thing to do even though it is unlikely to yield any beneficial result and/or is expected to yield a negative result. We are also more apt to speak of acting "on principle" in such cases. Think of a high school student who stands and says the Pledge of Allegiance when it has become optional while all her classmates remain seated. Think of Rosa Parks who refused to yield her seat to a white person because she was tired of being a victim of injustice. In some cases, those who protest systemic injustices have hopes of changing things for the better, as, for example, was the case of the members of the White Rose, a nonviolent, intellectual resistance group in Nazi Germany, and was also the case of Parks when she appealed her conviction. However, such actions are often done solely because the person is determined not to act contrary to what their reason or conscience dictates as the thing to do, despite the predictable outcome being ridicule, ostracization, job loss, physical harm, or even death.

One of the major reasons why certain people attribute morality to animals is that they deny the need for reasoning in moral decision-making and affirm that the basis of morality is emotions such as sympathy. However, it is clear that sympathy blindly followed can lead to morally bad actions, such as enabling people or neglecting to discipline them. Moral principles are needed to judge when sympathy and other emotions ought to be checked

17 See *ST* I, q. 49, a. 5, ad 2:

> Particular doable things, in which prudence sets order, especially recede from the condition of being intelligible, and so much more to the extent that they are less determinate and certain. For those things that pertain to art, granted that they are singulars, are, nevertheless, more determinate and certain, whence for the most part counsel is not taken regarding them for the sake of certitude, as is said in bk. III of the *Ethics*. And although in certain other intellectual virtues reasoning is more certain than it is in prudence, nevertheless it is particularly required for prudence that man be capable of reasoning well (*bene ratiocinativus*), so that he may be able to apply well universal principles to particulars which are varied and uncertain.

or fostered, and these are available only to animals that are able to grasp the meaning of abstract, universal propositions.[18]

The Nature of Reason: Its Object and Natural Perfection

My main argument against morality in the animal kingdom stands or falls on certain truths concerning the nature of reason; first and foremost, that it is immaterial. The immateriality of the intellect is witnessed to by our ability to apprehend immaterial things, such as "rights," "science," and "God."[19] As a consequence of being an immaterial knowing power, intellect, unlike the senses, has no inherent limit as to what it is able to know: any and every intelligible being falls under its purview.[20] However, so long as our soul is united to our body, our intellect is limited by its dependence on sense experience. Thus, although the proper object of intellect, as such, is being, the proper object of the human intellect is said to be the nature of material things, insofar as we arrive at ideas starting from sense experience, and things that cannot be perceived by sense can only be known by us through some form of negation. This is why Aristotle famously said: "As the eyes of bats are to the blaze of day, so is the reason in our soul to the things which are by nature most evident of all."[21] As Aquinas explains:

> A knowing power is proportioned to the knowable. Whence the proper object of the angelic intellect, which is entirely separate from the body, is intelligible substance separated from the body; and through intelligible

18 Perhaps there is some sense in which sympathy is necessary for morality, but I do not intend to investigate this here. Even if one grants that it is, this fact by itself does not negate the need to be able to grasp moral principles.

19 This is one of the arguments that Aquinas gives for the incorporeal nature of the intellect in *SCG*, bk. 2, chap. 48. I give other arguments in chapters 2 and 4.

20 Although Aquinas frequently speaks of the possible intellect as being in potency "ad omnia intelligibilia," he does add some qualifications. He maintains that the separated soul is able to understand other "separated substances," but not as perfectly as these beings are able to understand themselves, given that the separated soul is the least among them; see *Q. DA*, a. 17. He also maintains that no created intellect can naturally know the divine essence; however, created intellects, unlike the senses, can be raised by God to such knowledge (which even then falls short of unqualified comprehension). See *ST* I, q. 12, a. 4, ad 3.

21 Aristotle, *Metaphysics*, bk. 2, chap. 1, 993b7–10, in McKeon, *The Basic Works of Aristotle*. See *ST* I, q. 84, a. 8: "The proper object proportioned to our intellect is the nature of a sensible thing." See also *In Meta.*, bk. 2, lec. 1, n. 13.

> things of this sort it knows material things. However, the proper object of the human intellect, which is conjoined to the body, is the "whatness" or nature existing in a material body; and through the natures of visible things of this sort it ascends to a certain cognition of invisible things.[22]

The limitations of our intellect due to the dependency of thinking on imagining and sensing render us incapable of fully grasping the natures of the beings that are most perfect, that is, immaterial substances, and above all, God, but we can achieve "a certain cognition" of them.

By contrast, even the most perfect senses, the interior senses, are inherently limited. The senses of themselves are ordered to knowing certain accidents belonging to particular beings, not "being." They are incapable of grasping the "whatness" (*quod quid est*) or nature of material things, knowledge of which is the means whereby the intellect arrives at a distinct knowledge of being. It is only in a rational being that the knowledge the senses bring can be further ordered to knowing what things are. In nonrational animals, sense knowledge of beings can only be ordered to action.

Now, since the intellect is in potency to knowing all things, rational beings naturally desire the actualization of this potency, for therein lies their perfection.[23] And despite the limits on the human intellect stemming from its dependence on sense experience, the natural orientation of our intellect is toward knowledge of the things most intelligible by nature. A sign of which is, as Aristotle observes, that "although our grasp of the eternal things is but slight, nevertheless the joy which it brings is, by reason of their excellence, greater than that of knowing all things that are here below; just as the joy of a fleeting and partial glimpse of those whom we love is greater than that of an accurate view of other things, no matter how numerous or how great they

22 *ST* I, q. 84, a. 7. See also *ST* I, q. 84, a. 8.

23 See *In Meta.*, bk. 1, lec. 1, n. 1: "Therefore he [Aristotle] first proposes that there is in all human beings a natural desire to know (*sciendum*). A threefold reason can be given for this. First, because everything whatsoever naturally desires its perfection. . . . Since therefore the intellect, by which man is what he is, considered in itself is in potency to all things, nor is it reduced in act in regard to them before it understands. . . . Thus, naturally each and every human individual desires science." See also *In Meta.*, bk. 1, lec. 1, n. 3: "For every natural thing whatsoever has an inclination to its proper operation: as the hot thing to heating and the heavy that it move downward. The proper operation of man as man is to understand. . . . Whence, the desire of man naturally inclines to understanding."

are."[24] We can know that separated substances exist, albeit with difficulty, and something about their properties, albeit largely by negation.[25] And we naturally desire such knowledge, as it is what most perfects our intellect.[26]

The natural desire that rational beings have to perfect their intellect by acquiring knowledge about what is results in them spontaneously asking questions about things, questions that are ordered to acquiring knowledge for its own sake.[27] In the case of rational animals, the first questions that occur to them are about the material things that they sense. This is why the questions children ask are about sensible things: What are shadows made of? Where do babies come from? Why do some dogs have one eye of one color and another of another color? And so on, ad infinitum.[28] An animal species whose members did not ask these kinds of questions could not be rational.

Do Animals Trained to Use Symbols Ask Speculative Questions?

People do not generally think that insects and other simpler animals (e.g., coral) are candidates for moral agency, as they do not exhibit much by way of flexible, learned behavior, but for the most part act invariably in the same

24 Aristotle, *Parts of Animals*, 644b33–35. See also *ST* I, q. 12, a. 1, and *ST* I-II, q. 94, a. 2: "There is in man an inclination to the good according to the nature of reason, which is proper to man; as man has a natural inclination to this, that he knows the truth about God, and to this that he lives in society."

25 See *In Librum Boethii de Trinitate*, q. 6, aa. 3 and 4.

26 See *SCG*, bk. 3, chap. 25: "Therefore, the end of the intellect is the end of all human acts. The end and good of the intellect is, however, the true; and consequently, the ultimate end is the first truth. And, therefore, the ultimate end of the whole human being, and of all his operations and desires, is to know the first truth, which is God."

27 To say that children spontaneously ask questions is, of course, not meant to deny that they must first learn language and hear others use it to ask questions; nor is it meant to deny that they generally first ask certain types of questions (e.g., "what" questions) and only later other types of questions (e.g., "why" questions). All that is meant by saying that children spontaneously ask questions is that once they master the language needed, they form questions on their own in order to satisfy their desire to know.

28 See "Mothers Asked Nearly 300 Questions a Day, Study Finds," *The Telegraph*, March 28, 2013, http://www.telegraph.co.uk/news/uknews/9959026/Mothers-asked-nearly-300-questions-a-day-study-finds.html: "The five toughest questions mothers get asked: 1) Why is water wet? (35 per cent) 2) Where does the sky end? (34 per cent) 3) What are shadows made of? (33 per cent) 4) Why is the sky blue? (20 per cent) 5) How do fish breathe under water? (18 per cent)."

way, and such behavior is readily attributed to genetic/physiological determinations, and not to a reflected decision. It turns out that some of these animals have greater cognitive capacities than we initially suspected. Bees, for example, can learn to do match-to-sample tasks.[29] Nevertheless, it is reasonable to think that the more likely candidates for moral agency are the animals whose behavior is less dictated by instinct, namely, apes, cetaceans, and certain birds.

Certain individuals of the animal species in question have been taught symbolic means of communication. However, they do not employ the symbols they have learned in order to gain knowledge for the sake of knowledge. The questions they ask are not speculative, but are practical, and for the most part are tantamount to requests or commands for specific things.[30] For example, the chimpanzee Lana signed: "?Lana drink this [Coke] out-of room."[31] Lana was not signing simply for the sake of knowing whether she may drink the Coke that was in the room adjoining the one she was in; she was signing in order to be allowed to drink it. Duane Rumbaugh, who ran the Lana project, acknowledges that "so far as the computer program was concerned, *?* was the functional equivalent of *Please*, and hence the two lexigrams coupled together were redundant."[32] Rumbaugh then notes that Lana eventually used one or the other when "making requests of people." The point of such questions can be equally well expressed in the form of a command. "May I have a banana?" and "Could you please tickle me?" do not express anything essentially different for the ape than "Give banana" and "Tickle me."

Sometimes Lana's requests were elicited by problems such as not getting the food or drink she wanted. For example, one day the bread dispenser was not working. After making a few misguided requests, Lana asked "Beverly

29 See Martin Glurfa et al., "The Concepts of 'Sameness' and 'Difference' in an Insect," *Nature* 410 (April 19, 2001): 930–33.

30 The questions the first humans asked were most likely practical ones, such as "Are there any berries left on the bushes by the stream?" and "Has the predator gone away?" I am focusing here on speculative questions because they unambiguously express a desire for knowledge, unlike practical questions, which are sometimes veiled requests or commands.

31 Rumbaugh and Gill, "Lana's Acquisition of Language Skills," in Rumbaugh, *Language Learning*, 173–74.

32 Rumbaugh and Gill, "Lana's Acquisition of Language Skills," 171. Note that the majority of apes in language studies are not taught to use the question mark. They do respond to Wh-questions (who, what, where, etc.) and so they are familiar with the words needed to ask questions seeking knowledge for its own sake.

move behind room period," which was an appropriate request as technicians had to go behind Lana's room in order to fill the various dispensers. Now perhaps Lana hit upon that specific request by chance, but "in subsequent formal tests where equipment failures were intentionally staged, Lana reliably came forth with the request that the technician move behind the room."[33] Although such a request (or perhaps command) is more mentally demanding than simply asking for bread (as it requires the ape to first make an association between the location of the technician and the dispensers working, and then to use the symbols that it has learned by association to request that the technician move to the appropriate place so that a dispenser will resume working), it neither depends on universal knowledge nor expresses a desire for knowledge for its own sake.

Yet another type of question Lana would ask is for the name of something.[34] For example, a trainer named Tim put candies in a box and showed them to Lana, who knew the symbol for "can," but not for "box." First Lana asked for the can. When that did not work, she asked for the bowl. When that did not work, she asked: "?Tim give Lana name-of this." Tim responded: "Box name-of this." Lana then said "yes," followed by "?Tim give Lana this box."[35] If we are correct in understanding "?Tim give Lana name-of this" to have been a request for the name of a thing, plainly Lana's question was not ordered to gaining knowledge for its own sake, but rather to acquiring useful knowledge.

Alex, the African Grey parrot, also asked for names of things. While looking at itself in the mirror, it asked "What color?" Alex was told that "that's grey; you are a grey parrot." Alex, after repeating the question five times, learned the word "grey."[36] Alex also "simultaneously learned the color 'orange'

33 Rumbaugh and Gill, 172.

34 See Rumbaugh, "Language Behavior of Apes," in Sebeok and Umiker-Sebeok, *Speaking of Apes*, 249 and 250: "To date, at least, she [the chimpanzee Lana] has not used expressive language to expand her horizons *except to ask for the name of something which she then requested by the name given*"; italics added.

35 Rumbaugh, *Language Learning*, 176–77.

36 See Steven M. Wise, *Drawing the Line: Science and the Case for Animal Rights* (Perseus Books, 2002), 107. Alex knew from previous experience that color names are useful for getting things it wants, as it was trained by means of the Model/Rival method. See Irene M. Pepperberg, "Cognitive and Communicative Abilities of Grey Parrots," *Applied Animal Behaviour Science* 100, nos. 1–2 (2006): 78. This is how the Model/Rival method works: In the parrot's presence, one human asks questions, e.g., "What's here?," "What color?" and the other human answers. If the one who responds get the answer wrong, he is scolded and the item is removed

and the name 'carrot' when he asked a student eating a carrot what color it was and what it was called. Henceforth he reliably identifies . . . 'orange,' and he added carrots to the list of vegetables he requests from time to time."[37] These questions, however, are about names and not about things. The parrot did not gain new knowledge of the colors grey and orange when it was told their names. It gained the ability to name them, and same for the carrot. There is a difference between asking a question to learn a name and asking it to understand a thing. For example, a person visiting a laboratory could ask: "What is that?" and be told that it is a centrifuge, but then go on to ask, "What is a centrifuge?" It is the latter question that is seeking knowledge about things.[38]

Do animals ever ask questions other than as a means to an end? Does their use of symbols in their questions require cognitive abilities other than those employed by animals that push a specific button to get a reward? One looks in vain at transcripts of signs produced by animals for a question seeking knowledge for its own sake.[39] And the likelihood that the key transcript has been overlooked is greatly reduced in light of the fact that the ape researchers involved in teaching apes to communicate using symbols are keenly aware that their research has bearing on the differences between human and nonhuman animals; thus, if the apes were asking questions that displayed a humanlike desire for knowledge for its own sake, the chances that no ape researcher noticed this is next to nil. Ape researcher Herbert Terrace questioned David Premack's claims about the linguistic competence

---

from sight; and if he gets the answer right, he is praised and rewarded with the item in question. The bird is thus motivated by hopes of getting a like reward when it is questioned. The parrot's experience, then, is that learning the names of things is useful for getting something it wants.

37 Theodore Xenophon Barber, *The Human Nature of Birds* (St. Martin's Press, 1993), 7.

38 A classmate of mine recounted that his parrot asked, "What doing?" when he was cleaning its cage, and that the next time he cleaned the cage the parrot said, "cleaning cage." While it is unclear what the motive of these behaviors was, there is no reason to think that the parrot was seeking knowledge for its own sake.

39 Many of the animals that use symbols respond to Wh-questions but never use them to ask such questions. For example, the chimpanzee Dar was reported as being able to respond to Wh-questions (e.g., Who made sound?), but the signs for such questions did not form part of its active vocabulary. See James B. Rimpau, et al., "Expression of Person, Place, and Instrument in ASL Utterance of Children and Chimpanzees," in Gardner et al., *Teaching Sign Language to Chimpanzees*, 252 and 253. The same is reported in regard to the chimpanzees Washoe, Tatu, Moja, and Loulis; see Leeds and Jensvold, "The Communicative Functions of Five Signing Chimpanzees."

of the chimpanzee Sarah on the grounds that the chimp did not ask questions.[40] Premack recognized the legitimacy of this criticism and tried to blame Sarah's failure to ask questions on the training program, claiming that it gave the chimp no opportunity to ask questions (which ran up against the fact that Sarah sometimes walked off with the tokens and wrote out all the questions and answers that had been taught her, but no new questions).[41] Given that Terrace and Premack were renowned pioneers in the area of symbol usage by apes, it is highly unlikely that other ape researchers would be ignorant of their views on this matter. Thus, if there were cases of apes asking questions seeking knowledge for its own sake, we can be reasonably sure that ape researchers would report this; to my best knowledge there are no such reports.[42]

Not only do the animals not ask speculative questions, they also are not known to ask questions about moral action. Their questions are restricted to requests for objects and actions and for names.

In striking contrast to linguistically trained apes, the blind and deaf Helen Keller, upon being taught sign language, eventually came to ask questions about things, and not just about the names of things:

40 See Terrace, "Is Problem-Solving Language?," in Sebeok and Umiker-Sebeok, *Speaking of Apes*, 404.

41 See Terrace, "Is Problem-Solving Language?," 404.

42 See Joseph Jordania, *Who Asked the First Question? The Origin of Human Choral Singing, Intelligence, Language and Speech* (Logos, 2006). In this text, Jordania independently formulated the argument that animals' failure to ask questions is a sure sign of their incapacity for abstract thought. Jourdania has extensive knowledge of the literature on the language experiments with apes and finds that there is no record of them asking a question seeking knowledge for its own sake. My position differs from his insofar as my position emphasizes that the type of question indicative of a rational being is one that seeks knowledge for its own sake. Jordania recounts an incident where the ape Lana asked "?move food into room" when the dispenser was broken. Jordania, *Who Asked the First Question?*, 336. He claims this is "the only case that it was claimed that an ape asked a question," and he feels a need to explain it away by saying it does not make sense for an ape to ask a machine a question. The question the ape asked does not surprise me at all, since it is a practical question bearing on a particular. The ape wants food, the dispenser is not working, and so the ape asks that the food be brought into the room. And the ape almost certainly addressed this request to one of the technicians, as it had been trained to ask them to load food into the machine; indeed, experimenters sometimes intentionally did things like put water instead of the usual milk in the drink dispenser in order to provoke Lana to sign. Thus, the question Jordania dismisses is exactly the sort of request one would expect from an ape; it is not a question seeking knowledge for its own sake.

> I had now the key to all language, and I was eager to learn to use it. Children who hear acquire language without any particular effort; the words that fall from others' lips they catch on the wing, as it were, delightedly, while the little deaf child must trap them by a slow and often painful process. . . . At first, when my teacher told me about a new thing I asked very few questions. My ideas were vague, and my vocabulary was inadequate; but as my knowledge of things grew, and I learned more and more words, my field of inquiry broadened, and I would return again and again to the same subject, eager for further information.[43]

The apes that were subjects in the language studies had normal vision and hearing and could see and hear all sorts of things that ordinarily evoke wonder in a human child. And yet none of them asked a single question seeking knowledge for its own sake.

Reasons Proposed for Why Apes Fail to Ask Speculative Questions

Agustín Fuentes suggests that the lack of such behavior on the part of animals may not be due to their lack of reason, but rather because there is an inherent incompatibility between animal language and human language:

> The decades of attempts to teach apes to talk or to acquire and use human language failed because the construction, patterning, and system of language is distinctively human and not ape. In trying to get apes to use a species-specific human system, we were asking the wrong question. . . . The apes in these experiments became adept at using aspects of a human-imposed means of communication to do things that mattered for the apes (request food, drink and favored items, direct movement and manipulate social interactions and hierarchies between humans the captive apes, etc.). But they did not engage in the symbolic, grammatically, temporally, and intersubjectively dense meanings humans infuse into conversation—the apes communicated but did not talk.[44]

43 Helen Keller, *The Story of My Life*, https://www.holloway.com/g/helen-keller-the-story-of-my-life/sections/chapter-vi.

44 Celia Deane-Drummond et al., "The Evolution of Morality: A Three-Dimensional Map," *Philosophy, Theology, and the Sciences* 3, no. 2 (2016): 130.

Fuentes maintains that the attempt to teach apes language failed, though they were capable of communicating about the "things that mattered" for them, the reason being that the patterning of the language that people tried to teach them was distinctively human. Fuentes implies that if an ape patterning of language had been used, then the apes would have learned to "talk." I maintain that the reason the apes were not conversing is not because of the patterning of language "imposed" on them, but because of their inability to make a connection between a symbol and an idea, an ability that belongs solely to rational beings. It is only once this connection is made, and a sufficient vocabulary built up, that a person can seek to acquire new ideas for the sake of knowledge, even if at first ungrammatically.

One might object to the idea that we could learn other beings' languages on the grounds that their sensory perception of the world may differ significantly from ours (e.g., the dog lives in a world of smell that we don't), and what they view as important in the world may differ as well (whence even human languages differ in their vocabularies). This is how some people interpret Wittgenstein's statement: "If a lion could talk, we could not understand him."[45] This view fails to note the commonalities in human and nonhuman animals' lives, and similarities as to things that are important, some of which are rather obvious, for example, the desire for food. One might object that the lion does not experience the emotion of desire for food in exactly the same way that humans do. But even the same human individual does not always experience her desire in an identical manner from day to day, for example, one's desire to eat a delicious meal the first day it is served often differs from one's desire to eat it for the third day in a row. Yet we consider it reasonable in both cases to speak of desire. Similarly, gazelles and lions might desire different foods, but they both have desires. Given the importance that food plays in an animal's life, an animal language would have to contain words both for food and for expressing the desire for food. We could then understand a lion that said, "I'd like to eat you." That humans, unlike other animals, often attribute cultural meanings to food (as in the case of matzo), does not mean that we do not share with them a common need for food. It is this

45 Ludwig Wittgenstein, *Philosophical Investigations*, trans. G. E. M. Anscombe (MacMillan, 1953), 223e.

common need—and many others—that provides solid grounds for thinking that humans and animals should be able to communicate with each other.[46]

It is instructive to think about how different the lives of people with autism are from those without it. For example, Temple Grandin tells us that she has "four simple emotions of happy, sad, fearful, or angry," and never feels "mixtures of these emotions."[47] Even though Grandin does not understand emotions such as envy or how people can feel two emotions at once (e.g., love-hate), she can understand that envy names an emotion that she does not feel and that people claim to feel more than one emotion at a time, though she never experiences this. Her case brings out how there can be shared vocabulary and meaning at a general level, even when one individual's life, as to the details, is very different from another's. And we see that some animals, such as dogs, in some way share in the emotional life of humans, and indeed are sometimes more responsive to their masters' emotional states than people are.

Without doubt differences in sensorial capacities would be a hindrance in learning an animal or extraterrestrial language, but they would not be insurmountable. We see this in the case of Helen Keller, an individual who was barred from acquiring language through hearing, which is the sensory channel through which humans ordinarily learn language, and who was also barred from acquiring language though the sense that predominates when it comes to human knowledge of the world, namely, sight. Yet despite these sensory obstacles Helen did learn language. She did so because, being rational, she had the natural aptitude to understand the connection between symbols (pressed into her hand) and the ideas that she had. Helen could have learned an extraterrestrial language in the same manner that she was taught English.

W. V. O. Quine in *Word and Object* raises many valid points as to how hard it would be to decipher the meaning of a foreign language by observing

46 Notice how five-year-old Erin asks several questions seeking knowledge for its own sake using a limited vocabulary that consists largely of words that apes can and often do learn: "'Dad . . . why do spiders like to bite people? Do spiders like to bite people? We have spiders in the house. I saw one. Does *that* spider there like to bite people? One time . . . Daddy, one time there was a spider on Mommy's sweater. Was *that* spider going to bite her? It was black. Not the sweater. The sweater was her red sweater. . . . Looks nice! Was it going to bite her? Do we taste good? Like chocolate?'" Clark Elliott, *The Ghost in My Brain: How a Concussion Stole My Life and How the New Science of Brain Plasticity Helped Me Get It Back* (Penguin Books, 2016), 199.

47 Grandin, *Thinking in Pictures*, 164.

how foreign speakers use it. However, he seems to work on the assumption that the individuals who speak different languages would not want to communicate and so would not try to help each other understand what various words mean. Apes are motivated to communicate their desires for food and the like to humans, and thus to learn the symbols that we have invented in hopes of establishing communication with them. In any case, apes are observed to learn to correctly associate specific symbols with specific things, so at the level of memory the correct links have been formed, despite the obstacles Quine mentions. If these animals had ideas, they, like Helen Keller, would naturally link those symbols with their ideas and not just with their memories or images.

I conclude, then, that if apes have invented their own language, and do not simply communicate via signals they make instinctually or by imitation, this would mean that these animals understand the connection between ideas and arbitrary signs. But as argued above, if this were so, then they could learn another language (understood as a system of arbitrary signs expressing ideas), and then they would ask questions seeking to gain new ideas about reality. Their failure to do so, despite their learning to associate a specific symbol with a specific type of thing, shows that they do not have language at all.

Could a Rational Animal Lack Speculative Reason?

I once heard it proposed that it is possible that apes are rational but only possess practical reason. This is an unusual proposal in that the person who suggested it maintains that the intellect is immaterial, and that it, unlike the senses, grasps the universal.[48] Her idea was that maybe there could be a rational intermediary lying between rational animals such as ourselves who ask speculative questions and nonrational animals.

One might argue that Aristotle seems to associate speech not first and foremost with expressing truths about the way things are, but about the way they ought to be, that is, moral truths: "And whereas mere voice is but an

48 It is far more typical for those who attribute reason to nonhuman animals to understand reason to be some type of sense power, the possession of which is explainable by natural evolutionary causes. From this perspective, speculative thought—philosophy, science, the fine arts—are often viewed as by-products of our superior problem-solving capabilities.

indication of pleasure or pain, and is therefore found in other animals . . . the power of speech is intended to set forth the expedient and inexpedient, and therefore likewise the just and the unjust."[49] Aristotle concludes from this that humans are by nature political animals. This suggests that perhaps an animal could exist that was only able to use speech to express practical truths.

Further support for this view seems to come from Aquinas's affirmation that

> the knowledge (*scientia*) of doable things pertaining to prudence is more natural to man than the knowledge (*scientia*) of things able to be contemplated (*speculabilium*); whence certain individuals are found to be naturally prudent, but not naturally possessing science (*scientes*), as is said in the *Ethics*, bk. 6. And for this reason, men do not forget prudence as readily as science.[50]

What is meant by the affirmation that knowledge of practical things is more natural to humans than knowledge of speculative things? The life according to practical reason is more proportionate to our nature insofar as we are body-soul composites and not pure spirits. This is true of all human beings. In addition, to the extent that moral action directly concerns singulars, and singulars are known through the senses, it is possible for human individuals to be better or worse disposed for moral knowledge as a result of their particular physical constitution. Aquinas, commenting on the aforementioned passage in Aristotle's *Ethics*, notes:

> Since the aforesaid habits [related to prudence] concern singulars, it is necessary that in some manner they belong to the sensitive faculties which operate through bodily organs. And therefore, the said habits seem to be natural: not that they are entirely from nature, but from the natural disposition of the body certain are in readiness for these habits, so that upon a little experience they are completed in them; which does not happen in regard to the intellectual habits, which are about the natures of things, for example, geometry or metaphysics. . . . Not that some according to nature are not more apt for [knowing] the latter than others, but this is according to a remote disposition, rather than to a proximate one.[51]

49 Aristotle, *Politics*, bk. 1, chap. 2, 1253a10–15, in McKeon, *Basic Works of Aristotle*, trans. Benjamin Jowett.

50 *De Verit.*, q. 18, a. 7, ad 7.

51 *In Ethic.*, bk. 6, lec. 9, no. 16; see also no. 17.

Practical knowledge is ultimately fully practical when it bears directly on a singular, which is not true of speculative knowledge, which concerns universals. While both speculative reason and practical reason draw their principles from singulars known through sense experience, a prudential decision requires not only a grasp of the appropriate universal principles, but also a recognition of how they apply to a specific singulars.[52] Though the habit of prudence is primarily a perfection of the practical intellect, it is also a perfection of the cogitative faculty, which is a sense power.[53] Some individuals, due to their physical make-up, have a cogitative faculty that is better disposed to acquiring a perfection of this sort. Think of how certain people have a knack for parenting each of their very different children, a knack conspicuously missing in others.

Both Aristotle and Aquinas maintain that the higher animals have a share in prudence, for they too recognize things useful or harmful to them.[54] In addition, a person's physical constitution may make the acquisition of prudence easy for him, while at the same time causing him to lack aptitude for speculative matters.[55] It seems possible, then, for there to be a rational animal that is an intermediary of sorts between nonrational animals and rational animals like ourselves; they exceed the nonrational animals by their possession of prudence in the strict sense, while falling short of humans like us by their lack of capacity for speculative thought.

Prudential knowledge, however, does not only involve singulars, which are objects of the senses, but presupposes moral principles as well. The first principles of the practical intellect are immediately known, as are those of the speculative intellect:

52 See *In Ethic.*, bk. 6, lec. 9, no. 19.

53 See *In Ethic.*, bk. 6, lec. 7, no. 21: "Prudence, through which particular reason is perfected to rightly assessing the singular intentions of things doable, more pertains to this sense, that is, the interior sense [than to the proper senses]." Aquinas also speaks of the importance of another internal sense in prudence and indeed argues that it is a quasi-integral part of prudence. See *ST* II-II, q. 49, a. 1: "Prudence applies universal knowledge to particulars which pertain to sense; whence many things which pertain to the sensitive part are required for prudence, among which is memory."

54 See *In Ethic.*, bk. 6, lec. 7, no. 21: "Whence even brute animals that have good natural assessment of what is damaging or beneficial are said to share in prudence."

55 Experience shows that people who are good at theoretical matters are often devoid of common sense, something that is needed to make good practical decisions, and vice versa.

> For it is manifest that in the intellective part there is the possible intellect, which is in potency to all intelligible things, in the knowledge of which intellectual virtue consists; and there is the agent intellect, by whose light things become intelligible in act; of which certain things immediately from the beginning become naturally known to man without study or inquiry. And things of this sort are the first principles, not only in speculative matters, such as "every whole is greater than its part," and the like, but also in practical matters, such as "evil is to be avoided," and the like. These things that are naturally known are, however, the principles of all subsequent knowledge which is acquired through study; whether it is practical or speculative.[56]

Given that the intellect by nature is "in potency to all intelligible things," one might wonder whether knowledge of practical first principles arises before knowledge of speculative first principles, or vice versa, or whether there is no particular order in the acquisition of first principles.

One might argue that the first principles of the practical intellect are more known than those of the speculative intellect, insofar as life according to practical reason is more natural to the composite being that we are:

> Prudence includes knowledge of universals and of singular doable things to which the prudent person applies the universal principles. Therefore, as to the universal knowledge, reason stands in the same way to prudence and to speculative knowledge. For the first universal principles of both are naturally known, . . . except the common principles of prudence are more connatural to man; for as the philosopher says in bk. X of the Ethics, "The life that is according to speculative truth is higher than that according to human nature (secundum hominem)."[57]

Yet on further investigation there is reason to think that knowledge of speculative first principles is prior. As Aquinas notes:

> Something happens to be self-evident (*per se notum*) in two ways: one way in itself and not according to us, and another way in itself and according to us. For a given proposition is self-evident when the predicate is included in the notion of the subject, as [in the affirmation] "man is an animal," for animal belongs to the notion of man. If, therefore, as to a given predicate and subject, it is known to all what they are, the

56 *De Virt.*, q. 1, a. 8.

57 *ST* II-II, q. 47, a. 15.

> proposition will be self-evident to all, as is plain in [the case of] the first principles of demonstration, whose terms are certain common things that no one can be ignorant of, such as being and nonbeing, whole and part, and the like. If, however, it is not known by some what the predicate and subject are, the proposition in itself will be self-evident, but not to those who are ignorant of the subject and predicate of the proposition.[58]

There are certain concepts that all normal human beings naturally form, because there are certain realities that are thrust upon us, the first of which is being. We cannot experience anything without experiencing something that is. And there are any number of other things that we come into contact without any investigation on our part because these things are so general, and hence, widespread, for example, wholes and parts (we cannot be ignorant that we ourselves are wholes made up of parts), motion (we cannot be ignorant that we move), and so forth. We cannot help but form concepts of these things (they "fall" into our minds[59]), and once we do, we are led to immediately recognize certain speculative truths, such as that a thing cannot both be and not be at the same time and in the same respect, and that the whole is greater than its part. And we form these concepts and propositions, at least in the case of being, before we form concepts and propositions concerning the good (which is what is first apprehended by practical reason):[60]

> Being" is prior to "good" according to its notion. For [since] the notion that is signified through a name is what the intellect conceives about the thing, and signifies through the voice, therefore what is prior according to notion is what falls prior in the conception of the intellect. Being is the first thing that falls in the conception of the intellect, for everything whatsoever is knowable insofar as it exists in act (as is said in book 9 of

58 *ST* I, q. 2, a. 1. See also *Q. DA*, a. 14, arg. 16: "All or most of the individuals that belong to a species arrive at the proper operation of the species. But a very small number of human beings arrive at the point of having understanding (*sint intelligentes*). Therefore, to understand is not the proper operation of the human soul." Ibid., ad 16: "Granted that few arrive at perfect understanding, nevertheless all arrive at some manner of understanding. For, it is manifest that the first principles of demonstration are the common conceptions of the soul, which are perceived by the intellect."

59 See *Expositio libri Boetii De ebdomadibus*, lec. 1; *De Verit.*, q. 21, a. 1.

60 See *ST* I-II, q. 94, a. 2: "Just as being is the first thing that falls in apprehension simply speaking, so too good is the first thing that falls in the apprehension of practical reason, which is ordered to a work; for every agent acts for an end, which has the notion of good." See also *De Virt.*, q. 1, a. 6, ad 5: "The truth of the practical intellect is the good, which is the end of operation."

> the *Metaphysics*). Whence "being" is the proper object of the intellect, and in this way it is the first intelligible, as sound is the first audible.[61]

Thus, the intellect conceives speculative truth before it conceives practical truth. And one cannot get around this by claiming, perhaps, that a rational being could be limited at the sense level to possessing a cogitative sense (and corresponding memory) such that it only picked out and retained singulars that are good or bad, and not other singulars, for even then the good and the bad are good and bad *things*.

The concept "being" and the principle of contradiction are not the only speculative concepts and principles that precede practical reasoning; there are others as well. Acting justly presupposes that one has the notion of equality; for example, one could not recognize that giving unequal compensation to people who did equal work was unfair if one did not have the notion of equality.[62] Acting temperately and bravely presupposes knowing certain truths about human nature, for example, the purposes that concupiscible and irascible emotions are meant to serve in human life.

A similar conclusion can be drawn in regard to questions; that is, a rational being could not be limited to asking practical questions alone. We experience wonder—which leads us to ask questions—when something occurs that is contrary to our expectation and its cause is hidden.[63] Certainly the earliest humans experienced the particular form of wonder that is provoked by things whose magnitude exceeds or appears to exceed one's ability to resist them—terrifying things, such as floods, plagues, swarms of locust, earthquakes, etc.[64] In the face of these things, early peoples composed myths that provided a way of understanding these phenomena and that allowed people to in some sense cope with them (e.g., they could propitiate the gods who supposedly were in control of these phenomena). The wonder

61 *ST* I, q. 5, a. 2. See also *ST* I, q. 16, a. 4, esp. ad 2; *ST* I-II, q. 9, a. 1; *De Verit.*, q. 21, a. 4.

62 See *Expositio De ebdomadibus*, lec. 1:

> For there are conceptions of the soul that are common to all human beings, such as: if equals are taken from equals, what remains are equals. . . . Since a common conception of the soul, or a principle that is self-evident (*per se notum*), is a proposition where the predicate belongs to the notion of the subject, then if the thing that is signified by the subject and the predicate falls in the knowledge of all, as a consequence the proposition is self-evident to all; for example, what equal is is known to all, and similarly what it is to subtract, and therefore the aforesaid proposition is known to all.

63 See *De Pot.*, q. 6, a. 2; *ST* I-II, q. 105, a. 7.

64 See *ST* I-II, q. 41, a. 4.

about these phenomena was practical, insofar as the knowledge people sought about these things concerned how they could protect themselves from them; it was the wonder of "What are we to do?"[65] However, at the same time, humans were exposed to many wonders that were not harmful or threatening: rainbows, tides, phases of the moon, harvest moons, shooting stars, flowers that close at night; and since these are in some way out of the ordinary, people's wonder, as a desire simply to know, would have been naturally aroused by them, just as it is in us.

Now one might insist that the rational soul is the substantial form of a body, and so a life in which we use both mind and body is more proportioned to us,[66] in addition to which factually most people spend their time making a living and raising their families, while few devote it to the pursuit of speculative truth. Indeed, Aquinas speaks of there being multiple potential obstacles impeding the pursuit of speculative knowledge, and even offers the widespread character of these obstacles as a reason for why God needs to reveal his existence to us.[67] So why couldn't there be a type of rational animal, none of whose members *pursued* speculative truth?

The impediments to the pursuit of speculative learning that Aquinas most frequently names are the lack of leisure, laziness, and a physical make-up that renders learning difficult.[68] However, as he observes, these various impediments are obstacles not so much to asking questions as they are to obtaining answers:

> And therefore, man naturally desires knowledge (*scientiam*). Nor does the fact that some men do not undertake the study of this science disprove it, since frequently those who desire some end are diverted from pursuing that end from some cause, either on account of the difficulty of arriving at it, or on account of other business. In this manner, granted all men desire knowledge, nevertheless not all undertake the study of knowledge, because they are held back by other things, either by

65 See *In Meta.*, bk. 2, lec. 2, no. 2: "The end of the practical is some work, for even if practical people, that is, those who do something, intend to know how the truth stands in certain things, nevertheless they do not seek it as the ultimate end."

66 See *Nicomachean Ethics*, bk. 10, chap. 6, 1177b26, and *In Ethic.*, bk. 10, lec. 11, nos. 8 and 13.

67 See *ST* II-II, q. 2, a. 4, *De Verit.*, q. 14, a. 10, and *In Meta.*, bk. 1, lec. 1.

68 Regarding physical make-up affecting one's ability to learn speculative truths, see *De Verit.*, q. 14, a. 10 (*pravitatem complexionis*); *SCG*, bk. 1, chap. 4 (*complexionis indispositionis*); *ST* I, q. 85, a. 7.

> pleasures, or by the necessities of the present life, or yet again they avoid the labor of learning on account of laziness.[69]

The truth of this can be seen by examining one by one each of the factors Aquinas frequently names as impediments to acquiring speculative knowledge.[70] As for lack of leisure, while individuals in a given society may be so focused on merely staying alive that they do not attend to anything other than what is apt to foster survival, this is not true of the children who are too young to work or to work continuously. At any rate, this is no excuse for the linguistically trained apes for not asking speculative questions, as all their needs from birth through adulthood are taken care of by humans.

As for laziness, seeking answers is often difficult, but asking questions about unusual natural phenomena is easy, for example, why does a shooting star move as it does, unlike the other stars?[71] Having a physical make-up that renders one inapt for intellectual pursuits offers the most plausible explanation for how there could be a rational being that asked practical questions but not speculative ones. While it is not possible for there to be a rational being capable of formulating practical questions but not speculative ones, it seems that perhaps there could be one that was so dense that it would never do the latter.[72] One might also claim that a being might have a physical make-up that resulted in a total lack of interest in pursuing any speculative knowledge. And, in fact, certain individuals display a seemingly innate apathy toward learning for its own sake. However, if either of these things were true of a species of rational being, then that species would exist in vain, for "a thing would exist in vain, if it was left destitute of its proper act, for everything is for the sake of its operation."[73] For again, the "end and good of the intellect is the true: and consequently the ultimate end is the first truth."[74] The intellect, whose very nature is to know intelligible being, would be rendered vain if it

69 *In Meta.*, bk. 1, lec. 1.

70 See *SCG*, bk. 1, chap. 4.

71 There are questions that are difficult to formulate, as they arise as the result of a dialectical investigation or scientific inquiry; certainly, these are not the first questions people ask.

72 It would have knowledge of the first principles of the speculative intellect, but this knowledge would have been acquired naturally, rather than deliberately sought.

73 *De Verit.*, q. 24, a. 10, arg. 10.

74 *SCG*, bk. 3, chap. 25.

were deprived of its proper act due to the absence of any ability or desire to actualize its potential.

One might maintain that there are exceptions to the principle that "nature does nothing in vain."[75] However, if the intellect is indeed immaterial, then it requires an immaterial cause, namely, God. And God does not create things in vain. Although God is entirely free in what he chooses to create, and does not owe anything to any creature, nevertheless,

> in every creature whatsoever a conditional debt is taken from its parts and properties and accidents on which the creature depends as to its being or as to some perfection of it: as, supposing that God wants to make a human being, it is due from this supposition that soul and body be joined in it, and sense perception, and other means of aid, both intrinsic and extrinsic be bestowed on it. In all things, if one considers things rightly, God is not said to be the debtor of the creature, but of fulfilling his own disposition.[76]

To create a species of rational animal incapable of actualizing its potential to know intelligible being, and above all to know God, because of inadequate internal senses or because of an inherent (i.e., natural) absence of desire to know speculative truth, would be contrary to God's wisdom.

One might argue that a being capable of practical reasoning alone could know God as it could grasp the Fourth Way, which is based on goodness. However, this view does not hold up to scrutiny. The Fourth Way begins: "For there is found in things something more and less good. But more and less is said about diverse things according as they approach in diverse ways to something that is the maximum, as what is hotter approaches more to what is maximally hot."[77] The principle "more and less is said about diverse things according as they approach in diverse ways to something that is the maximum" transcends the practical order, and so could not be fully known to a being only capable of practical reasoning. Moreover, it is difficult to see how this principle could be known from practical matters (be they moral or artistic), as there does not seem to be a bravest person to whom less brave persons approach in different ways. This problem becomes even more acute in regard to the following assertion made in the Fourth Way: "What is said

75 See Aristotle, *On the Soul*, bk. 3, chap. 9, 432b22: "Nature does nothing in vain."

76 *SCG*, bk. 2, chap. 28.

77 *ST* I, q. 2, a. 3.

to be the maximum in some genus is the cause of all the things that belong to that genus, as fire which is maximally hot is the cause of all hot things." The problem becomes more acute because this is a speculative principle, and also, it is not the case that the bravest person is the cause of the bravery of less brave individuals.

Alternately, one might object that the beings in question could come to know that God existed through moral arguments; however, these arguments are not the work of practical reason, but are metaethical considerations concerning the foundation of morality and belong to speculative reason (*pace* Kant).

Lastly, one might argue that the beings in question could know God through faith. However, even the knowledge of God through faith is primarily speculative, for God is not an object of our operation, but rather is the One Who Is. As Aquinas notes:

> It stands that the object of faith is not an operable truth, but the uncreated truth, in regard to which there can only be an act of the speculative intellect. Whence faith is in the speculative intellect, although it is as a remote occasion for doing something: whence operation is not attributed to faith except by the mediation of love.[78]

De Waal's Argument in Favor of Animal Rationality

Frans de Waal maintains that

> animals just can't afford to blindly run after their impulses. Their emotional reactions always go through an appraisal of the situation and judgment of available opportunities. This is why they all have self-control. Furthermore, in order to avoid punishment and conflict, the members of a group need to adjust their desires, or at least their behavior, to the will of those around them. . . . So even though personally I am not a big believer in free will, we do need to pay close attention to the way

78 *De Verit.*, q. 14, a. 4. See *ST* II-II, q. 4, a. 2, ad 3: "Faith is in the speculative intellect as in a subject as is patently manifest from the object of faith. But because the first truth, which is the object of faith, is the end of all our desires and acts . . . whence it is that it works through love; as also the speculative intellect by extension becomes practical, as is said in III *De Anima*." See also *ST* I, q. 1, a. 4, s.c.

> cognition may override inner urges. Fighting the impulse to take one course of action and replacing it with another that promises a better outcome is a sign of rational agency.[79]

According to what de Waal says here, animals control their emotions in order to gain some concrete benefit (such as the reciprocation of a favor) or to avoid some concrete harm (such as being bitten). The reason a male chimpanzee does not act on its desire to mate is because the alpha male nearby is liable to attack it. Its restraint is not due to a moral principle. The same is true of animals that delay gratification in order to get a bigger or better reward.[80]

De Waal, in deeming such restraint to be a sign of rational agency, fails to distinguish two different meanings of the word "rational." "Rational" can refer to something that results from reasoning in the strict sense, which necessarily involves abstract principles, such as concluding that one should protest this war because large numbers of civilians are being killed. In this sense, a person's behavior is "rational" when it is in accord with the dictates of her reason and it is "irrational" when it departs from it, and this is so regardless of whether her reasoning is correct or not.[81]

"Rational" can also refer to adopting a means or course of action that is apt to ultimately lead to a desired outcome. Rational behavior in the latter sense can result from sensory knowledge alone, be it experiential or innate or some combination of the two, as well as from reasoning in the strict sense. For example, the chimpanzee desirous of mating knows either experientially or instinctively that acting on this feeling in the presence of the alpha male will result in its being attacked. In this situation, not acting on this feeling is the "rational" thing to do, given that it would not lead to the desired outcome.

I have argued earlier that "rational" in the first sense applies only to humans and not to other animals. It seems that de Waal would have to agree that we differ from other animals in that we can choose to act on principle even though the ultimate outcome of doing so may well be some concrete harm to ourselves. Animals make mistakes about what actions are apt to bring about the best ultimate outcome. However, not only is there evidence

79 De Waal, *Mama's Last Hug*, 230–31.

80 See de Waal, 226–27, for examples of animals restraining their immediate desire in order to get a bigger or better reward.

81 See *ST* I-II, q. 19, a. 5: "Whether the will dissenting from erring reason is bad" and a. 6: "Whether the will agreeing with erring reason is good."

that they do not adopt maladaptive courses of action on principle, but in addition natural selection would eliminate such behaviors. It is only humans who control their emotions in order to abide by moral convictions despite a foreseeably bad result, such as being sent to a gulag.

De Waal fails to appreciate the role that abstract principles play in human decision-making. He points to "the screaming protests, the marches, the violence, the endurance of police beatings and water cannons," as evidence that the "absence of fairness and justice shakes us to the core, something that no amount of elegant abstract reasoning will ever accomplish."[82] However, affirming that people are capable of doing things because they conclude on the basis of abstract principle that doing these things is right does not mean that they must always do so in the absence of emotion. Given that we are body-soul composites it is to be expected that there will be interaction between desires we have due to our rationality and our emotions. For example, helping someone in need often generates warm feelings.[83] But it is quite possible for us to help someone in need, even when the person is unpleasant and ungrateful, solely because we think it is the right thing to do.[84] Dorothy Day is often quoted as saying: "There are two things you should know about the poor: they tend to smell, and they are ungrateful."[85] I think it is safe to conclude that Day advocated for the poor primarily on the basis of principle and not on the basis of emotion. People will sometimes do things that they take no joy in not because of fear of punishment, but because they think it is their duty or responsibility to do so. For example, a professor might feel very bad about giving a failing grade to a student who has had a rough semester and yet will do so solely in order to be fair to the other students. The force of abstract reasoning is also indicated by the expression, having the "courage of one's convictions," which is used to describe people

82 De Waal, *Mama's Last Hug*, 219.

83 See *ST* I-II, q. 77, a. 6: "The motion of the higher powers [namely, reason and will], if they are vehement, overflow in the lower powers, for the will is not able to intensely move toward something without some emotion (passio) being excited." See also *Super Sent.*, bk. 4, d. 15, q. 4, a. 2, qc. 1.

84 As Aristotle observes, people who freely do good to others always gain a greater good than what they give, as they perfect their character, which is a good of the soul. We do not call people "selfish" for this reason, but rather when they deprive others of external goods, such as money or promotions. See Aristotle, *Nicomachean Ethics*, bk. 9, chap. 8.

85 "83 Notable Quotes By Dorothy Day, The Founder Of Catholic Worker Movement," wisdomly.net. https://www.wisdomly.net/dorothy-day-1255.php. Accessed May 13, 2025.

who overcome fear of a prison sentence, or of death, or of some other grave harm in order to stay true to their principles.

The force of principle is also seen in the case of the moral virtues of temperance and courage. Both these virtues involve moderating emotion in light of reason (the former, the desire for pleasure and the latter, fear and confidence). We are able to ask ourselves, "Should I feel this way, and should I act on this feeling?" and what measures the "should" is moral principle. It is abstract reasoning that allows us to put the brakes on our emotions. De Waal fails to see this as differentiating us from other animals.

Up until now, I have opted to treat moral behavior by looking to reason rather than to free will. Here I will make a few brief comments about free will. I maintain that free will is rooted in reason. An animal has no choice but to follow whatever emotion is strongest in it. If an animal desires to grab food from a conspecific it fears, either its desire will outweigh its fear or vice versa, and whichever is the case will determine how it acts. Same in the case of its hope of getting a greater reward by forgoing acting on its desire to eat what is currently before it. Even in those cases where animals attempt to distract themselves from a present reward to gain a greater one, they do so only to the extent that they feel it is worth it.[86] Their actions inevitably fluctuate in direct correspondence to the fluctuation of their emotions. They are not freely choosing what they do. As I have argued, we are capable of acting on principle, independently of our emotions and even contrary to them. Our ability to act in accord with abstract moral principles does not force us to act in any given way. Knowing that stealing is wrong does not force us to not steal. Our ability to act in accord with or contrary to such knowledge frees us from having our behavior determined by our emotions.

86 De Waal gives interesting examples of animals exhibiting self-control by apparently distracting themselves. For example, a chimpanzee watching candies continually falling into a container knows that when it lifts the container, the candies will stop coming. The longer it waits before it lifts the container the more candies it gets. Apparently, some chimpanzees will look at toys to reduce their desire to lift the container; see de Waal, *Mama's Last Hug*, 227.

Arguments That Seemingly Undermine the Role of Moral Principles in Moral Decision-Making

Some suggest that all moral acts depends on emotion, basing this view on research on psychopaths and people with certain forms of brain damage. In regard to psychopaths, Larry Arnhart maintains that

> there is no evidence that psychopaths have any deficit in their capacity for abstract rationality or pure thought. Their immorality comes not from any defect of abstract reasoning, but from their emotional poverty. They cannot be moral, because they lack the social emotions—such as sympathy, guilt, and shame—that sustain moral conduct.[87]

As for brain-damaged persons who lack emotion, both de Waal and Arnhart bring up the case of Elliott, a patient who after undergoing damage to his frontal lobe went from being a successful businessman, husband, and father to an unemployed drifter who was briefly married to a prostitute after his wife divorced him.[88]

De Waal describes Elliott thus:

> While Elliott was articulate and intellectually sound, witty even, he had become emotionally flat, showing no hint of affect in many hours of conversation. Elliott was never sad, impatient, angry, or frustrated. This lack of emotion seemed to paralyze his decision making. It might take him all afternoon to make up his mind about where and what to eat, or half an hour to decide on an appointment or the color of his pen.[89]

Arnhart describes people with frontal lobe damage thus:

> People with such damage show no loss of intellectual capacity, at least at the level of abstract reasoning. They show no impairment of memory or knowledge. . . . Yet they are unable to make good practical decisions

87 Larry Arnhart, *Darwinian Natural Right: The Biological Ethics of Human Nature* (State University of New York Press, 1998), 229. See also Arnhart, 228: "[Psychopaths] cannot reason well about their lives because their desires are too shallow to move them consistently toward any goal. Without deep desires, they lack the motive power to make or enforce any practical decision conforming to any coherent pattern of life. Reason without desire cannot move us."

88 See Arnhart, 225.

89 De Waal, *Mama's Last Hug*, 205.

> that are socially acceptable and personally advantageous. This weakness in their practical reason seems to come from their inability to feel the social emotions. The poverty in their feelings impedes their reasoning. They cannot think clearly about practical decisions because they cannot feel strongly about the consequences of their decisions.[90]

The claim is what is lacking in the moral decision-making of psychopaths and those with frontal lobe damage is not the ability to reason but to feel emotion.

I maintain that focusing on a very small number of abnormal people's behavior in place of looking at what is the case of most people is not a good way to understand human behavior. For that reason, I am not going to investigate these cases in depth but will limit myself to showing that they can be understood in a manner that is compatible with the thesis that a grasp of moral principles is essential to moral decision-making.

The view that psychopaths "cannot be moral, because they lack the social emotions," does not as such deny that moral behavior also depends on the application of moral principles. The latter is what is crucial to seeing that animals are not moral beings. However, this view does give at least equal importance to emotion and to the application of moral principles in moral behavior, and this stands in opposition to my claim that humans can act on principle alone. In response, it should first be noted that not everyone agrees that psychopaths cannot be moral; some hold that they simply choose to act in an immoral manner, a manner that is facilitated but not necessitated by their lack of affect.[91] And as for those with frontal lobe damage, it is not clear from the examples that de Waal gives concerning Elliott that such people are incapable of moral decision-making, as these examples concerned things that had no ostensible moral content, such as what to eat for lunch. Was Elliott unable to decide whether he should pay for his groceries? Antonio Damasio, who was Elliott's physician at one point, describes Elliott's behavior

90 Arnhart, *Darwinian Natural Right,* 225.

91 See Susan Krauss Whitbourne, "Psychopaths Don't Care If They Hurt You: This Is Why," *Psychology Today*, June 3, 2017, https://www.psychologytoday.com/us/blog/fulfillment-any-age/201706/psychopaths-dont-care-if-they-hurt-you-is-why:

> We can't say that people high in psychopathy are unable to make moral choices, then, but it does appear justified to say that they will feel less anguish when they have to do so. The rest of us don't want to cause harm to others and feel stressed when forced to do so, but those high in psychopathy seem to be able to make the 'utilitarian,' logic-based choice without feeling particularly distraught.

at greater length.[92] The only thing Damasio mentions that suggests that Elliott had a problem with moral decision-making was Elliott's decision to go into business with a disreputable character despite warnings from friends.[93] Elliott's main problems, according to Damasio, were with planning for the hours ahead of him[94] and with keeping the big picture in mind when executing tasks.[95]

In any case, it is possible to attribute some role to emotion in moral decision-making while still holding that moral reasoning is essential for moral decision-making, as well as also holding that moral decision-making may occur when emotion is absent. Aquinas observes that:

> As the Philosopher says in bk. 6 of the Ethics [1142a 26], prudence does not consist in an exterior sense, by which we know proper sensibles, but in an interior sense which is perfected through memory and experience so as to promptly judge about particulars that are experienced. Nevertheless, this is not in such a manner that prudence is in the interior sense as in its principal subject; rather it is principally in reason. However, through a certain joining it [prudence] extends to a sense of this sort.[96]

Aquinas is speaking about the cogitative power, which was mentioned earlier. The cogitative power is the sensory faculty by which humans recognize singulars as having a certain nature, for example, "this is a dog," and "that is water."[97] The cogitative power is needed both to provide the minor premise in practical reasoning and to grasp the conclusion thereof; for example, the intellect knows the universal truth, "Taking things belonging to others without their consent is morally wrong," while the cogitative recognizes *this pen is a thing that belongs to another*, and thus the intellect concludes to something

92 See Antonio Damasio, *Descartes' Error: Emotion, Reason, and the Human Brain* (Penguin Books, 1994), 34–51.

93 See Damasio, *Descartes' Error*, 37.

94 See Damasio, 37.

95 See Damasio, 36: "One might say that Elliot had become irrational concerning the larger frame of behavior, which pertained to his main priority, while within the smaller frames of behavior, which pertained to subsidiary tasks, his actions were unnecessarily detailed."

96 *ST* II-II, q. 47, a. 3, ad 3.

97 See *In DA*, bk. 2, lec. 13, n. 16: "For the cogitative apprehends individuals as existing under the common nature; which happens to it insofar as it is united to the intellective power in the same subject; whence it know this man according as it is this man, and this wood according as it is this wood."

recognized by the cogitative: therefore, *taking this pen without the other's consent is morally wrong*. Prudence requires not simply knowing that one should not harm others but also recognizing that that this specific act here and now is harmful to someone.[98] Thus, although Aquinas situates prudence in reason, he sees the virtue of prudence to be intimately connected with the cogitative power, specifically as perfected through memory and experience.

So, what does emotion have to do with this? For one, emotion help us remember things. Consider a mother deciding what kind of sandwich to fix for her kindergartener's lunch. She can know that some children have nut allergies and that young children sometimes exchange food, but she is more likely to apply this knowledge if she has seen the emotionally distressing event of a child undergoing anaphylactic shock due to eating peanut butter than if she had not witnessed such an event. In general, we retain things in our conscious memory because they are emotionally charged, and thus to the extent that memory perfects the cogitative power which is required for judging particular things to be morally good or bad, emotion can be conducive to prudence, while not being absolutely necessary for it.[99]

Imagine that the woman who had seen the child in anaphylactic shock did not feel distressed by it. In this case, she would not be any more likely than the person who had not witnessed such an event to be attentive to what

98 See *De Verit.*, q. 10, a. 5:

> In another manner [the mind is joined in an accidental manner to singulars], according as the motion which is from the soul to things begins in the mind and proceeds to the sensitive part, according as the mind rule the lower powers. And in this manner, it joins itself to singulars by means of particular reason, which is a certain power of the sensitive part which composes and divides individual intentions (which is also known by another name, the cogitative power), and which has a determinate organ in the body, namely, a chamber in the middle of the head. For the universal conviction [sententiam] that the mind has about things to be done cannot be applied to a particular act except through some intermediary power that apprehends the singular, such that in this manner a certain syllogism comes to be, the major of which is universal, which is the conviction held by the mind; the minor, however, is singular, which is the apprehension of particular reason; the conclusion is the choice of the singular work, as is clear through what is said in bk. 3 of *De Anima*.

99 Here is another example that illustrates the help that emotion can provide to the cogitative. Two people may hold on principle that one should tithe to give to the poor. The one who will more readily apply that knowledge is the one who has witnessed the dire situation of the poor firsthand, as opposed to the person who has not, because the emotion attached to having viewed this concrete harm thus helps keep the importance of acts of charity in the front of his mind. "I will never forget the pitiful sight of people living in cardboard boxes." Such memories help us identify things in the present as things to be done or avoided.

she put in her young child's school lunch. But again, having the emotional experience is not essential to avoiding behaviors known to harm others. This mother still could avoid putting a peanut butter sandwich in the lunch box based on her general knowledge that it may harm other children. How does this apply to psychopaths? It is commonly said that psychopaths tend to be indifferent to the emotions and suffering of others. They don't feel distress at others' distress. This may make it more difficult for them to recognize a particular harm as a harm, but it does not render them incapable of doing so.[100]

A second consideration as to how a lack of emotion may affect one's moral agency concerns how one first learns about harm, which, generally speaking, is by being a victim of it. The Golden Rule and its variants presuppose knowledge of how one wants oneself to be treated or not treated. When one is young, one's first experiences of harm typically involve pain or the deprivation of pleasure; being smacked by a sibling or parent or being deprived of dessert. It is often said that psychopaths in general are not much affected by their own pain and have little or no fear of experiencing pain (though not all research supports this view).[101] If so, this would be a hindrance in recognizing that inflicting pain on others is a harm. While I do not think this is an insurmountable obstacle to moral agency—consider, for example, that one does not have to have been raped to recognize it as a harm—it would make it more difficult for the person to recognize a particular action as inflicting harm.

Turning now to those whose lack of emotion is due to frontal lobe damage, if we concede, for the sake of the argument, that they are paralyzed in their moral decision-making, something Damasio says hints at the possibility that the problem lies in a defect within their cogitative power: "the defect appeared to set in at the late stages of reasoning, close to or at the point at which choice making or response selection must occur."[102] This point is the actual application to something here and now, something which again is known through the cogitative. The emotions can not only affect

100 See Whitbourne, "Psychopaths Don't Care If They Hurt You." See also Christian Keysers, "Inside the Mind of a Psychopath—Empathic, But Not Always," *Psychology Today*, July 24, 2013, https://www.psychologytoday.com/us/blog/the-empathic-brain/201307/inside-the-mind-psychopath-empathic-not-always.

101 See Guillaume Durand and Erika Motsumoto Plata, "The Effects of Psychopathic Traits on Fear of Pain, Anxiety, and Stress," *Personality and Individual Differences* 119 (December 2017): 198–203.

102 Damasio, *Descartes' Error*, 50.

the cogitative power by rendering particulars memorable, but the cogitative power can also affect the emotions, or at least so thinks Aquinas, who put the cogitative sense in parallel with the estimative power in animals:

> For the sense appetite [the emotions] are apt to be moved in nonhuman animals by the estimative power, as the sheep, judging the wolf to be an enemy, feels fear. In humans, . . . what takes the place of the estimative power is the cogitative power, which is called by some "particular reason." It puts together individual intentions. Whence the sense appetite [the emotions] in humans is apt to be moved by it.[103]

A person using the cogitative power recognizes, for example, that this religious sister gave a classmate detention for talking in class and that that religious sister gave another classmate detention for talking in class. The cognitive power, when working properly, puts these things together and they are stored in the person's memory. As a result, the sight of a nun produces a fear of talking in class. As was mentioned earlier, some people have a natural aptitude that allows them to readily pick up on things of this sort. At the other end of the spectrum are people who tend to be oblivious to such things. Not everyone picks up that talking in class when a religious sister is present is asking for trouble.[104] So perhaps the defective decision-making ability of people with frontal lobe damage is not rooted in their lack of emotion but in some deficiency affecting their cogitative power, which in turn impacts on their ability to feel emotion; in this case, the lack of emotion is concomitant with the defect in the cognitive power, but is not a cause of the defective decision-making.[105]

In sum, I do not think that looking at rare aberrant cases is the best way to understand human moral decision-making. In any case, an examination of these cases shows that emotion may in some way be implicated in our ability to make moral decisions, but acknowledging this does not compel us to reject the view that the ability to grasp moral principles is essential for moral decision-making.

103 *ST* I, q. 81, a. 3.

104 See Proverbs 23:3: "The one clever by reason of experience sees evil and hides himself; the naïve go forward and are afflicted with harm."

105 Note that Damasio says of Elliott, "In spite of being confronted with the disastrous results of his decisions, he did not learn from his mistakes." Damasio, *Descartes' Error*, 38.

Conclusion

My argument is that the animals that are the most likely candidates for moral agency, when taught to use symbolic forms of communication, fail to ask speculative questions. Since rational beings naturally ask such questions, the animals' failure to do so shows that they lack reason. Moral agency depends on reason. Moral agents act knowingly in accord with universal moral principles or contrary to them. Consequently, animals cannot be moral agents.

Epilogue

Some will legitimately be somewhat skeptical of my conclusion in the absence of plausible explanations for why some animals sometimes act as if they were altruistic or just. I do not pretend to be able to explain with certitude the various seemingly altruistic or fair actions displayed by animals. However, there are several causes, proposed by biologists and others, that plausibly explain what motivates a lot of the seemingly moral behavior of animals.

Some cases can be explained by the presence of prosocial emotions in social animals,[106] that is, an innate desire to be helpful toward and cooperative with other group members, something which increases the chances that group efforts will be successful. Accompanying, and indeed presupposed by, these prosocial emotions are cognitive abilities allowing the animal to recognize needs and intentions. Prosocial emotions are apparently triggered in some cases even by members of other species that in some way resemble theirs. This explains cases such as the gorilla that brought a toddler who fell into its enclosure to safety, dolphins who rescue humans who are drowning or being threatened by sharks, and chimpanzees that retrieve items humans have dropped.

A behavioral corollary to helping behavior is punishing behavior. Individuals thereby deter others from exploiting them. Certain animals have the cognitive ability to identify things such as not getting a proportional

106 Aquinas, commenting on Aristotle, talks about the need for a certain emotional disposition in social animals, e.g., they cannot be bellicose. *Sententia libri Politicorum*, bk. 1, lec. 1, nos. 35 and 36. Aquinas maintains that animals have natural virtues, e.g., lions exhibit behavior that appears courageous, *In Ethic.*, bk. 10, lec. 12, n. 14, and *De Virt.*, q. 1, a. 8, ad 10, but these virtues are not true virtues due to the absence of prudence. *De Virt.*, q. 1, a. 6, ad 4. Animals' lives are much more uniform than ours and so it is possible for them to have fixed emotional tendencies driving behaviors that in most circumstances are beneficial to them.

recompense as harmful to them. While they recognize concretely what is just, they do not know it as an instantiation of a universal principle of justice, for example, that those who contribute equally to the attainment of a collective good ought to receive an equal share of it. Their actions are not principled but driven by the emotion of anger (or fear of reprisal in cases where they received a greater reward than another without having expended more effort).[107]

Other cases of seemingly moral behavior can be explained by animals' tendencies to form emotional attachments. There is evidence that stable social bonds lead both to better health and increased reproductive fitness.[108] We already see in dogs the importance that an animal's emotional ties to others has for it; dogs sometimes become depressed and even die after their master dies, even though their physical needs are met by someone else. Apes form relationships with other apes that in some ways resemble human friendships,[109] and they can become attached to humans as well. It is not surprising then that in such cases they defend one another or that they display affection toward an individual that helped them in the past.

The maternal instinct seems to explain some of the "altruistic" relationships between animals of different species, such as the case of a cat that nursed a baby squirrel.[110] Since generally mother animals only come into close contact with their own offspring, there is little selective pressure for fine-tuning the maternal instinct to be triggered solely by their own offspring; this offers an explanation of why it is triggered in some of the unusual cases where a female does come across a baby of another species.

107 See de Waal, *Mama's Last Hug*, 214:

> Being resentful about another's success may seem petty, but in the long run it keeps one from being duped. If you and I often go out hunting together and you always claim the best chunks of meat, I need to either vociferously object to the way you are treating me or else start looking for a new hunting buddy. . . . Sensitivity to reward distribution helps ensure payoffs for both parties, which is essential for continued cooperation. It is probably no accident that the animals most sensitive to inequity—chimps, capuchins, and canids—hunt in groups and share meat.

108 See Robert M. Seyfarth and Dorothy L. Cheney, "The Evolutionary Origins of Friendship," *Annual Review of Psychology* 63 (2012): 170.

109 See Dorothy L. Cheney and Robert M. Seyfarth, *Baboon Metaphysics* (University of Chicago Press, 2007), 87–88.

110 See Anna Swartz, "Orphaned Animals Who Were Adopted by a Different Species," *Dodo*, January 28, 2015, https://www.thedodo.com/inspiring-animal-families-958705512.html.

Of course, some animals help humans as a result of being trained to do so. Examples of such animals include sheep dogs, service dogs, and avalanche dogs. (The latter are both trained to locate humans covered with snow and to dig them out.)

It is hard not to remain surprised, however, at the number of friendships of a sort between individuals belonging to different species, especially ones where the maternal instinct cannot be at play, for example, a male boxer dog that grooms a baby goat that was abandoned by its mother.[111] It surprises us because we assume that animals are not going to expend effort on things that are not going to increase their reproductive fitness. However, if my argument is correct, animals are unable to reflect on the potential cost of their actions. They are not like humans who reflect on whether they should opt to remain celibate and dedicate their lives to providing healthcare to the poor or who consider whether they should adopt a child or have another of their own. Rather, certain animals' ability to form emotional bonds simply proves to be more flexible than what is conducive to their reproductive success in certain specific cases.

In sum, while certain animals perform behaviors such as helping or punishing conspecifics or even heterospecifics, an analysis of the language studies show that they lack the ability to grasp universal moral principles, and thus their behavior in such cases is not moral. Rather it is explained by their ability to recognize concrete benefits and harms, and to respond emotionally to them in a way that on the whole promotes survival and reproductive success.

111 See Swartz, "Orphaned Animals."

Part III

THE HUMAN ANIMAL: LANGUAGE

7

Does Knowing What Things Are Require Language (As a System of Physical or Imaginable Signs)?

A number of authors in the Aristotelian-Thomistic tradition have taken up a variety of questions concerning language. Some of them offer a comprehensive AT account of language and some compare aspects of this account to the accounts of contemporary philosophers.[1] What

1 This note will provide a summary overview of works by Thomists on language. Mortimer J. Adler, in *Some Questions about Language* (Open Court, 1976), 14, maintains that the two primary problems that philosophy of language needs to solve are "the factors that must be operative for any mark or sound to become a meaningful word in any language" and "what is meant by any meaningful word." John O'Callaghan, in *Thomist Realism and the Linguistic Turn: Toward a More Perfect Form of Existence* (University of Notre Dame Press, 2016), 12, proposes to "explore how each tradition approaches the crucial Aristotelian text [in *De Interpretatione*] that purports to enunciate how the capacity for words to be about the world involve the 'mind' and what criticism involving this text might representatives of one tradition direct at another." Bernard Lonergan speaks at times about the relationship between the exterior word and the inner word. For example, he notes in *Verbum: Word and Idea in Aquinas*, ed. Frederick Crowe, SJ, and Robert Doran, SJ, vol. 2 in *The Collected Works of Bernard Lonergan* (University of Toronto Press, 1997), 14, that "the inner word is the efficient cause of the outer word." However, Lonergan's main focus is the nature and origin of the inner word. Tilman Anselm Ramelow, in "Language Without Reduction: The Linguistic Turn," *Angelicum* 85, no. 2

I propose to do is much more limited in scope.[2] I intend to address the question of whether thought is prior to language or language to thought. I became interested in the question upon reading an article by the Thomist, Nicanor Austriaco, OP, in which he affirmed that "our natural kind [human being] can be defined by our developmental capacity for language, which I suggest is necessary for abstract thinking."[3] Austriaco's claim motivated me to articulate arguments in favor of thought being ultimately prior to language. Some of my arguments were drawn from Aquinas and some from contemporary sources, while others are original with me. The latter, in some cases, are responses to objections raised by Austriaco, who was my interlocutor in a debate held on this question.[4]

Language is generally understood to consist of words and rules for putting the words together to make sentences (grammar). I am going to focus

(2008): 497, proposes the following: "Without any claim to completeness, this article is trying to highlight some of the features of an Aristotelian and Thomist understanding of language, and how they can help to categorize modern positions and by doing so contribute to an understanding of some of their problems." Other Thomistic authors consider whether there is any Thomistic equivalent to the nominalist and modern concepts of mental language; see, for example, Joshua P. Hochschild, "Mental Language in Aquinas?," in *Intentionality, Cognition, and Mental Representation in Medieval Philosophy*, ed. Gyula Klima (Fordham University Press, 2015): 29–45.

2 To my best knowledge, Fr. Anselm Ramelow, OP, is the only Thomist who directly addresses the question of whether language is prior to thought or thought to language in *Beyond Modernism?: George Lindbeck and the Linguistic Turn in Theology* (Ars Una, 2005): 68–113. Some of the arguments I offer are drawn from him.

3 Nicanor Pier Giorgio Austriaco, OP, "Defending Adam After Darwin: On the Origin of *Sapiens* as a Natural Kind," *American Catholic Philosophical Quarterly* 92, no. 2 (Spring 2018): 337. David Braine also argues that what differentiates us from animals, first and foremost, is language, rather than thinking or some form of thinking, such as reasoning. See *The Human Person: Animal and Spirit* (Notre Dame University Press, 1992), chap. 10, section 1: "Language as What Differentiates Human Beings from Other Animals," 351–67.

4 See Nicanor Pier Giorgio Austriaco, OP, "Thomistic Thoughts About Thought and Talk," *American Catholic Philosophical Quarterly* 95, no. 1 (2021): 117–30, and "On the Limits of Abstraction: A Response to Professor Marie George," *American Catholic Philosophical Quarterly* 95, no. 1 (2021): 145–48. See Marie George, "Does Knowing What Things Are Require Language (As a System of Physical or Imaginable Signs)?," *American Catholic Philosophical Quarterly* 95, no. 1 (2021): 131–44 and "A Rambutan by Any Other Name Would Taste as Sweet: Response to Professor Nicanor Pier Giorgio Austriaco, OP," *American Catholic Philosophical Quarterly* 95, no. 1 (2021): 149–53. See also Marie George, "Aquinas's Teachings on Concepts and Words in His Commentary on John Contra Nicanor Austriaco, OP," *American Catholic Philosophical Quarterly* 94, no. 3 (2020): 357–78.

on words in addressing the questions of whether language is necessary for knowing what things are.[5]

Language is an Artifact and As Such is Produced in View of a Final Cause

Words are artifacts; they are not produced naturally. Humans do not naturally speak any language, and it is humans who invent vocabularies. This is not to deny that humans by nature tend to invent language, just as they tend to make music and to form political societies. The fact remains, however, that humans speak different languages, which would not be the case if the production of any determinate language was natural. By contrast, the moans of the sick, smiling, and the like, are natural signs, as they are the same for all.[6]

Language, like all human artifacts, has a purpose or purposes. The purposes that language serves are to organize our thoughts and to express our thoughts to others.[7] In the absence of a purpose or final cause, that is, having thoughts or concepts to organize and/or express, we would not invent language.[8] Therefore, concepts are prior to language.

One might object and say that language also serves to express things other than our thoughts, such as our emotions ("I am angry") or what we want done ("please give me an apple"). However, in these cases as well, what we express is expressed by the intermediary of concepts. We use words to think about or express our emotions, insofar as those words refer to concepts of emotions. We can't think to ourselves or express to others that we are angry in the absence of a concept of what anger is. Similarly, when we ask for an apple, we employ the word "apple" knowing that it names not one specific apple alone, but any and every apple, that is, "apple" as conceptualized as a certain kind. Perhaps ceremonial usages of language, such as "How are you?" do not refer to concepts but are more like a bow or handshake.

5 Arguably the purpose of grammar is to clarify what the words in a sentence taken together mean (e.g., man, ate, dog); space does not allow for a discussion of this point.

6 See Aquinas, *Expositio libri Peryermeneias*, bk. 1, lec. 2, n. 8: "Those sounds that signify naturally, such as the moans of the sick, and other things of this sort, are the same for all."

7 I am taking "concept" to be synonymous with "thought."

8 See *ST* I, q. 5, a. 2, ad 1: "The causality of the final cause is first, for an agent does not act except for an end, and by the agent matter is moved to form, whence it is said that the end is the cause of causes."

However, the vast majority of our speaking to ourselves or to others directly involves concepts.

To clarify what I mean by thoughts or concepts: I understand a thought or concept to be knowledge of a nature apart from the principles of individuation that belong to the members sharing that nature. The concept of something is knowledge of what that being is that abstracts from the specific features that make the individual or individuals possessing that nature to be the individuals that they are. For example, the concept of "stone" is knowledge of what a stone is, knowledge that abstracts from the specific features that make individual stones to be the specific stones that they are, and similarly for other concepts. Thus, the concept of stone applies to all individual stones, whereas one's knowledge of particular stones insofar as they are particular stones does not apply to other stones; this latter knowledge is had through the senses (the "stoneness" of this stone is not the "stoneness" of that stone).

One last clarification: Language may consist of signs that are produced both exteriorly (such as a specific gesture or articulated sounds) and also interiorly in the imagination prior to being exteriorized or it may consist of signs that are only imagined.[9] For the sake of simplicity, I am going to talk about vocal signs, imagined or exteriorized, though what I say would apply to tactile or gestural signs as well.[10]

The considerations above clarify but do not alter my opening argument, which, again, is that we cannot intend to invent words in the absence of knowing their purpose, which is to organize and express concepts of what things are. If we had no concepts, then we could not intend to invent words.[11]

The Natural Process of Concept Formation Must Occur Prior to Language

The position that knowing what things are requires language entails the denial that there is a purely natural process by which humans arrive at

9 On words as imagined, see *ST* I, q. 34, a. 1 and *De Verit.*, q. 4, a. 1.

10 I take no stance on what modality the first human language had (gestural, aural, both or other) as it does not affect my main thesis.

11 The view that language is prior to reason was articulated in the eighteenth century by Johann Gottfried Herder. For a history of this view, see Ramelow, *Beyond Modernism?*, 68–70.

concepts of what things are, as doing so would always require the intervention of something artificial, that is, a word.

If one had no concepts at all it would be impossible to consciously set for oneself the goal of acquiring them. One cannot have consciously sought to know everything one knows because to consciously seek to know something presupposes that one knows that there is such a thing as knowledge about things, which cannot be the case if one is devoid of knowledge of any thing. Thus, there must be some means by which concepts are arrived at other than through investigation.

There is good reason to reject the Platonic notion that our concepts are come upon by recollection. This theory leaves unexplained why there is progress in human knowledge over time, as the same scientific truths that we supposedly recollect today could equally well have been recalled by the ancients. Another problem with the view that all our concepts are simply recollected is that it entails the highly implausible position that we have forgotten the self-evident truths that we previously knew (e.g., that the whole is greater than the part).

The evidence lies in favor of the Aristotelian view that concepts originate from sense experience. We form the concept "apple" only after sensing individual apples. When people lack a sense, they are unable to form concepts of things that are known through that specific sense; as Aquinas notes, the person blind from birth never arrives at concepts of the things treated in optics.[12]

While the formation of concepts depends on sensing, it requires more than sensing. The senses only give us knowledge of the particular. They do not give us universal knowledge of the natures of things. So there must be some type of natural process by which we arrive at concepts starting from sense knowledge. Again, whatever this process is, it goes on in the absence of investigation or reasoning, as these presuppose concepts. I am going to refer to this process as "abstraction."

Certain concepts then simply "fall" into the intellect as a result of this natural process. The first of these concepts is "being." One cannot have a concept of anything without recognizing that it is a being.[13]

12 See *ST* I, q. 84, a. 3.

13 See *ST* I, q. 5, a. 2: "What falls first in the conception of the intellect is being, for anything whatsoever is knowable insofar as it exists in act."

It is hard to know with certitude what other concepts were arrived at by the humans who invented language prior to their inventing language. It seems reasonable to think that they would have concepts of accidents that cannot escape our observation and are important for survival, such as certain of the proper sensibles (e.g., hot and cold) and the common sensibles (motion, location, etc.). It also seems that starting from sense experience they would form concepts of substances important to their lives, such as water, food, humans, various plants and animals, etc. For example, sensing deer on a number of occasions seems to suffice for the mind to form the concept "deer." In cases like this, how could lack of a word interfere with our natural capacity for abstraction?

The first concepts of substances that prelinguistic humans formed were inevitably imperfect, as is the case with people today. The first concepts of substances that we form are vague, as can be seen from the fact that we have sufficient knowledge of what things are to identify at least some specific individuals of a kind, while being unable to define the kind.[14] Since our intellects start out in potency to knowing what things are and our actually knowing what they are is arrived at from what we sense, our first knowledge of things is very much tied to the sensible accidents that we perceive. These accidents vary as to what they reveal of the nature of the thing. For example, a thing's shape generally reveals more about it than does its color. Thus, in some cases our vague knowledge of a thing is based on something that is a property of the thing, that is, an accident that flows from the thing's nature, for example, we know that stars shine. In other cases, however, our vague concepts of substances are mixed with what we mistake to be an essential accident, but which in fact falls outside the nature; for example, we may think that twinkling is a property of stars and that being white is a property of swans. People often think that shooting stars are stars because they look similar to stars and that the sun is not a star because it looks different from other stars.

Now one might say that the people named above do not have a concept of swan, shooting star, star, and sun. But if that was so, how could they ever learn that shooting stars are not stars and that the sun is a star and that being white is not a proper accident of the swan? While in the case of the swan,

14 I understand a definition to be speech which makes known in a distinct way what a thing is. It seems one could use the word "definition" to name by analogy the composition of thoughts themselves. I tend to think that words are not always necessary in order to arrive at a definition, understood in this manner.

further observation would allow a person to realize that being white does not belong to the nature of swan, it is unlikely that the errors concerning shooting stars and the sun would be cleared up in the absence of language allowing us to discuss and communicate our ideas concerning astronomy and physics with others. Nevertheless, in the absence of the initially formed vague idea there would be nothing to discuss.

Thus, I maintain that there is a difference between the unconscious process by which we go from sense experience to intellectual knowledge (concepts) and the conscious process by which we seek to clarify the vague concepts that we arrive at through the natural process, as that latter is a purely intellectual activity. While the latter activity may often or even always require words, when it comes to the former, it is impossible that this is always the case.

The Correct Use of the Word "Concept"

Nicanor Austriaco denies that abstraction (understood as a process by which concepts are arrived at starting from sense experience) yields actual concepts, and for this reason maintains that language is always prior to concepts. He asserts:

> The process of abstraction is not complete until a perfect concept is realized, in the same way that the process of habituation is not complete until perfect virtue has been attained. As I see it, imperfect concepts are only concepts in potency, in the same way that imperfect virtue is only virtue in potency.[15]

In this statement Austriaco acknowledges that concepts can be either imperfect or perfect but affirms that the former are not concepts in act. He compares them to imperfect virtue.

There is an ambiguity as to what is meant by "imperfect concept." The person who knows "animal" but is ignorant that jackals exist, by knowing "animal" only has a concept of jackal in potency (i.e., as to its genus). He does not have a perfect concept of jackal. Indeed, it is questionable whether he even has an imperfect concept of jackal; rather, by knowing "animal" he has knowledge of jackal in remote potency, that is, if he were to see a jackal, he

15 Nicanor Austriaco, OP, personal communication in response to my article "Aquinas's Teachings on Concepts and Words."

would recognize it to be an animal. This seems to be what Austriaco has in mind. But there is another way of understanding "imperfect concept," that is, in the case where a person has a vague concept of a thing's nature, as is manifested by her ability to correctly identify individuals sharing that nature (at least in most cases), while being unable to define the nature in question, for example, a person can identify animals and dogs without being able to define "animal" and "dog." Perhaps there is yet another type of situation that involves imperfect concepts. Cognitive scientist Jean Mandler references evidence from studies that show that very young children overgeneralize: "Even at age 2, as many as 30% of common nouns are still understood too broadly, for example, understanding (and using) the word *dog* to included foxes, and the word *cake* to include pies."[16] These children apparently perceive characteristics that the domestic dog and fox share in common and they are associating the word "dog" with animals having those shared sensible accidents. They are perceiving generic characteristics belonging to the dog family and not what is proper to the domestic dog. So do they have the concept "domestic dog?" They are able to correctly identify domestic dogs as dogs, but they misidentify foxes as being domestic dogs. Is this situation finally different than the situation of those who have a vague concept of domestic dog, but cannot define domestic dog? It seems not. Until one can define a kind, one is liable to mistake things that have a different nature as being of that kind. For example, a person who has a vague concept of animal might think that a barnacle is a plant. So, it seems that a person who thinks that foxes are dogs does have a vague idea of dog, while lacking a sufficiently clear idea of dog to distinguish it from a fox. It is this sort of vague idea that I regard as an imperfect concept.

One might object that the problem with children using words imprecisely may not be due to an imperfection in concept formation but rather to unfamiliarity with how certain words are used. For example, in the case of children who call pies "cakes," how would we know if children are failing to distinguish the proper accidents of cakes relative to pies (i.e., they have an imperfect concept), as opposed to not knowing the appropriate word for a pie (i.e., they understand that cakes differ from pies, but have not yet acquired the word "pie") or alternately, whether they are actually intending to indicate

16 Jean M. Mandler, "Thought Before Language," *TRENDS in Cognitive Sciences* 8, no. 11 (November 2004): 512.

all pastries by the use of the term "cake" but lack the word for the more general term "pastry," while still accurately distinguishing cake from pie?

I think this objection has substance. I concede that I may be mistaken in the case of particular instances that I name, as I agree that the misuse of words is sometimes not due to some imperfection in one's concept but rather in one's failure to grasp the word's meaning. For example, when I was little, I used to think that "dearth" meant a lot of, only later to learn that it means the opposite. I had the concepts of a lot and of a little, but I matched the word "dearth" to the wrong concept. The notion of "false friends" in language learning also illustrates a misuse of words that is not due to imperfect concept formation. A "false friend" is a word in a foreign language that closely resembles a word in one's native tongue, and for this reason is apt to be misused. For example, the Spanish word, "embarazada" looks like the English word "embarrassed," but in fact means pregnant. In this case, when adult English speakers misuse the word, it is not because they do not have concepts of embarrassment and pregnancy but rather, they mistake the meaning of the Spanish word.

Nevertheless, there is reason to maintain that in some cases misuse of language is due to some imperfection in concept formation. Consider, for example, the fact that Aquinas did not think that our sun is a star.[17] Even nowadays, people are sometimes surprised to learn that our sun is a star. This is due to imperfect concept formation. People note the extreme brightness of our sun and/or it large size in contrast to the relative dimness and/or smallness of the stars and fail to recognize that if our sun was much more distant it would appear like the stars do. While they correctly note that stars and the sun are bright, they fail to recognize that how bright a thing appears depends in part on the distance from the viewer, and similarly for size. It is also clear that imperfect concept formation was at the basis of the misnomer, "shooting star." This name presumably arose because people took emitting light to be a proper accident of stars, since that is the most obvious observable similarity between burning meteoroids and stars.

Austriaco compares imperfect concepts to imperfect virtue. If we take imperfect virtue in the sense of the state of a person who exercises self-control and is getting close to being truly virtuous, but who still falls short, as he does not always do the right thing promptly and with pleasure, as it the case of the those who have a fixed state of character (L. *habitus*), we can see

17 See *In Meta.*, bk. 7. lec. 13, n. 9.

a relevant difference between imperfect virtue and imperfect concepts. It is possible to perform an act of moral virtue without possessing moral virtue in act; for example, a person who does not possess the virtue of chastity can perform chaste acts, but not in the manner that the chaste person performs them. However, it is impossible to think without possessing a concept in act. Thus, when one carries on an intellectual discourse ordered to clarifying vague concepts, the latter must exist in act; otherwise, there would be nothing in one's intellect to be clarifying. While imperfect or vague concepts are in potency to further clarification, the intellect forming them is knowing a nature in act; thus, these concepts cannot be merely potential. It is similar to a sketch being an actual picture, but in potency to being completed.

In addition, if in forming imperfect concepts we were not actually thinking anything, we could never know that our attempts at clarifying our concepts failed. This point was made earlier. A person who initially thinks that a shooting star is a star is able to learn this is not the case, and he is not talking about something different when he now says: "A shooting star is not a star." Indeed, it seems that our first vague concept of what a thing is generally is *more certain* than our more distinct concept. People often disagree about whether something has been correctly defined while agreeing about what they are trying to define.

To maintain that the word "concept" applies in the fullest sense to a perfect understanding of a nature does not entail denying that imperfect concepts are concepts produced in act by the person thinking them.[18] A perfect concept is more deserving of the name concept than an imperfect one, just as a finished drawing is more deserving of being called a picture of X than the sketch of X is. However, a sketch of X is still a picture of X, and similarly for an imperfect concept.

I maintain that denying that imperfect concepts are concepts in act (in which case the intellect is knowing in act), is a misuse of the word "concept," and thus it is by linguistic subterfuge that the position that knowing what things are always requires language is maintained (that is, on the

18 See *In Libros Physicorum*, https://www.corpusthomisticum.org/iopera.html. bk. I, lec. 1: "And because to know something indistinctly stands between pure potency and perfect act, therefore, since our intellect proceeds from potency to act, what first occurs to it is vague, rather than distinct."

additional assumption that the formation of perfect concepts always requires language).[19]

It is important to note that even if we set aside the disagreement as to what constitutes the appropriate use of the word "concept," it leaves unaffected the argument given in section 2 that shows that we must arrive at knowledge of what certain things are through the natural process of abstraction, and thus that knowing what things are does not, in every case, require language.

The Denial That Concepts Are Prior to the Invention of the First Words Leaves Unexplained How the First Words Were Invented

A reason offered above for why concepts must be prior to language is that in the absence of a final cause (be it that of organizing one's thoughts or communicating them to others) people would lack a motivation to make up words. If we set this problem aside and consider only what the agent does to form words, we again see that concepts must be prior to language.

First, someone had to arrive at the concept of naming before inventing names. Although prior to arriving at the concept of naming a person may have associated in memory a certain thing with a certain sound, for example, ocean waves with the sound "swoosh," the person would have to recognize that this sound could be used to signify "ocean wave" before deciding to do so.

Secondly, once one has the concept of naming, before naming a specific kind of thing, one has to think to oneself: "What shall I call this?" (and this applies to the act of naming itself). So, for example, when a scientist discovers a new species, she asks herself: "What shall I name it?" Here the knowledge of a kind precedes the invention of the name. The same has to be the case, however, of the first names people invented. They had concepts of kinds of things, such as plants and food or specific foods, and then asked themselves what they were going to call these things, and then decided on some word.

19 The assumption that the formation of perfect concepts always requires language is questionable, as the concepts of things that we directly sense, such as hot and cold, do not seem to admit of further clarification. "Hot" and "cold" name sensible qualities, but the only way to differentiate them from other sensible qualities is by pointing to experience.

That the above must be the case becomes even clearer when one considers alternatives offered for the origin of language. It cannot be the case that imagining or articulating sounds all of a sudden produces a new concept, for example, a person imagines or makes the sound "tree" and this causes the concept of tree to form as a result, for there is no necessary connection between the sound "tree" and the concept of tree, as trees are called by other names in other languages. The connection is one that needs to be forged, and it can only be forged by one who has the concept of tree and the concept of naming.

It has been suggested that we began to form words as a result of imitating sounds that things naturally produce, given that such sounds naturally bring to mind the things in question. Certain words have been formed using sounds that are connected with the thing named, for example, whisper and buzz. However, onomatopoeia is involved in the invention of a very limited number of words. More importantly, even in the case of those words, their signification is not automatic: We need to make a choice as to what they signify. Does "buzz" signify the sound a bee makes or the bee itself? Does whisper signify the sound whispering makes or a type of speech in which the vocal cords are not employed?[20] The one inventing the word has to make a decision. The same is true for iconic gestures.[21] For example, does spreading two palms facing each other with the little fingers touching mean "open a book" or "book?" One might suggest that deictic gestures, such as pointing to oneself, are unambiguous. Yet there is no reason that one could not choose to use that gesture to signify something other than oneself.[22]

There are other theories similar to the onomatopoeia theory, such as that language arose from sounds that commonly accompany emotional

20 As Steven Pinker notes: "Onomatopoeia, where it is found, is of no help, because it is almost as conventional as any other word sound. In English, pigs go 'oink'; in Japanese, they go 'boo-boo.'" Steven Pinker, *The Language Instinct* (Harper Perennial, 2007), 146.

21 Iconic gestures become language if the intention of the one gesturing is to consistently use that same gesture to signify a given concept. Since vocal signs can be produced and imagined more rapidly than gestural ones, it is not surprising that, if gestural language came first, it was supplanted by vocal language.

22 See Pinker, *The Language Instinct,* 147: "The sign [in ASL] for 'you' is a point to one's partner." However, just as very young children confuse "me" and "you," sometimes calling themselves "you," similarly children using ASL will point to the other person to mean "me," thus "treating the gesture as a pure linguistic symbol; the fact that it pointed somewhere did not register as being relevant."

reactions, for example, "ew" in the case of disgust.[23] And there are words that have been formed based on such sounds, for example, "owie" (an American slang expression for a minor injury) comes from the sound sometimes made upon being mildly injured. However, "owie" could name a minor injury or a specific minor injury or something entirely unrelated. What it names depends on a decision to use that sound to name a specific concept, and such a decision clearly presupposes having that concept.

Austriaco proposes that words may have originated from vocal sounds that our animal ancestors used to enhance their survival. He maintains that it is reasonable to think that our prelinguistic hominin ancestors had some vocal communication system that linked phantasms to vocal sounds, similar to that which is found in animals with smaller brains, such as vervet monkeys. These monkeys use different alarm calls for different predators; for example, they emit one call when an eagle is spotted and another when a snake is spotted. Austriaco proposes that a rational being could

> transform this vocal communication system into a language. Here, the phantasms would be replaced with concepts, and the vocal sounds would be replaced with words. In fact, the vocal sounds would have become words in that the same particular sounds that were once linked to particular phantasms would now be able to signify the concepts abstracted from those same phantasms. Note that the final cause for these first words would have been inherited from our brute hominin ancestors and would not have been invented by Adam and his descendants: In the same way that vocal sounds enhance survival, words would have done the same.[24]

This view fares no better than the theories of the origin of language mentioned above in establishing a priority of language over thought. If we concede that an animal call is tied to some phantasm, this phantasm does not determine what that sound will signify if a human decides to make a word out of it. For example, the phantasm of a wolf is also that of a predator, a danger on the ground, a carnivore, etc. The human who decides to turn the sound of a call into a word must decide on the specific concept he wants to express by that sound.

23 See Steven Mithen, *The Singing Neanderthals: The Origins of Music, Language, Mind and Body* (Harvard University Press, 2007), 203.

24 Austriaco, "On the Limits of Abstraction," 148.

Note also that Austriaco's claim that the final cause for words formed in this manner is inherited from our animal ancestor is misleading. Humans can remember or imagine people being harmed by predators, and upon judging this to be undesirable, can discern that communicating with others may help them escape this harm. Preventing conspecifics from being harmed by predators is a final cause or goal that humans and some animal species share in common. However, when people invent a word or words to serve this purpose, the final cause of the specific word(s) invented is not shared with animals. When humans decide to repurpose the cry or call that they have inherited from their brute hominin ancestors (e.g., "woo-hoo"), they also have to decide which concept they are going to signify by it. Is it "wolf" or "carnivore" or "predator" or "run," etc.? The final cause of the word "woo-hoo" meaning wolf is different from the final cause of the word "woo-hoo" meaning predator, because in each case the word is formed in order to signify a different concept, and this is so even when the initial motivation for coining the word is to communicate with others so that they may escape harm.

The Denial That Concepts Are Prior to the Invention of the First Words Leaves Unexplained Many Other Experiences That Commonly Occur Concerning Language

How could we ask "What is that called?" if we did not know what the thing is, at least in some vague way? In such cases, this knowledge is clearly prior to the word for that thing.

Sometimes we have a concept of something in mind but can't remember the name. Similarly, we are sometimes aware that we can't find the right word to express our thoughts or that the words we are using are not the right ones to convey our thoughts. The facts that we seek the right words to express our thoughts and we recognize that we don't always come up with them shows that in some cases thought is prior to language.[25]

Our ability to translate words from one language to another also shows that concepts are prior to words. How could one know that the word "tree" in

25 Pinker offers another reason to think that thought must precede language: "When we hear or read, we usually remember the gist, not the exact words, so there has to be such a thing as a gist that is not the same as a bunch of words." Pinker, *The Language Instinct*, 47.

English should be translated as "arbre" in French other than by reference to a concept of what that thing is that is known independently of a sign for it?[26]

Accounts of Individuals Who Acquired Language Much Later Than Is Usual

We have accounts of individuals who did not begin to acquire language when they were babies, but only much later in life. If abstraction is a natural process that is not language dependent one would expect that these individuals had quite a few concepts, given their age, despite their lack of language.

The story of Helen Keller, who was both blind and deaf, is well known. On the day that Keller realized that that the sign her teacher traced in her hand signified something (namely, water), she began to ask for the names of other things, and she learned thirty words that very first day.[27] How could Keller ask for the names of other things, if she did not have concepts of them?

One might object that animals sometimes ask what things are called. For example, the African Grey parrot, Alex, asked a student who was eating a carrot, "What's that?" and "What color?" However, the parrot only used the words it learned to ask for things. It never used them in a way that showed that the words signified concepts for it. By contrast, Keller says:

> At first, when my teacher told me about a new thing I asked very few questions. My ideas were vague, and my vocabulary was inadequate; but as my knowledge of things grew, and I learned more and more words, my field of inquiry broadened, and I would return again and again to the same subject, eager for further information.[28]

Here Keller claims to have vague ideas prior to learning words and that words helped her increase her knowledge about the things that she, at first,

26 As Tilman Anselm Ramelow, OP, notes, the very fact that we recognize that translations may be imperfect or inaccurate indicates that we have concepts that are independent of language, for our concepts are what allow us to compare a text to its translation. See Ramelow, "Language Without Reduction," 507. Similarly, our ability to compare languages as to their capability of expressing certain thoughts also shows the independence of thought from language. Ramelow, *Beyond Modernism?*, 72.

27 Biography.com, "Helen Keller: Biography," last updated July 17, 2024, https://www.biography.com/activist/helen-keller.

28 Helen Keller, *The Story of My Life*, https://www.holloway.com/g/helen-keller-the-story-of-my-life/sections/chapter-vi.

only vaguely understood. Assuming that her account is accurate, it shows that Keller was not learning vocabulary simply by associative memory in view of getting treats; she already had vague concepts to which she then associated the words she learned. Having learned words allowed her to ask questions to augment her conceptual knowledge of the world, something never seen on the part of animals capable of using symbolic forms of communication.

The case of Ildefonso also indicates that concepts are prior to language. Ildefonso was deaf and lacked language.[29] When he was twenty-seven, Susan Schaller began to teach him language. Initially Ildefonso simply mimicked Susan's gestures. Eventually he recognized the sign for "cat" to be a sign, and then went on to ask for the names of things such as desks and clocks by touching them or pointing at them. One day, when Susan was teaching him the names for colors, she signed "green" and Ildefonso responded by mimicking hiding. There was a story he was trying to convey, but he lacked the words to do so. At a later time, using a combination of words and mime, he was able to convey to Susan that he had had frightening encounters with border patrolmen (who wore green and drove green vehicles).[30] Though language allowed him to express more clearly what had happened, he had concepts of hiding, vehicle, having pockets searched, etc. prior to learning words.[31]

Ildefonso's deaf adult friends also had concepts despite their lack of language. These friends had developed a small number of common signs. However, they told stories principally using mime, acting out what their life was like in the villages they came from. So, for example, one man conveyed a hatred of plowing and described oxen.[32] It would be hard to deny that this man had a concept of what oxen are, despite not having a word for them. Another man, using mime, described how his wife only gave birth to girls.[33] It is absurd to think that his lack of language had prevented him from forming concepts of child, childbirth, and female.

One might counter that there are cases of human individuals who were deprived of language in childhood and who showed no clear sign

29 Ildefonso's story is recounted by Susan Schaller in *A Man Without Words* (Summit Books, 1991).

30 Schaller, *A Man Without Words*, 93.

31 Schaller, 157: "Ildefonso asked me about greed, before he knew the sign." He also knew what begging was before he had a word for it. Schaller, 79.

32 See Schaller, 184.

33 See Schaller, 186.

of possessing concepts of what things are. Their failure to form concepts seems attributable to their lack of language. First, there are very few records of people who fit this description. Most language-deprived individuals do eventually learn to produce simple, if ungrammatical, sentences.[34] Secondly, correlation does not prove causal connection, and there is another possible explanation for these individuals' apparent failure to form concepts, namely, deficiencies on the part of their internal senses. There is reason to think that unless one can retain what one has sensed in one's memory, one is not going to be able to form a concept of that thing. It may also be the case that a certain amount of grouping of like experiences goes on in the interior senses prior to abstraction, and that such grouping is needed for abstraction. Individuals that are brain damaged may not have the memory or collative ability required for abstraction. Feral children are generally abandoned children, and mental disabilities are a motive to abandon a child; alternately, the trauma of abandonment and the lack of interaction with people may have affected normal mental development. Thus, a disability affecting the interior senses that provide the intellect the sensory knowledge from which it abstracts provides an alternate explanation for the absence of concepts in the rare language-deprived person who appears to lack concepts. In any case, an individual incapable of learning language could not be the originator of a language. So the existence of such individuals does not show that language is prior to thought.[35]

If Thought Is Prior to Language, Why Does It Seem We Can't Think Without Words?

In the case of many of us, and perhaps all of us, when we make a conscious effort to think without words they generally come to mind despite our efforts. This leads some people to think that thought always depends on language.

34 Pinker notes that individuals who were deprived of language when they were young later have problems with grammar rather than with vocabulary and communication. It appears that there is a sensitive period for developing grammar. Pinker, *The Language Instinct*, 297–301.

35 There are quite a few scientific papers involving experiments with infants arguing that thought precedes language. See, for example, Mandler, "Thought Before Language," and Susan J. Hespos and Elizabeth S. Spelke, "Conceptual Precursors to Language," *Nature* 430 (July 22, 2004): 453–56.

It seems that the heavy reliance we have on words arises from our need to talk to each other combined with the benefits that words afford with respect to rapidity of thought and remembering ideas.

Early humans managed to survive only with great difficulty. They faced the challenges of finding food, protecting themselves from the elements and from predators, making tools, etc. A certain amount of cooperation between parents was needed to ensure that their offspring would survive; and a certain amount of cooperation with other families, if not absolutely necessary, was helpful for achieving this end. Gestures, such as are used for communication between individuals who do not speak the same language, only go so far. Thus, the invention of language was motivated by the advantage it offers when it comes to coordinating activities ordered to survival.[36] Language was not first invented to reflect upon the natures of things, as survival held priority. It seems unlikely that language was invented simply so that an individual could mentally form a plan, as words are unnecessary for planning. For example, nothing prevents a person from imagining that the next morning she will take a container and walk on a certain path to the woods to pick berries. It is when the person wants to send someone else to perform this task or when she wants others to come with her that words become helpful, as they are a more effective way of communicating than is some form of pantomime.

Once we invent or learn from others names for things, it is hard to see or sense something that we have a name for without the name spontaneously coming to mind. Although we may forget the names of things on certain occasions, our habitual usage of words when communicating with others engrains them in our memories.

Perhaps the most troubling thing about this reliance on words is that when we are thinking to ourselves they appear to replace images that are likenesses of things. It seems we must necessarily have the latter in mind if we are going to "completely and truly" understand a material nature. I think Aquinas is correct when he maintains that it belongs to the notions of

36 Terrance Deacon holds that language first arose to ensure marital fidelity, something that is important for reproductive success, as it increases the likelihood that offspring will receive the care they need. Terrance Deacon, *The Symbolic Species* (W. W. Norton, 1997), 400–401. I will not address his chapter-length argument here. I am not rigidly wedded to the view that language first arose to coordinate activities such as hunting, tending the fire, etc. On both Deacon's account and my account, language first arose as a means of communication concerning things conducive to the survival of our species.

material natures that they exist in some individual that is individuated by matter.[37] One does not truly and completely conceive "stone" if one does not refer the concept to some particular stone, real or remembered/imagined. In the case of material things, our senses are our point of contact with reality, allowing us to recognize a true concept from a false one.

Words seem to usurp the place that images which are likenesses of real things play in our intellectual knowledge. Words definitely cannot replace images that are determinate likenesses insofar as the latter are needed in order for our thoughts to be connected to reality. And certainly experience shows that words are apt to be employed in a way that does not conform to reality. Speech taken by some for sublime thought is sometimes gibberish, and linguistic fallacies may well be the most common type of fallacy. Words, however, have a certain aptitude to evoke the needed images. People do not first and foremost make up names for imaginary beings (e.g., centaurs). They make up names for concepts that they naturally tie to the particulars from which the concept arose. They are aware of the utility of names for identifying particulars. Again, words were initially invented, at least for the most part, not to discuss the natures of things, but to speak about practical matters that necessarily bear on particulars. Thus, while words signify concepts, their formation is also tied to particulars, and so it is not surprising that upon hearing a single word naming a kind of material thing, people, in general, automatically form an imagined likeness of that thing. In the case of humans, such as ourselves, who learn a language that has already been invented, as children we often learn words from others in conjunction with hearing them used in regard to particulars. For example, a mother points to her nose repeatedly, while saying "nose" and calls the green round things the child is fed "peas." Words, then, have an aptitude not only to call to mind (i.e., the intellect) the concept they signify, but also to trigger the formation of an appropriate image. And words are more quickly imagined than likenesses of things. We can imagine the statement, "cats are animals," more quickly than imagining a cat and focusing on that which makes it sentient, such as its activity of seeing. This makes words handy shorthand for images.

Words sometimes help us recall a specific line of thought. When we have arrived at concepts as the result of dialoguing with others or from reading books, our recall of these concepts is often tied to the words that were employed, granted, not necessarily always to the exact words. For

37 See *ST* I, q. 84, a. 7.

example, for Aristotelians, thought about motion spontaneously conjures up Aristotle's words, "the act of the potential insofar as it is potential,"[38] through which what motion is is more clearly understood. Given that our intellectual knowledge originates in sense experience, it is not surprising that the senses (including the inner senses) would aid the intellect in the recall of ideas as well.

We have become habituated to thinking in terms of words from an early age because people are continually speaking to us. In addition to allowing for fluent communication, this habit is beneficial insofar as the sensory memory of words assists us in remembering concepts. Although this practice does pose the risks that we fall into linguistic fallacies or end up merely mentally throwing around words, this need not occur. Words have the aptitude to evoke the images needed in order to fully understand the natures of material things, and they offer the advantage that they can be imagined much more rapidly than the latter.

If Thought Is Prior to Language, Why Does Language Shape Our Discourse?

It is hard to talk about things if we do not have words for them. Consider how hard it would be to discuss the nature of "accident" as opposed to "substance" in a language that has no word for accident or to discuss being *qua* being in a language that has no word for being. Different groups of people had different priorities in forming vocabularies. The ancient Greeks, for example, coined more words for virtues and vices than are found in most, and perhaps all, other languages, and peoples who lived in northern climes have invented more words for snow and things snow-related than those living at the equator. Having words facilitates our discussion of the things whose concepts they signify, and the lack thereof sometimes makes us prone to fall into error. Consider how much easier it is to clarify the concept of the capital sin of "acedia" when one is not limited to the word "sloth." "Sloth" is commonly understood to name indolence or laziness, which tends to mislead people as to acedia's true nature.[39] Acknowledging that arriving at certain thoughts

38 Aristotle, *Physics*, 201a10–12.

39 An interesting example of how language can help or hinder occurred during discussions concerning the Assumption of Mary. Some English-speaking persons suggested that Mary died but was never dead. (In other words, the same instant that was the end of her life was

is facilitated or hindered by language, however, does not show that language is ultimately prior to thought, as it does not address how the words used in discourse originated.

I agree that language is generally prerequisite to clarifying a vague concept so as to perfectly know a thing's nature. I see this need as being rooted in the kind of intellect we have, that is, one that comes to know things starting from sense experience. As a result, our first concepts are vague. In order to clarify them, we generally need to dialogue with others and/or read what others have written, as some of us notice one thing about a thing and others something else and of these things it is not immediately apparent what is essential and what is accidental, and for this reason lone individuals reasoning by themselves are apt to fall into error. We generally need to pool our knowledge together and cull out incorrect conclusions drawn from it before a perfect concept can be arrived at.[40] This ordinarily requires talking to others. Thus, without words, we generally could not arrive at the precise knowledge of what a thing is that is expressed by a definition. Nevertheless, if the words did not already mean something, that is, signify concepts of something, they could not help us arrive at precise knowledge of what things are.

Conclusion

In sum, there are many reasons to hold that concepts, albeit vague ones, are prior to language. First, knowledge of an artifact's purpose is required to invent an artifact. If the purpose of language is to organize or express concepts, then the formation of words presupposes knowledge that there are such things as concepts, which is only possible to the one who possesses a concept. Secondly, the agent who invents a word has to have both the concept of naming, as well as having in mind a concept of what she intends to signify by that word. A person could not invent the name "deer" in the

the beginning of her resurrected life, similar to a point at which two line segments meet at an angle can be viewed as the end of one of the line segments and the beginning of the other.) However, French-speaking persons had difficulty understanding what they were proposing, as in French there is only one expression ("elle est morte"), rather than there being separate expressions for saying that she died and for saying that she is dead.

40 See Aristotle, *Metaphysics*, bk. 2, chap. 2, 993b12–15: "It is just that we should be grateful, not only to those with whose views we may agree, but also to those who have expressed more superficial views; for these also contributed something, by developing before us the powers of thought." (W. D. Ross translation)

absence of a concept of this animal. Thirdly, it is not possible to consciously seek to know everything one knows because to consciously seek to know something presupposes that one knows that there is such a thing as knowledge about things. Thus, the first intellectual knowledge we arrive at must occur through a natural process. The position that language is prior to all concepts without qualification entails the denial that there is a purely natural process by which humans form concepts starting from sense experience. In other words, according to this view, our natural ability to form concepts is inherently deficient, and this defect can only be remedied by something artificial, namely, language. Lastly, the facts that we can ask what something is called, that we can know that we are forgetting the name of something, and that we can translate from one language to another all show the priority of thought over language.[41]

41 Elsewhere, I argue that Aquinas might agree that an imagination capable of inventing suitable signs, along with the ability to organize them, is a disposition necessary for the reception of the rational soul. If so, he would accept in a qualified way that the capacity for forming abstract concepts presupposes the capacity for language, that is, by way of disposition. See George, "Aquinas's Teachings on Concepts and Words," 372–76.

Part IV

THE DIFFERENCE BETWEEN PLANTS AND ANIMALS

8

A Defense of the Distinction Between Plants and Animals

Aristotle divided the realm of material living beings into nonsentient living things (plants), sentient, nonrational living things (animals), and rational animals (humans), and Aquinas concurs with this division. While the difference between humans and animals has received extensive attention by neo-Thomists, the difference between plants and animals has been largely neglected.[1] This is understandable since until fairly recently there has been little reason to reexamine the categories of plant and animal. However, nowadays it has become increasingly common to find mainstream scientists who claim that plants are sentient.[2] There is even a scientific society founded in 2005 in order to promote the study of

1 I have only seen one neo-Thomist address the question of plant sentience: Nicanor Austriaco. See Nicanor Pier Giorgio Austriaco, OP, "Immediate Hominization from the Systems Perspective," *The National Catholic Bioethics Quarterly* 4, no. 4 (2004): 729–30.

2 Some of the biologists who affirm that plants are sentient include František Baluška, Paco Calvo, Daniel Chamovitz, Monica Gagliano, and Stefano Mancuso. And then there are even biologists who go so far as to attribute intelligence to plants, e.g., see Anthony Twewavas, "Aspects of Plant Intelligence: An Answer to Firn," *Annals of Botany* 93, no. 4 (2004): 353–57. Note that there are many plant scientists who disagree with those affirming that plants are sentient. See Jon Mallett et al., "Debunking a Myth: Plant Consciousness," *Protoplasma* 258

the underlying causes of sensing in plants.[3] In this chapter I will give reasons to uphold the Aristotelian division of plant and animal, and I will show that the claims made by those who hold that plants are sentient involve faulty reasoning.[4] At stake is our understanding of what constitutes the most fundamental divisions of living things.

What Does it Mean to Sense?

The living thing that we know first and best is ourselves. We know what sensing is, at least in a confused way, because we ourselves sense. What does it mean to sense? It means to know individual colors, sounds, and other sensibles. Since we have another kind of knowledge, that is, intellectual knowledge, I am going to use the word "aware" in speaking about sense knowledge. Thus, to see is to be aware of specific instances of color (if only of color on a grey scale), and smelling is awareness of this or that odor, and so forth.

(2021): 459–76. See also Lincoln Taiz et al., "Reply to Trewavas et al. and Calvo and Trewavas," *Trends in Plant Science* 25, no. 3 (March 2020): 218:

> At a recent conference the question was raised of why we had bothered to publish an article making such an obvious point: that plants are fundamentally different from animals. The answer is that, due to the heavy media coverage, we felt that it had become necessary to counter the growing public perception that plant biologists had demonstrated that plants have emotions, cognition, and carry out intentional acts as animals do, whereas the overwhelming majority of plant biologists reject such zoocentric paradigms of plant behavior. The photoautotrophic lifestyle of plants dictated an alternative pathway to evolutionary fitness. Instead of subjective consciousness, plants evolved adaptive behavior that is genetically determined by natural selection and epigenetically determined by environmental factors.

3 The Society for Plant Neurobiology, founded in 2005, is now called the *Society* of *Plant* Signaling and Behavior. See František Baluška and Stefano Mancuso, "Plant Neurobiology as a Paradigm Shift Not Only in the Plant Sciences," *Plant Signaling and Behavio*r 2, no. 4 (2007), abstract: "Emerging research document that plants sense, memorize, and process experiences and use this information for their adaptive behavior and evolution."

4 Woese et al. deny that plants and animals are fundamental divisions of living things: "Our present view of the basic organization of life is still largely steeped in the ancient notion that all living things are either plant or animal in nature. Unfortunately, this comfortable traditional dichotomy does not represent the true state of affairs," Woese et al., "Towards a Natural System of Organisms," 4576. Woese et al. support their rejection of the plant-animal dichotomy by noting that evolutionary and molecular differences between other categories of living things, e.g., between Monera (prokaryotes) and plants are far greater than those between plant and animal. I am going to restrict my defense of the plant-animal dichotomy to the cases where it is denied on the grounds that plants too are sentient.

It is not possible to define sensing in terms of something better known. Aristotle attempts to define it partly in terms of what it is not: it is the reception of sensible forms of things without the matter. Much has been written on what Aristotle means to convey and I do not intend here to enter at length into the debate. Briefly, I think that Aristotle means to contrast sensing with a purely physical change. A coal heats a poker. The poker does not turn into coal, but it becomes like the coal in being hot. The poker receives the same type of accidental form that the coal has, but not the matter of the coal. However, it receives this accidental form in the same manner that the coal possesses it: it, like the coal, is hot. By contrast, sensing is not a matter of the sense coming to possess the same type of accidental form in the same manner. Rather, the more the sense become physically like the thing it senses, the less sensitive it becomes; for example, when one's hand becomes the same temperature as the water it's in, one no longer feels the temperature of the water. For this reason, John of St. Thomas understands "the reception of form without matter" to refer to the knower's receiving the form of another as other while remaining itself: feeling an object's heat is other than becoming hot oneself.[5] Thus, if one is to claim that a being is sentient, it is necessary to provide evidence that something more than a physical change occurs in it.[6]

We humans not only sense, but sense that we sense. I'm going to use the word "consciousness" to refer to our awareness that we are sensing. We often sense qualities, quantities, and position without being conscious that we are doing so; for example, when walking, we often avoid tripping on uneven pavement without being consciously aware that we are sensing the unevenness. If we are sensing something, however, we can become conscious that we are doing so.

Many Life Activities in Humans Do Not Involve Sensing

In addition to knowing that we sense, we also know that food nourishes us and that we grow—or have grown. We have no consciousness of these activities, which indicates that they do not involve sense perception. We know

5 See John of St. Thomas, *Cursus Philosophicus Thomisticus* (Marietti, 1937), part 4, q. 4, a. 1.

6 In order to for humans to see red, red light has to hit the cones in their eyes, which results in it being converted into electrical signals that are transmitted to their brains via the optic nerve. Seeing or the awareness of color, however, is not reducible to this physical chain of events.

that we grow not because we sense ourselves growing, nor because we sense the underlying processes which result in growth. We know we grow because of comparisons we make, for example, "I am now taller than Mom" and "My pants don't fit any more." Similarly, while we are aware of how food tastes and feels, we are not aware of what goes on in nutrition once we swallow the food. We are aware of feeling weak if we don't eat, and sometimes of our belly bloating; and we know that excretion in some way depends on eating, and there are other clues as well. But exactly what goes on in nutrition does so without us sensing it; and this is also the case for the production of sperm and the maturation and release of eggs. These vegetative activities would not go on any better for us being aware of them; indeed, being aware of them would be distracting.

It would seem then that since nutrition, growth, and the production of germ cells go on in us without sensation, then there is no need for sensation in order for other organisms to perform these activities. From the point of view of finality, there is reason to think that other organisms are not going to be endowed with sense perception to execute these same fundamental activities, for this would be superfluous.[7]

The Directional Character of Certain Life Activities of Plants

The reasoning above seems to overlook a pertinent fact about plant growth. It is not plants' growth per se that has motivated some scientists to assert that plants are sentient; it is instead the fact that their growth is directional and variable. Compare the growth of an animal with bilateral symmetry, for example, a dog, with the growth of a tree. If development takes place normally, the dog will eventually have one head, a torso, and four legs, the legs being very close in size and placed in determinate locations on the torso. A tree of a given species, on the other hand, does not have a determinate

7 Stated in evolutionary terms, an organism using energy and materials to produce an unneeded sensory apparatus would be at a disadvantage as to surviving and leaving offspring. Species that originated in areas where a given sense no longer serves its purpose, e.g., cavefish, typically lose it. It must be noted, however, that selection is not the only driver of evolution, and so it is not absolutely impossible that sentience arise as an accessory for a given vegetative activity. However, it is strange to think that organisms that have fewer types of cells and are less structured would have a sensory organ for performing activities such as nutrition and growth when more complex organisms do not.

number of branches and where the branches are placed on different individual trees varies, as does their size and orientation. The number, size, and orientation of the branches is not predetermined by internal factors, as is the case of the number and arrangement of the dog's parts but depends in large part on the light that is available.[8] Indeed, trees have the challenge of growing their branches in such a manner so as not to obstruct light from their other branches. It seems then that trees (and other plants) need to know where the light is so that their branches and/or leaves grow in the manner most apt to sustain their lives. And the same seems to be true with root growth toward water. The plants seem to have to know which way their roots should grow. And there are other direction-specific responses in plants, such as the hypersensitive response (discussed below).

One could also add here as being problematic, plants' seasonal responses, such as losing leaves in the winter, growing new leaves in the spring, and flowering at the right time. Doesn't the plant have to know when to do these things? For the sake of brevity, I will focus mainly on directional growth. However, consulting a plant physiology book would show that the general point that I will make concerning directional growth also applies to plants' temporal responses.

Before I go on to respond to the question raised by the directional character of plant growth, I would like to first address some other activities of plants that might seem to require sensation.

Defense from Harmful Agents, Adaptation, and Homeostasis Do Not Necessarily Require Sensation

Here we will examine whether plants need to sense in order to adapt or to defend themselves from harmful agents or for homeostasis.

In the case of adaptation, biologist Nicanor Austriaco maintains: "Modern biologists would challenge this account [i.e., that there is a nutritive soul that is other than the sensitive soul] because all living things have to respond and to adapt to their environments to survive, and they do this by

8 Some organisms that have radial symmetry do have a somewhat indeterminate number of arms (or rays). This is the case of certain starfish that start out with five arms but can grow up to as many as fifty. These organisms, however, do not grow directionally as do plants, which grow toward something outside of themselves, such as light or moisture.

sensing different external cues. Thus, all living things must have sensitive souls."[9]

Many adaptations, however, take place without sensation, for example, acclimatization to both altitude and temperature. What happens in the case of acclimatization to altitude is that the body needs a certain amount of oxygen to carry on vital processes, but the lower pressure of higher altitudes "makes it more difficult for oxygen to enter our vascular systems."[10] Adaptation consists in changes in the body that help overcome this difficulty. What are these changes?

> When we travel to high mountain areas, our bodies initially develop inefficient physiological responses. There is an increase in breathing and heart rate to as much as double. . . . Later, a more efficient response normally develops as acclimatization takes place. Additional red blood cells capillaries are produced to carry more oxygen. The lungs increase in size to facilitate the osmosis of oxygen and carbon dioxide. There is also an increase in the vascular network of muscles which enhances the transfer of gases.[11]

9 Nicanor Austriaco, personal communication. Indeed, it is not hard to find biologists who base the claim that plants sense on their need to adapt to changes in the environment. For example, biologist Daniel Chamovitz asserts:

> Rootedness is a huge evolutionary constraint. It means that plants can't escape a bad environment, can't migrate in search of food or a mate. So plants had to develop incredibly sensitive and complex sensory mechanisms that would let them survive in ever changing environments. I mean if you're hungry or thirsty you can walk to the nearest watering hole. . . . But plants are immobile. They need to see where their food is. They need to feel the weather, and they need to smell danger. Gareth Cook, "Do Plants Think?," *Scientific American* (June 5, 2012). (https://www.scientificamerican.com/article/do-plants-think-daniel-chamovitz/).

Note that a subsidiary argument sometimes offered for plant sentience is the plant's ability to adjust its response in function of multiple stimuli present in the environment: "The plant lives in a vast interactive sphere, both above and below the Earth, filled with chemical compounds that supply countless tidbits of information. It is exposed to numerous interactions, and that is why it must also be constantly aware of what is going on around it." Massimo Maffei, quoted in "The Silent Scream of the Lima Bean," congressional report, Chemical Ecology, *Max Planck Research* 4 (2007): 65. However, a response to multiple stimuli need not involve sentience, as is plain in the case of cells within the body, as they receive multiple signals from other cells affecting their development and growth. (The fact that plants respond to external factors is no reason to assume sentience, as will be illustrated by the cases of the melanocytes and acclimatization to altitude.)

10 Dennis O'Neil, "Adapting to Hight Altitude," On-line tutorial, https://www2.palomar.edu/anthro/adapt/adapt_3.htm.

11 O'Neil, Human Biological Adaptivity.

The changes producing the acclimatization are not triggered by sense perception of lower air pressure; it is the lower air pressure itself that triggers them, and they go on without our sensing them. Thus, it is not true that adaptation always requires sensation.[12]

Even machines are capable of changing behavior in response to environmental changes so as to function better. For example, one can train Siri to more accurately convert one's voice to text. Thus, observation of this type of response, independent of other knowledge of the being in question, does not even allow one to conclude that the being is alive, much less sentient.[13]

Plants are able to adapt to many stressful conditions. However, research on how they do so does not propose accounts that involve sensing but rather biochemistry. Here is a typical example, taken from the abstract from a paper on cold acclimation:

> Molecular as well as biochemical mechanisms underpinning plant cold acclimation are very complex and interwoven. The cold-impacted plants try to modulate expression of variety genes controlling cell membrane lipid composition, mitogen-activated protein kinase cascade, total soluble proteins, polyamines, glycinebetaine, proline, reactive oxygen species (ROS) scavengers, cryoprotectants, and a large number of cold responsive factors.[14]

Homeostasis is maintained without sensation. For example, sodium and glucose levels in blood are regulated without being sensed. As for defense from enemies, while doing so sometimes requires sensation, there are many examples when it is not required; for example, our immune system fights off germs without us being aware of it.

12 Another example of adaptation not involving sensation is the resetting of our internal circadian clock. We do not sense what does this, which is why it took us a while to figure out strategies to overcome jet lag. And as Vincent Torley notes, phenotypic plasticity is another example of adaptation that does not involve cognition on the plants' part, but rather simply results from the activation one of a "built-in set of possible phenotypic responses" by an environmental cue. Vincent Torley, "Excursus—Plants," http://www.angelfire.com/linux/vjtorley/plants.html.

13 Here the problem of the ambiguity of vocabulary arises once again. One might say that even machines are capable of adapting, understood as changing behavior in response to environmental changes so as to function better. Our natural tendency to extend words to name like things results in a loss of precision and an increased potential for equivocation.

14 R. John et al., "Some Key Physiological and Molecular Processes of Cold Acclimation," *Biologia Plantarum* 60, no. 4 (2016): 603.

In principle, then, a living thing could adapt and defend itself from foreign invaders without sentience, and thus having sentience for the purpose of doing so would be superfluous. Some reason would have to be given for why a specific defense or a specific adaptation required sensation.

How Does One Judge That a Living Thing, Other Than Human, Senses?

Certainly, observing its behavior is a key element. The behavior is not the sense perception, but certain behaviors would be inexplicable in the absence of sense perception. Some behaviors are directly connected to sensing, for example, looking, listening, and sniffing. These behaviors are voluntary attempts to sense something or to continue to sense something. Then there are behaviors other than those of directing the senses that could not be accomplished in the absence of sensation. One example is an earthworm holding something in the right orientation to get it into its hole; as Darwin observes: "If worms are able to judge . . . having drawn an object close to the mouths of their burrows, how best to drag it in, they must acquire some notion of its general shape."[15] Plainly, in observing the organism's behavior one needs to determine what is provoking or stimulating the behavior—is it the visible, the audible, etc.? Bats catch insects, but not because the insects are visible. One needs to narrow down what the organism is responding to, by observing it in situations where other things it could be responding to are eliminated.

The presence of an organ similar to our sense organs is also helpful for determining that an organism senses. The fact that dogs have eyes is a big clue that they see. Though some organs have somewhat similar appearances, but different functions, such as the swim bladder in fish that resembles a lung but is used to control the fish's position in water, highly structured organs are unable to carry on different activities.[16]

15 Charles Darwin, *The Formation of Vegetable Mould Through the Actions of Worms* (1881), 97, *Darwin Online*, https://darwinonline.org.uk/content/frameset?pageseq=1&itemID=F1357&viewtype=text.

16 Though obviously not just any molecules and structures will allow for the perception of a given sensible, I do not know whether we know enough to be sure in advance of the sort of molecules and structures that are necessary. For example, are neurons necessary for sense perception? Note that while similarity between known sense organs and what is found in

Even when an organism's organ is not like ours, we sometimes manage to recognize it on the basis of studies we do that allow us to connect a specific structure that we observe with the responses of the organism to something that we know exists, as is the case, for example, of the lateral line found in fish by which they sense movements and pressure changes in the surrounding water and the ampullae of Lorenzini which sharks and certain other animals use to sense electricity. Sometimes we posit the presence of an organ on the basis of what we suspect is a sentient response. For example, our discovery that migratory birds orientate themselves toward magnetic north preceded investigation into the organ by which this is accomplished.[17] Every case of sensing requires a sense organ.

Sensation Is Not Needed to Explain Directional Plant Responses to External Agents

With these criteria in mind, let us now consider plants in more detail. At the basis of claims that plants are sentient are their various responses to things outside of them, especially when those responses are directional, as is the case of growth toward light or toward water.

First, it should be noted that growth in one part of an organism but not in a corresponding part can occur in response to external causes without sensation being present. People who use hand tools often form calluses on the hand wielding those tools but not on the other hand, and calluses are formed by the growth of extra layers of skin. Similarly, muscle growth in one arm may be greater than in another due to differences in usage.

To evaluate the view that directional growth requires sensing on the part of plants, let us consider whether plants that grow toward light have an organ for sensing light. Austriaco argues:

> The tip of the coleoptile[18] is the part of the young, growing plant that allows the plant to sense and respond to light . . . specifically blue light . . .

---

putatively sensing organisms is a sign that the latter indeed senses, the lack of similarity does not definitively rule out the possibility that the organism is sentient.

17 See Roswitha Wiltschko and Wolfgang Wiltschko, "The Discovery of the Use of Magnetic Navigational Information," *Journal of Comparative Physiology A: Neuroethology, Sensory, Neural, and Behavioral Physiology* 208, no. 1 (2022): 9–18.

18 The coleoptile is the protective sheath that covers the emerging shoot.

> by growing in the direction of the light.[19] If you cut off the tip . . . then the plant will ignore the blue light and continue to grow straight up. In the same way, I can destroy the few light sensing cells in a worm, and when I do this the worm will ignore the light. . . . If you know that you are disrupting sensing in the worm because it now responds differently to light by removing the light sensing organ then you have to say that you are also disrupting sensing in the plant because it now responds differently to light after you disrupt its sense organ.[20]

However, a 2013 article explains what occurs in purely photo-biochemical terms.[21] The blue light photoreceptors in the coleoptile tip, called phototropins, consist of a protein with two chromophores embedded in it. Chromophores absorb photons and this changes their structures, which change has an effect on the protein in which they are embedded, which in turn triggers chemical changes leading to an auxin gradient, which causes asymmetric growth (auxins are growth hormones). It is not the plant's seeing blue, but rather the absorption of a photon and the subsequent changes that this causes that leads to growth. Plainly, if one removes any part of the chain that leads ultimately to growth, growth will not occur. But this has no bearing on whether a sensing of light has taken place. Some reason has to be given

19 The fact that a being's response arises from a specific stimulus within a category (e.g., it responds to blue light and not red) is not sufficient evidence that it is sentient, as there are machines that respond in this manner, e.g., transferring voice to text for someone speaking English but not for someone speaking Chinese.

20 Nicanor Austriaco, personal communication.

21 See Tim Hohm et al., "Phototropism: Translating Light into Directional Growth," *American Journal of Botany* 100, no. 1, 47: "The blue light photoreceptors in the coleoptile tip] (phot1 and phot2 in Arabidopsis) . . . are light-activated protein kinases. The kinase activity of phototropins and phosphorylation of residues in the activation loop of their kinase domains are essential for the phototropic response. These initial steps trigger the formation of the auxin gradient across the hypocotyl that leads to asymmetric growth." See also David Goodsell, "Molecule of the Month, Phototropin," *PDB-101* (Training and Outreach Portal of Protein Data Bank), March 2015, http://pdb101.rcsb.org/motm/183. Note that the cones and rods of the human eye contain photoreceptors with an overall similarity to the phototropins of plants, as they consist of a chromophore bound to a protein, with light causing a change in the chromophore that induces a conformational change in the protein it is embedded in. Unlike plants, human have an organ of sight, the eye along with part of the brain, the visual cortex. One might argue that plants' blue light receptors should be considered an organ since they are similar to the odor molecule receptors that lie in the nasal cavity that constitute the organ of smell. This overlooks the fact that the organ of olfaction is not simply the receptors but also includes part of the brain.

for why sensing blue must be added to the chain of physical causes that are proposed as an explanation for the differential growth.[22]

From the point of view of finality, the plant isn't going to react any better for seeing the light than we would digest our food better if this was a sensed process.

The 2011 discovery that melanocytes (the skin cells that produce melanin) contain rhodopsin, a light receptor found in the eye, puts in sharp relief the gratuitousness of attributing sight to plants.[23] Activation of this receptor "unleashes calcium ion signals that instigate melanin production."[24] Plainly, we do not see with our skin. Similarly, the activation of the plant's light receptors causes a series of biochemical reactions resulting in teleological response. There is no reason to say that the plant sees, any more than there is to say that we see with our melanocytes.[25]

22 A less prosaic reason for maintaining that plants see than their growing toward light is found in the case of the Boquila vine, which mimics the leaves of other plants. It seems that Boquila has to see what the plant leaves they mimic look like in order to mimic them. According to Gionoli et al., "*Boquila* is able to mimic the leaves of over a dozen tree species when growing onto them or in close proximity. Moreover, an individual *Boquila* plant associated with two different tree species can mimic both of them. Leaf mimicry by *Boquila* has been characterized in terms of leaf size, shape, colour, orientation, petiole length, and leaf tip spininess." Ernesto Gianoli et al., "Endophytic Bacterial Communities Are Associated with Leaf Mimicry in the Vine *Boquila trifoliolata*," *Science Reports* 11, no. 22673 (2021), https://doi.org/10.1038/s41598-021-02229-8. A hypothesis alternate to sight is the horizontal gene transfer hypothesis, according to which genes from the mimicked plant are transferred into and then expressed by Boquila. According to Gianoli et al., "Our results suggest the involvement of bacterial agents in leaf mimicry in *Boquila*, yet we are still far from proving the HGT [Horizontal Gene Transfer] hypothesis." White and Yamashita in a 2022 paper argue against the HGT hypothesis and in favor of the sight hypothesis in light of their experiment in which Boquila imitated a plastic plant. See Jacob White and Felipe Yamashita, "*Boquila trifoliolata* Mimics Leaves of an Artificial Plastic Host Plant," *Plant Signaling & Behavior* 17, no. 1 (2022), e1977530. However, plant scientists Ernesto Gianoli and John Pannell were highly critical of how the experiment was done; see Christie Wilcox, "Can Plants See? In the Wake of a Controversial Study, the Answer's Still Unclear," *New Scientist* (November 30, 2022), https://www.the-scientist.com/news-opinion/can-plants-see-in-the-wake-of-a-controversial-study-the-answer-is-still-unclear-70796. In any case, there are very few plants that mimic the leaves of other plants. So even if Boquila sees—and so is really an animal—this does not show that your average plant sees.

23 See Nadine L. Wicks et al., "UVA Phototransduction Drives Early Melanin Synthesis in Human Melanocytes," *Current Biology* 21, no. 22 (November 2011): 1906–11.

24 "Skin 'Sees' UV Light, Starts Producing Pigment," *News from Brown*, November 3, 2011, https://news.brown.edu/articles/2011/11/melanin.

25 I learned about rhodopsin in melanocytes from Robert Todd Caroll's 2016 four-part article, "Debunking Plant Sentience," which unfortunately is no longer available on the internet. Skin

The same type of explanation that is given for plants' growth toward blue light is proposed in other cases of their directional growth. For example, plants need to detect where water is in order to send out roots. We don't entirely know how roots grow toward water, but the type of explanation that is advanced by scientists is along the lines of moisture triggering a physical or chemical change that in turn sets "in motion a signaling cascade leading to cell elongation."[26] There is no evidence that the plants need to sense wetness.[27]

Another asymmetrical response of plants to outside agents is the hypersensitive response. According to plant biologist, Peter Balint-Kurti, "The plant hypersensitive response (HR) is a rapid localized cell death that occurs at the point of pathogen penetration and is associated with disease resistance."[28] The plant kills some of its own cells in order to deprive the pathogen attacking it of nutrition.[29] The explanation scientists offer for this response is not in terms of the plant feeling or tasting or otherwise sensing the pathogen but rather in terms of pathogen effector molecules binding to receptors on the plant, thereby initiating a complex signaling cascade in the attacked cells that ultimately leads to cell death at the infection site.[30]

---

cells are not the only cells that have nonvisual light receptors. Nonvisual light receptors are found both in the eye (they regulate the circadian rhythm), as well as in the central nervous system and in internal organs. See Thomas W. Cronin and Sönke Johnsen, "Extraocular, Non-Visual, and Simple Photoreceptors: An Introduction to the Symposium," *Integrative and Comparative Biology* 56, no. 5 (2016): 758–63. See also, Thomas Cronin, "Seeing Without Eyes — The Unexpected World of Nonvisual Photoreception," *The Conversation*, August 9, 2017, https://theconversation.com/seeing-without-eyes-the-unexpected-world-of-nonvisual-photoreception-79166.

26 Daniela Dietrich, "Hydrotropism: How Roots Search for Water," *Journal of Experimental Biology* 69, no. 11 (May 2018): 2766.

27 One plant motion that does not involve growth is the opening and closing of the stomata (i.e., pores defined by two guard cells) that allows for gas exchange. Part of the explanation for how the stomata open is that "blue light activates a proton pump in the guard cell plasma membrane," and this causes "ion and water uptake in the guard cell protoplasts, which in the intact guard cells provide a mechanical force that drives increases in stomatal apertures. In the absence of a rigid cell wall, the guard cell protoplasts swell." Lincoln Taiz and Eduardo Zeiger, *Plant Physiology*, 2nd ed. (Sinauer, 1998), 524. The plant need not sense blue light in order for the light to activate the proton pump. (Protoplasts are cells that do not have a cell wall.)

28 Peter Balint-Kurti, "The Plant Hypersensitive Response: Concepts, Control and Consequences," *Molecular Plant Pathology* 20, no. 8 (August 2019): 1163.

29 See Ankita Thakur et al., "Hypersensitive Responses in Plants," *Agricultural Review* 40, no. 2 (April-June 2019): 113.

30 See Thakur et al., "Hypersensitive Responses," 113. See also, Balint-Kurti, "The Plant Hypersensitive Response," 1163.

Equivocation Is Sometimes Involved in Claims That Plants Are Sentient

Accounts of how plants achieve directional growth often include terms such as "gravisensing,"[31] and "mechanosensation."[32] We need to examine the various ways in which words such as "sensing" are used. A "sensor" changes in response to some specific external thing and generally this change is set up so as to trigger another change, such as a device being turned on; for example: "A thermostat is a component which senses the temperature of a system so that the system's temperature is maintained near a desired setpoint."[33] Of course, the thermostat is not aware of hot and cold. Changes in heat energy cause a physical change in part of the thermostat, and this change causes other changes ultimately completing or breaking a circuit, resulting in a device going on or off. The same is true for other sensors; they do not sense, that is, they are not aware of motion, moisture, carbon monoxide, etc. These devices are typically tools for our senses, alerting us to the presence of sensible things that we cannot or cannot readily sense. And that is why we call these devices sensors and why we sometimes also say that they sense. This usage of "sense" is plainly equivocal. For the sake of clarity, I am going to arbitrarily use the word "detect" to name a noncognitive change in response to a specific thing, which change has some utility and restrict my use of "sense" to awareness of color, sound, etc.

I acknowledge that using "detect" in the aforesaid way is not an ideal solution as it obscures differences between what plants do and what artificial things do. For example, the detection of moisture in wood by a moisture

31 See, for example, Daisuke Kitazawa et al., "Shoot Circumnutation and Winding Movements Require Gravisensing Cells," *PNAS* 102, no. 51 (December 20, 2005): 18742–47.

32 Plants need mechanosensation for activities such as the growth of their roots, growth in response to wind, and trap closure in the case of the Venus Flytrap. This leads some to say that plants sense. See, for example, Jennifer Bohm, et al., "The Venus Flytrap *Dionaea muscipula* Counts Prey-Induced Action Potentials to Induce Sodium Uptake," *Current Biology* 26, no. 3 (February 8, 2016): 287: "During evolution, plants developed senses to recognize mechanical forces." However, there is mechanosensation that is plainly nonsentient; it plays a role in "fundamental cell functions including cell division, motility, and differentiation." W. H. Goldmann, "Mechanosensation: A Basic Cellular Process," *Progress in Molecular Biology and Translational Science* 126 (2014): 75–76. Thus, some reason would have to be given to show that sentience is required for the mechanosensation of plants.

33 "Temperature transmitters," https://sauermanngroup.com/en-INT/measuring-instruments/transmitters/temperature-transmitters. Accessed May 13, 2025.

meter does not benefit the meter itself but rather helps us, whereas the detection of moisture by the plant's root allows the plant to grow toward the water it needs to maintain itself. This difference highlights a problem with language. There is no special word that names an interaction between a living thing and something in its environment that leads to a nonsentient teleological response. The words that scientists typically use are "sense" and "perceive." Some scientists recognize that these words have been transferred from naming awareness in animals and are not univocal.[34] Thus, when they use these words in regard to plants, they are not affirming that plants are aware of sensible qualities. For example, Mithöfer and Boland say: "To successfully combat aggressors, plants must be equipped with a sophisticated sensory system to perceive signals fast and efficiently from their environment and thereby detect potential enemies and subsequently translate and integrate such signals into appropriate biochemical and physiological responses."[35] Yet Mithöfer, when asked whether he thought plants are sentient, responded: "The data available are not that clear yet. In my opinion I'd say NO."[36] Some scientists, however, seem to take such words univocally. One wonders whether Austriaco is not misled by the limitations of language when he reasons: "All living things have to respond and to adapt to their environments to survive, and they do this by sensing different external cues. Thus, all living things must have sensitive souls."[37] In any case, later on, we will see a clear instance where the equivocal use of "memory" vitiates one researcher's reasoning concerning plant sentience.

34 "Perception" is another word that, like "sensing," is sometimes used to name activities that occur independent of sensation. Scientists talk about "the perception of a signal by a specific receptor"; this "perception" consists in the binding of the extracellular signaling molecules to receptors located on the cell, which binding causes a conformational change in the receptor, which triggers changes within the cell. The simple fact that a receptor binds the extracellular signaling molecule does not establish that sense perception is taking place, as in many cases it is known to occur without sense perception. Thus, statements such as: "We will also discuss advances in herbivore recognition, namely, the perception of insect-derived signals by specific binding proteins" cannot be taken as evidence that plants are sentient. Axel Mithöfer and Wilhelm Boland, "Recognition of Herbivory-Associated Molecular Patterns," *Plant Physiology* 146 (March 2008): 825.

35 Mithöfer and Boland, "Recognition of Herbivory-Associated Molecular Patterns," 825.

36 Axel Mithöfer, personal communication.

37 Nicanor Austriaco, personal communication. One wonders to what extent the scientist's habit of using technical terms that have only one meaning makes them prone to assuming that words in general only have one meaning.

Faulty Reasoning Based on the Correlation of Plant Responses with Accidents Sensed by Us

People are more inclined to make unjustified leaps from detection to sensation when we happen to sense an accident (in the Aristotelian sense of "accident") than in cases where we do not. For example, since we do not smell CO_2, no one claims that plants smell it, whereas since we can hear the sound of a caterpillar chewing, at least when it is amplified, some people maintain that when plants increase chemical defenses against caterpillars in response to exposure to this sound, and not to other sounds, it must be because the plants hear.[38] Yet evidence that the plants have a sense organ for hearing is lacking.[39] Moreover, the research paper on this topic is entitled: "Plants Respond to Leaf Vibrations Caused By Insect Herbivore Chewing."[40] Sound waves are mechanical waves. They cause things that lack hearing to move. Thus, it may simply be the case that the jiggling of the plant by the sound waves triggers a series of reactions in the plant that ultimately results in an increase of defense chemicals in the leaves. Those who claim that hearing is involved need to provide evidence beyond the fact that the plant responds to specific sound waves.

Another example where the fact that something can be sensed by us paves the way to the assumption that it is sensed by the plant is the case of Daniel Chamovitz's attribution of the sense of smell to dodder plants. Dodders, when placed between a wheat plant and a tomato plant, preferentially grow toward the tomato, and similarly when exposed to the volatiles of these plants.[41] The dodders were then exposed to some of the individ-

38 See, for example, Janet Fang, "Plants Can Hear Themselves Being Eaten," *IFL Science*, July 4, 2014, https://www.iflscience.com/plants-and-animals/plants-can-hear-themselves-being-eaten/. The paper of M. Gagliano et al., "Tuned in: Plant Roots Use Sound to Locate Water," *Oecologia* 184, no. 1 (2007): 151–60, is also interpreted by some to show that plants hear. However, the paper gives no evidence that the plant does more than respond to certain vibrations that are audible to organisms that hear.

39 Carel ten Cate, in response to Monica Gagliano's call for studies on acoustic communication in plants, notes that the advantages of such communication presupposes the possession of sophisticated sensory mechanisms, "mechanisms not known from plants." "Acoustic Communication in Plants: Do the Woods Really Sing?," *Behavioral Ecology* 4, no. 1 (2013): 799.

40 H. M. Appel and R. B. Cocroft, "Plants Respond to Leaf Vibrations Caused by Insect Herbivore Chewing," *Oecologia* 175, no. 4 (2014): 1257–66.

41 See Cook, quoting Daniel Chamovitz, in "Do Plants Think?": "In one classic experiment scientists showed that dodder prefers tomato to wheat because it prefers the smell." Centuries

ual compounds in the wheat and tomato volatiles one by one. It turns out that "one compound present in the wheat blend, (Z)-3-hexenyl acetate, is repellent, providing a plausible explanation for the lower attractiveness of the wheat blend."[42] However, the simple fact that the compound is repellant and smellable by us does not show that the plant smells it. It may simply cause a nonsentient physiological reaction in the plant, as occurs in other cases when ligands external to the plant bind with plant receptors.[43]

Chamovitz, after mentioning that ethylene receptors have been found in plants, goes on to say: "Plants detect a volatile chemical in the air, and they convert this signal (albeit nerve-free) into a physiological response. Surely this could be considered olfaction."[44] However, a paper by Caren Chang describes the ethylene-signaling pathway in detail.[45] Put in general terms, ethylene binds to a receptor which then causes a series of other biochemical

---

earlier, Theophrastus maintained that plants smell: "When the vine is near cabbage or bay its shoot curves its tip and (as it were) turns back because of the pungency of the odour. For the vine is sensitive to smell." *De Causis Plantarum*, bk. II, ed. and trans. Benedict Einarson and George K. K. Link (Harvard University Press, 1990), vol.1, sec. 18.4, at 353.

42 Mark C. Mescher et al., Article Addendum "Plant Host Finding by Parasitic Plants: A New Perspective on Plant to Plant Communication," *Plant Signaling & Behavior* 1, no. 6 (November/December 2006): 285.

43 There is no reason to say that plants taste the saliva of the insects chewing on them. While it is true that not many elicitor and receptor pairs are known in the case of herbivory, they are not entirely unknown. (The elicitors in the case of herbivory are called HAMPs, which stands for herbivore-associated molecular patterns.) According to Santamaria et al., "Examples of well-characterized plant receptors of HAMPs," include "the tomato receptor-like kinase SISERK1, the A. thaliana L-type lectin-receptor kinase LecPRK-1.8, and LRR receptor-like kinase BAK1 (brassinosteroid insensitive-associated kinase)." M. E. Santamaria et al., "Plant Perception and Short-Term Responses to Phytophagous Insects and Mites," *International Journal of Molecular Science* 19, no. 5 (2018): 9. Researchers, despite having meager success so far in finding receptors in plants for chemicals in insect saliva, continue to look for them; they do not turn to sentience to explain plant responses to herbivory. And as for pathogen/microbial–plant interactions, they "are well established in terms of activated receptors between interacting partners." Massimo E. Maffei et al., "Natural Elicitors, Effectors and Modulators of Plant Responses," *National Products Report* 29 (2012): 1300. For a list of plant receptors for bacterial, fungal, and oomycete pathogens, see Yusuke Saijo et al., "Pattern Recognition Receptors and Signaling in Plant-Microbe Interactions," *The Plant Journal* 93, no. 4 (2018): 596.

44 Daniel Chamovitz, *What a Plant Knows: A Field Guide to the Senses*, rev. ed. (Scientific American, 2017): 48.

45 Caren Chang, "Q&A: How Do Plants Respond to Ethylene and What Is Its Importance?," *BMC Biology* 14, no. 7 (2016), https://bmcbiol.biomedcentral.com/articles/10.1186/s12915-016-0230-0. See also Hongwei Guo and Joseph R. Ecker, "Plant Responses to Ethylene Gas Are Mediated by SCFEBF1/EBF2-Dependent Proteolysis of EIN3 Transcription Factor," *Cell* 115, no. 6 (December 2003): 667–77.

changes in the plant. There is no organ involved, nor is there any need for the plant to be aware of the odor of the ethylene in order for it to respond to the ethylene.[46]

It is even clearer that sensing is not involved when one considers the details of how the plant responds to ethylene. The plant itself may both produce ethylene and be exposed to ethylene from without. Ethylene diffuses across cell membranes. The receptors for ethylene are not on the surface of the plant's cells but rather are located within the cells, in the endoplasmic reticulum.[47] When these receptors bind the ethylene the plant itself produces, this does not result in sensation, any more than when the plant's receptors bind other chemicals the plant produces (e.g., jasmonic acid receptors with jasmonic acid). There is no difference in what occurs when the plant's ethylene receptors bind ethylene that comes from an outside source than when they bind ethylene from an internal source. Thus, sensation does not occur in the former case anymore that it does in the latter. This example makes it clear that the fact that something from the outside triggers a reaction in a plant is no reason to conclude that it is sensed by the plant.[48]

46 Austriaco offers this as support for the notion that plants have a primitive sense of smell:

> Finally, and most spectacularly, Arimura et al., in Japan, have demonstrated that lima bean plants communicate with each other and with insects. These authors showed that a lima bean plant that is under attack by spider mites emits volatile substances that prompt neighboring and distant lima bean plants to undergo physiological changes, that will protect them from a future attack of these mites. Furthermore, they also demonstrated that this same plant when it is being attacked emits signals that attract predatory mites that will feed upon the original infestation of spider mites. Austriaco, "Immediate Hominization," 729–30.

As in the case of plants' responses to ethylene, there is no reason to say here that the interaction between a plant and a volatile involves sensation. There is also no evidence at all that the plants are aware of communicating with other plants or insects.

47 See Chang, "Q&A: How Do Plants Respond to Ethylene?"

48 If every receptor-ligand interaction resulted in sensation, the millions of such interactions going on inside our bodies between our cells would constitute separate acts of awareness. Some reason needs to be given beyond the occurrence of such interactions if one is to assert that sensing is occurring. Some people may alternately claim that it is the individual cells that are sensing in the strict sense of sensing, but in doing so they reduce us to a mere collection of cells and deny our per se unity. Regarding receptor-ligand interactions within the body, see Jordan A. Ramilowski et al., "A Draft Network of Ligand–Receptor-Mediated Multicellular Signalling in Human," *Nature Communications* 6 (2015): 7866 | DOI: 10.1038/ncomms8866, abstract: "Cell-to-cell communication across multiple cell types and tissues strictly governs proper functioning of metazoans and extensively relies on interactions between secreted ligands and cell-surface receptors. Herein, we present the first large-scale map of cell-to-cell communication between 144 human primary cell types. We reveal that most cells express tens

I note that the authors of the paper that established that the dodder "uses volatile cues to find its host" make no claim about it smelling odors.[49] Similarly, the researchers who experimented with vibrations made by caterpillars make no claim that the plants hear sounds.[50] Their silence indicates that those who are making such claims need to bring additional evidence to the fore.

What Is Learning and How Does It Relate to Sensing?

At first sight it seems that if a being learns, this is a sure indication that it senses. Is it possible, though, to define learning in the sense relevant to our discussion in a way that does not include sense perception in its definition? [51] It seems not. Learning means going from nonknowing to knowing (either that something is true or how to make or do something). If a thing is incapable of knowing anything to start with, then it cannot learn in this sense of learn.

If a thing cannot change its responses to things, plainly it cannot learn to do something. However, if it can change its responses, this does not necessarily mean that it can learn in the sense of going from being ignorant to knowing. This is clearest in the case of machine learning, for example, Spotify "learns" the kinds of songs a user likes based on those the user has previously

---

to hundreds of ligands and receptors to create a highly connected signalling network through multiple ligand-receptor paths."

49 J. B. Runyon, M. C. Mescher, and C. M. De Morales: "Volatile Chemical Cues Guide Host Locations and Host Selection by Parasitic Plants," *Science* 313, no. 5795 (2006): 1965–76.

50 See Appel and Cocroft, "Plants Respond to Leaf Vibrations Caused by Insect Herbivore Chewing," abstract:

> We asked whether acoustic energy generated by the feeding of insect herbivores was detected by plants. We report that the vibrations caused by insect feeding can elicit chemical defenses. *Arabidopsis thaliana* (L.) rosettes pre-treated with the vibrations caused by caterpillar feeding had higher levels of glucosinolate and anthocyanin defenses when subsequently fed upon by *Pieris rapae* (L.) caterpillars than did untreated plants. The plants also discriminated between the vibrations caused by chewing and those caused by wind or insect song. Plants thus respond to herbivore-generated vibrations in a selective and ecologically meaningful way.

51 We are plainly not talking here about learning that requires an intellect. Nor are we talking about "learning" in the sense of adaptive changes that do not involve cognition, such as when one's body is said to learn to adjust to a new mattress or to learn to adjust to seasonal changes in the length of day and night.

liked or disliked. Thus, evidence must be given that like changes in activity or response are due to sensing.

If one has learned to do something, ordinarily one can do it at some later time. That means one has to remember how one does it. "Memory" is a word with multiple meanings. In one sense, one can only remember things one knows. In another sense, a computer is said to have a memory because it encodes information which can subsequently be retrieved. But plainly computers don't know anything. How is one going to determine that a plant remembers something in the former sense, when one is not sure that it knows anything to start with?

Do Plants Have Memory?

Biologist Daniel Chamovitz articulates typical claims concerning plant memory:

> Plants definitely have several different forms of memory, just like people do. They have short term memory, immune memory and even trans-generational memory! I know this is a hard concept to grasp for some people, but if memory entails forming the memory (encoding information), retaining the memory (storing information), and recalling the memory (retrieving information), then plants definitely remember. For example a Venus Fly Trap needs to have two of the hairs on its leaves touched by a bug in order to shut, so it remembers that the first one has been touched. But this only lasts about 20 seconds, and then it forgets.[52]

The main problem here is that the definition of memory applies to computer memory (which does not involve life) and to immune system memory (which does not involve sensation), as well as to memory of something that has been sensed. Such a broad definition, embracing both sentient and non-sentient activities, is plainly unhelpful in determining whether plants have the sort of memory that depends on sensation.[53] I mentioned earlier

52 Cook, quoting Daniel Chamovitz, in "Do Plants Think?"

53 People who talk about plant memory sometimes tell us that the word "memory" names for them something that does not necessarily involve cognition: "Bruce et al. (200&) suggested that the use of the term 'memory' in plants implies a cognitive function. However, neither learning, memory nor indeed intelligence are words limited to biological, let alone, cognitive processes. For example, computers possess memory, and the more advanced ones can learn." Anthony Trewavas, "What is Plant Behaviour?," *Plant, Cell & Environment* 32, no. 6 (2009): 610.

how it is not uncommon for those who argue in favor of plant sentience to use words that have more than one meaning as though they had only one, as if such use of words offered support for plant sentience. We see this here in the case of Chamovitz, who fails to distinguish different meanings of the word "memory."

Chamovitz claims that the Venus Fly Trap has a memory on the grounds that in order for one of its traps to shut, a second hair has to be touch within twenty seconds of a first hair being touched; if the second hair is touched later than that, the trap will not close. Thus, it seems that the plant must remember that a first hair has been touched in the last twenty seconds in order for it to close. However, Chamovitz himself provides an explanation for trap closing that does not invoke knowledge on the part of the plant:

> The first touch of a hair activates an electric potential that radiates from cell to cell. This electric charge is stored as an increase in ion concentrations for a short time until it dissipates within about twenty seconds. But if a second action potential reaches the midrib within this time, the cumulative charge and ion concentrations pass the threshold and the trap closes.[54]

Here is another example of a claim about plant "memory." Chamovitz describes plant phytochrome as acting like a "light-activated switch: the red light turns on flowering; the far-red light turns it off." He goes on to say: "On a more philosophical level, we can say that the plant remembers the last color it saw." Chamovitz then continues:

> Warren L. Butler and his colleagues had demonstrated that a single photoreceptor in plants was responsible for both the red and the far-red effects. . . . In its simplest model, phytochrome is a light-activated switch. Red light activates phytochrome, turning it into a form primed to receive far-red light. Far-red light inactivates phytochrome, turning it into a form primed to receive red light.[55]

Those who use "memory" with so broad a meaning generally have little to say about whether "memory," taken in the sense that does involve cognition, is found in plants.

54 Chamovitz, *What a Plant Knows*, 141. See also Alexander G. Volkov et al., "Kinetics and Mechanism of *Dionaea muscipula* Trap Closing," *Plant Physiology* 146, no. 2 (February 2008): 694–702.

55 Chamovitz, *What a Plant Knows*, 19. Phytochrome is a photoreceptor that allows the plant to detect the length of nights, important for activities such as flowering.

The evidence Chamovitz provides does not support the claim that sensory memory is involved, but rather the opposite. A physical change happens which renders the phytochrome primed to receive one or the other types of red light, just as when one flips a light switch, the switch is now primed to complete or break the circuit. The switch does not need to remember the last position it was in.

Habituation

Habituation is commonly presented as the lowest form of learning. It is typically defined as

> the decrease of a response to a repeated eliciting stimulus that is not due to sensory adaptation or motor fatigue. Sensory adaptation (or neural adaptation) occurs when an organism can no longer detect the stimulus as efficiently as when first presented and motor fatigue occurs when an organism is able to detect the stimulus but can no longer respond efficiently. In contrast, habituation is a learned adaptation to the repeated presentation of a stimulus, not a reduction in sensory or motor ability.[56]

Examples of sensory adaptation include how loud sounds eventually become less perceptible and odors less or no longer noticeable due to changes in the sense organs. Examples of habituation include a person situated under a flight pattern, though initially momentarily distracted by a plane flying overhead and also by the subsequent plane, eventually stops noticing the planes; and a person, upon hearing a tone repeated at intervals, eventually exhibits almost no skin conductance response.[57]

Is Sensing Necessary for Habituation?

A number of experiments have been done that indicate that plants can be habituated. In one done in 1965, mimosas stopped closing in response to water droplets falling on them, and it was not because they were tired, as

56 This Wikipedia definition succinctly sums up what can be found in more authoritative sources. See, for example, R. Thompson, "Habituation," in *International Encyclopedia of the Social & Behavioral Sciences,* ed. Neil J. Smelser and Paul B. Bates (Elsevier Ltd., 2001), 6458. Note that I do not take up here sensitization, which is generally understood to be a phenomenon related to but the opposite of habituation.

57 The skin conductance response refers to the skin becoming a better conductor of electricity.

they closed upon being touched.[58] In a more recent experiment, done in 2014, mimosas were dropped 4–6 inches.[59] Initially they folded up their leaves, but after a number of repetitions, they stopped doing so. This was not due to fatigue, as shaking them resulted in them closing.[60]

Those who favor the view that plants are sentient rightly point out that our habitual ways of thinking about plants can be an obstacle to considering objectively what plants are able to do. I think it is also the case, however, that it has become customary to regard habituation solely as a form of "true" learning (i.e., learning that involves sensing). However, just as there is a need to distinguish nonsentient machine learning from true learning, there is a need to distinguish nonsentient habituation from habituation that depends on sensing. This is because machines can act in a manner that fits the description of habituation, that is, they cease responding to inputs that are repeated. There are word processors that autocorrect words that they "perceive" as being misspelled. Some of them have a feature such that if one deletes two times a word that has been autocorrected and puts the originally typed word back in, the processor now perceives this word as part of its dictionary, and it no longer responds to it by correcting it.[61] It is as if it has gotten used to the word. Also, there are robots that have been programmed to "habituate." They cease responding to things that they repeatedly encounter and turn to

58 Eric Holmes and Gail Gruenberg, "Learning in Plants," *Worm Runner's Digest* 7, no. 1 (1965): 9–12. Similar experiments using mechanical and electrical stimulation were done by Wilhelm Pfeffer, *Physiologische Untersuchungen* (Leipzig: W. Engelmann, 1873) [English: *The Physiology of Plants*, trans. Alfred J. Ewart (Clarendon, 1906)] and J. C. Bose, *Plant Response* (Longmans, 1906). All these experiments are recounted by Charles I. Abramson and Ana M. Chicas-Mosier, "Learning in Plants: Lessons from *Mimosa pudica*," *Frontiers in Psychology* 7, no. 417 (March 2016): 2.

59 Monica Gagliano et al., "Experience Teaches Plants to Learn Faster and Forget Slower in Environments Where It Matters," *Oecologia* 175, no. 1 (2014): 63–72.

60 Some question Gagliano et al.'s experiment. "The available data on Mimosa does not contain studies investigating a wide range of intertribal intervals. Until such data are available and correlated with underlying physiological data, it is difficult to separate sensory adaption from habituation." Abramson and Chicas-Mosier, "Learning in Plants," 4. See also Robert Biegler, "Insufficient Evidence for Habituation in *Mimosa pudica*: Response to Gagliano et al. (2014)," *Oecologia* 186, no. 1 (2018): 33–35.

61 Note that there is no reason one could not program the computer to require three or more changes on the user's part before it stopped responding by autocorrecting the new word.

novel things.[62] Thus, a decreased response to a repeated stimulus by a plant does not show that the plant senses.

From the point of view of finality, a reaction triggered by a stimulus that is biologically unimportant is a waste of energy regardless of whether the reaction is to something sensed or to something merely detected. Thus, from this point of view, it is not surprising that something resembling habituation in animals would arise in non-sentient living things.

Here again the problem of appropriate vocabulary arises. "Habituate" is now used in an extended sense that applies to robots and other machines, in a way similar to the extension of the word, "memory." While prior to now, the word "habituation" was used solely to name a form of true learning, there is now a need to distinguish a new sense that applies to its unknowing machine counterpart. And then to avoid confusing the plant's reduced reaction to a repeated stimulus with similar changes on the part of a machine or an animal, we need to distinguish yet another sense of "habituation."

Associative learning

Associative learning involves making a connection of sorts between two things, resulting in a new or improved behavior. It seems to be more likely to require knowledge than habituation which only leads to a diminishment of a typical response. Associative learning is commonly divided into classical conditioning and operant conditioning.

Classical conditioning

In classical conditioning, an organism begins to expect the arrival of an unconditioned stimulus (US) (i.e., something that naturally elicits a certain response) upon presentation of a conditioned stimulus (CS) (i.e., something that does not naturally elicit a response). The classic case of classical conditioning is Pavlov's dogs, which formed an association between a tone (CS)

62 See M. H. Lee, Q. Meng, and F. Chao, "Developmental Learning for Autonomous Robots," *Robotics and Autonomous Systems* 55, no. 1 (2007): 753–54: "Habituation mechanisms are used to reduce excitation with repetition and time and so attention is attracted by novelty and decays with familiarity. This motivation mechanism automatically attempts to repeat actions that accompanied the most exciting stimuli until eventually attention shifts away when familiarity has been gained." See also, Carolina Chang, "Using Sensor Habituation in Mobile Robots to Reduce Oscillatory Movements in Narrow Corridors," *IEEE Trans Neural Networks* 16, no. 6 (2005): 1582–89.

and the arrival of food (US), as witnessed by their salivating upon hearing the tone.

In the case of Pavlov's dogs, we know that dogs hear tones and that they remember things (e.g., where their water dish is), and so we recognize that the dog upon hearing a tone repeatedly followed by the arrival of food eventually associates the two. We take this as a model for classical conditioning. And so we tend to exclude a priori the idea that an organism could make associations between things that it merely detects, as opposed to senses and remembers.

There is an experiment that has been done with plants that seems to show that they are capable of classical conditioning. A garden pea shoot was placed in a Y-shaped tube at the point where the top of the Y forks. A puff of air was used as the conditioned stimulus, as in a test prior to the main experiment it did not affect the direction of growth of any of the plants, as predicted by the last direction in which the plant had detected blue light. Blue light was the unconditioned stimulus, as plants grow in the direction of blue light. The plants were divided into two groups. The puff of air was then delivered from one fork or the other and this was followed by a burst of blue light either from the same fork in the case of one group or from the other fork in the case of the second group. After a number of repetitions, the plants were tested. Sixty-two percent that had received a puff of air followed by blue light in the same tube, when given a puff of air grew in that tube, and 69 percent of those that had received the blue light in the opposite tube, when given a puff of air, grew in the opposite tube, as is consistent with classical conditioning.[63]

There are two problems with Gagliano et al.'s experiment. The first concerns the experiment itself, and the second concerns the interpretation of the results.

Kasey Markel questions the way in which Gagliano et al.'s experiment was done in a 2020 publication in which he recounts his unsuccessful attempt to replicate its findings. According to Markel, a major problem with the experiment was that "Gagliano *et al.* reported that in the absence of fan stimuli, pea plants always grow towards the last one-hour presentation of light, whereas we find their growth to be only slightly biased towards

63 Monica Gagliano et al., "Learning by Association in Plants," *Scientific Reports* 6, no. 1 (2016): 38427.

the last presentation of light."[64] Markel acknowledges that there is a remote chance this was due to Gagliano et al. using a different strain of peas. Another problem Markel notes is that 40 percent of plants have to be discounted, either because the morning of the test they already had grown into one tube before being exposed to the fan or because they had not grown into either tube the day after the test.

Taiz et al. also question the control in Gagliano et al.: "In our view a 100% response to the previous day's US is not expected."[65] They go on to note that if the control response is not 100 percent, then the "significance of the 65% response to the CS would have been greatly diminished, although not necessarily abolished."[66]

Barry Adelman, in his 2018 review of conditioning experiments with plants, also questions Gagliano et al.'s experimental procedure, as well as noting that the experiment has not been replicated.[67] Adelman's overall assessment of the conditioning experiments that have been done is "at best we have a 'maybe,' a few demonstrations, but more replications and extensions are needed, as well as better indications of the conditions under which respondent conditioning does and does not occur in plants."[68]

64 Kasey Markel, "Lack of Evidence for Associative Learning in Pea Plants," eLife 9 (2020), e57614.

65 Lincoln Taiz et al., "Plants Neither Possess nor Require Consciousness," *Trends in Plant Science* 24, no. 8 (2019): 680. See also Taiz et al., 680:

> The growing tip typically undergoes strong circumnutation in the dark, which weakens in light or during phototropic bending. In the dark, circumnutation increases and the tip gradually reverts to vertical growth due to the effects of gravitropism. The presence of the Y-maze adds another level of complexity to the experiment. If the shoot tip happens to enter the arm of the Y-maze where light was last presented during the previous day's training session, it would be mechanically prevented from reverting to vertical growth and would therefore resume growth the next day in the same arm. In this case, the control plants would appear to grow toward the arm where light had previously been presented, whereas in the absence of the Y-maze the control would grow randomly.

66 Taiz et al., 680.

67 See Barry Adelman, "On the Conditioning of Plants: A Review of Experimental Evidence," *Perspectives on Behavior Science* 41 (2018): 439. In this 2018 review of conditioning experiments with plants, Adelman notes that there were only six experiments of this sort in the literature, two of which gave positive results and one mixed results. In the case of the latter, one of which was Gagliano et al.'s, Adelman finds reason to question the results.

68 Adelman, "On the Conditioning of Plants," 439.

As to the interpretation of the pea experiment's results, we tend to assume that the plants felt the puffs of air and saw the blue light and remembered, even if unconsciously, that the former is associated with the arrival of the latter, similar to what happened with Pavlov's dogs and the bell followed by the delivery of food. It is especially tempting to do so, given the fact that we cannot explain in detail how this altered response occurs in plants. Yet, in the absence of a reason to hold that the plants do not merely detect the pressure of the puff and detect the colored light, this assumption is ultimately just that, an assumption. What the plant does resembles learning, but there is no reason to say that it is true learning.

Also relevant here is the fact that rats with spinal cords severed from their brains exhibit behavior typical of classical conditioning. As Jon Mallett et al. explain:

> During the training, the mild shock to the leg [conditioned stimulus] is given just before an antinociceptive shock to the tail [unconditioned stimulus], the latter being a shock that naturally diminishes tail flick in response to the focused heat. With learning, the leg shock diminishes this tail flick when given alone.[69]

In other words, in the trained animal, application of the conditioned stimulus, the mild leg shock, results in the response typical of the unconditioned stimulus, the antinociceptive shock, namely, tail flick is diminished without the unconditioned stimulus being applied. Since the spinal cord is disconnected from the brain, the rat is not aware of the leg shock or the tail shock. Thus, true learning is not occurring, despite the appearance thereof. This provides a further reason against concluding that plants sense solely on the grounds that they act in a manner consistent with classical conditioning.

In addition, the fact that robots have been constructed that "learn" in the manner of classical conditioning shows that what appears to be a form of true learning can occur in the absence of sentience.[70]

69 Mallett et al., "Debunking a Myth: Plant Consciousness," 468.

70 Ben Kröse and Joris van Dam, "Neural Vehicles," in *Neural Systems for Robotics*, ed. Omid Omidvar and Patrick van der Smagt (Academic Press, 1997), 280:

> The learning method is based on a model of "classical conditioning," a well-studied phenomenon in the behavioral sciences. Assuming that the system is capable of triggering an "unconditioned" response (UR) to stimuli from a basic set of unconditioned stimuli (US), the learning methods allow the system to develop associations between the set of USs and other stimuli which have no "genetically" preassigned value

Operant Conditioning

Operant conditioning occurs when an organism's behavior is shaped by punishment or reward. As yet there have been no claims of operant conditioning in plants. Indeed, it is hard to imagine how such conditioning could occur.[71] A pigeon learns through trial and error to press a certain sequence of buttons to get a grain reward and a dog learns to shake hands through "shaping," that is, being rewarded for successive approximations of the desired behavior. How could such training regimes be applied to a plant? In any case, if plants were observed to act in a manner consistent with operant conditioning, we must keep in mind that there are many papers in the field of robotics reporting the successful production of robots that are able to "learn" in a manner resembling operant conditioning.[72] If operant conditioning can be

---

> (conditioned stimuli, CS). The learning method was successfully applied to an obstacle avoidance task, where the US-UR reflex consisted of avoidance movements upon collision detection, and the CS was the output of a range sensor. After about 300 steps of the system, the avoidance movements were totally induced by the range sensor.

See also, Andreas Bühlmeier and Gerhard Manteuffel, "Operant Conditioning in Robots," in Omidvar, *Neural Systems for Robotics*, 199: "This learning paradigm, called classical conditioning, can be explained by one simple adaptive element and one delay element. The reflex is formed by a fixed US input weight, and conditioning occurs when the delayed CS coincides with the US. Figure 7.2 shows a simple circuit to explain the basic effect of conditioning with one fixed and one modifiable synapse (*w*)." See also Bühlmeier and Manteuffel, 213–16.

71 See Abramson, "Learning in Plants," 2:

> If a researcher is interested in studying operant conditioning, for example, a reward must be found that can be administered quickly, does not produce rapid satiation, and is effective over several presentations. Many learning paradigms require an established sequence of behavior that requires the delivery of time sensitive feedback. For example, one of the basic issues in operant conditioning is how to reward a behavior that does not naturally occur. One strategy is to reward successive approximations of the target response. This process, known as shaping, requires a reward to be administered at a precise time for producing a small piece of the desired action. Over time, the successive approximation comes together to produce the final outcomes. For this type of training, plants present unique challenges because they often appear to be inactive, making small behavioral changes difficult to see and relate to consequence.... Before a learning experiment can be designed, researchers must know what will motivate a plant and for how long.

72 Here is a sample of the fairly extensive literature on operant conditioning in robots: Xiaoping Zhang et al, "A Self-Learning Sensorimotor Model Based on Operant Conditioning Theory," 2015 IEEE Advanced Information Technology, Electronic and Automation Control Conference (IAEAC), 572–76 (this paper described how the robot they made learned how to shake hands); André Cyr et al., "Operant Conditioning: A Minimal Components Requirement in Artificial Spiking Neurons Designed for Bio-Inspired Robot's Controller," *Frontiers in Neurorobotics* 8, no. 21 (2014), doi: 10.3389/fnbot.2014.00021; Paolo Gaudiano and C. Chang,

mimicked by nonliving things, it would not be surprising that nonsentient living things can do so as well.

An Argument in Favor of Plant Sentience Drawn from Motile Unicellular Organisms

Arthur S. Reber offers an argument in favor of plant sentience, after which he goes on to respond to it. He first posits that evolution is generally conservative; once a feature that evolves proves to be adaptive, it is rarely lost.[73] He then points out that there is reason to think that motile bacteria are sentient. He concludes, then, that plants too should be sentient, given that bacteria are their ancestors and sentience is adaptive.

Reber goes on to respond to this argument:

> But it [sentience] is metabolically expensive; there's a lot of biological cost invested in being able to key in on, represent, and react to these many features of the environment. If a species lays down roots, abandons its motile way, it may just find that this aspect of existence is no longer worth the biological effort. It might turn out to be more effective from a natural-selection point of view, to focus instead on other forms and functions, ones that have a more immediate evolutionary benefit.[74]

Unlike Reber, I am agnostic as to whether any motile unicellular organisms are sentient (and regard the question as very difficult to answer). However, when it comes to understanding plants' activities, no matter what activity I consider, I find either that researchers have discovered an adequate explanation in terms of biochemistry or that that they are seeking that kind of explanation. Regardless of whether sentience is an ability that plants lost

---

"Adaptive Obstacle Avoidance with a Neural Network for Operant Conditioning: Experiments with Real Robots," *Proceedings 1997 IEEE International Symposium on Computational Intelligence in Robotics and Automation CIRA '97: Towards New Computational Principles for Robotics and Automation*, doi: 10.1109/CIRA.1997.613832. Cyr and Gaudiano studied the neural systems that underpin learning in organisms and took their inspiration from them.

73 It is debatable as to whether evolution is generally conservative. There is no doubt that traits are sometimes lost, e.g., sight in animals that are cave-dwelling. It may be the case that loss is less common than retention of features but is still not rare. In any case, Reber's counterargument turns on the fact that traits are lost when they no longer afford an advantage to the organism.

74 Arthur S. Reber, "Sentient Plants? Nervous Minds?," *Animal Sentience* 11, no. 17 (2018): 2.

or whether is one that they never had, the evidence presented throughout this paper indicates that they do not possess it.

A Clarification Concerning Sense Organs

At this point, I would like to make explicit something that I have been assuming all along as to what constitutes a sense organ. A sense organ is comprised of parts that interact for the purpose of knowing, which is an activity other than any response the organism may make to what it knows. A receptor that changes in response to something outside of an organism and that is simply the first part of a pathway leading to a determinate response is not a sense organ. We have seen clear examples of the latter, namely, the melanocytes in humans and the blue light receptors responsible for plant growth toward light. By contrast, when blue light strikes the cones of human eyes, we know that our seeing blue is not the same as any response we might have upon seeing it. When we see blue, we know it is present. Any response of ours to seeing blue is something that is in addition to our being aware of blue.

Another clarification concerning what a sense organ is can be illustrated by examining the case of sight. Though the organ of sight is typically said to be the eye, the eye is only part of the organ of sight. This can be seen from the fact that if one's optic nerve is cut or seriously damaged, one cannot see. The organ of sight is composed of the eye, the optic nerve, the primary visual cortex (which is part of the brain) and any other parts that are necessary for vision. Similarly, the organ of smell is not just the olfactory receptors that are in the nose but also includes the olfactory cortex (which is part of the brain), among other parts.

In the case of some organisms, one can readily tell that an activity of sensing is going on rather than a nonsentient reaction being triggered because the former does not always lead to any action. For example, cows turn their heads and look at passersby, but they do not always move in response; sometimes they do, sometimes they don't. And they look at other things as well, without necessarily reacting to them. By contrast, we neither observe plants gazing at blue light nor is the interaction between it and the blue light something that goes on independently of a determinate response. Rather, the plant's blue light receptors (phototropins) undergo a conformation change upon being struck by photons of blue light, which change causes other biochemical changes ultimately resulting in growth toward the light.[75]

I mention here in passing a question that would require a separate chapter, if not chapters, to treat, namely, whether very simple organisms, such as nematode worms and coral, sense or merely detect stimuli. I will limit my treatment here to talking about some of the difficulties involved in answering this question, with an eye to providing a better understanding of the nature of sense organs.

One problem in determining whether simple organisms sense is that in many cases they exhibit uniform responses to external stimuli. For example, nematode worms move toward certain volatile organic molecules and away from others.[76] When the worm's receptors bind to these molecules a specific reaction typically ensues.[77] This makes it unclear whether what goes on is only the triggering of a reaction or whether there is an act of sensing as

75 It should be noted that phototropins are responsible for things other than growth toward light (i.e., phototropism). See Shin-ichiro Inoue et al., "Phototropin Signaling and Stomatal Opening as a Model Case," *Current Opinions in Plant Biology* 10, no. 5 (2010): 587: "Phototropins . . . transduce light signals into diverse responses, including phototropism, chloroplast movement, nuclear positioning, stomatal opening, rapid inhibition of hypocotyl growth, leaf flattening, leaf positioning, sun tracking, and destabilization of *Lhcb* and *rbcL* transcripts." The authors acknowledge that it is unknown why phototropins are responsible for diverse responses. They propose that this is due to a difference in the proteins with which the phototropins interact, as a number of the latter have been identified. Inoue et al., 591. In other words, the activation of the phototropins appears to be the first step in a variety of different biochemical pathways. There is no reason to think that the diverse responses they are responsible for are due to sensing.

76 See C. I. Bargmann, E. Hartwieg, H. R. Horvitz, "Odorant-Selective Genes and Neurons Mediate Olfaction in C. elegans," *Cell* 74, no. 4 (1993): 515–27.

77 I had initially written that, "When the worm's receptors bind to these molecules a specific *behavior* typically ensues," and later amended the sentence, substituting reaction for behavior. The reason for this is that while the word "behavior" is sometimes used in a broad sense that applies even to inanimate things, most of the time its usage is restricted to beings that act voluntarily. In the latter sense, the dissolution of salt in water, the plant's growing toward light, and a reflex are not behaviors. "Voluntarily" here is to be understood to include both acts that proceed from free will and acts such as that of a dog getting up and walking to its food dish—the dog does this when it feels hungry. Behavior thus involves more than just sensing; it involves wanting of some sort. In the case of simple organisms such as nematode worms, it is not obvious how one could determine that they wanted something through observation. Aquinas argues on general grounds that living things that possess knowledge will necessarily have an inclination following upon that knowledge; see *ST* I, q. 80, a. 1. I do not intend to examine his view here. However, if it were determined that nematodes sense, assuming Aquinas is correct, then they would have to have some desire, and one could speak of nematode behavior in the strict sense of the word.

well. These worms are not like the dog that we can see sniffing another dog without its sniffing necessarily resulting in some specific response.[78]

A second reason that it is hard to know whether simple organisms sense is that their nervous systems are extremely simple. This makes it hard to judge whether part of their nervous system along with the receptors that change in response to things outside of the organism constitute an organ. We know in our own case that we are aware of hot and cold, and scientists have discovered thermoreceptors whose activation is the first step in sensing heat;[79] however, part of the brain as well is required in order for us to feel temperature.[80] Thus, the organ of touch in us is constituted by the thermoreceptors, the relevant part of the brain, and what connects the two. Some organisms, such as coral, have nerve nets, but do not have a brain, and others such as nematode worms have little by way of a brain—the entire nervous system of the most-studied nematode worm, *C. elegans*, consists of 302 neurons. These facts call into question whether either of these organisms have an organ that allows them to be aware of the odors and/or tactile qualities that they respond to. It may be the case that their responses are not due to sensing but are due to a reflex arc or to something resembling a reflex arc.[81] A reflex arc is a neural pathway mediating a reflex. A reflex is a response to a stimulus before one is aware of that stimulus, as, for example, when we instantly pull our hand off a hot stove or when our foot jerks upward when our bent knee is struck with a hammer. Reflex actions in vertebrates do not involve the brain but do involve neurons, some of which are found in the spinal cord. Thus, the presence of neurons in simple animals may not guarantee that the animals are able to sense.[82]

78 This is not to deny that in some cases of sensing a determinate response almost inevitably follows. For example, mice automatically flee the smell of a cat.

79 See Darren W. Logan, "Hot to Touch: The Story of the 2021 Nobel Prize in Physiology or Medicine," *Disease Models and Mechanisms* 14, no. 10 (2021), abstract: "The 2021 Nobel Prize in Physiology or Medicine was awarded to Ardem Patapoutian and David Julius for their research on receptor channels responsible for the perception of touch and temperature."

80 See M. Vestergaard et al., "The Cellular Coding of Temperature in the Mammalian Cortex," *Nature* 614 (2023): 725–31.

81 Nicanor Austriaco, OP, defended this view in "*Plants Too Have Sensitive Souls*," presented at the 2019 Annual Meeting of the American Catholic Philosophical Association.

82 This raises the further question: What about organisms that are much simpler than nematode worms, as they lack neurons, such as the unicellular organism, the paramecium? Do they sense? There are unicellular dinoflagellates in the family Warnowiaceae that appear to have an eye.

My intention in discussing simple animals here is not to ascertain whether they sense or not but to clarify how we determine what does and does not constitute a sense organ. If one were to object that my denial that plants are sentient entails the denial that certain simple animals are sentient, I would respond that I do not know enough about these organisms to judge whether they are sentient. If they turned out to be plants, this obviously would not eradicate the category plant.

Conclusion

I rest my case that plants, at least most of them, lack sentience.[83] Most of the life activities that go on in us without sentience and that would not be carried on any better with sentience are reasonably thought to go on in plants as well in a nonsentient manner.[84] These activities include nutrition, gamete production, adaptation, resisting foreign invaders, and homeostasis. While clearly, I could not cover in detail every activity that plants perform, as this book would end up being the length of a plant physiology book, relatively few activities suggest themselves as needing sensation to account for them. The two main ones that do are, first, directional responses and seasonal responses, which make it seem that plants have to know in what

83 My thesis that plants and animals are fundamentally different kinds of living things would not be affected if it turned out that we have misclassified a given species of living thing, e.g., if a species of carnivorous plant was shown to be an animal.

84 I have been arguing that plants ensure their survival exclusively through biochemistry and not by also sensing. It is interesting that the number of genes that humans have is estimated to be between twenty thousand and twenty-five thousand, whereas the number of genes the average plants has is estimated to be thirty-two thousand (https://www.crops.org/news/science-news/exploring-first-50-sequenced-plant-genomes/). When it was discovered that *Daphnia* (the water flea) has thirty-one thousand genes, one reason proposed to explain why they have so many more than humans is that *Daphnia* live in a changeable aquatic environment, one that they can't really escape from, given they do not swim that fast, and a large genome affords them a wide variety of biochemical ways of dealing with changes in the water. By contrast, most animals can deal with changes in their environment by simply moving elsewhere, and so they are not so reliant on biochemical strategies by which they alter themselves. Plants are even more restricted in their ability to move elsewhere than are *Daphnia*, and so it makes sense that they deal with environmental challenges using a wide array of biochemical responses. Consequently, it is not surprising that so many plants have a large number of genes, as the latter are needed for these biochemical responses. While it is not the case that every plant has more genes than every animal, for example, the model plant *Arabidopsis thaliana* has ~twenty-five thousand genes, whereas the puffer fish has ~thirty-five thousand, still the average plant has a strikingly large number of genes when compared to many animals.

direction to grow or change or when to do something, such as flower; and second, changes in the plants' responses to external stimuli, which makes it seem that they learn.

As for the first, while it is the case that scientists have yet to discover the causes of many directional activities in plants, such as their roots growing toward water, in the cases where such activities are fairly well understood, they are not explained in terms of awareness on the part of the plant. As we have seen, directional growth toward light results from photo-biochemical changes that take place in the absence of an organ, and that also would not proceed any better if the plant were to be aware of them. Similarly, the hypersensitive response, which occurs in the part of the plant that is attacked by pathogens, is due to molecules from pathogens binding to plant receptors, causing further biochemical reactions in the plant and not from the plant tasting or otherwise being aware of the pathogen molecules. While I did not cover plants' seasonal changes, the photo-biochemical explanations given for them can be readily found in the literature.[85]

As for the second potential exception, putative learning, as I have shown, even nonliving things can mimic the various forms of learning, from habituation to the various forms of associative learning. For this reason, pointing to a new or better behavior that a plant displays does not offer sufficient justification for the claim that it senses. Moreover, since learning depends on sensing, if there is no evidence to begin with that the plant senses, this is a reason to doubt that it engages in true learning when it appears to do so.

Those claiming that plants are sentient typically make a variety of false assumptions, probably the most common of which is that if a living thing responds in a teleological way to something in its environment (e.g., parasitizing another plant in response to volatiles produced by that plant), it must sense that thing.[86] People are especially prone to make this assumption when what the plant responds to has a quality we sense, such as an odor.

85 See Stephen D. Jackson, "Plant Responses to Photoperiod," *New Phytologist* 181 (2008): 517–31; Young Hun Song et al., "Photoperiodic Flowering: Time Measurement Mechanisms in Leaves," *Annual Review of Plant Biology* 66 (2015): 441–64.

86 Rafał Kupczak, for example, supports his claim that plants are sentient in this manner: "As shown above, in recent years extremely selective and efficient orientation processes have been discovered in plants. Their tendency to orientate in the environment results from the construction of specific structures (sensors) that monitor changes in certain selected parameters of the environment." Rafał Kupczak, "Selected Aspects of Biophilosophical Controversies in Complex Plant Behaviour Research," *Studia Philosophiae Christianae* 53, no. 2 (2017): 137–38.

Certain usages of language give the false appearance of supporting the notion that plants are sentient.[87] Words such as "sense" and "memory," which originally named ways of knowing in animals, have been transferred to also name things that nonsentient beings do, based on a resemblance. Consequently, using such words without distinguishing their meanings leads to question-begging assertions concerning plant sentience. The lack of words for activities that resemble in certain ways both those of animals and of machines but are in fact plant-specific exacerbates this problem.[88]

One wonders if Kupczak is not also misled by the lack of a precise term for the receptors involved in plants' selective and ecologically meaningful responses.

87 A number of plant biologists note how those promoting the notion that plants are sentient co-opt language typically used for animals to further their purposes. For example, Taiz et al. note in "Reply to Trewavas et al. and Calvo and Trewavas," 218:

> In any case, complexity *per se* is no proof for nervous systems. Again, cognition-related terms are used to suggest the existence of neuronal-like representations in plants. However, the use of such terms is not based on proven cognitive processes, but are at best mere metaphors similar to the term "memory cells" in immunology, which compares adaptive immunity to a learning process but does not seriously claim that immune systems have consciousness, cognition, or sentience.

88 See Taiz et al., "Plants Neither Possess nor Require Consciousness," 685–86:

> Why is anthropomorphism resurgent in biology today? In the most extreme case, all forms of life, even prokaryotes, are said to possess consciousness. This new wave of romantic biology appears to be inspired by a justifiable concern about humanity's continuing ecological degradation of the biosphere. . . . PN (plant neurology) has its roots in plant ecology and its philosophical offshoot, the Gaia hypothesis, rather than in plant physiology, and an ethical perspective permeates its intellectual foundation.

Part V

INTELLIGENT LIFE BEYOND EARTH

9

Aquinas on Intelligent Extraterrestrial Life

Both as a philosopher and as a theologian, Aquinas took an interest in the question of whether there are intelligent material beings other than humans in the universe. As a philosopher he sought to understand the order of the universe, which entails ascertaining the beings that are in the universe. As a theologian he sought knowledge of created beings insofar as it leads to a greater understanding, admiration, and love of the creator, and also insofar as it frees one from superstitious beliefs that pose an obstacle to faith in God.[1]

Although Aquinas was unable to approach the question of the existence of intelligent extraterrestrial life from the scientific perspective of our day, he does raise some generally overlooked philosophical questions regarding such beings. His theological reflections are helpful for addressing the popular claim that the discovery of intelligent extraterrestrial life would spell the end of Christianity. Aquinas's position is that it is possible that ETs of a certain

1 See *SCG*, bk. 2, chaps. 2 and 3.

sort exist, but improbable that they do.[2] I will consider first Aquinas's philosophical positions on the possibility of ET life, then his theological views thereon, and close with his arguments regarding the probability of ET life.

The Possibility of Extraterrestrial Life: Philosophical Considerations

When people today think of ET life, they generally imagine another earthlike planet inhabited by beings with odd-looking faces who are brainier than ourselves. Aquinas never considers ETs as inhabitants of another earthlike planet. This is because he thinks that there cannot be a more than one world like ours.[3] His views on the material composition of the universe further restrict what he considers possible as far as ET life is concerned. He thinks that celestial bodies are made of a single incorruptible element, while the earth is the only place where corruptible elements are found. Thus, his only candidate for ETs is the celestial bodies themselves, which some philosophers thought might be animate. He does, however, consider the possibility of the existence of rational beings other than humans that are composed of the earthly elements. Though he would necessarily imagine them as dwelling on the earth, we may take his arguments as applicable to the possibility of their existence on another planet.

The arguments against an intellectual substance being united to a *single* element are straightforward:

> If some intellectual substance is united to one of the simple bodies [corruptible elements] as form, either this being will have intellect alone or it will have other powers such as those which pertain to the sensitive or nutritive part as is the case in man. If, however, it has intellect alone, it would be vain for it to be united to the body. For every form of a body has some proper operation through the body. The intellect, however, does not have some operation belonging to the body except according as it moves the body. The motions of the elements are from natural movers, namely, from the things which generate them, and they do not move themselves; whence there is no need as far as their motion is concerned

2 Henceforth ET will be used as an adjective in place of "intelligent extraterrestrial" and will also be used as a noun to name beings of this sort.

3 See *In Libros Aristotelis De Caelo et Mundo,* Leonine ed. (Rome: Society for the Propagation of the Faith, 1886), bk. 1, chap. 9, lec. 19. See also, *ST* I, q. 47, a. 3.

> for them to be animate. If on the other hand the intellectual substance which is supposed to be united to an element or part of it has other parts of the soul [in addition to intellect], it will be necessary to find in a simple body a diversity of organs; which is incompatible with the body's simplicity. Therefore, an intellectual substance cannot be united as form to some element or part thereof.[4]

The argument against the possibility that there exists another body besides ours composed of many elements is less convincing:

> For if it [an intellectual substance] were united to another body, either it would be united to a mixed body or to a simple body. It cannot however be united to a mixed body, because it is necessary that that body be of the most balanced make-up according to its genus among the other mixed bodies, since we see that mixed bodies have nobler forms to the extent that they arrive at a more temperate mixture; and thus that body which has the most noble form, as an intellectual substance, would have to be of the most temperate mixture, if it is a mixed body; whence we even see that softness of flesh and goodness of touch which demonstrate balance of constitution are signs of a good intellect. The most balanced constitution is the constitution of the human body. It is necessary, therefore, that if an intellectual substance is united to some mixed body, it be of the same nature as the human body. The form of this being would be of the same nature as the human soul, if it be an intellectual substance. There would not therefore be a difference according to species between this animal and man.[5]

In this passage Aquinas seems to ignore the possible existence of beings with a rational soul who have better or additional external or internal senses. If they did exist, would they belong to the same species as we do?

Aquinas is actually addressing the question of whether there could be a rational being with better or additional senses when he speaks of the need for human beings to possess a body that has the most balanced mixture of elements. To understand Aquinas's position here, one must realize that although he thought that there was no best possible world, he did hold that the things in this world were as good as they possibly could be, given

4 *SCG*, bk. 2, chap. 90.

5 *SCG*, bk. 2, chap. 90.

the overall constitution of the world.[6] The human body was thus as well disposed as it could be for the rational soul and its operations given the constraints of the elements available in the world. Thus, in response to the objection that "since man is the most noble animal, the human body ought to be disposed in the optimal manner as to those things which are proper to animals, namely, sense and motion,"[7] Aquinas says that

> touch, which is the foundation of the other senses, is more perfect in man than in any other animal; and it is for this reason that it was necessary that man have the most balanced complexion among all the animals. Also, man surpasses all the other animals as to the interior sense powers. . . . From which it happens by necessity that as to some of the exterior senses man falls short of some other animals. For example, man has the worst sense of smell among all the animals. For it was necessary that man have the biggest brain in proportion to his body among all the animals so that the operations of the interior sense powers in him which are necessary for the operation of the intellect would be more readily exercised. . . . The magnitude of the brain on account of its moistness is an impediment to smell which requires dryness.[8]

The rest of Aquinas's response is to the effect that any inferiority in the human body is an unavoidable side effect of something needed to insure the good functioning of the internal senses and the "perfect equality of complexion" required for a good sense of touch.[9] One gathers from this that Aquinas thought that there was one perfect balance of elements and arrangement of organs in a human body (albeit varying within a certain range),[10] and that

6 See *ST,* I, q. 25, a. 6, ad 3:

> The universe cannot be better, supposing these things, on account of the most fitting order attributed to them by God, in whom the good of the universe consists. If some one of them would be better, it would corrupt the proportion of order; just as if one chord was more than duly stretched, it would destroy the melody of the cithara. Nevertheless, God could make other things, or add other things to the things already made; and thus there would be a better universe.

7 *ST* I, q. 91, a. 3, obj. 1.

8 *ST* I, q. 91, a. 3, ad 1.

9 Aquinas insists in many places on the importance of "perfecta complexionis aequalitate," which ensures that humans have the best sense of touch. See *Q. DA, unicus,* a. 8: "Whether the Rational Soul Ought to Be United to Such a Body of the Sort That the Human Body Is."

10 Aquinas is not ignorant that there is a certain range in human composition. See *Sent.* II, d. 15, q. 2, a. 1: "For when some make-up [*complexio*] is assigned to some genus, this is not

the presence of any other organs or even better organs would be incompatible with the balance that is needed for two or three things that humans need in order to be human, namely, a good sense of touch, a good memory and imagination,[11] and perhaps upright posture.[12]

The modern scientific evidence for the evolution of life forms provides reason to believe that there could be more than one body plan for a rational being. The evolutionary process itself is a kind of material constraint that Aquinas was not aware of. The "making over," so to speak, involved in producing a new life form from its predecessor could account for certain imperfections in the human body, just as the need for a good imagination has as a necessary undesirable side effect that areas of the brain devoted to other functions in animals have to be reduced in humans. The question is, then, would an intelligent being with a variation of the human body plan be a human being? Aquinas is not really able to consider this as a possibility. However, his minimal criteria for what constitutes a human being gives us some idea of what he might have said had he been aware of the evidence for evolution:

> But finger, foot, and hand, and other parts of this sort are outside an understanding of "man," whence the essential notion of man does not depend on them and man can be understood without them. For whether it has feet or not, so long as there is affirmed a conjunct of rational soul and body mixed from the elements with the proper blending that such a form requires, it will be a man.[13]

This text maintains that there are some components of humans that are not essential to our nature and thus do not enter into the definition of "human," whereas there are others that cannot be dispensed with. A human being could exist without hands or feet but could not exist without a mixed body that has the proper mixture of elements that a rational soul as form requires, namely, that which is requisite for an excellent sense of touch. As

according to some indivisible grade, but with a certain latitude; so what is found beyond certain limits no longer preserves the make-up belonging to that genus. But there is much diversity between those limits. . . . Nevertheless, there is some level of heat or cold that the human make-up cannot withstand."

11 See *Q. DA*, a. 8.

12 See *ST* I, q. 91, a. 3, ad 3.

13 *In Librum Boethii de Trinitate*, q. 5, a. 3.

mentioned above Aquinas also regards a large brain as a necessary component of human beings. He also names bones, which are needed for upright posture.[14] We are still left wondering whether Aquinas would rank a being that fit the above criteria and that was endowed with an extra sense or bigger brain than ours in the same species as us or only in the same genus.[15]

Up to now I have considered whether it is possible for another human-type body to exist. However, what determines the species of a thing is its form, which in the case of living things is the soul. It remains to be considered whether there is something about the rational soul that prevents it from existing as the form of more than one species. On this point it is helpful to see why separated substances and the human soul are not put in the same species:

> Further, any thing whatsoever has its proper being according to the *ratio* of its species; for of those things of which there is a diverse *ratio* of being, there are diverse species. The being, however, of the human soul and of the separated substance are not of one *ratio;* for a body is not able to share in the being of a separated substances as it can share in the being of a human soul according to which it is united to the body as form to matter. The human soul therefore differs in species from separated substances. Moreover, the species of a thing is perceived from the proper operation of it; for operation demonstrates power [*virtutem*], which indicates the essence. The proper operation, however, of separated substances and the intellectual soul is to understand; however, the mode of understanding of separated substances and of the soul is totally other; for the soul understands by taking from the phantasms, which is not the case of separated substances, which do not have bodily organs in which the phantasms must necessarily be. Therefore, the human soul and separated substances are not of one species.[16]

Both our hypothetical ETs and humans would have a rational soul that is the form of the body and that knows by abstracting concepts from sense experience.

14 See *ST* III, q. 5, a. 2: "Carnes et ossa in hominis definitione poni oportet."

15 I do not intend here systematically to address the question of how a species is determined according to Aquinas. This is a difficult task which demands separate treatment, and so I will continue to skirt the issue as I examine the question of the possibility of another species of human-type life.

16 *SCG*, bk. 2, chap. 94. See *Sent.* II, d. 3, q. 1, a. 6: "Utrum angelus et anima differant specie."

The multiplicity of angelic forms suggests that there might also be a multiplicity of human forms.[17] Yet, according to Aquinas

> that there is only one species of rational animal, while there exist many species of irrational animal, arises from the fact that the rational animal is constituted from this that corporeal nature reaches the highest thing it can attain to, [namely], the nature of spiritual substance which [in turn] attains its lowest [grade]. There is only one highest grade, as well as lowest grade, of one nature.[18]

This argument does not address the possibility that there could be a group of human-type beings more capable of understanding than another due to better senses. In fact, Aquinas even seems to think that there is room for doubt on the point because after he says that "there is only one highest grade, as well as lowest grade, of one nature" he ends by saying "although it could be said that there were many species of rational animal, if one would posit that the celestial bodies were animate."[19]

When Aquinas, in the *Summa Contra Gentiles*, apparently excludes the possibility that several species of human beings could exist, his concern is to refute the erroneous views that demons are physical animals made of bronze and that the elements are animate, and that angels and demons by nature

17 See *ST* I, q. 50, a. 4, obj. 2: "More and less does not cause a diversification of species. But angels do not appear to differ from one another except according to more and less, namely, according as one is simpler than another, and is of more perspicacious intellect. Therefore, angels do not differ in species." Aquinas responds (ad 2): "More and less, according as it is caused from the intensification and remission of one form does not cause a diversification of species. But more and less according as they are caused from forms of diverse grades do thus cause a diversification of species; for example, if we say that fire is more perfect than air. And in this manner angels are diversified according to more and less."

18 *De Spir. Creat.* 8, ad 10.

19 *De Spir. Creat.*, a. 8, ad 10. This last statement, despite being couched in hypothetical terms, is somewhat odd since Aquinas holds that celestial bodies are simple, and thus would not have sense organs as animals must have. See *Q. DA*, a. 8, ad 12: "The body of man could not be a simple body, neither a heavenly body on account of the passibility of organic senses, and above all the sense of touch; nor a simple elementary body: because in an element there are contraries in act. It is necessary, however, that the human body be brought to a middle [state]." See also, *SCG*, bk. 2, chap. 70. One cannot get around this by saying that movement is also an animal characteristic because while it is true that only animals move locally, not all animals do so, whereas all sense; sensing is thus the defining characteristic of animals. A further problem is that not only would such a being not be an animal, it also would not be rational either, strictly speaking, since reason is distinguished from pure intelligence by its dependency on sense experience.

had bodies.[20] If he were presented with an intelligent individual that had a sixth sense and an exceptional memory, would he say that it was the same species, or that it and we were only generically the same?[21] I do not see any room to say that he would deny that the beings in question are human, at least in the generic sense, given that they have the requisite sensitive body and an intelligence which starts off tabula rasa and arrives at ideas starting from sense experience.

Aquinas's other candidate for an ET is an animated celestial body. His views on this subject might seem of merely historical interest given that we know that the stars and planets are not composed of a fifth incorruptible element. However, it is useful to see how Aquinas reasons when faced with a possible addition to the chain of being.

Aquinas thinks that the most plausible view concerning the movement of the heavenly bodies is that it is caused by lower-ranking separated substances that are not united to those bodies as their forms.[22] However, he does seriously entertain the possibility that these separated substances are united to the heavenly body as their forms.[23] In the *Disputed Question on Spiritual Creatures*, after giving one argument pro and another con, he asserts that "the

20 See *SCG*, bk. 2, chap. 90.

21 The capacity to interbreed is important for modern science in determining species. To my knowledge, Aquinas says very little about reproduction in relation to species. He determines that men and women do not belong to different species on the grounds that male semen could not produce both sexes if they were not of the same species. It does not however follow from this that if a human cannot reproduce with an alien that the two are not of the same species. Aquinas was aware that the mule is an offspring of a horse and an ass. However, this does not help much in determining whether there could be another species of humans because Aquinas regards horse and ass as two species to start with, and he does not provide us with the criteria whereby he determined this.

22 See *De Spir. Creat.*, a. 6:

> It ought to be said further that it is contrary to the incorruptibility of the heavenly bodies that they be animate as are lower bodies which are rendered vegetative and sensitive through the soul. It is therefore to be denied that celestial bodies are animate in the same manner in which these lower bodies are animated. It is nevertheless not to be denied that heavenly bodies are animate, if what is understood by animation is nothing other than the union of mover to mobile.

23 See *De Verit.*, q. 5, a. 9, ad 14:

> Or it can be said that the soul is the perfection of the human body both as form and as mover; the heavenly body which is perfect does not require another spiritual substance which will perfect it as form, but which will perfect it as motor only. Although some held that the movers of the orbs were joined to them as their forms; which is left in doubt by Augustine. Damascene, however, says the contrary.

opinion on each side has the *ratio* of probability."[24] Though in that disputed question he finds the argument for a negative conclusion more compelling, in the *Disputed Question on the Soul,* after extensive discussion, he says in the response to an objection:

> If, however, it [the separated substance] only possesses intellect [and not sense] it is nevertheless united to the body as form not for the sake of intellectual operation, but for the sake of the execution of its active power.[25]

It is somewhat surprising that Aquinas entertains as possible that an intellectual substance be united to a celestial body, since this does not seem consistent with his position that the difference between the human form or soul and angelic forms is that the latter does not have the ability to share its being with a body.[26] Perhaps Aquinas thinks that the human soul may not be the only immaterial form that can be united to a body after all, for in another place he says:

> This thing able to be perfected that is the human body corresponds to the soul, [whereas] to an angel either no body corresponds or that of another species such as a bronze body as Augustine . . . seems to say.[27]

On the supposition that the heavenly bodies are animate, Aquinas never envisages them as an *intermediary* between humans and angels. We have already seen that he seems open to ranking them with humans, but more often he maintains that "if the celestial bodies are animate, their souls

24 *De Spir. Creat.*, a. 6.

25 *Q. DA,* a. 8, ad 3.

26 See *SCG*, bk. 2, chap. 94, cited above. See also *Q. DA*, a. 3: "Belonging to the notion of the human soul is that it is unitable to a human body, since it does not have in itself the complete species; but what makes up the whole of the species is in the composite itself. Whence that the soul be unitable to this body or that body multiplies it according to number, not, however, according to species."

27 *Sent.* II, d. 3, q. 1, a. 6 ("Utrum angelus et anima differant specie"). The passage reads:

> Praeterea, eidem formae vel perfectioni respondet idem perfectibile. Sed anima et angelus sunt quaedam formae, prout communiter omnes substantias a materia separatas formas dicimus, quorum formae materiales sunt imagines, ut Boethius dicit. Cum ergo animae respondeat hoc perfectibile quod est corpus humanum, angelo vero vel nullius vel alterius speciei, ut corpus aereum, secundum quod Augustinus videtur dicere, vel etiam corpus caeleste secundum opinionem Avicennae et quorumdam philosophorum; videtur quod anima et angelus non sunt unius speciei.

belong to the society of the angels."[28] The reasons for classifying them in this manner is that they lack a sensitive body and they have an angelic mode of understanding.

What can we conclude from Aquinas's hesitancy and at least apparent inconsistency on the issues concerning animated celestial bodies? The fact that his preferred authorities (Aristotle and St. Augustine) do not adopt the position that he thinks is most plausible alerts him to the difficulty of determining the answer. He recognizes that the arguments given on both sides contain probability. Unable to come up with evidence sufficient to allow him to decide the question with certitude, he remains open to the possibility that the opposite position to his own might be true.

Aquinas also takes care to avoid speaking in such a manner as would prejudice divine wisdom. As a philosopher he maintains that the works of nature manifest intelligence while themselves lacking it, and as a Christian believing in divine Providence he is even more firmly convinced that natural things are not junk.[29] Thus, although the existence of ensouled heavenly bodies appear to him unlikely because they do not fill an obvious gap in the hierarchy of beings in the universe, he still sees a need to postulate some goodness that would be proper to them, in case they do exist. We see this in the passage quoted above from the *Disputed Questions on the Soul,* where he says that such a being would be "united to the body as form not for the sake of intellectual operation, but for the sake of the execution of its active power, according to which it is able to attain to likeness to God as to causality, by [causing] the motion of the heavens."

28 *Q. DA,* a. 8, ad 5. The objection states "that if they are animate, in eternal beatitude there would be not only angels and men, but also a certain middle nature." See *De Spir. Creat.,* q. 1, a. 6, "Whether a spiritual substance is united to a heavenly body," and s.c. 3:

> The heavenly society of the blessed consists of angels and souls. But the soul of the heavens, if the heavens are animate, would be contained under neither group. Therefore, there would be some rational creatures which could not be sharers in beatitude, which seems to be unfitting. [ad s.c. 3:] If the heavenly bodies are animate, the spirits governing them are to be counted in the society of the angels.

29 Aquinas does exclude some combinations as absolutely impossible, for example, an animate body made only of air.

Theological Concerns

Aquinas does not see the existence of ETs as posing difficulties to the faith. While his treatment is unfortunately limited by what he considers to be possible ETs (namely, animated heavenly bodies), he does make some generally applicable points.

In one passage, Aquinas goes so far as to say that to make a pronouncement on the existence of animated celestial bodies is of no concern to the faith:

> According to what Aristotle says, it is the case that it is necessary to posit an intellect united to the body as form. According to the opinion of Aristotle, it is therefore the case that the heavens are composed from an intellectual soul and a body. . . . It will be necessary to say then that the intellect according to its substance is united to the heavenly body as form. . . . What is being said, however, about the animation of the heavens we do not say as asserting it according to the teaching of the faith, to which it is of no concern at all [nihil pertinet] whether this matter is said to be thus or otherwise; whence Augustine [says] (Enchird. c. 58): "Nor am I certain whether the sun and moon and other stars belong to the same society, namely, that of the angels; the brightness of the bodies notwithstanding, they do not appear to have sense or intelligence."[30]

One reason why Aquinas does not think the existence of ETs is of concern for the faith is that the faith and Sacred Scripture are ordered to our salvation, and not to instructing us in cosmology or science in general. It is for this reason that scripture sometimes omits mention of certain things, as happens, for example, in the book of Genesis in regard to the creation of the angels:

> Augustine says that "the angels were not left out in the first creation of things, but are signified by the name 'heaven,' or even 'lights.'" Therefore, however, either they were left out, or they were signified by the names of corporeal things because Moses habitually spoke to uneducated people who were not yet able to grasp [things of an] incorporeal nature; and thus, if it had been expressed to them that there were things above all corporeal nature, it would have been for them an occasion of idolatry,

30 *SCG*, bk. 2, chap. 70.

> to which they were prone, and from which Moses chiefly intended to call them back.[31]

Knowledge of extraterrestrials is of no more concern for the faith than is knowledge about animated celestial bodies. It belongs to science and not to faith to catalogue the different beings in the material universe. Moreover, just as untimely knowledge concerning angels was apt to pose an obstacle to the faith of early uneducated believers, this could also be the case with ETs, on the supposition that they exist.

Of course, it does pertain to the theologian to defend the teachings of the faith. The specific manner in which Aquinas envisages ETs does not suggest any conflict with scripture since that sort of ET would be ranked with the angels.[32] The existence of ETs as people today typically envisage them, however, does raise questions. For example, if ETs are generically human, how is one to understand 1 Corinthians 15:22–23: "Death came through one man and in the same way the resurrection of the dead has come through one man. Just as all men die in Adam, so all men will be brought to life in Christ"?[33] If Aquinas had recognized the possibility of ETs as we envisage them, he would have seen it as the theologian's duty to treat these questions.

Aquinas does make at least two applicable observations. Following scripture, he insists that all humans have Christ as their head:

> Moreover, the one who is not harmed by sin, is not in need of redemption. If therefore there would be someone who was not born in original sin, aside from Christ, there would be someone who was not in need of the redemption accomplished by Christ; and thus Christ would not be the head of all men, which is not fitting according to the faith. Therefore, neither ought one to hold that someone can be born without original sin.[34]

31 *ST* I, q. 61, a. 1, obj. 1 and ad 1. See *De Substantiis Separatis,* c. 17.

32 See *Q. DA,* a. 8 ad 5; cited above with *De Spir. Creat.,* a. 6.

33 To my mind the most problematic text is Colossians 1:15–20: "As he is the Beginning, he was first to be born from the dead, so that he should be first in every way; because God wanted all perfection to be found in him and all things to be reconciled through him and for him, everything in heaven and everything on earth when he made peace by his death on the cross." This could be explained by saying that fallen ETs were redeemed through Christ's death on earth. Another alternative is that they never fell.

34 *Sent.* II, d. 31, q. 1, a. 2. See *SCG,* bk. 4, chap. 83:

> Furthermore, if after the resurrection there will be generation of human beings, either those who are generated will be later corrupted, or they will be incorruptible and immortal. If, however, they will be incorruptible and immortal, a number of unsuitable

This raises the question of what, if any, problem this position would pose were generically human ETs to be discovered.

The argument that Aquinas gives for the possibility of other incarnations is another contribution that he makes to the theological ET debate:

> On Whether One Divine Person is Able to Assume Two Human Natures: That which is able [to do something] in one case and not in another has its power limited to one. The power of a divine person is, however, infinite, nor can it be limited by something created. Whence it ought not be said that a divine person assumed one human nature in such a manner that it could not assume another. For it would appear to follow from this that the personality of the divine nature would be so bounded by [*comprehensa*] one human nature that its personality could not assume another, which is impossible, for the uncreated cannot be bounded by the created. It is manifest therefore that whether we consider the divine person according to power, which is the principle of the union, or according to its personhood which is the term of the union, it must be said that the divine person over and beyond the human nature that it has assumed is able to assume another numerically different human nature.[35]

Thus far I have considered Aquinas's arguments regarding ET life chiefly with an eye to its possibility. Now I would like briefly to examine a few arguments Aquinas gives in other contexts to the extent they can be applied to the question of the probability of ET life.

A philosophical argument for the improbability of ET life can be derived from considering the order of the universe:

---

consequences follow. First, it will be necessary to hold that those men are born without original sin, since the necessity of dying is a punishment consequent upon original sin; which is contrary to what the Apostle says in Romans 5:12, that "through one man sin was transmitted to all men, and through sin, death." Whence it would follow that not all were in need of the redemption which is from Christ, if some were born without original sin and without the necessity of dying; and thus Christ will not be the head of all men; which is contrary to the view of the Apostle who says in 1 Corinthians 15:22 that "as all died in Adam, so too all are made alive in Christ."

35 *ST* III, q. 3, a. 7. See also ad 2: "The assumed nature, however, as to something stands in the manner of a vestment, granted that there is not a likeness on all points, as was said above. And therefore, if a divine person would assume two human natures, on account of the unity of the supposit, one would speak of 'one man having two human natures.'" For a contemporary defense of Aquinas's view on multiple incarnations, see Timothy Pawl, "Brian Hebblethwaite's Arguments Against Multiple Incarnations," *Religious Studies* 52 (2016): 117–30. See also Timothy Pawl, "Thomistic Multiple Incarnations," *The Heythrop Journal* 57 (2016): 359–70.

> The order of the universe includes in itself both the conservation of the diverse things instituted by God, and the motion of them; because according to these a twofold order is found in things, namely, according as one thing is better than another, and according as one thing is moved by another.[36]

For Aquinas, if there were no interaction between us humans in our world and the ETs in their world the universe would be deficient as to one kind of order, though it still would have the order of hierarchy. Aquinas regards rational beings as the principal parts of the material universe, and consequently he sees their ordering as more essential to the good order of the universe than the ordering of other material beings in the universe.[37] For this reason, while he would not see a lack of interaction between humans and the elements of distant galaxies as being prejudicial to the order of the universe, he would see a lack of interaction between rational beings as being such. Consequently, Aquinas would regard the existence of a universe lacking interaction among its principal parts (i.e., rational beings) to be unlikely.

Another philosophical argument for the improbability of ET life is based on a notion that Aquinas uses to argue that this world is the only one, namely, that uniqueness is a desirable characteristic:

> The third objection is as follows: It is better to multiply the best things than those which are less good; but the world is the best thing; therefore, it would be better for there to be many worlds than it is for there to be many animals and many plants. And to this it ought to be said that this

36 *ST* I, q. 103, a. 4, ad 1.

37 See *In Meta.*, bk. 12, lec. 12, n. 7:

> Aristotle manifests that not all things [in the universe] are ordered in a similar way by way of an example. For diverse grades of order are found in a home or family: As ranked under the head of the household, the first grade belongs to the children, the second grade to the servants, and the third grade to the domestic animals which serve in the home, such as dogs and other animals of this sort. These diverse grades stand in diverse ways to the order of the household, which is imposed by the head governing it. It is not admissible that the children do things haphazardly and without order, but all, or most, of the things they do are ordered. This is not so in the case of the servants or of the domestic animals, because they share little in the order, which is to the common good. Rather much is found in their case that is contingent and happens by chance. And things are this way because these individuals have little connection with the ruler of the household, who aims at the common good of the household.

See also Albertus Magnus, *De Caelo et Mundo*, vol. 5 of *Opera Omnia* (Monasterii Westfalorum, 1971), 69: "The good of the worlds is not perfect without communication of its citizens."

> itself belongs to the goodness of the world: that it be one; because one has the notion of good: for we see that something is cut off from its proper goodness through division.[38]

One could similarly argue that one human species is enough, since it would reflect God's goodness by being unique.

Another argument against the probability of ETs derives from an argument Aquinas uses to refute the position that there are many worlds, based on a characteristic of intelligent agents. In responding to the objection that "it would be better that there exist many worlds rather than one, because many good things are better than fewer,"[39] Aquinas points out that

> no agent intends a material plurality as an end; because a material multitude does not have a fixed term, but of itself tends to infinity; infinity, however, is contrary to the notion of "end." When it is said, however, that many worlds are better than one, this is said according to material multitude. This sort of better, however, does not belong to the intention of God as agent, because for the same reason it could be said that if he made two, it would be better that there were three; and thus, ad infinitum.[40]

38 *De Caelo,* bk. 1, chap. 9, lec. 19. This argument is already found in Plato's *Timaeus,* and perhaps Aquinas took it from there: "To the end that this world may be like the complete and living Creature in respect of its uniqueness, for that reason its maker did not make two worlds nor yet an indefinite number, but the Heaven has come to be and is and shall be hereafter one and unique." Plato, *Timaeus* 3la, b, in *The Collected Dialogues of Plato,* ed. Edith Hamilton and Huntington Cairns, trans. Benjamin Jowett (Pantheon Books, 1961). A number of authors maintain that the discovery of ET life would prove Christianity is false since it would imply that there were many Adams and many incarnations. Thomas Paine is a noteworthy proponent of this view, as we shall see in chapter 10. See Thomas Paine, quoted by Michael J. Crowe, in *The Extraterrestrial Life Debate 1750–1900: The Idea of a Plurality of Worlds from Kant to Lowell* (Cambridge University Press, 1988), 163:

> From whence, then, could arise the solitary and strange conceit that the Almighty, who had millions of worlds equally dependent on his protection, would quit the care of all the rest and come to die in our world, because, they say, one man and one woman had eaten an apple! And, on the other hand, are we to suppose that every world in the boundless creation had an Eve, and apple, and serpent, and a redeemer? In this case, the person who is irreverently called the Son of God, and sometimes God himself, would have nothing else to do than to travel from world to world, in an endless succession of deaths, with scarcely a momentary interval of life.

Of course, this is not the only possible scenario, even if ET life existed in great numbers. However, it does accord with Aquinas's claim that uniqueness is a kind of perfection.

39 *ST* I, q. 47, a. 3, obj. 2.

40 *ST* I, q. 47, a. 3, ad 2. See *De Caelo,* bk. 1, c. 9, lec. 19: "If God would make other worlds, either he would make them like this world or unlike. If they were completely alike, they would exist

God could have populated the universe with any number of reproductively isolated groups of rational animals, but there is no motivation for him to make more than one human race, since simply having more than one for the sake of having more than one is not something an intelligent being would aim at. The weakness of this argument is that it does not exclude God's creating other groups of human beings who would differ by more than the insignificant differences characteristic of the different races. And indeed, Thomistic positions on the diversity of being in the universe seem to lean in the direction of an affirmative answer to the question of whether ET life is probable. Aquinas maintains that

> God produces things for the sake of communicating his goodness to creatures, and through them to represent his goodness. And because it cannot be adequately represented through one creature, he produces many and diverse creatures, so that what is lacking to one for the purpose of representing divine goodness, is filled up by others; for the goodness which exists simply and uniformly in God, in creatures is multiple and divided. Whence the whole universe more perfectly shares in and represents divine goodness than any other creature whatsoever.[41]

Of the diverse beings that God creates, Aquinas holds that it "certainly agrees with the affluence of divine goodness that those things which are more noble are more abundantly produced in being."[42] A question remains as to whether the greater abundance of more noble things refers to the number of individuals within a species or to the number of species or types. Aquinas addresses this question when discussing the number of angels:

> The Platonists were saying that to the extent that something is closer to the first principle to that extent it is smaller in multitude; just as to the extent that a number is nearer the unit to that extent it is less in multitude. And this opinion stands up well as to the number of orders: three assist, while six minister. But Dionysius held . . . that the multitude of angels transcends lower bodies in greatness by something immense, so that the higher incorporeal natures transcends all corporeal natures because what is better is more intended by God and more multiplied.

in vain: which does not belong to his wisdom."

41 *ST* I, q. 47, a. 1.

42 *De Pot.*, q. 6, a. 6. See *SCG*, bk. 2, chap. 92, which also says that there should be more of better things, giving as the reason that the lower are for the sake of the higher.

> And according to this, since those assisting are superior to those ministering, there are more assistants than ministers.[43]

According to these principles, there should be fewer sorts of humans than animals, and more individual humans than animals, but the latter is not the case. And if one regards humans as the lowest of separated substances, again the principles fail to apply: There should be more sorts of the lower form, that is, humans, and fewer individual humans than angels, but the former is not the case. Ultimately, Aquinas seems to acknowledge that the numbers of created things are not dictated by necessary rules:

> It does not therefore appear to be universally true that the more imperfect difference of a genus is multiplied in more species. For body is divided into animate and inanimate: nevertheless, there appear to be more species of animate bodies than inanimate, especially if the heavenly bodies are animate, and all the stars differ from one another in species. But even in plants and animals there is the greatest diversity of species, so it is even in the whole universe of things that to the extent that something is superior among beings, to that extent it has a greater formal multitude, which is judged according to the distinction of species: and in this Dionysius's saying is saved; it has less, however, material multitude, which is judged according to the distinction of individuals in the same species, in which the saying of the Platonists is saved. That there is, however, only one species of rational animal when there exist many species of irrational animals comes from the fact that rational animal is constituted from corporeal nature attaining its highest grade and spiritual substances attaining its lowest grade. The supreme grade, however, of a nature, and also the lowest grade, is only one: although it could be said there were many species of rational animal, if one held that the celestial bodies were animate.[44]

Aquinas notes that there are more species of animals than species of elements. It is not clear whether he ever also noticed that there are more species of insects than species of cats or of boars. This fact, and the preceding observation of the comparative numbers of animals and elements make it plain that there are no absolute rules concerning the numbers of the different sorts of beings. In any case, it is apparent, especially from the last sentence

43 *ST* I, q. 112, a. 4, ad 2.

44 *De Spir. Creat.*, a. 8, ad 10.

in the passage above, that Aquinas is proceeding inductively in order to establish what, if any, principles are operative here, rather than deriving these principles deductively. The principles he arrives at are not then of such a certain character as to exclude the possibility that there exist more than one species of human being. And Aquinas is open to this possibility, as one can see from the last sentence in the quotation. If God indeed does create more of the higher sorts of beings, this could serve as the basis of a very weak argument in favor of the probability of ET life.

Summary

Aquinas calls to our attention that one sort of ET that could exist is a separated intelligence joined to a body as its mover. He himself thinks that there are intelligent beings of this sort that move the heavenly bodies. He notes, however, that "animate" is said equivocally of the heavenly bodies as moved by spiritual substances and of plants, along with animals.[45] The spiritual substances animate the heavenly bodies like a puppeteer animates puppets; they are not united to these bodies as their forms.

As for the other sort of ET, which would consist of a separated substance united to a body as its form, Aquinas argues that it is extremely unlikely that a pure intelligence be united to a body as its form, since the pure intelligence, as far as its activity of knowing is concerned, in no way profits from its union to the body. However, an intellectual substance of the rational sort is suitably united to a body since an intelligence of this sort can only acquire its ideas through sense experience.

Aquinas points out that the sort of body the composite being must have is specified to some extent by the requirements of the intellectual substance that is united to it. The body cannot be a simple body such as air or iron, because sense organs require a balance of elements, and indeed, a most subtle blend of elements; otherwise, the being will lack a good sense of touch and well-functioning internal senses that provide reason with the starting points it needs for forming ideas. Aquinas further points out that rational beings need not have fingers, hands, and feet as humans do; he holds that even humans would still be human without them.

Aquinas does not favor the idea that other human-type beings exist because he thinks that the human soul represents the very lowest type of

45 See *ST* I, q. 70, a. 3.

intelligence, whereas the human body represents the very highest material body. However, he does remain open to the possibility.

From a theological standpoint, Aquinas maintains that there is no reason for concern here because it is not the task of scripture to classify the beings in the universe. Yet he explicitly denies that it is probable that other human-type bodies exist, for the reason noted above. There are two other probable arguments that can be drawn from Aquinas, one against and one in favor of the existence of other human-like creatures. On the one hand, the human species would reflect God's goodness in a special way by being unique, while, on the other, it is befitting to God's goodness that he create more of better creatures. Aquinas leans in the direction of the former view but realizes that the latter could in fact be the case. By doing so, he gives us an example of the circumspection that this matter demands.

10

ET Meets Jesus Christ: A Hostile Encounter Between Science and Religion?

The Copernican Revolution brought with it the realization that there are other suns in the universe, which in turn paved the way to speculation that the planets orbiting them might be populated with intelligent beings. In no time at all, some began to wonder whether the existence of intelligent extraterrestrials (ETs) was compatible with the Christian message. The political philosopher Thomas Paine (1737–1809) is perhaps the best-known proponent of the incompatibility thesis. He was adamant that: "the two beliefs cannot be held together in the same mind; and he who thinks that he believes in both has thought but little of either."[1]

Paine, of course, was eager to find reasons to discredit organized religion. Paine, however, was not alone in endorsing an either/or position in regard to belief in ETs and Christianity. Philosopher William Whewell (1794–1866), a Christian believer, also embraced this dichotomy. Whewell

1 Thomas Paine, *The Age of Reason* (Prometheus Books, 1984), 52.

reasoned that the specialness of the human race (and planet Earth) would be lost if there were other planets inhabited by intelligent life forms:

> The earth . . . can not, in the eyes of any one who accepts this Christian faith, be regarded as being on a level with any other domiciles. It is the Stage of the great Drama of God's Mercy and Man's Salvation. . . . This being the character which has thus been conferred upon it, how can we assent to the assertion of Astronomers, when they tell us that it is only one among millions of similar habitations?[2]

Nowadays it has become increasing popular to oppose Christianity to belief in the existence of ETs. For instance, physicist Paul Davies maintains that "it is hard to see how the world's great religions could continue in anything like their present form should an alien message be received."[3] And philosopher Willem B. Drees presents us with a dichotomy that suggests (paradoxically) that a loving response to extraterrestrials might require us to set aside traditional Christian beliefs: "But that is not to say that extraterrestrials are to be conformed to traditional theological schemes; Bethlehem does not have to be the center of the universe. It is more important to be open-minded, loving, responsible."[4]

Facile Solutions to the Compatibility Question

Of course, many do not agree that the existence of ETs is opposed to the Christian message. A couple of common approaches used to show that there is no incompatibility, however, fall short of their goal. One of them consists in noting that God is all-powerful and the universe is an immense place, from which it is inferred that there would be nothing surprising about God populating other planets. The problem with this approach is that it passes over all the difficulties in reconciling the two beliefs, difficulties that led Paine and others to conclude that the two were incompatible. At a meeting held by the Pontifical Academy of Science on the ET question, the science fiction writer Robert Sawyer criticized the response of one of the participants on

2 William Whewell, *Of the Plurality of Worlds*, ed. Michael Ruse, rev. ed. (1853, repr. The University of Chicago Press, 2001), 44, 45.

3 Paul Davies, *Are We Alone?* (Basic Books, 1995), 54, 55.

4 Willem B. Drees, "Bethlehem: Center of the Universe?," in *God for the 21st Century*, ed. Russell Stannard (Templeton Foundation Press, 2000), 69.

this very score: "It was basically a spiritual as opposed to an explicitly Christian reply, and it amounts to nothing more than saying that in this whole vast universe, sure, there might be other intelligences. The hard response would be to deal with the issue in explicitly Christian terms."[5] Talk about the size of the universe and what God is able to do fails to address the doubts about the existence of ETs that arise from Christian beliefs in the Incarnation, Redemption, and lordship of Christ.

Another common move in the ET-Christianity debate is to point out that the purpose for which scripture was written is human salvation, and to conclude from this that scripture does not say anything that has bearing on the existence of other intelligent beings in the universe. The fact of the matter, however, is that scripture does tell us about intelligent beings other than humans, namely, the angels and devils. But more importantly, God is certainly free to reveal to us how humankind's savior Jesus Christ relates to all created beings, purported ETs included. God, if he so chooses, can also reveal to us how the redemption wrought by Christ fits into his plan for the entire universe. And indeed, scripture does contain statements that extend beyond the confines of planet Earth. Thus, there is absolutely no reason to reject in advance the possibility that scripture says something that has a bearing on the ET question.

Scripture and the ET Question

The ET-Christianity debate cannot be settled without looking at scripture. Only in this way can we address claims of the sort made by Thomas Paine:

> Though it is not a direct article of the Christian system that this world that we inhabit is the whole of the habitable creation, yet it is so worked up therewith from what is called the Mosaic account of the Creation, the story of Eve and the apple, and the counterpart of that story—the death of the Son of God, that to believe otherwise, that is, to believe that God created a plurality of worlds at least as numerous as what we call stars, renders the Christian system of faith at once a little ridiculous.[6]

5 Michael McAteer, "The Truth Is Out There," *The Star* (Toronto), Saturday, August 17, 2002, Life Section, K14.

6 Paine, *The Age of Reason*, 52.

There are a number of passages in scripture which support the notion that the central event in the universe's history was the Incarnation, Death, and Resurrection of Christ. The creation account in Genesis culminates with the creation of Adam and Eve, and at the time of their fall, God promises that the offspring of the woman would one day crush the head of the serpent, foretelling the Good News that the son of a woman would conquer the devil, freeing man from the sin and death that the devil ushered into the world. One could say that this story is a story of importance only to us on Earth. A number of scripture passages, however, indicate that it is the heart of the plan for the entire cosmos:

> I, who am less than the least of all the saints, have been entrusted with this special grace, not only of proclaiming to the pagans the infinite treasure of Christ, but also of explaining how the mystery is to be dispensed. Through all the ages, this has been kept hidden in God, the creator of everything. Why? So that the Sovereignties and Powers should learn only now, through the Church, how comprehensive God's wisdom really is, exactly according to the plan which he had from all Eternity in Christ Jesus our Lord (Eph. 3:8–12).[7]

> The one who rose higher than all the heavens to fill all things is none other than one who descended (Eph. 4:10).

> He has let us know the mystery of his purpose, the hidden plan he so kindly made in Christ from the beginning to act upon when the times had run their course to the end: that he would bring everything together under Christ, as head, everything in the heavens and everything on earth (Eph. 1:8–10).

While there is doubtlessly a variety of views on these texts among the different Christian faith communities, the Catholic Church, for one, has traditionally understood these texts to indicate that the reason for the original creation was the new creation in Christ:

> Creation is the foundation of "all God's saving plans," the "beginning of the history of salvation" that culminates in Christ. Conversely, the mystery of Christ casts conclusive light on the mystery of creation and reveals the end for which "in the beginning God created the heavens

7 All Biblical quotations are taken from the Jerusalem Bible translation.

> and the earth": from the beginning, God envisaged the glory of the new creation in Christ.[8]

Now some might argue that it is not Christ as man, but only as the divine Word, who plays a central role in all of creation. However, several passages in scripture indicate that Christ—not only as God, but also as man—is the central figure in the cosmos.

> His state was divine, yet he did not cling to his equality with God, but emptied himself to assume the condition of a slave, and became as men are; and being as all men are, he was humbler yet, even to accepting death, death on a cross. But God raised him high and gave him the name which is above all other names, so that all beings in the heavens, on the earth and in the underworld, should bend at the name of Jesus and that every tongue should acclaim Jesus Christ as Lord, to the glory of God the Father (Phil. 2:6–11).
>
> "You have put him in command of everything." Well then, if he has "put him in command of everything," he [God] has left nothing which is not under his command. At present it is true, we are not able to see that "everything has been put under his command," but we do see in Jesus one who was "for a short while made lower than the angels and is now crowned with glory and splendor" because he submitted to death (Heb. 2:8, 9).
>
> He [God] has put all things under his [Christ's] feet, and made him, as ruler of everything, the head of the Church; which is his body, the fullness of him who fills the whole creation (Eph. 1:22).

Multiple Incarnations?

Paine appears to be quite correct when he says that Christianity teaches that the central story of the cosmos is Christ's redemption of fallen man by his death on the cross. It does not, however, follow immediately from this that there is no room for any other sort of intelligent being in this story. After all, Christians believe that there are other such beings, the angels and devils. Just as Jesus Christ is Lord and head of the angels, he could in principle be

8 *Catechism of the Catholic Church* (Apostolate for Family Consecration, 1994), no. 280. See also nos. 2174 and 315.

Lord and head of other intelligent beings as well. Paine, however, raises the following objection against this being the case:

> Are we to suppose that every world in the boundless creation had an Eve, and apple, and serpent, and a redeemer? In this case, the person who is irreverently called the Son of God, and sometimes God himself, would have nothing else to do than to travel from world to world, in an endless succession of deaths, with scarcely a momentary interval of life.[9]

It is undoubtedly true that the Word of God could have become incarnate multiple times. Uniting his person to human nature certainly did not exhaust his infinite power, and so he can become incarnate over and over again.[10] In addition, Paine's assumption that God would not leave fallen races unredeemed seems eminently reasonable in light of God's goodness and mercy, albeit some debate this point. Nevertheless, Paine's multiple redeemers are not the only solution for the redemption of fallen races. For Christ's sacrifice on the cross is infinite in its saving power, and thus could have made satisfaction for any number of fallen races. And in fact Colossians 1:18–20 indicates that Christ is the savior of all of the fallen who are saved:

> As he is the Beginning, he was first to be born from the dead, so that he should be first in every way; because God wanted all perfection to dwell in him and all things to be reconciled through him and for him, everything in heaven and everything on earth when he made peace by his death [literally "blood"] on the cross (Col. 1:18–20).

Are Humans the Only Beings in Need of Salvation?

Simply acknowledging that Christ's sacrifice on Calvary could in principle save other fallen beings says nothing one way or the other about whether such beings exist. Further scrutiny of scripture, however, turns up a passage that speaks against the existence of ETs:

9 Paine, *The Age of Reason*, 59, 60.

10 See Aquinas, *Sent.* II, d. 31, q. 1, a. 2: "On Whether One Divine Person Is Able to Assume Two Human Natures." See also, *ST* III, q. 3, a. 7 (quoted above in the main text).

> As it was his purpose to bring a great many of his sons into glory, it was appropriate that God, for whom everything exists and through whom everything exists, should make perfect, through suffering, the leader who would take them to their salvation. For the one who sanctifies, and the ones who are sanctified are of the same stock; that is why he openly calls them brothers. . . . Since all the children share the same blood and flesh, he too shared equally in it, so that by his death he could take away all the power of the devil, who had power over death, and set free all those who had been held in slavery all their lives by the fear of death. For it was not the angels that he took to himself; he took to himself descent from Abraham (Heb. 2:10–17).

One might be inclined to take the line about the one sanctifying and the ones who are sanctified being of the same stock to establish that there are no fallen ETs. But the Greek text does not actually say "stock"; instead it simply says *henos* (one), and indeed some have interpreted this sentence to say that Christ and humans are from the same Father—which certainly could be said of ETs.[11]

The next lines are more telling, however. They say that the Word took on the same blood and flesh as humanity *since* the children were all of the same blood and flesh, so that by his death he could set free all those who had been held in slavery. Clearly Paul means to extend what was promised to the descendants of Abraham to all human beings. The Jews were awaiting a messiah for the chosen people, but Paul emphasizes that the Word had become man because the human race as a whole (and not just the Jews) was descended from one set of first parents. But how could such a claim be extended to ETs? It does not make any sense to say that the Word shared in human nature in order to free ETs and humans from the slavery of sin and death, *because* the children share the same blood and flesh, when ETs have no share in that heritage.

Romans 5:15–19 supports this reading of Hebrews 2:14 insofar as it speaks of the correlation between sin coming into the world through one man (Adam) and salvation coming into the world through another man (Christ):

11 Aquinas comments on Heb. 12:11: "But all, namely, the one himself who sanctifies and we who are sanctified are from one, namely, from the Father." "Ad Hebraeos" in *In Epistolas S. Pauli*, chap. 2, lec. 3 (no. 130 in the Marietti edition).

> Adam prefigured the One to come, but the gift itself considerably outweighed the fall. . . . If it is certain that death reigned over everyone as the consequence of one man's fall, it is even more certain that one man Jesus Christ, will cause everyone to reign in life who receives the free gift that he does not deserve, of being made righteous. Again, as one man's fall brought condemnation on everyone, so the good act of one man brings everyone life and makes them justified. As by one man's disobedience many were made sinners, so by one man's obedience many will be made righteous (Rom. 5:15–19).

This passage repeats over and over the correspondence between one fallen human and one human redeemer. This one-to-one correspondence between fallen and redeemer would be lost if fallen ETs were also to have Christ as redeemer. Moreover, Christ is not the new ET, and a fallen ET does not "prefigure the One to come." The biblically affirmed parallel between Christ and Adam would be lost if there was some other race out there in need of Christ's redeeming grace.

Other considerations, as well, make it plain that Paine is not wrong to see that there are tensions between Christian belief and belief in ETs existence. The more one looks at how carefully all the details of the central story of the universe, Christ's story, is fitted to its human beneficiaries, the more the introduction of any other kind of material rational being appears as something that would be superfluous and out of place.

Scripture Seems to Indicate That We Are Alone

If it is the case that Christ is the savior of all the fallen, and if he came only to save humans, and if God would not leave fallen material rational species unredeemed, it follows that there are no other fallen material rational species in the universe.

One could come back and say that humans and ETs are both human, meaning, they are both rational animals. This is a fair point, but they still lack biological unity with earthly humans. We humans and these other rational animals constitute independent families. Even though the effects of Christ's Death and Resurrection could be applied to them, it then could not be said that they were saved by one of their own, and thus Christ's sacrifice does not offer a satisfying solution to the "divine dilemma" their case poses.

The "divine dilemma" generated by original sin is this: God in his mercy did not want the human race to be lost on account of original sin. Although

God in his graciousness could simply have remitted the sin, mankind would not have fulfilled what justice demands by way of satisfaction. At the same time, no human being could ever make adequate satisfaction for an offense against the infinite God. It is only the God-Man, Jesus Christ, who is capable of making infinite satisfaction for this human debt. Applying this to the case of fallen ETs, if they were saved by the God-man Christ, justice would not have been perfectly respected. That is, a member of the fallen ET race—and not a member of Adam's race—would have to make reparation for the sin of that race for strict justice to be served.

Yet another undesirable consequence that would follow if Christ was savior to ETs can be gathered from the following passage from Hebrews:

> It was essential that he should in this way become completely like his brothers so that he could be a compassionate and trustworthy high priest of God's religion, able to atone for human sins. That is, because he himself has been through temptation he is able to help others who are tempted (Heb. 2:17, 18).

Perhaps the translation here of the Greek "*opheile*" as "essential" is unnecessarily strong; an alternate translation is "beneficial." Even then this passage provides a reason why the savior should be cut from the same cloth as the saved. For if he was not, they could make excuses for their bad behavior, claiming that Christ was made of sterner stuff than they, and so they could hardly be expected to resist the same temptations he was able to resist. Put in somewhat different terms, it would be difficult for ETs to take as role model someone whose natural capacities were different than their own.

In a similar vein, it seems that one of the purposes of the Incarnation was so that we would no longer see God as someone distant, but as someone who was our friend. One need not espouse cosmic racism or be oblivious to the suffering of animals to acknowledge that it would be hard, if not impossible, to fully appreciate the sufferings of a savior of an alien race and to feel the same degree of love toward him that we spontaneously feel toward a savior of our own race. Even if an ET savior did not look all that different than us, still our inability to fully fathom an alien being's capacities for experiencing things and his reactions to them would make him a less-than-satisfying savior. The ideal savior both understands us as a result of his own experience and can be understood by us in terms of our experience, rather than through extrapolation or guessing. This is what underlies the popularity of devotions addressed to Christ's Sacred Humanity, such as to the Sacred Heart and the Holy Face.

Does Scripture Definitively Exclude ET Existence?

At this point, it might appear that Paine was right after all in claiming that belief in ETs is incompatible with belief in Christ. However, there are two reasons why one need not concede Paine's point. First, none of the above speaks against the possibility that *unfallen* ETs exist. Second, while a strong probable case against fallen ET existence can be elaborated on the basis of scripture, the only passage that could be taken to definitively eliminate them is Hebrews 2:14. Still, a Christian may choose to reject the above interpretation of Hebrews 2:14, for it is not an official teaching of any Christian religion. It may, in fact, be a correct interpretation, and if so, there is a necessary conflict between belief in *fallen* ETs and Christian belief. But again, given that no church has endorsed the above reading of Hebrews 2:14, a believer who rejected this interpretation plainly could not be accused of heresy.

Perelandra

Many of us have been enchanted by C. S. Lewis's portrayal of the temptation of the first mother of another race on the fictive planet Perelandra. Less well-known is his essay "Religion and Rocketry" in which he entertains the notion that "man is the only lost sheep" among intelligent races, the others never having lost their primeval innocence. But how realistic is the notion of an unfallen race? We do not have much to go by to settle this question, but what we do have indicates this is unlikely. According to Christian belief, some of the angels fell, and angelic nature is a far more perfect nature than human nature. Any other material rational being would possess a nature inferior to the angelic nature. Thus, it seems more likely than not that some member of such a race would fall.

Another thing to be taken into consideration is that when beings possess an inherently fallible nature, it is reasonable to expect that at least some of them will fail at some time. Material beings such as ourselves need to acquire habits if we are to consistently choose the good. Before we acquire virtue, we all too easily make bad choices. God could in principle create a race of material beings that would remain unfallen, but their existence would border on miraculous—like fire that did not burn. And even then, one might still wonder whether God in his wisdom would choose to create a race in which the contrast between good individuals and bad individuals would be entirely absent.

One also could argue that unfallen ETs fit poorly into God's plan for the universe, which centers on Jesus Christ. After all, Christ would be neither their savior, nor the most suitable role model for them, nor their brother and friend in the way he is our brother and friend.

On the other hand, one could argue that ET existence would add richness to the universe, which would then contain unfallen, in addition to fallen, material rational beings. Moreover, even if the unfallen ETs could not have as close a relationship as we have with our brother, Christ, they could have an intimate friendship with God (both before and after the Word's incarnation) if he was present to them the way that he was present to Adam and Eve before the Fall. Or perhaps the situation could be somewhat like that of a mother with several children, one of whom is terribly sick. The mother would spend much more time with the sick child, and do many things especially for him, not because she loved him more than her other children, but simply because his condition required her additional attention.

It appears, then, that the existence of unfallen ETs cannot be ruled out. At the same time, there are reasons for doubt.

Human Specialness

Another reason commonly given to support the notion that belief in ETs is opposed to belief in Christ is that the discovery of ETs would prove Christianity mistaken as to the special place it assigns to humans. In the words of Paul Davies:

> Four hundred years ago, the Roman Catholic church burned Giordano Bruno at the stake for heresy. Among other things, he proposed the existence of an infinite number of inhabited worlds. Since this ran counter to the doctrine of man as God's supreme and special creation, Bruno was undermining a key tenet of the Christian faith at that time.[12]

12 Paul Davies, "Biological Determinism, Information Theory, and the Origin of Life," in *Many Worlds*, ed. Steven J. Dick (Templeton Foundation Press, 2000), 15.

Davies is entirely mistaken about the "key tenet" Bruno was supposedly undermining. The existence of ETs does not run counter to what Christians believed then or believe now about man "as God's supreme and special creation."

Humans are special because unlike nonrational beings we are created in the image of God. As a consequence, nonrational beings are ordered to us as to an end. This would not change if ETs were discovered. They too would be created in the image of God and nonrational beings would be ordered to them as well. There is an equality of dignity among those who share the definition of human regardless of disparity as to physical or intellectual ability, so if ETs proved to be more intelligent that would not mean that nonrational creation is ordered more to them, any more than it is ordered more to more intelligent humans than less intelligent ones. Their discovery would not cause us to slip a notch when it comes to being a goal to which the rest of material creation is ordered.

Similarly, related doctrines taught by some Christian religions concerning the special creation of human souls, and the special providence that is shown us would not change if ETs were discovered, and indeed the doctrines would also hold true of ETs in virtue of their possessing a rational nature.

Humans are also special as being the agents that will bring the universe to its final completion. This is first and foremost true because Christ, the savior of all, was a human being. Regardless of whether or not the Word has been incarnate more than once, it will remain the fact that a human being was the savior of all the fallen. Without the redemption wrought by Christ, the universe could not achieve its destiny of giving glory to God. Humans, by responding to Christ's grace, contribute to the realization of this destiny.

It may be that we are also special as being the only race whose nature a divine person united to himself. Even if it does turn out that there are other races of rational animals, superior to us in intelligence and virtue, it still would not be that surprising that we were favored in this way, and they were not, given that God uses the weak to confound the strong—Christ was born in a stable, the child of a poor couple, and it was said of him: "What good can come from Nazareth?" So it wouldn't be surprising if ETs, upon learning about the Incarnation, were to shake their heads in disbelief: "What good can come from planet Earth?"

The human race is certainly not special because of the exceptional wisdom and virtue of its members, for most lack these qualities. We must not forget that the reason that the Word became flesh was to save sinners. As C. S. Lewis puts it:

> They [non-Christians] seem to think that the Incarnation implies some particular merit or excellence in humanity. But of course it implies just the reverse: a particular demerit and depravity. No creature that deserved Redemption would need to be redeemed. They that are whole need not the physician. Christ died for men precisely because men are *not* worth dying for; to make them worth it.[13]

Does Scientific Research Provide Reason to Think ETs Exist?

Our considerations above show that ETs do not pose a threat to the various forms of specialness which Christianity attributes to humans, and that ETs can be fit into the Christian vision of the universe, albeit not very readily. The arrival of ETs, far from causing the collapse of Christianity, would not even require a change in any of its central tenets. That being said, it is interesting to note that, contrary to popular belief, much of contemporary science does *not* support ET existence.

In order for ETs to exist, there must be a planet that is inhabitable, life must take hold on it, and it must evolve to the point of intelligence. What evidence do we have for determining the likelihood of each of these things?

The Origin of Life

In the past, the Miller-Urey experiments were sometimes touted as providing evidence that it was easy for life to begin.[14] In 1952, Stanley Miller

13 C. S. Lewis, "Religion and Rocketry," in *Fern-Seed and Elephants*, ed. Walter Hooper (Fontana, 1975), 88–89.

14 See Simon Conway Morris, *Life's Solution: Inevitable Humans in a Lonely Universe* (University of Cambridge Press, 2003), 60:

> Those familiar with investigations into the origin of life may be surprised that no detailed mention has been made of the now-classic experiments by Stanley Miller and Harold Urey, which are still routinely cited (especially . . . in the undergraduate text book) and seem to be dramatic evidence of the ease with which simple organic compounds can be synthesized under conditions closely similar to those found on early Earth.

(who worked in Harold Urey's laboratory) passed a spark through reducing gases that he thought were likely to compose the earth's early atmosphere. The result was numerous simple carbon compounds which, when dissolved, were concentrated into amino acids, simple acids, purines, and pyrimidines, which are constituents of living things.[15] To conclude from this, however, that life arises easily is problematic from a logical point of view. There is a big difference between the formation of some of the chemicals found in life as we know it, and an actual living thing. Having the ingredients does not ensure getting the final product (and this is even more the case when one only has some of the ingredients). Although origin-of-life researchers have since discovered additional sources for organic molecules, such as meteorites,[16] and have developed hypotheses for how organic molecules eventually resulted in a living thing,[17] it is an undisputed fact that no one knows how life began.

If we do not know how life began here (assuming it did begin here), we are not in a good position to estimate how likely it is to have begun elsewhere. Some try to argue in an inductive manner that it is probably easy for life to arise under suitable conditions, basing their argument on what happened on planet Earth. Life perhaps only took around two hundred million years to appear, and perhaps as little as ten to twenty million years.[18] There are some, however, who regard this relatively short delay as evidence that life did not begin on earth, but elsewhere. Francis Crick and L. E. Orgel are two of the better-known scientists who hold it likely that life was seeded from space.[19]

Our uncertainty as to whether life did in fact originate on Earth casts a shadow of doubt over any kind of generalization about the ease with which life arises, starting from the case of our planet. And even if we were sure that life originated here, to reason inductively to the conclusion that life generally originates quickly, starting from one case, is plainly a hasty generalization.

15 The Urey-Miller experiments continue to receive attention in our day. See, for example, Joaquín Criado-Reyes et al., "The Role of Borosilicate Glass in Miller-Urey Experiment," *Scientific Reports* 11, no. 1 (2021): 21009.

16 See Yasuhiro Oba et al., "Extraterrestrial Hexamethylenetetramine in Meteorites —A Precursor of Prebiotic Chemistry in the Inner Solar System," *Nature Communications* 11, no. 1 (2020): 6243.

17 For one version of the RNA hypothesis for the origin of life, see Bruce Alberts et al., "The RNA World and the Origins of Life," *Molecular Biology of the Cell*, 4th ed. (Garland Science, 2002), https://www.ncbi.nlm.nih.gov/books/NBK26876/.

18 See Conway Morris, *Life's Solution*, 18, 73, 74.

19 See Francis Crick, *Life Itself: Its Origin and Nature* (Simon and Schuster, 1981).

As Ernan McMullin points out, various additional factors invoked in the extrapolation of how much life is out there in no way compensate for our fundamental ignorance concerning how readily life originates.[20] People will call upon the long periods of time to justify the population of other planets. However, if the origin of life is extremely improbable, the amount of time in question may still fall short of what would be necessary. Again, what we need to know, and do not know, is whether the origin of life is extremely improbable or not. Similarly, the large numbers of planets will also not result in hordes of ETs if life originates only under very special conditions.[21] Invoking the uniformity of nature, as ET proponents often do, affords no help to their cause, because again we do not know how likely it is for the conditions sufficient for life to arise to obtain—life may be uniformly absent in the universe with the exception of the earth.

How Readily Do Complex Life Forms Evolve?

It is plainly not enough for life to originate for there to be ETs; it also must evolve to the very high level of complexity requisite for intelligence. Here, too, our present state of knowledge does not allow us to make a reliable estimate of how likely this complexification is to occur on other planets. It took about 2.3 billion years after life originated to get the first animals, about half of the life of the Earth. In any case though, a single instance is not an adequate basis for extrapolation.

Moreover, it would be hard to deny that contingent events have had a role to play in the evolutionary history of our planet; at best we might be able to come up with the statistical chances of such events occurring, for example, how often a large meteorite will strike the planet, but even then, the timing of these events might be crucial to how life evolves. What if the meteorite that helped usher the dinosaurs out had not hit? Or what if it had hit much later? In both cases, we might not be here. Evolutionary biologist Steven Jay Gould thinks the contingent elements in evolution are so great that it is highly unlikely that human(-like) intelligence would evolve again on planet Earth, if one could go back in time and watch things evolve

20 See Ernan McMullin, "Persons in the Universe," *Zygon* 15, no. 1 (1980): 69–89.

21 See Ernan McMullin, "Life and Intelligence Far from Earth: Formulating Theological Issues," in Dick, *Many Worlds*, 166.

anew.[22] Another evolutionary biologist, Simon Conway Morris, disagrees with Gould. Conway Morris argues that once life got a foothold on earth, eventually humans would appear, contingent elements notwithstanding. The basis of his argument is that certain features essential to humans have evolved over and over, for example, eyes and advanced cognitive abilities, and so eventually they would come together in a human-type being.[23] While I think that this argument has merit, it doesn't amount to a proof.

The Rare Earth Hypothesis

Turning to numerical estimates made of habitable planets, some of the same sorts of problems arise estimating them as do with estimating the probability of life originating and complexifying. One big problem, as Michael Crowe points out, is that a planet may be similar to earth without it being similar in those ways crucial for life to begin and complexify—we do not know yet what all the crucial factors are.[24] Until then, finding earthlike planets is not equivalent to finding planets where life is able to arise and evolve.

Of late, the Rare Earth hypothesis has enjoyed increasing popularity among scientists. This hypothesis proposes that features that make the earth habitable are unlikely to be found on another planet. Probably the most cited feature is the earth's unusually large moon.[25] Without such a moon, the angle of the axis around which the earth spins would wobble chaotically, and this would cause drastic changes in climate.[26] Rare Earth proponents maintain that the chances are very slim that other earthlike planets have such a moon,

22 See Stephen Jay Gould, "The Evolution of Life on Earth," *Scientific American* 271, no. 4 (1994): 85–91.

23 See Conway Morris, *Life's Solution*, 96:

> But does the demise of the dinosaurs as a portal to mammalian success really pass muster? Possibly not, and for two reasons, one particular and one general. . . . The second and more general reason is the main theme of this book, that of evolutionary convergence. As all the principal biological properties that characterize humans are convergent, then sooner or later, and we still have a billion years of terrestrial viability in prospect, 'we' as a biological property will emerge." See Conway Morris, 147–73, concerning the eye and 246–60 concerning large brains and advanced cognition.

24 See Crowe, *The Extraterrestrial Life Debate*, 552, 553.

25 See Peter D. Ward and Donald Brownlee, *Rare Earth* (Copernicus Books, 2000) 50, 223–24, and 234.

26 See Ward and Brownlee, *Rare Earth*, 266. See also Bruce Jakosky, *The Search for Life on Other Planets* (Cambridge University Press, 1998), 116.

and as a consequence these planets would lack a climate sufficiently stable to continuously support life.[27] Another commonly cited feature of our solar system is that it contains a planet like Jupiter which "cleans our solar system of dangerous Earth orbit–crossing asteroids and comets."[28] There is reason to think that Jupiter-like planets are not all that common.[29]

Despite the growing body of literature in favor of the Rare Earth hypothesis, scientists are far from arriving at a consensus on this issue. Some, for example, argue that the moon is neither necessary for life to develop on a planet, and/or that such moons in any case are not rare.[30] Others question the importance of Jupiter in our solar system.[31] And some dispute the other evidence offered for the Rare Earth position. Until these debates are settled, realistic estimates of the number of habitable planets cannot be made.[32]

The Drake Equation—A Mathematical Way of Saying "Who Knows?"

Probably most of us have common across the famous Drake equation into which one plugs various variables and out pops an estimate of the number of ET civilizations.[33] When one realizes that two of the values that need to be filled in are the number of earthlike planets and the fraction of these planets where life emerges, one realizes that "the Drake Equation is just a mathematical way of saying who knows."[34]

Historically biologists have on the whole been more skeptical than the physical scientists as to ETs' existence, doubtlessly because they are more acutely aware that the question of the origin of life has no easy answer,

27 See Christopher B. Kaiser, "Extraterrestrial Life and Extraterrestrial Intelligence," *Reformed Review* 51 (Winter 1997–98): 77–91.

28 Ward and Brownlee, *Rare Earth*, 240.

29 See Robert Naeye, "Are We Alone in the Universe?" *Astronomy* 24, no. 7 (1996): 39.

30 See David Darling, *Life Everywhere* (Basic Books, 2001), 96–98.

31 See Darling, *Life Everywhere*, 107.

32 See Conway Morris, *Life's Solution*, chap. 5.

33 Frank Drake and Dava Sobel, *Is Anyone Out There?* (Delacorte Press, 1992), 52.

34 Jakosky, *The Search for Life on Other Planets*, 285. Heidi Manning, in "Yes, We Will Meet Them: The Drake Equation Tells Me So," in *Astrotheology*, ed. Ted Peters (Cascade Books, 2018) acknowledges that "the remaining variables in the Drake Equation are known with far less certainly" (138) and that: "One factor that the Drake equation does not account for is the possible habitable galactic zone" (143). These things argue against her confident subtitle.

and that once it does originate, that it subsequently develops to the level of human complexity is far from certain. However, at least one physicist of note argued on scientific grounds against ETs' existence. His name: Enrico Fermi.

The Fermi Paradox

In 1950, Enrico Fermi, while eating lunch with three other physicists, abruptly asked, "Where is everybody?," the "everybody" meaning intelligent extraterrestrials.[35] According to one of the three who was there, Herbert F. York, Fermi "followed up with a series of calculations on the probability of earthlike planets, the probability of life given an earth, the probability of humans given life, the likely rise of technology, and so on. He concluded on the basis of such calculation that we ought to have been visited long ago and many times over."[36] Thus, the fact that they are not here indicates that they are not out there.

Those who reject the Fermi Paradox and maintain that ETs do exist propose a variety of reasons for why they have not yet communicated with us. Physicist Stephen Webb lists fifty of them.[37] The "excuses" range from all the ETs have gone extinct to the cost of space travel is too exorbitant to "they are here." Of course, search-for-extraterrestrial-intelligence (SETI) proponents favor the possibility that they are trying to communicate with us, but we as yet have not had the luck to detect their signals.

There is a lot of speculation involved both in the Fermi Paradox itself and in attempts to refute it. Consider, for example, one of the explanations that is advanced for why ETs have not arrived, namely, that it not feasible for them to implement the technology available with the goal of travel to another planet. In the first place, one might wonder whether scientists who buy into the Fermi Paradox are not overly sanguine in supposing that the requisite technology will exist in ET civilizations. One of the more popular scenarios for the colonization of space in the literature was proposed by Barrow and Tipler. It involves "self-replicating universal constructor[s] with intelligence comparable to human intelligence" being launched to other stellar systems in every direction. Once the universal-constructor probes (called

35 See Eric M. Jones, "Where is Everybody?," *Physics Today* 38, no. 8 (1985): 12.

36 See Jones, "Where is Everybody," 13.

37 Stephen Webb, *If the Universe Is Teeming with Aliens, Where Is Everybody? Fifty Solutions to Fermi's Paradox and the Problem of Extraterrestrial Life* (Copernicus Books, 2002).

von Neumann machines) arrived in their new stellar system, they could construct more copies of themselves along with rockets to launch them, and the same process would repeat itself every time a probe got to a new planet.[38] Alternately, the probes could construct fertilized eggs and artificial wombs in which they could grow.[39]

It seems to me that the proponents of the Fermi Paradox are overly optimistic about the feasibility of galactic colonization. As Paul Davies notes:

> Tipler's assumptions about the feasibility of constructing von Neumann machines—in effect, living computers with superhuman intelligence added—strike me as being exceedingly simplistic. We have absolutely no idea what obstacles of principle may exist to frustrate such attempts, let alone the practicalities. The same applies to space travel: the recent failure of the Mars Observer mission underscores how vulnerable technology is in space. The assumption that a man- (or alien-) made machine could operate flawlessly over millions of years in a hostile environment stretches credulity.[40]

Although there may be more realistic alternatives to Barrow and Tipler's scenario, it seems that any attempts to colonize space will inevitably entail mistakes leading to disaster and frustration, putting at least a damper on future attempts, and possibly putting an end to them in some cases. Then again perhaps ET technology is bound to eventually become so advanced that insuring ET astronauts' safety would no longer be an issue. The issue can be further argued back and forth, but it should be clear that while the Fermi Paradox does cast scientific doubt on the existence of ETs, it is far from being an open-and-shut case.[41]

It is also too early to rule out the possibility that ETs have forgone expensive and dangerous space travel and in its place adopted the cheaper means of contacting other intelligent life forms via electromagnetic communication. We have not been listening very long for such communication from space. The first attempt to do so was in 1960, when Francis D. Drake and his

38 See John D. Barrow and Frank J. Tipler, *The Anthropic Cosmological Principle* (Oxford University Press, 1986), 79.

39 See Barrow and Tipler, *The Anthropic Cosmological Principle*, 580.

40 Davies, *Are We Alone?*, 72.

41 Physicist Hugh Ross argues that interstellar space travel is impossible. Hugh Ross, "Interstellar Space Travel," in Hugh Ross, Kenneth Samples, and Mark Clark, *Lights in the Sky & Little Green Men* (NAVPRESS, 2002), 55–64.

colleagues at the National Radio Astronomy Observatory listened for radio signals from two nearby stars (Project Ozma). Since then, there have been more than sixty projects that search for radio transmissions in our galaxy that would have the telltale signature of intelligence.[42] The scientists who do the listening make reasonable assumptions about ET transmissions, but of course they could be mistaken, and this could explain why contact has yet to be made. It is generally thought that ET transmitters would most likely choose radio waves because they are less susceptible to interstellar absorption and scattering than other frequencies.[43] The wavelengths preferentially searched for by most SETI projects were chosen according to criteria that we believe ETs would also be aware of.[44] Assuming that we are looking in the right way, the search for extraterrestrial intelligence has not even been carried on for seventy-five years, and so it is premature to conclude that ETs are not out there.

Webb astutely teams up the Fermi Paradox with the Rare Earth evidence to make a plausible science-based case against ET existence. Without denying that speculation is involved in both of these considerations, it is interesting how the two point in the same direction.

Responses to the Apparent Absurdity of the Vast Amounts of Uninhabited Space

It might seem that there would be no point to the immense size of the heavens if Earth was the only place in the universe populated by intelligent beings. However, William Whewell explains why this is not a reason to conclude that ETs exist. Whewell first notes that "a single case of success among many of failure is exactly the order of nature in the production of life."[45] In light of this, Whewell concludes that there would be nothing unusual about only one planet in the universe bringing forth intelligent life. Whewell establishes his general principle inductively, looking to cases such as ova in animals: "The female is stocked with innumerable ovules, capable of becoming living things: of which incomparably the greatest number end as they began, mere

42 Webb, *If the Universe Is Teeming with Aliens, Where Is Everybody?*, 100.

43 See George W. Swenson, Jr., "Intragalactically Speaking," *Scientific American* (July 2000): 44.

44 See Drake and Sobel, *Is Anyone Out There?*, 43.

45 Whewell, *The Plurality of Worlds*, 224.

ovules."[46] Sir Arthur Eddington later gives essentially the same argument based on "profligacy" in nature, such as the enormous number of acorns produced in order that one oak grow.[47] Eddington concludes that it would be just like nature to scatter a million stars in order to produce a single kind of rational being.

Another response to the argument that there would be no point to the immense size of the universe if it were only to be inhabited by one kind of rational being can be formulated by looking to God's nature rather than the workings of nature. God is the ultimate artist, and his works cannot be lacking in beauty. Magnitude is typically an element of beauty; think of Yosemite Falls or the Rockies or a building with high ceilings, as opposed to, respectively, water running from the kitchen faucet, the mound of dirt and pebbles left by a mole, and a building with average height ceilings. The universe must be a thing of grandeur. Otherwise, it would not be the case that the "heavens declare the glory of God, the vault of heaven proclaims his handiwork" (Ps. 19). And this is true whether the universe is inhabited by one intelligent material species or by many.

ET Proponents Who Resort to Personal Attack

A tactic employed by ET proponents with a certain frequency is a form of fallacious reasoning that goes by the name of "circumstantial ad hominem." This fallacy falls in the category of "personal attack." What it amounts to is instead of addressing the argument that one's opponent is proposing, one simply dismisses it on the grounds that the opponent stands to gain something if his conclusion is accepted. The typical form the argument takes is something like this: "You maintain that ET intelligence does not exist, for if it did exist then you stand to lose, since your species would no longer be unique in the universe. Therefore, your argument concluding that ET intelligence does not exist is incorrect." Kenneth Delano employs this sort of argument:

> With the jealousy of a spoiled only child, the human race is upset by the suggestion that it may have to share its cosmic domicile with others. To make their instinctive reaction seem less like childish resentment, many

46 Whewell, 223.

47 Sir Arthur Eddington, quoted by Annie Dillard in *Pilgrim at Tinker Creek* (Harper's Magazine Press, 1974), 175.

> think of themselves as being "Defenders of the Faith" in denying the possibility of intelligent beings existing on other worlds.[48]

Now, instead of attributing bad motives to one's opponent and using that as an excuse to dismiss his argument, one should evaluate the argument and provide reasons for rejecting it. Even if the person was ultimately rejecting ET life because it would be a blow to his ego if his species was not number one in material creation, this is not a reason to ignore any arguments that he has offered. Sad to say, this gross fallacy is not uncommon. Rabbi Barry Friedman asserts: "It would be an incredible conceit of egotism to think we're the only form of life."[49] Physicist Russell Stannard claims "that although, for all we know, intelligent life in the cosmos might be unique to planet Earth, that smacks of arrogance."[50]

The Greatness of Man, the Smallness of Man

While it would constitute a personal attack to dismiss a person's claim to excellence on the ground that the person was conceited, it is not a personal attack to ask whether in fact his claim has merit. Thus, it is a fair question whether or not taking the position that ET life does not exist, or is unlikely to exist, implies a mistaken estimation of the eminence of the human race in the cosmos.

What is at the root of the doubts about the status of our race is the paradoxical smallness and greatness of man, about which Pascal spoke so eloquently. Humans on the whole are moral mediocrities, in addition to which most lack very penetrating intellects, and fail to acquire any great learning. On the other hand, we, unlike the rest of creation on Earth, have the capacity to understand the whats and whys of things in the material universe. Our ability to contain the entire universe in our minds was one reason why the Greeks called man a "microcosm." The Greeks were not alone in their appraisal of human capabilities. The biologist Christian De Duve, in response to the question "What is the meaning of the universe?," asserts that "[it] is found in the structure of the universe, which happens to be such

48 Kenneth J. Delano, *Many Worlds, One God* (New York Exposition Press, 1977), 8.

49 Barry Friedman, quoted by Todd Halvorson and Robyn Suriano, "Finding Other Life Wouldn't Shake Most Faiths," *Florida Today*, 1999, Online Special Report.

50 Russell Stannard, "Our Place in the Scheme of Things," *Research News*, December 2000, 22, reprinted from *The Tablet*, May 13, 2000.

as to produce thought by way of life and mind. Thought, in turn, is a faculty whereby the universe can reflect upon itself, discover its own structure, and apprehend such immanent entities as truth, beauty, goodness, and love."[51] It is natural for human beings, as material beings, to be impressed by the sheer vastness of the heavens and number of the stars: "What is man that you are mindful of him?," exclaims the psalmist viewing the heavens. Nevertheless, when all is said and done, the stars are just big balls of fire, whereas we are beings who are not only able to see the stars, but in addition can reflect on their worth.

Christianity, looking at man from a supernatural standpoint, also recognizes his smallness and greatness. In the first instance, humans have a certain greatness because we are created to the image of God. However, the reason why the eternally begotten Son of the Father became man was not because humans were so wonderful. It was because we were sinners. The sin of Adam and Eve was followed by Cain's murder of his brother, and as the race continued to grow in number so did their evil ways. By the time of the flood, "Yahweh saw that the wickedness of man was great on the earth, and that the thoughts in his heart fashioned nothing but wickedness" (Gen. 6:5, 6). Thus, Christ did not come because we were an exemplary race, but rather because "we were still helpless when at his appointed moment Christ died for sinful men. It is not easy to die even for a good man . . . but what proves that God loves us is that Christ died for us while we were still sinners" (Rom. 5:7–9).

The ultimate greatness of humanity comes first and foremost from the unity of the person of the Word with a human nature. Secondarily, and as a result of Christ's sacrifice, Christians are able to live Christlike lives, "to become true images of the Son" (Rom. 8:29)[52]—and herein also lies our greatness. In the words of 2 Corinthians: "And we, with our unveiled faces reflecting like mirrors the brightness of the Lord, all grow brighter and brighter as we are turned into the image that we reflect; this is the work of the Lord who is spirit" (2 Cor. 1:18). One human being in the state of grace is of greater value than the entire material universe—and this is Christ's work.

A person could concede that the value of the material universe does not compare with that of a single godly human, but still find it hard to believe

51 Christian de Duve, *Vital Dust* (Basic Books, 1995), 301.

52 See 1 John 3:2.

that God would create this immense and beautiful universe for but a single mediocre species. Ultimately this is no stranger a notion than that the Son of God become a member of this same mediocre race and is directly connected to it. What reason would compel the Most High to mass produce multiple material races in his image, instead of creating one such race, unique and never to be repeated? Some suggest that if intelligent life arose in many places in the cosmos, rather than in just one, this would give us more reason to believe that a Cosmic Designer engineered the universe to produce life. However, it would not be contrary to God's wisdom if he chose to make the universe an instrument of producing one race that he intended to bring to perfection through the unique gift of the Incarnation, Death, and Resurrection of his only-begotten Son. The sculptor who turns out one unique masterpiece is not a lesser artist than the artisan who mass produces statuettes from a mold. It is a source of amazement to look at the myriad stars in the sky and think that perhaps only one planet around one sun harbors intelligent life. But it is not inherently absurd that this be the case. God can certainly order the universe this way. I have argued on theological and philosophical grounds that he in fact has—which is not to deny, *pace* Paine, that Christians are free to adopt the opposite view without prejudice to their faith.

11

Would St. Thomas Aquinas Baptize an Extraterrestrial?, Revisited

In his article, "Would St. Thomas Aquinas Baptize an Extraterrestrial?," Edmund Lazzari maintains that Aquinas would disagree with those who would baptize a fallen extraterrestrial on the grounds that they "disregard the necessity of a human nature for incorporation into the Mystical Body of Christ," baptism being the means by which human beings are so incorporated.[1] Lazzari maintains that, "because of the crucial role that that assumption of a human nature plays . . . in Thomistic soteriology, it is not possible to simply transfer the effects of the life of Jesus Christ to other intellectual beings who are not sharers in human nature."[2]

I first intend to show that Aquinas does not hold that one must have a human nature to belong to the Mystical Body. Secondly, I intend to show that while the effects of Christ's death and resurrection are not such as to be automatically applicable to intelligent extraterrestrials (ETs), much less to be automatically transferred to them through baptism, Aquinas would maintain

1 Edmund Michael Lazzari, "Would St. Thomas Aquinas Baptize an Extraterrestrial?," *New Blackfriars* 99, no. 1082 (July 2018): 440, abstract.

2 Lazzari, "Would St. Thomas Aquinas Baptize an Extraterrestrial?," 451.

that God is capable of ordering things in these ways. I will also show that while Lazzari is not justified in denying on Thomistic grounds the possibility that baptism would incorporate ETs in the Mystical Body and allow them to receive salvific grace from Christ, what he says gives reason to think that Aquinas would regard such occurrences as highly unlikely, insofar as they do not fit with what is known through revelation about God's saving action in the universe.

Does Aquinas Hold That Membership in Christ's Mystical Body is Limited to Humans?

Let us examine the possibility of the potential membership of ETs in the Mystical Body by looking at a passage Lazzari considers, namely, *Summa Theologiae*, III, q. 8, a. 4. This is a key passage, for here Aquinas unambiguously affirms that beings other than human, namely, the angels, belong to the Mystical Body of the Church with Christ as their head. In response to the question of "whether Christ is head of the angels," Aquinas affirms:

> As was said [a. 1, ad 2] it is necessary to posit one head where there is one body. However, one multitude ordered to one [end] according to distinct acts or offices is called one body by way of likeness. It is manifest, however, that men and angels are ordered to one end, which is the glory of divine fruition. Whence, the mystical body of the Church does not only consist of men, but also of angels. Christ is the head of this whole multitude, for he stands nearer to God and more perfectly shares his gifts not only than men do, but also than angels do; and not only do men receive from his inflowing, but also angels. For it is said in Eph. 1:20 that "he placed him," namely, God the Father [placed] Christ, "at his right hand in heaven, above every power and sovereignty and virtue and domination and every name which is named not only in this age, but in the future, and he subjected all things under his feet." And therefore, Christ is not only the head of men, but also of the angels. Whence, it is read in Matt. 4 that "the angels came and ministered to him."[3]

3 *ST* III, q. 8, a. 4.

> Respondeo dicendum quod, sicut dictum est, ubi est unum corpus, necesse est ponere unum caput. Unum autem corpus similitudinarie dicitur una multitudo ordinata in unum secundum distinctos actus sive officia. Manifestum est autem quod ad unum finem, qui est gloria divinae fruitionis, ordinantur et homines et Angeli. Unde corpus Ecclesiae mysticum non solum consistit ex hominibus, sed etiam ex Angelis. Totius

Aquinas sees two things as establishing that the angels belong to the Mystical Body of the Church with Christ as their head. First, what legitimates speaking of a body by way of likeness is that a group of many are ordered to one end according to distinct acts or offices (as is the case, for example, of a legislative body). Secondly, what is essential to a head is that it is the primary cause of the influx of something into the body's other members. Aquinas affirms that these two things hold true of Christ in regard to both us and the angels. The angels together with humans are ordered to one end, the beatific vision.[4] And Christ fulfills the requirement of head in regard to both angels and humans due to the primacy of the causal influence he exercises in their regard. Since one body can only have one head, angels and humans belong to the same Mystical Body of Christ.

In an objection, Aquinas explicitly raises the question of whether difference in nature precludes Christ *as man* from being head of the angels: "It seems that Christ, as man, is not head of the Angels. For head and members are of one nature, but Christ, according as he is man, is not like in nature with the Angels, but only with men."[5] Aquinas responds that

> the influence of Christ over all men is principally as to their souls, according to which humans agree with angels in the nature of the genus, granted not in the nature of the species. And by reason of this conformity Christ is able to be called the head of the angels, granted the conformity fails as to what is bodily.[6]

Let us consider whether what Aquinas says in *ST* III 8.4 concerning the angels is applicable to ETs. Although God need not order the ETs to the beatific vision, he can certainly choose to do so. And Aquinas would

autem huius multitudinis Christus est caput, quia propinquius se habet ad Deum, et perfectius participat dona ipsius, non solum quam homines, sed etiam quam Angeli; et de eius influentia non solum homines recipiunt, sed etiam Angeli.

4 Beings that are sentient, but not rational, cannot experience the beatific vision, and so cannot be incorporated into the Mystical Body; see *ST* I, q. 12, a. 4, ad 3: "The sense of sight, because it is entirely material, in no manner can be elevated to something immaterial. But our intellect or the angelic intellect, because it is in some manner according to nature elevated from matter, is able to be elevated higher to something beyond its nature through grace."

5 *ST* III, q. 8, a. 4, obj. 1.

6 *ST* III, q. 8, a. 4, ad 1.

hold that it is more likely than not that God would so choose.[7] Although God need not redeem fallen ETs, he can certainly choose to do so; Aquinas would also see this as being what God is more likely to do.[8] Now, there is nothing to prevent Christ from exercising causal influence in regard to ETs, as he does in the case of the angels. This influence would be more like the influence he has on humans, given that ETs, unlike angels, have souls. The lack of bodily conformity, which Aquinas dismissed as being a barrier to Christ's headship as man over the angels, would for the same reason not be an obstacle in the ET's case, for there would be agreement as to the spiritual element of their nature.

A question that I will later return to is whether Christ's influence on the ETs can be such as to redeem them. Let us first look at how Lazzari understands *ST* III 8.4:

> St. Thomas does say that the functioning of all makes a metaphorical body. His point in this passage is to establish the headship of Christ over the angels and not that the angels are part of the *Mystical* Body of Christ (i.e. requiring the sacraments).[9]

The Mystical Body of Christ is not other than the Mystical Body of the Church. Again, contrary to what Lazzari claims, Aquinas affirms in the

7 On the hypothesis that ETs exist, Aquinas would regard it as reasonable to think that God would give them the gift of grace, which orders them to the glory of divine fruition. For the reasoning he uses to answer the question of whether angels were created in grace is applicable to ETs. Aquinas notes that: "one cannot discover an efficacious reason for which of the [two opposite] opinions be truer, because the beginning of creatures depends on the simple will of the Creator, which is impossible to investigate by reason." *Sent.*, II, dist. 4, q. 1, a. 3. However, he goes on to say: "Nevertheless according to agreement with other of his [God's] works, one can sustain one side as more probable than the other." Using the latter mode of reasoning, Aquinas argues in a sed contra:

> It pertains to divine freedom to infuse grace into all who are capable of grace, unless something resisting is found in them, much more than he gives natural form to any disposed matter. But angels from the beginning of their creation had the motion of free will, and there was nothing in them impeding [the infusion of grace]. Therefore, it seems that he immediately infused grace in them. (*Sent.* II, d. 4, q. 1, a. 3, sed contra 3).

8 See *Sent.* III, dist. 1, q. 1, a. 2, s.c.: "It was not suitable that one of the most noble creatures be entirely frustrated in achieving its end. But human nature is among the noblest natures. Since, therefore the whole [nature] was corrupted through sin in the first parent and was so deprived of the beatitude for which it was made, it was fitting that it be repaired." Since ETs are material rational beings, the same reasoning applies to them.

9 Lazzari, "Would St. Thomas Aquinas Baptize an Extraterrestrial?," 455n57.

passage in question that "the mystical body of the Church does not only consist of men, but also of angels." And again, Aquinas does not see the lack of likeness to Christ as to his bodily nature as preventing a rational creature from being a part of Christ's Mystical Body. Lazzari, in referring to "the functioning of all," does not clearly identify the reasons Aquinas gives for why the angels are part thereof. Aquinas specifically states that they are members of a multitude ordered to the same end (the "glory of divine fruition," or the beatific vision), and that Christ as man exercises causal influence over them—two things, again, that could hold true for ETs.

Toward the very end of his article, Lazzari acknowledges that Aquinas in *ST* III 8.4 holds that the angels are incorporated into Christ's Mystical Body, and more or less concedes that Aquinas could then envisage ETs as part of Christ's Mystical Body:

> It certainly seems as though being incorporated into the mystical Body of Christ by baptism requires a human nature because this is the remedy for the human fall, which, as we saw must be distinct from an extraterrestrial one. However, St. Thomas does say that the angels have been incorporated into the mystical body of Christ in an analogous way because of their unity of will with God. It is possible that the unity of will (cooperating with grace) could also suffice for extraterrestrial life forms to be incorporated into the mystical body of Christ without needing a human nature. This will in union with the divine will may even be meritorious for salvation, as the patriarchs were saved by the desire for Christ.[10]

Aquinas does not say in *ST* III 8.4 that the angels are incorporated into the Mystical Body of the Church in an analogous way. Nor does Aquinas explicitly mention unity of will with God as being the cause of their incorporation, granted they would not belong to the company of the blessed if their will was not in union with God's will. The primary issue, however, is that Lazzari, in affirming the possibility that fallen ETs are members of Christ's Mystical Body, largely dismantles his main argument, which is that only through being incorporated into Christ's Mystical Body can the salvation

10 Lazzari, 456. Note that if the ET fall was prior to Christ's death and resurrection, Aquinas would hold that the ET individuals living at the time could not be saved by Christ as instrumental cause of grace, but rather would be saved, as were the patriarchs, by faith in a future savior. Similarly, Aquinas would reject the notion that the angels received the grace moving them to submit themselves to God (thereby gaining their beatification) from Christ as man, as this event occurred before the Incarnation.

Christ wrought on the cross flow to the ETs.[11] Note how Lazzari shifts from categorically affirming the impossibility of a fallen nonhuman rational being from sharing in Christ's salvific grace through baptism to saying that "it certainly seems" so.

Before considering the reason Lazzari offers for denying that that Christ as man could exercise causal influence over ETs by applying the fruits of his Passion to them, let us look at another passage where Aquinas speaks about the headship Christ as Man exercises over the angels, in order to be sure that some essential point has not been overlooked.

De Veritate 29.4: "Whether the grace proper to the head belongs to Christ in his human nature"

Aquinas speaks in greater detail about Christ's headship in an earlier work, the *De Veritate*, than he does in the *Summa Theologiae*. He opens his discussion by noting that "head" first names a part of a natural living body and then is transferred to name something in the spiritual realm; thus, we need to consider the relation of a physical head to the body's members if we are to understand in what manner Christ is head of the Church. Aquinas then explains that the basis of the word being transferred to name other things is one or more similarities to the three characteristics of a living body's head: dignity or eminence of what is like in nature, union of order to one end, and continuity by way of influence. He goes on to say:

> Christ, according to his human nature, is called head of the Church in these three ways. For he is of the same nature according to species with the rest of men; and in this manner it belongs to him to be head by reason of dignity, according as grace is found more abundantly in him. There is also a unity of order in the Church, according as the members of the Church serve one another and are ordered to God; and in this manner Christ is said to be the head of the Church as governor. There is also a certain continuity in the Church by reason of the Holy Spirit, who, one and the same in number, fills and unites the whole Church; whence

11 See Lazzari, 450: "Christ's Passion redeems us by our being incorporated into His mystical body and thus our sharing in His saving actions."

> also Christ according to human nature is said to be head by reason of influence.[12]

Aquinas then points out that to flow into (*influere*), as applied in the spiritual realm, can be understood in two ways: "In one way, as principal agent; and in this manner it belongs only to God to cause an influx of grace in the members of the Church." The other way is to cause this influx in an instrumental manner. This is true of Christ's humanity, insofar as "his humanity was an organ, as it were, of his divinity."

Aquinas then addresses the manner in which Christ is the head of the angels:

> Christ according to the last two conditions of head [i.e., governance and influence] is able to be called head of the angels according to human nature, and head of both human and angels according to his divine nature; but not according to the first, unless fellowship (communitas) is taken as to the nature of the genus, according as man and angel come together as to their rational nature, and further by the community of analogy, according as it is common to the Son with other creatures to receive from the Father, as Basil says; by reason of which he is called the first born of every creature (Col. 1:15).

Christ, as to preeminence over those like in nature, is not able to be called head of the angels according to what is specific to human nature, but is able to be called head according to what is generically shared by angels and humans, namely, an intellectual nature; in addition, he can be called head by reason of the analogous manner in which everything that exists receives from the Father. In these same ways, Christ, in his human nature, could be head of the ETs, in addition to being their head by way of governance and influence.

Aquinas makes some further comments in the *De Veritate* about Christ's headship over the angels in response to an objection that reads:

> The good angels and men belong to one Church. However, there is one head of one Church. Therefore, since Christ is not the head of the good angels, who never sinned, nor are conformed to him in nature, it seems that neither did he exist as head of men according to his human nature.

12 *De Verit.*, q. 29, a. 4. All the quotations in this section are drawn from this text.

Aquinas does not respond by denying that the angels belong to the one Church, but rather says:

> Christ is not only head of the angels according to his divine nature, but also according to his human nature; for he illuminated them according to his human nature, as Dionysius says. . . . whence also Col. 1:16 says that he is the head of every sovereignty and power.[13]

Aquinas does then add some qualifications as to how Christ is the head of the angels:

> Nevertheless, the humanity of Christ stands other to the angels than to men as to two things. First, as to conformity in nature, through which he belongs to the same species as men, not angels. Secondly, as to the end of the Incarnation, which was done principally for the sake of the liberation of man from sin; and in this manner the humanity of Christ was ordered to the influence which he exercised in men, as to an end intended; the influx, however, in the angels was not [intended] as the end of the Incarnation, but as a consequence of the Incarnation.

The first qualification, concerning likeness in nature, has already been discussed. The second qualification concerns Christ's influence on the angels; he did not redeem them nor does his grace come to them through the sacraments. Whatever effects that Christ as man has on the angels was not the end for which he took on human nature.[14] If one conceded that Christ's sacrifice redeemed ETs, the question would arise as to whether their redemption should be regarded as an end or as a consequence.

We have seen then that what Aquinas says about Christ's headship of the mystical body in the *De Veritate* accords with what he says in the *Summa Theologiae*.

13 *De Verit.*, q. 29, a. 4, ad 5.

14 In *ST* III, q. 8, a. 4, Aquinas speaks of Christ as man illuminating the angels. Aquinas speaks of another effect that Christ's Incarnation, Death, and Resurrection had on the angels in *Super Epistolas S. Pauli*, ad Ephesios, no. 2: "The effect of this hidden plan was to restore all things. For insofar as all things are made for the sake of man, all things are said to be restored. . . . *All things* he says *which are in heaven*, i.e., the Angels—not that Christ died for the Angels, but by redeeming man, the fall of the Angels was repaired."

It Appears That the Effects of Christ's Passion Are Inapplicable to ETs

Lazzari acknowledges that Aquinas holds that rational beings other than humans can become incorporated into Christ's Mystical Body. Why then does he deny that the salvific grace that comes to us instrumentally through Christ's Death and Resurrection could also come to ETs? He justifies his position by invoking "the Chalcedonian necessity of a common nature for salvation." Aquinas appears to agree with this view: "The action of one is not able to sufficiently pass over to another, except insofar as the former has some fellowship with the latter, which can be through sharing in nature or being joined in affect."[15] Aquinas goes on to say that the latter form of fellowship, since it is accidental, rather than essential, is insufficient to have an effect upon human nature. He also affirms that the action of a pure man is insufficient to effect a change in human nature. Aquinas thus concludes that "only Christ is able to sufficiently merit for others."[16]

Lazzari's case seems to be further strengthened by Aquinas's reliance on St. John Damascene's dictum: "What is not assumable is not healable" (*quod est inassumptibile, est incurabile*[17]). Aquinas directly quotes it six times and paraphrases it at least once.[18] He relies on it to argue that Christ should have assumed a sex, a human intellect, and a human will. For example, in regard to the question of whether Christ ought to assume a human intellect, he says:

> Secondly, it [the non-assumption of a human mind] opposes the utility of the Incarnation, which is the justification of man from sin. For the human soul is not capable of sin, nor of the grace that justifies, except through the mind. Whence it was chiefly fitting that the human mind be assumed. Whence Damascene says in Bk. III [c. 6, *On the Orthodox Faith*]

15 *Sent.* III, d. 19, q. 1, qc. 1.

16 *Sent.* III, d. 19, q. 1, qc. 1.

17 Note that Aquinas worked with an inexact translation of Damascene. Damascene states categorically "for what is not assumed, is not healed" ("to gar aproslepton, atherapeuton"). This axiom was articulated earlier by Gregory of Nazianzus in *Epistola*, 101 and is more commonly attributed to him. (The Greek text is taken from Saint John of Damascus, *On the Orthodox Faith*, trans. Norman Russell [St Vladimir's Seminary Press, 2022], 175.)

18 Aquinas quotes Damascene's dictum three times in objections, twice as a sed contra, and once in the body of an article. And in *ST* III, q. 3, a. 1 he paraphrases it: "Et ideo conveniens fuit ut carnem sumeret ex materia ab Adam derivata, ut ipsa natura per assumptionem curaretur" (so that through assumption, the nature itself would be healed).

> that the Word of God assumed a body and an intellectual and rational soul, and he adds afterwards that "the whole was united to whole that He might in His grace bestow salvation on the whole of me. For what is unable to be assumed, is unable to be healed."[19]

What Is Unable to Be Assumed Is Unable to Be Healed" in Context

Aquinas's usage of Damascene's dictum needs to be understood in the context of the resolution of a prior question, namely, whether the Incarnation was necessary. As Lazzari correctly points out, Aquinas holds that it was not necessary, but rather it was fitting, that the Word become incarnate and die for our salvation: "God through his omnipotent power could have repaired human nature in many other ways [than through the Incarnation]."[20] Having acknowledged this, Aquinas goes on to quote Augustine, who affirms that there was "no more suitable manner to heal our misery" than through the Incarnation. Thus, whenever Aquinas addresses questions such as whether Christ should assume a human will or a human body, etc., it needs to be understood that he is doing so in a context in which God's decision to redeem human beings by the Incarnation, Death, and Resurrection of the Word Incarnate is taken to be fitting rather than necessary. Therefore, that God act in a way in keeping with this decision also carries with it fittingness rather than necessity. This can be seen from one of the passages in which Aquinas invokes Damascene's dictum. In response to the question of whether Christ should have assumed a sex, Aquinas presents as a *sed contra*: "Moreover, what is not assumable is not curable, as Damascene says. But sex, in which original sins chiefly reigns, is especially in need of healing."[21] Note the language Aquinas then uses in the corpus:

19 *ST* III, q. 5 a. 4: "Secundo, repugnat utilitati incarnationis, quae est iustificatio hominis a peccato. Anima enim humana non est capax peccati, nec gratiae iustificantis, nisi per mentem. Unde praecipue oportuit mentem humanam assumi. Unde Damascenus dicit, in III libro [De Fide Orthodoxa], quod Dei verbum assumpsit corpus et animam intellectualem et rationalem, et postea subdit, totus toti unitus est, ut toti mihi salutem gratificet idest, gratis faciat, quod enim inassumptibile est, incurabile est."

20 *ST* III, q. 1, a. 2.

21 *Sent.* III, d. 12, q. 3, a. 1, qc. 1, s.c. 2.

> Christ came to repair human nature, which he repaired through assumption [of that nature]; and therefore it was necessary (oportuit[22]) that he assume whatever is a per se consequence of human nature, namely, all the properties and parts of human nature, included among which is sex; and therefore it was befitting (decuit) that he assume a sex.[23]

Aquinas does not use the language of absolute necessity, but rather of fittingness. It appears, then, that the correct way of understanding the dictum "what is not able to be assumed is not able to be healed" is as indicating that, on the supposition that God determined that a fallen nature was to be healed by means of a divine person assuming that nature, it is fitting that the divine person assume the fallen nature in its integrity, rather than in a piecemeal fashion. Understanding the dictum in this manner fits with how Aquinas speaks in regard to whether Christ should assume a true body:

> The first reason [for why the Son of God ought to assume a true body] is taken from the notion of human nature, to which it pertains to have a true body. Therefore, on the supposition, drawn from what was said before, that it is fitting that the Son of God assume human nature, it follows that he would assume a human body.[24]

Damascene's dictum, as Aquinas understands it, is not meant to exclude the possibility that human beings could have been saved in many other ways.[25] Thus, it need not be understood to exclude the possibility that fallen ETs be saved by a divine person united to a human nature.

22 "Oportuit" can be translated as "it is proper or becoming" rather than as "it is necessary." Even if one translates it in this passage as "it is necessary," it still could be understood in a sense that falls short of absolute necessity; see *SCG*, bk. 4, chap. 54 (quoted in a later note).

23 *Sent.* III, d. 12, q. 3, a. 1, qc. 1.

24 *ST* III, q. 5, a. 1. Here is another similarly qualified statement: "As Augustine says in *De Trinitate* 13, God could have taken on man elsewhere than from the stock of that Adam who bound the human race by his sin. But God judged it better to assume vanquished human nature—through which he would vanquish the enemy of the human race—from the very same race." *ST* III, q. 4 a. 6.

25 St. John Damascene qualifies the Incarnation as fitting, not as necessary; see *An Exposition of the Orthodox Faith*, bk. 3, chap. 1.

Is It Possible for God to Apply Christ's Sacrifice to Rational Beings Other Than Human?

The crucial question that remains is whether or not God could choose to accept Christ's sacrifice in reparation for the sin of another generically similar species. Again, Aquinas affirms that God could have saved the human race in many different ways, and the same would be true in the case of ETs. Is it impossible for the God-man to be an instrumental cause of ET salvation?

Given that it is possible for God to save a fallen rational species in ways other than by Incarnation, what precludes God from doing so in the case of fallen ETs by means of the God-man's sacrifice on the cross? Does the difference in nature render it impossible for Christ to be a universal redeemer for all of the fallen, regardless of their nature?

We have seen that Aquinas would hold that ETs are able to be incorporated in Christ's Mystical Body. We have also seen that Aquinas holds that Christ as man exercises causal influence over the angels who are members of his Mystical Body, despite the difference in nature. The only thing that could preclude God from choosing to let ETs share in the salvific effects of Christ's Death and Resurrection would be if doing so involved a contradiction or, in other words, it would have to be the case that there can be no such thing as redemption of a fallen nature by a divine person who is incarnate in another nature.[26] There is nothing contradictory, however, in the notion of Christ as man redeeming ETs.

One might concede that the ET elect could be saved individually through grace coming instrumentally from Christ's sacrifice on Calvary, while denying that this sacrifice healed their nature.[27] Christ is the new

26 God cannot make the past to never have been because there is no such thing (an event cannot both have been and not have been), nor can he create another God, as God is the uncreated one. See *De Pot.*, q. 1, a. 3.

27 See *ST* III, q. 14, a. 4 and ad 1:

> Christ assumed human defects in order to make satisfaction for the sin of human nature, to which end it was necessary that he have the perfection of knowledge and grace in his soul. Therefore, Christ ought to have assumed those defects which follow from the common sin of the whole nature, so long as they were not incompatible with the perfection of knowledge and grace. Thus, it was not fitting that he assume every human defect or infirmity. . . . There are defects of a third kind which are commonly found in all men due to the sin of the first parent, such as death, hunger, thirst, and other things of the sort. Christ took upon himself all these defects. . . . When Christ healed the passibility and corruptibility of our body by assuming it, as a consequence he healed all other defects [i.e., the ones that were not fitting for him to assume].

Adam, not the new ET. However, God could by divine fiat accept the death and resurrection of Christ as healing the fallen ET nature, as this does not involve contradiction.[28] What Aquinas says is true in the case of the angels, namely, that they are generically like us in nature, would be even more true of the ETs,[29] and thus the need Aquinas speaks of for there to be "some fellowship in nature" for the action of one (Christ) to pass into another (ETs) is met.[30]

It is certainly true that the "divine dilemma" in regard to the fallen ETs would not be solved were Christ's sacrifice to save them, as then it would not be an ET who made satisfaction for the race's sin.[31] Still, it is not impossible for God to waive the need for an ET to make satisfaction. Indeed, Aquinas would hold that God could forgive the fallen ETs without demanding any satisfaction whatsoever.[32]

28 Aquinas does hold that certain acts by a divine person could not secure human salvation. He says that "if his [Christ's] body was not a true body but an imaginary body, then he did not undergo a true death either. . . . And in this manner, it would also follow that the true salvation of man did not ensue; for it is necessary for an effect to be proportioned to its cause." *ST* III, q. 5, a.1. A fake atonement is in nowise meritorious; paying the price of sin in false currency is no payment at all.

29 Angels and humans can be considered as species belonging to the same genus insofar as both are intelligent beings (albeit the manner of their intellectual knowing is quite different). If ETs exist, both they and us would be species belonging to the genus rational animal, that is, on the assumptions that we and they would be unable to interbreed, and that biological species are in part defined by reproductive isolation. Thus, in the case of ET existence, intelligent being would be the genus of pure intelligences (angels) and rational animals, and rational animal would be the genus of human being and ET. (Rational animal would be a species vis-à-vis intelligent being and it would be a genus vis-à-vis human and ET.)

30 *Sent.* III, d. 19, q. 1, qc. 1. This passage was quoted earlier in the main text.

31 See *SCG*, bk. 4, chap. 54:

> The order of divine justice so stands . . . that sin is not remitted by God without satisfaction. No one purely human, however, could make satisfaction for the sin of the entire human race, because anyone who is purely human is something less than the entire ensemble of the human race. It was necessary, therefore, so that the human race could be freed from the sin common to it that someone would make satisfaction who would be a human being, to whom the satisfaction pertained, and someone beyond human, so that the merit would be sufficient for satisfying for the sin of the entire human race. As far as the order of beatitude, there is no one greater than man except for God; for angels, granted that they are superior as to the condition of their nature, are not nevertheless as to the order of the end, because they are made blessed in the same way as humans. It was therefore necessary that God become man in order to destroy the sin of the human race so that man might attain beatitude.

32 See *ST* III, q. 46, a. 2:

> For if he [God] had wanted to free man from sin without [man] making any satisfaction, he would not have acted contrary to justice. For a judge cannot dismiss a

Here lies the central difference between Lazzari's view and mine. I acknowledge that it is within God's power to allow ETs to be saved as an effect of Christ's sacrifice on the cross, be it by healing their nature or through grace given to them only individually, whereas he denies it.

Similarly, I hold that it falls within God's power to use baptism as the means by which fallen ETs would be incorporated into the Mystical Body. Indeed, given that ETs and humans would belong to the same Church, the expectation would be that we would share the same sacraments.[33]

In regard to baptism, Lazzari shows hesitancy in categorically denying the possibility that ETs could be saved through baptism: "Since baptism is the remedy of original sin for human beings, it seems as though one must have a human nature to undergo baptism."[34] He is right to qualify that statement, as the conclusion does not follow with necessity. Take a parallel case: Since X is a remedy for digestive problems in humans, therefore one must be human in order for X to remedy one's digestive problems.

Lazzari is correct to think that transference of Christ's merits to ETs would not automatically occur.[35] The Word's Incarnation, Death, and Resurrection is suited in all its details to human salvation, but not to ET salvation.[36] What Lazzari fails to see, however, is that it is not impossible for God to choose to apply the effects of Christ's salvific acts to ETs.

> fault without punishment and preserve justice when his place is to punish a fault committed against another, be it against another man or against the whole republic or against a higher ruler. But God does not have some superior, but he himself is the supreme and common good of the universe. And therefore, if he remits sin, which has the notion of fault from this that it is committed against him, he causes injury to no one; just as any man who remits an offense committed against himself without satisfaction [being made], does not act unjustly, but mercifully.

33 *ST* III, q. 64, a. 2, ad 3:

> The Apostle and their successors are vicars of God as to the regimen of the Church instituted through faith and the sacraments of faith. Whence, just as it is not permitted to them to constitute another Church, so too it is not permitted to them to hand on another faith or institute other sacraments; rather the Church of Christ is built by the sacraments which flowed from the side of Christ hanging on the cross.

If God were to apply the salvific effects of Christ's cross to ETs, he most likely would do so through baptism, given that ETs and humans would belong to the same Church. However, as institutor of the sacraments, God could determine that fallen ETs be incorporated in the Mystical Body in a manner other than by baptism.

34 Lazzari, "Would St. Thomas Aquinas Baptize an Extraterrestrial?," 451.

35 See *ST* III, q. 64, a. 2, s.c.: "Only God can institute sacraments."

36 See *De Rationibus Fidei*, c. 5: "The mode of repair ought to be such that it is suited to the nature to be repaired and to the wound."

The Element of Truth in Lazzari's Position

While Aquinas would not deny the possibility that ETs be saved through Christ's Death and Resurrection, he would regard a divine decision to order things this way as highly unlikely in light of what God has revealed to us concerning his salvific activity in the universe. There are many things that God could do that he does not do because it does not befit his wisdom, for example, he could annihilate a thing, but this does not befit his wisdom.[37] Aquinas says about the Incarnation:

> Granted that the will of God suffices for doing all things, nevertheless divine wisdom requires that individual things be provided for by God in ways that befit them; for it [divine wisdom] appropriately instituted proper causes for each particular thing. Whence, granted that God by his will alone could bring about in the human race all the benefits which we say have come from the incarnation of God . . . , nevertheless it was suited to human nature that benefits of this sort were brought about by God made man, as is apparent in a certain measure from the reasons adduced.[38]

Aquinas gives dozens of reasons for the Word's incarnation as man, some concerning the reparation of our nature and others concerning how Christ serves as an example for us, motivating us to live in accord with God's will, as is necessary for our salvation.[39] In the *Summa Contra Gentiles*, Aquinas, after listing multiple benefits that accrue to us humans due to the Incarnation, concludes: "Someone can conceive from these and other like reasons that it was not unfitting that God, by divine goodness, become man, but rather it was most expedient for human salvation."[40] ETs, however, would not be the recipients of many of the benefits that accrue to us as a result of the Incarnation; to give two examples:

> Since the perfect beatitude of man consists in divine fruition, it was necessary that the affect of man be disposed to desiring divine fruition. . . . The desire for the fruition of something is caused, however, by love of that thing. Therefore, it was necessary that man, as tending toward perfect beatitude, be led to love what is divine. Nothing, however, induces

37 See *ST* I, q. 104, a. 3; *ST* I, q. 104, a. 4, ad 1; and *De Pot.*, q. 5, a. 4.

38 *SCG*, bk. 4, chap. 55.

39 See *ST* III, q. 1, a. 2 and *SCG*, bk. 4, chap. 55.

40 *SCG*, bk. 4. chap. 55.

> us to love someone as the experience of that person's love towards us. The love of God for human beings cannot be demonstrated in a more efficacious manner than by this that he wanted to be united to man in person; for it is proper to love to unite the lover with the beloved to the extent that this is possible. It was therefore necessary for man, as tending to perfect beatitude, that God become man.[41]

Here is the second example:

> Since friendship consists in a certain equality, those who are highly unequal are seen to be unable to be joined in friendship. Therefore, to this end that there would be a more familiar friendship between man and God, it was expedient that God become man, since man is naturally a friend to man, and when we know God in this visible manner, we are borne away to love of what is invisible.[42]

There are many other benefits that accrue to human beings as a result of the Incarnation that would be absent to fallen ETs if Christ were to be their savior. Aquinas would certainly grant that if ETs were saved through Christ, they would have gained the greatest possible benefit. Yet, upon considering how the Incarnation, Death, and Resurrection of Christ are so carefully tailored in so many details to human benefit alone, Aquinas would regard it as unlikely that God would intend Christ's salvific actions to apply to other rational beings. As Aquinas says in a passage quoted earlier: "[Divine wisdom] appropriately instituted proper causes for each particular thing." God does not act in an arbitrary and whimsical manner, but "orders all things sweetly" (Ws 8:1). When one compares human salvation through Christ to ETs' salvation through Christ and considers the myriad benefits that accrue to humans due to God adopting this plan that are absent to the ETs, it is hard to see ET salvation through Christ as God acting "in keeping with the proper causes for each particular thing." The question raised earlier comes up here: If one conceded that Christ's sacrifice redeemed ETs, should their redemption

41 *SCG*, bk. 4, chap. 54. Note that Aquinas distinguishes two senses of "necessary":

> Something is said to be necessary for some end in two ways; in one way as that without which it is not possible, as food is necessary for the preservation of human life; in another way, as that through which one more suitably arrives at an end, as a horse is necessary for a journey. That God become incarnate in order to repair human nature was not necessary in the first way, for God through his omnipotent power could have repaired human nature in many other ways. *ST* III, q. 1 a. 2.

42 *SCG*, bk. 4, chap. 54.

be regarded as the primary end of the Incarnation or only as a consequence of human redemption? Either response seems problematic.

Conclusion

Again, it is one thing to argue that it does not seem fitting that God redeem ETs through Christ's sacrifice, and it is another to say that he is unable to do so. If Lazzari had restricted his thesis to the improbability of fallen ET salvation through Christ, rather than the impossibility of ET salvation through Christ, and had focused on whether fallen ET salvation through Christ is in keeping with what we know about divine wisdom, he would have been able to make a Thomistic case for the negative position.

The theologians Lazzari mentions who affirm that "any fallen intelligent extraterrestrial life would be incorporated into the sacrifice of Christ"[43] hold that God almost certainly would redeem a fallen ET species, but they are quite aware that he is under no obligation to do so. Colossians 1:18–20 gives them reason to hold that Christ is the universal redeemer: "As he is the Beginning, he was first to be born from the dead, so that he should be first in every way; because God wanted all perfection to dwell in him and all things to be reconciled through him and for him, everything in heaven and everything on earth when he made peace through the blood of the cross." Certainly, Christ's sacrifice is infinite in its saving power. As Aquinas puts it: "The passion of Christ was of such great power that it suffices for expiating all the sins of the entire world, even if there would be a hundred thousand worlds."[44] Since there is no contradiction involved in affirming that Christ is savior of ETs (for God can choose to apply the salvific graces of Christ's cross to generically similar beings), these theologians conclude that if fallen ETs exist, they are, most likely, redeemed by Christ. This view does not commit them to holding that the existence of fallen ETs is likely. Aquinas, arguably, would hold that the existence of ETs is unlikely.[45] However, if they were to be discovered, Aquinas, who agrees with the premises the aforementioned

43 See Lazzari, "Would St. Thomas Aquinas Baptize an Extraterrestrial?," 451n59. Lazzari names theologians Gerard O'Collins and Augustine Di Noia.

44 *In Symbolum Apostolorum*, a. 4. Aquinas says essentially the same thing in *Compendium theologiae*, bk. 1, chap. 215 and *Super Ioannem*, chap. 3, lec. 6 (no. 543 in the Marietti edition).

45 Aquinas would most likely regard fallen ETs' existence as unlikely on the grounds that God is unlikely to leave them unredeemed, and yet their redemption through Christ, though possible, is hard to reconcile with divine wisdom.

theologians rely on, would maintain that the effects of Christ's Death and Resurrection could be applied to fallen ETs, and he would not assume that it would be inappropriate to baptize them.

APPENDIX

A Very Brief Introduction to the Aristotelian-Thomistic Understanding of Substance and Accident

This appendix aims to give a basic understanding of the Aristotelian-Thomistic notions of substance and accident, as is helpful for understanding some of the considerations offered in this volume. It omits a number of distinctions (such as that between primary and secondary substance) and it does not engage in disputes with other currents of thought concerning the nature of substance and accident.[1]

For Aristotle and Aquinas, a fundamental division of being is into substance and accident.[2] The notions of "substance" and "accident" are under-

1 For an account of the Aristotelian notion of substance, see Richard J. Connell, "An Empirical Consideration of Substance," *Laval Théologique et Philosophique* 24, no. 3 (1978): 235–46 and by the same author, *Substance and Modern Science* (Center for Thomistic Studies, 1988). See also Warren Murray, "If T'were a Substance," *Philosophia Perennis* 1, no. 1 (1994): 113–32.

2 Aquinas makes reference to the division of being into substance and accident in many places; for example, in his *Commentary on Aristotle's Metaphysics*, bk. 5, lec. 9, n. 1 (no. 885 in the Marietti edition) he says: "Being . . . divides into the ten categories of which nine are of the genus, accident." The entire book of the *Categories* of Aristotle is devoted to explaining

stood in relation to one another. When we talk about what is (what exists), we in the first instance name things like dogs and trees rather than qualities or quantities, such as small and yellow. If someone were only to say "small" or "yellow," we would ask ourselves, "Small or yellow what?," which is not the case of when someone says "dog" or "tree." (In the latter case, we might ask, "What about them?") Dogs and trees are beings simply speaking, whereas small and yellow are beings in a qualified way. The former are substances, and the latter are accidents. Substances exist of themselves, whereas accidents exist in virtue of belonging to a substance.

When it is said that substances exist of themselves, this is not to deny that they may depend in some way on other beings for their existence (as we rely on oxygen and food), but rather it is to affirm that they exist separately from the beings upon which they depend. Also, while substances exist independent of a subject, this does not mean that they do not depend on a cause for their existence.[3]

"Accident" in the Aristotelian sense of the word corresponds to "characteristic." A characteristic has to be a characteristic of something. An accident can be defined as what exists in another as in a subject.[4]

Not only our manner of speaking but also our experience of change reveals to us the difference between substance and accident. This is most obvious to us in the case of ourselves. When we get a tan or a fever, or change position, we remain ourselves. Similarly, when an aging cat becomes emaciated, it changes shape and size but remains a cat. Accidents are modifications of a substance.

When scientists talk about substances, they are talking about the elements, such as iron, and compounds such as water. Aristotle's notion of

---

what substance and accident are, as well as what characterizes the nine accidents. The other major work in which Aristotle treats substance and accident at length is the *Metaphysics* (e.g., bk. 7, chap. 2, 1028b8–33).

3 See Connell, "An Empirical Consideration of Substance," 240: "Similarly, a substance is independent of a subject in its existence, but an independence of that kind is in no way absolute; substance is not independent in the sense that it is uncaused and needs nothing else to exist (and is therefore God) as Descartes, for example, would have it."

4 Accident comes from the Latin word "*accidere*" which means to fall to, to happen. "*Accidens*" implies contingency or chance, which is also the case of its Greek counterpart, *symbebēkos*. However, being contingent or by chance is not part of the definition of accident (understood as opposed to substance). Proper accidents are neither contingent nor possessed by chance. For example, the ability to reason is a proper accident of human beings and is necessarily possessed by all humans.

substance is broader: anything that is a being in an unqualified sense is a substance.[5] Aristotle notes that "substance is thought to be present most obviously in bodies. Hence we call animals and plants substances, and also natural bodies, such as fire, water, earth, etc., and all things which are parts of these or composed of these."[6]

In addition to the Aristotle's list of substances being longer than that of scientists, Aristotelian-Thomists maintain that some substances are more readily recognizable as substances than others. Arguably, Aristotle's list above begins with what are most obviously substances and ends with what are least obviously substances, granted that Aristotle himself does not affirm this.[7] To see this, we must first understand that substance names an individual thing, a thing that is one. As Aristotle notes: "All substance appears to signify the individual. This is indisputably true in the case of primary substance. It signifies this something. For it signifies what is indivisible in number."[8]

The very first substance that we recognize as such is the rational animal that is ourselves. I know myself to be one human individual who possesses various characteristics. When I get a suntan or learn something new or become plump, I remain who I am. I know that I am not a collection of things—organs, cells, or molecules—that have their own independent

5 We call substances "things" without qualification. A dog is a thing, an oak tree is a thing. Accidents, on the other hand, we only call "things" in a qualified way. Yellow and small are not nothing, but their existence is never independent of the subjects in which they inhere. See *In Meta.*, bk. 7, lec. 1, n. 12:

> Substance is the first being and is being simply speaking, and not being according to something, i.e., in a qualified way, as is the case of accidents. For to be white is not to be simply speaking, but to be in a qualified way. Which is manifest from this that when something begins to be white, we do not say that it begins to be simply speaking, but that it begins to be white. On the other hand, when Socrates begins to be a man, it is said, simply speaking, that he begins to be. Whence it is manifest that to be man signifies to be simply speaking, whereas to be white signifies to be in a qualified manner.

Note that God is not a substance; see *ST* I, q. 3, a. 5, ad 1: "The name 'substance' does not only signify what exists of itself . . . but it also signifies an essence to which it belongs to exist in such a manner, i.e., to exist of itself, which existence is nevertheless not its very essence. And in this way, it is manifest that God is not in the genus of substance."

6 *Metaphysics*, bk. 7, chap. 2, 1028b8–12. Loeb translation.

7 Aristotle goes on to question whether this list is accurate; see *Metaphysics*, bk. 7, chap. 2, 1028b13–16. However, he never rejects anything on it. Note that elsewhere, Aristotle enumerates substances in a different order; see 1017b10–13: "Substance means simple bodies, e.g. earth, fire, water and the like; and in general bodies and the things, animal or divine, including their parts which are composed of bodies."

8 *Categories*, chap. 5, 3b10–13 (translation mine).

existence. These things are parts of me. There is one "me" who has these parts.[9]

Since you are like me in appearance and activity, I recognize you to be a substance. Individual dogs and squirrels present themselves as being single substances with a variety of accidents. We observe that their various activities, many of which are similar to ours, serve the purpose of keeping the individual alive (as well as contributing to the continuation of the species). And we witness upon the death of each individual animal that it ceases to exist as a being whose parts are organized so that it can perform activities that keep it in existence and that it turns into beings, that is, a number of chemicals. We also recognize that plants are substances, albeit the unity that an individual plant has when compared to an individual animal is less obvious. For example, it is not obvious whether what seems to be individual trees when viewed from above the ground really are individual trees in the case when they are united by their roots and have the same genome. Still, we recognize a plant that grows from a seed to be a single plant, at least initially.[10]

As for the elements, they are less obviously substances than living things are; first, because it is difficult to identify them, as is clear from Aristotle's misidentification of them.[11] And secondly, compared to living things, it is much harder to recognize the individual substance, as elements are often encountered in groups, e.g., a fleck of gold contains many individual atoms of

9 See Charles de Koninck, *The Hollow Universe* (Les Presses de l'Université Laval, 1964), 63–64:

> That I am a swarm of sparsely scattered electric charges, rushing headlong in nearly empty space, the combined bulk of the swarm less than a billionth of myself, does not in the least distress me as a substance. Neither they, in their mad rush, nor I, have any doubts as to whom they belong. Though I keep on losing and acquiring them in billions, I sit here quite unperturbed by the frightful turmoil, nor do I feel any more divided up by their multiplicity than by having two eyes, two legs, a heart, all outside of my feet. I am a loose enough assemblage of limbs, but does that prevent me from being myself? Indeed, how could I be myself without these odds and ends? But if I were truly described by these multiplicities as such, if I deserved nothing more than Russell's collective name, then, speaking literally, I should always use the royal 'we': 'We' the bundle of events.

10 Scientific investigation shows that a seed is, in part, a dormant plant embryo.

11 Aristotle adopted the view of Empedocles, who maintained that the elements were earth, air, fire, and water; see *On Generation and Corruption*, bk. 2, chap. 3, 330b31.

gold. And one can even question whether an atom is a substance, as opposed to being composed of substances, such as protons.[12]

Lastly, parts of organisms and things composed of elemental parts are substances. The parts of organisms only imperfectly fall in the category of substance because while they do not exist in another as in a subject but rather make up the subject, they do not completely share in the nature of that subject. A dog's paw does not possess everything that belongs to canine nature.[13]

As for things composed of parts that are elements, not just anything so composed is a substance. For example, a smartphone may be made of over fifty elements but is no more than an aggregate of these substances. When Aristotle speaks of things composed of natural bodies, he most likely has in mind natural things that result from the union of elements. A contemporary example of such a thing is water, H_2o. The reason such things are listed last on the list of substances is that, unlike the case of living things, it is very hard to know whether composite nonliving natural things such as water are substances or whether they are simply an aggregate of elements. Do the hydrogen and oxygen in water continue to exist as substances or is water a substance, that is, is it a single being that possesses a determinate nature and has existence through itself (in which case, the hydrogen and oxygen do not exist in act in it but only in potency)?[14] If the latter is the case, it is the least readily recognizable kind of substance.

12 One could further question whether parts of atoms, such as protons, are substances or whether they are composed of substances, such as quarks.

13 See *Q. DA*, unicus, 1:

> An individual in the genus of substance is not only able to subsist of itself but also is something complete in some species and genus of substance; whence the philosopher also in the *Categories* names hand and foot parts of substances rather than first or second substances; for granted that they do not exist in another as in a subject (which is what is proper to substance), nevertheless they do not completely share the nature of the species; whence they are not in some species or in some genus, except by reduction.

See also, *In Meta.*, bk. 7, lec. 16, n. 1–6.

14 For a discussion of this point, see Murray, "If T'were a Substance," 128–29.

Bibliography

Abramson, Charles I., and Ana M. Chicas-Mosier. "Learning in Plants: Lessons from *Mimosa pudica*." *Frontiers in Psychology* 7, no. 417 (2016). https://doi.org/10.3389/fpsyg.2016.00417.

Adelman, Barry. "On the Conditioning of Plants: A Review of Experimental Evidence." *Perspectives on Behavior Science* 41 (2018): 431–46.

Adler, Mortimer. *The Difference of Man and the Difference it Makes*. Holt, Rinehart and Winston, 1967.

Adler, Mortimer. *Some Questions About Language*. Open Court, 1976.

Alberts, Bruce, Alexander Johnson, Julian Lewis, et al. *Molecular Biology of the Cell*. 4th ed. Garland Science, 2002.

Albertus Magnus. *De Caelo et Mundo*. Vol. 5 of *Opera Omnia*. Monasterii Westfalorum, 1971.

Alcock, John. *Animal Behavior*. Sinauer, 1998.

Anastasio, Alexandra. "Do Dogs Grieve the Loss of Their Human Owners?," https://www.akc.org/expert-advice/lifestyle/do-dogs-grieve/.

Andreas, Jacob, Gašper Beguš, Michael M. Bronstein, et al. "Toward Understanding the Communication in Sperm Whales." *iScience* 25, no. 6 (2022): 104393.

Andrews, Kristin. "Chimpanzee Mind Reading: Don't Stop Believing." *Philosophy Compass* 12, no. 1 (2016): e12394.

Appel, H. M., and R. B. Cocroft. "Plants Respond to Leaf Vibrations Caused by Insect Herbivore Chewing." *Oecologia* 175, no. 4 (August 2014): 1257–66.

Aquinas, St. Thomas. *In Aristotelis Libros: De Sensu et Sensato Commentarium*. Edited by Raymundi M. Spiazzi. Marietti, 1949.

Aquinas, St. Thomas. *Compendium Theologiae*. In vol. 1, *Opuscula Theologica*. Edited by Raymundi A. Verardo. Marietti, 1954.

Aquinas, St. Thomas. *De Causis*. https://www.corpusthomisticum.org/cdc01.html.

Aquinas, St. Thomas. *De mixtione elementorum ad magistrum Philippum de Castro*. https://www.corpusthomisticum.org/opx.html.

Aquinas, St. Thomas. *De Rationibus Fidei*. https://www.corpusthomisticum.org/ocg.html

Aquinas, St. Thomas. *De unitate intellectus*. https://www.corpusthomisticum.org/oca.html.

Aquinas, St. Thomas. *Expositio libri Boetii De ebdomadibus*. https://www.corpusthomisticum.org/cbh.html.

Aquinas, St. Thomas. *Expositio libri Peryermeneias*. https://www.corpusthomisticum.org/cpe.html

Aquinas, St. Thomas. *In Aristotelis Librum De Anima Commentarium*. Edited by P. F. Angeli and M. Pirotta. Marietti, 1959.

Aquinas, St. Thomas. *In Decem Libros Ethicorum Aristotelis ad Nicomachum Expositio*. Edited by Raymundi M. Spiazzi. Marietti, 1964.

Aquinas, St. Thomas. *In Duodecim Libros Metaphysicorum Aristotelis Expositio*. Edited by Raymundi M. Spiazzi. Marietti, 1950.

Aquinas, St. Thomas. *In Epistolas S. Pauli*. https://www.corpusthomisticum.org/che11.html

Aquinas, St. Thomas. *In Libros De Caelo et Mundo*. https://www.corpusthomisticum.org/iopera.html.

Aquinas, St. Thomas. *In Libros Physicorum*. https://www.corpusthomisticum.org/iopera.html.

Aquinas, St. Thomas. *In Librum Boethii de Trinitate*. Edited by Bruno Decker. Brill, 1959.

Aquinas, St. Thomas. *In Symbolum Apostolorum*. https://www.corpusthomisticum.org/csv.html.

Aquinas, St. Thomas. *Quaestio Disputata de Anima* in *Quaestiones Disputatae*. In vol. 2, Bazzi et al., *Quaestiones Disputatae*.

Aquinas, St. Thomas. *Quaestiones Disputatae*. Vol. 2. Edited by P. Bazzi, M. Calcaterra, T. S. Centi, E. Odetto, and P. M. Pession. Marietti, 1965.

Aquinas, St. Thomas. *Quaestiones Disputatae de Potentia*. In vol. 2, Bazzi et al., *Quaestiones Disputatae*.

Aquinas, St. Thomas. *Quaestio Disputata de Spiritualibus Creaturis*. In vol. 2, Bazzi et al., *Quaestiones Disputatae*.

Aquinas, St. Thomas. *Quaestiones Disputatae de Veritate*. In vol. 1 *Quaestiones Disputatae*. Edited by Raymundi M. Spiazzi. Marietti, 1964.

Aquinas, St. Thomas. *Quaestio Disputata de Virtutibus in Communi*. In vol. 2, Bazzi et al., *Quaestiones Disputatae*.

Aquinas, St. Thomas. Quodlibet VIII. https://www.corpusthomisticum.org/q08.html.

Aquinas, St. Thomas. *Scriptum super Sententiis*. https://www.corpusthomisticum.org/iopera.html.

Aquinas, St. Thomas. *Sententia libri Politicorum*. https://www.corpusthomisticum.org/iopera.html.

Aquinas, St. Thomas. *Summa contra Gentiles*. https://www.corpusthomisticum.org/iopera.html.

Aquinas, St. Thomas. *Summa Theologiae*. Edited by Instituti Studiorum Medievalium Ottaviensis. Commissio Piana, 1953.

Aquinas, St. Thomas. *Super Evangelium S. Ioannis*. Edited by P. Raphaelis Cai. Marietti, 1952.

Aristotle. *Categories*. Translated by Harold P. Cooke. Harvard University Press, 1973.

Aristotle. *History of Animals*. Edited and translated by D. M. Balme. 3 vols. Harvard University Press, 1991.

Aristotle. *Metaphysics*. Translated by H. Tredennick. Harvard University Press, 1980.

Aristotle. *Metaphysics*. In *The Basic Works of Aristotle*. Edited by Richard McKeon and translated by W. D. Ross, 689–926. Random House, 1968.

Aristotle. *Nicomachean Ethics*. Translated by H. Rackham. Harvard University Press, 1982.

Aristotle. *On the Generation of Animals*. Translated by A. L. Peck. Harvard University Press, 1963.

Aristotle. *On the* Soul. Translated by W. S. Hett. Harvard University Press, 2000.

Aristotle. *On the Soul*. In *The Basic Works of Aristotle*. Edited by Richard McKeon and translated by J. A. Smith, 535–603. Random House, 1968.

Aristotle. *Parts of Animals*. Translated by A. L. Peck and E. S. Forster. Harvard University Press, 1968.

Aristotle. *Physics*. In *The Basic Works of Aristotle*. Edited by Richard McKeon and translated by R. P. Hardie and R. K. Gaye, 218–394. Random House, 1968.

Aristotle. *Politics*. In the *Basic Works of Aristotle*. Edited by Richard McKeon and translated by Benjamin Jowett, 1127–1324. Random House, 1968.

Aristotle. *Posterior Analytics*. In *The Basic Works of Aristotle*. Edited by Richard McKeon and translated by G. R. G. Mure. Random House, 1968.

Arnhart, Larry. *Darwinian Natural Right: The Biological Ethics of Human Nature*. State University of New York Press, 1998

Arnold, Kate, and Klaus Zuberbühler. "Meaningful Call Combinations in a non-human Primate." *Current Biology* 18, no. 5: R202–3.

Augros, Michael. "Aquinas's Proof of the Human Soul's Subsistence." *The Aquinas Review* 27, no. 1 (2024): 1–28.

Aureli, Filippo, and Andrew Whiten. "Emotions and Behavioral Flexibility." In *Primate Psychology*, edited by Dario Maestripieri, 289–323. Harvard University Press, 2003.

Austriaco, Nicanor Pier Giorgio. "Immediate Hominization from the Systems Perspective." *The National Catholic Bioethics Quarterly* 4, no. 4 (2004): 729–30.

Austriaco, Nicanor Pier Giorgio. "The Specification of Sex/Gender in the Human Species: A Thomistic Analysis." *New Blackfriars* 94, no. 1054 (2013): 701–15.

Austriaco, Nicanor Pier Giorgio. "Defending Adam After Darwin: On the Origin of *Sapiens* as a Natural Kind." *American Catholic Philosophical Quarterly* 92, no. 2 (2018): 337–52.

Austriaco, Nicanor Pier Giorgio. "Plants Too Have Sensitive Souls." *Paper presented at the Meeting of the American Catholic Philosophical Association, Minneapolis, MN,* Nov. 30, 2019.

Austriaco, Nicanor Pier Giorgio. "Thomistic Thoughts About Thought and Talk." *American Catholic Philosophical Quarterly* 95, no. 1 (2021): 117–30.

Austriaco, Nicanor Pier Giorgio. "On the Limits of Abstraction: A Response to Professor Marie George." *American Catholic Philosophical Quarterly* 95, no. 1 (2021): 145–48.

Ayala, Francisco J. "Teleological Explanations." In *Philosophy of Biology*, edited by Michael Ruse. Macmillan Publishing Company, 1989.

Balint-Kurti, Peter. "The Plant Hypersensitive Response: Concepts, Control and Consequences." *Molecular Plant Pathology* 20, no. 8 (2019): 1163–78.

Baluška, František, and Stefano Mancuso. "Plant Neurobiology as a Paradigm Shift Not Only in the Plant Sciences." *Plant Signaling and Behavio*r 2, no. 4 (2007): 205–7.

Barber, Theodore Xenophon. *The Human Nature of Birds*. St. Martin's Press, 1993.

Bard, Kim A. "Neonatal Imitation in Chimpanzees (*Pan troglodytes*) Tested with Two Paradigms." *Animal Cognition* 10, no. 2 (2007): 233–42.

Bard, Kim A., and Takeshi Kishimoto. "Early Communicative Gestures in Human and Chimpanzee 1-Year-Olds Observed Across Diverse Socioecological Settings." *Learning & Behavior* 51, no. 1 (2023): 15–33.

Bargmann, C. I., E. Hartwieg, and H. R. Horvitz. "Odorant-Selective Genes and Neurons Mediate Olfaction in C. elegans." *Cell* 74, no. 4 (1993): 515–27.

Barr, Stephen M. "The Design of Evolution." *First Things* 156 (2005): 9–12.

Barrow, John D., and Frank J. Tipler. *The Anthropic Cosmological Principle*. Oxford University Press, 1986.

Behrens, Timothy E. "Differences Between Chimpanzees and Bonobos in Neural Systems Supporting Social Cognition." *Social Cognitive and Affective Neuroscience* 7, no. 4 (2012): 369–79.

Bengson, Jesse J., Todd A. Kelley, Xiaoke Zhang, et al. "Spontaneous Neural Fluctuations Predict Decisions to Attend." *Journal of Cognitive Neuroscience* 26, no. 11 (November 2014): 2578–84.

Beran, Michael J., Bonnie M. Perdue, Sara E. Futch, et al. "Go When You Know: Chimpanzees' Confidence Movements Reflect Their Responses in a Computerized Memory Task." *Cognition* 142 (2015): 236–46.

Bergman, Thore J., Jacinta C. Beehner, Melissa C. Painter, et al. "The Speech-Like Properties of Nonhuman Primate Vocalizations." *Animal Behaviour* 151 (2019): 229–37.

Berkman, John R. "Towards a Thomistic Theology of Animality." In *Creaturely Theology*, edited by Celia Deane-Drummond and David Clough. SCM, 2009.

Bertini, Marta, Guilia Annicchiarico, Chiara Bresciani, et al. "Playful Interactions and Facial Mimicry in Infant Bonobos (*Pan paniscus*)." *Ethology, Ecology & Evolution* 34, no. 3 (2022): 344–59.

Biegler, Robert. "Insufficient Evidence for Habituation in *Mimosa pudica*: Response to Gagliano et al. (2014)." *Oecologia* 186, no. 1 (2018): 33–35.

Biography.com Editors. "Helen Keller Biography." https://www.biography.com/activist/helen-keller.

Bodamer, Mark D., and R. Allen Gardner. "How Cross-Fostered Chimpanzees (*Pan troglodytes*) Initiate and Maintain Conversations." *Journal of Comparative Psychology* 16, no. 1 (2002): 12–26.

Bohm, Jennifer, Sönke Scherzer, Elzbieta Krol, et al. "The Venus Flytrap *Dionaea muscipula* Counts Prey-Induced Action Potentials to Induce Sodium Uptake." *Current Biology* 26, no. 3 (2016): 286–95.

Bok, Hilary. "The Implications of Advances in Neuroscience for Freedom of the Will." *The Journal of the American Society for Experimental NeuroTherapeutics* 4, no. 3 (2007): 555–59.

Bor, Daniel. "The Mechanics of Mind-Reading." *Scientific American*, July 1, 2010. https://www.scientificamerican.com/article/the-mechanics-of-mind-rea/.

Bose, J. C. *Plant Response*. Longmans, 1906.

Braine, David. *The Human Person: Animal and Spirit*. Notre Dame University Press, 1992.

Brooker, Robert, Eric P. Widmaier, Linda E. Graham, and Peter D. Stiling. *Biology*, 5th ed. McGraw Hill, 2019.

Brosnan, Sarah, Catherine Talbot, Megan Ahlgren, et al. "Mechanisms Underlying Responses to Inequitable Outcomes in Chimpanzees, *Pan troglodytes*." *Animal Behavior* 79, no. 6 (2010): 1229–37.

Brown, Warren S., Nancey Murphy, and H. Newton Malony, eds. *Whatever Happened to the Soul?* Fortress, 1998.

Budiansky, Stephen. *If a Lion Could Talk*. The Free Press, 1998.

Bühlmeier, Andreas, and Gerhard Manteuffel. "Operant Conditioning in Robots." In Omidvar, *Neural Systems for Robotics*.

Burrows, Anne M. "The Facial Expression Musculature in Primates and Its Evolutionary Significance." *BioEssays* 30, no. 3 (2008): 212–25.

Campbell, Neil A., Jane B. Reece, and Lisa A. Urry. *Biology*, 8th ed. Pearson Benjamin Cummings, 2014.

Carrasco, Lara, Sandra Posada, and Montserrat Colell. "New Evidence on Imitation in an Enculturated Chimpanzee (*Pan troglodytes*)." *Journal of Comparative Psychology* 123, no. 4 (2009): 385–90.

Catchpole, Clive. *Vocal Communication in Birds*. University Park Press, 1979.

Catechism of the Catholic Church. Apostolate for Family Consecration, 1994.

Chalmers, David. J. *The Conscious Mind: In Search of a Fundamental Theory*. Oxford University Press, 1996.

Chamovitz, Daniel. *What a Plant Knows: A Field Guide to the Senses*. Scientific American, 2017.

Chang, Caren. "Q&A: How Do Plants Respond to Ethylene and What Is Its Importance?," *BMC Biology* 14, no. 7 (2016). https://doi.org/10.1186/s12915-016-0230-0.

Chang, Carolina. "Using Sensor Habituation in Mobile Robots to Reduce Oscillatory Movements in Narrow Corridors." *IEEE Trans Neural Networks* 16, no. 6 (2005): 1582–9.

Cheney, Dorothy L., and Robert M. Seyfarth. *Baboon Metaphysics*. University of Chicago Press, 2007.

Chomsky, Noam. "Human Language and Other Semiotic Systems." In Sebeok and Umiker-Sebeok, *Speaking of Apes*.

Churchland, Patricia Smith. "I have no soul (and I'm okay with that)." *National Post*, August 8, 2013. https://nationalpost.com/opinion/patricia-smith-churchland-i-have-no-soul-and-im-okay-with-that.

Clay, Zanna, and Frans B. M. de Waal. "Development of Socio-emotional Competence in Bonobos." *PNAS* 110, no. 45 (2013): 18121–18126.

Clay, Zanna, Christine E. Webb, Teresa Romero, et al. "Comparative Perspectives of Empathy Development: Insights from Chimpanzees and Bonobos." In Dukes, *Oxford Handbook of Emotional Development*.

Coghaln, Andy. "Science: What Really Makes Water Wet?," *New Scientist*, February 15, 1997. https://www.newscientist.com/article/mg15320693-200-science-what-really-makes-water-wet/.

Coles, Nicholas A., Jeff T. Larsen, and Heather C. Lench. "A Meta-Analysis of the Facial Feedback Literature: Effects of Facial Feedback on Emotional Experience Are Small and Variable." *Psychological Bulletin* 145, no. 6 (2019): 610–51.

Connell, Richard J. "An Empirical Consideration of Substance." *Laval Théologique et Philosophique* 24, no. 3 (1978): 235–46.

Connell, Richard J. *Substance and Modern Science*. Center for Thomistic Studies, 1988.

Conway Morris, Simon. *Life's Solution: Inevitable Humans in a Lonely Universe*. University of Cambridge Press, 2003.

Cook, Gareth. "Do Plants Think?," *Scientific American*, June 5, 2012. https://www.scientificamerican.com/article/do-plants-think-daniel-chamovitz/.

Craver, Carl F., and William Bechtel. "Top-Down Causation Without Top-Down Causes." *Biology and Philosophy* 22 (2007): 547–63.

Criado-Reyes, Joaquín, Bruno M. Bizzarri, Juan Manuel García-Ruiz, et al. "The Role of Borosilicate Glass in Miller-Urey Experiment." *Scientific Reports* 11, no. 1 (2021): 21009.

Crick, Francis. *Life Itself: Its Origin and Nature*. Simon and Schuster, 1981.

Cronin, Thomas. "Seeing Without Eyes—The Unexpected World of Nonvisual Photoreception." *The Conversation*, August 9, 2017, https://theconversation.com/seeing-without-eyes-the-unexpected-world-of-nonvisual-photoreception-79166.

Cronin, Thomas W., and Sönke Johnsen. "Extraocular, Non-Visual, and Simple Photoreceptors: An Introduction to the Symposium." *Integrative and Comparative Biology* 56, no. 5 (2016): 758–63.

Crowe, Michael. *The Extraterrestrial Life Debate 1750–1900: The Idea of a Plurality of Worlds from Kant to Lowell*. Cambridge University Press, 1986.

Cyr, André, Munir Boukadoum, and Frédérick Thériault. "Operant Conditioning: A Minimal Components Requirement in Artificial Spiking Neurons Designed for Bio-Inspired Robot's Controller." *Frontiers in Neurorobotics* 8, no. 21 (2014). https://doi.org/10.3389/fnbot.2014.00021.

da Cunha, R. Vieira, and J. B. Relvas. "Who's Afraid of the Big Bad Neuroscience: Neuroscience's Impact on Our Notions of Self and Free Will." In *The Human Sciences After the Decade of the Brain*, edited by Jon Leefmann and Elisabeth Hildt. Elsevier/Academic Press, 2017.

Damascene, St. John. *An Exposition of the Orthodox Faith*. https://www.orthodox.net/fathers/exactidx.html.

Damasio, Antonio. *Descartes' Error: Emotion, Reason, and the Human Brain*. Penguin Books, 1994.

Damasio, Antonio. *The Feeling of What Happens*. Harcourt, Inc., 1999.

Darling, David. *Life Everywhere*. Basic Books, 2001.

Darwin, Charles. *The Formation of Vegetable Mould Through the Actions of Worms*. 1881. *Darwin Online*. https://darwin-online.org.uk/content/frameset?pageseq=1&itemID=F1357&viewtype=text.

Darwin, Charles. Notebook B, edited by John van Wyhe. http://darwin-online.org.uk/content/frameset?itemID=CUL-DAR121.-&viewtype=side&pageseq=38.

Darwin, Charles. *Origin of the Species*. Mentor Books, 1964.

Darwin, Charles. *The Descent of Man*. In *The Darwin Compendium*. Barnes & Noble Publishing, 2005.

Davies, Paul. *Are We Alone?* Basic Books, 1995.

Davies, Paul. "Biological Determinism, Information Theory, and the Origin of Life." In *Many Worlds*, edited by Steven J. Dick. Templeton Foundation Press, 2000.

Dawkins, Richard, and Steven Pinker. "Is Science Killing the Soul?," Guardian–Dillons Debate, Feb. 10, 1999. www.edge.org/documents/archive/edge53.html.

De Caro, Mario, and Hilary Putnam. "Free Will and Quantum Mechanics." *The Monist* 103 (2020): 415–26.

de Duve, Christian. *Vital Dust*. Basic Books, 1995.

De Koninck, Charles. *The Hollow Universe*. Les Presses de l'Université Laval, 1964.

De Koninck, Charles. "Introduction to the Study of the Soul." Translated by David Quackenbush. *The Aquinas Review* 23 (2019–2020): 29–33.

de Waal, Frans. *Good Natured: The Origins of Right and Wrong in Humans and Other Animals*. Harvard University Press, 1996.

de Waal, Frans. *Primates and Philosophers*. Princeton University Press, 2006.

de Waal, Frans. *The Age of Empathy: Nature's Lessons for a Kinder Society*. Three Rivers Press, 2009.

de Waal, Frans. *Mama's Last Hug*. W. W. Norton & Company, 2019.

Deacon, Terrance. *The Symbolic Species*. W. W. Norton & Company, 1997.

Deane-Drummond, Celia, Neil Arner, and Augustín Fuentes. "The Evolution of Morality: A Three-Dimensional Map." *Philosophy, Theology, and the Sciences* 3, no. 2 (2016): 115–51.

Decaen, Christopher. "Elemental Virtual Presence in St. Thomas." *The Thomist* 64, no. 2 (2000): 271–300.

Delano, Kenneth J. *Many Worlds, One God*. New York Exposition Press, 1977.

Descartes, René. *Principles of Philosophy*. Vol. 1 of *Descartes: Selected Philosophical Writings by René Descartes*. Edited by John Cottingham, Robert Stoothoff, and Dugald Murdoch. Cambridge University Press, 1988.

Dietrich, Daniela. "Hydrotropism: How Roots Search for Water." *Journal of Experimental Biology* 69, no. 11 (May 2018): 2759–71.

Dillard, Annie. *Pilgrim at Tinker Creek*. Harper's Magazine Press, 1974.

Dodds, Michael. "Top Down, Bottom Up or Inside Out? Retrieving Aristotelian Causality in Contemporary Science." Thomistic Institute, June 25, 1997. https://www3.nd.edu/~afreddos/papers/dodds.htm.

Dodds, Michael. "Hylomorphism and Human Wholeness: Perspectives on the Mind-Brain Problem." *Theology and Science* 7, no. 2 (2009): 141–62.

Dodds, Michael. "The Reality of the Soul in an Age of Neuroscience." *Nova et Vetera* 17, no. 3 (2019): 893–912.

"Dolphins Rescuing Humans." Dolphins-World, April 26, 2017. http://www.dolphins-world.com/dolphins-rescuing-humans/.

Drake, Frank, and Dava Sobel. *Is Anyone Out There?* Delacorte Press, 1992.

Drees, Willem B. "Bethlehem: Center of the Universe?," In *God for the 21st Century*, edited by Russell Stannard. Templeton Foundation Press, 2000.

Dukes, Daniel, ed. *Oxford Handbook of Emotional Development*. Oxford University Press, 2022.

Durand, Guillaume, and Erika Motsumoto Plata. "The Effects of Psychopathic Traits on Fear of Pain, Anxiety, and Stress." *Personality and Individual Differences* 119 (2017): 198–203.

Elliott, Clark. *The Ghost in My Brain: How a Concussion Stole My Life and How the New Science of Brain Plasticity Helped Me Get It Back*. Penguin Books, 2016.

Evers, Kathinka, and Mariano Sigman. "Possibilities and Limits of Mind-Reading: A Neurophilosophical Perspective." *Consciousness and Cognition* 22, no. 3 (2013): 887–97.

Fagot, Joël, E. A. Wasserman, and M. E. Young. "Discriminating the Relation Between Relations: The Role of Entropy in Abstract Conceptualization by Baboons (*Papio papio*) and Humans (*Homo sapiens*)." *Journal of Experimental Psychology: Animal Behavior Processes* 27, no. 4 (2001): 316–28.

Fang, Janet. "Plants Can Hear Themselves Being Eaten." *IFL Science*, July 4, 2014. https://www.iflscience.com/plants-and-animals/plants-can-hear-themselves-being-eaten/.

Farah, Martha J., and Paul Root Wolpe. "Monitoring and Manipulating the Human Brain: New Neuroscience Technologies and Their Ethical Implications." *The Hastings Center Report* 34, no. 3 (2004): 35–45.

Fedorenko, Evelino, and Rosemary Varley. "Language and Thought Are Not the Same Thing: Evidence from Neuroimagining and Neurological Patients." *Annals of the New York Academy of Sciences* 1369, no. 1 (2016): 132–53.

Ferrari, Pier Francesco, Annika Paukner, Consuel Ionica, et al. "Reciprocal Face-to-Face Communication Between Rhesus Macaque Mothers and Their Newborn Infants." *Current Biology* 19, no. 20 (2009): 1768–72.

Feser, Edward. *Scholastic Metaphysics: A Contemporary Introduction*. Editiones Scholasticae, 2014.

Feser, Edward. *Aristotle's Revenge*. Editiones Scholasticae, 2019.

Fisher, Madeline. "Exploring the First 50 Sequenced Plant Genomes." Crop Science Society of America, September 10, 2013. https://www.crops.org/news/science-news/exploring-first-50-sequenced-plant-genomes/

Flemming, Timothy M., Michael J. Beran, Roger K. R. Thompson, et al. "What Meaning Means for Same and Different: Analogical Reasoning in Humans (*Homo sapiens*), Chimpanzees (*Pan troglodytes*), and Rhesus Monkeys (*Macaca mulatta*)." *Journal of Comparative Psychology* 122, no. 2 (2008): 176–85.

Fouts, Roger. *Next of Kin*. William Morrow, 1997.

Fraser, Orlaith N., Daniel Stahl, and Filippo Aureli. "Stress Reduction Through Consolation in Chimpanzees." *PNAS* 105, no. 25 (2008): 8557–62.

Gagliano, Monica, Mavra Grimonprez, Martial Depczynski, et al. "Tuned in: Plant Roots Use Sound to Locate Water." *Oecologia* 184, no. 1 (2007): 151–60.

Gagliano, Monica, Michael Renton, Martial Depczynski, et al. "Experience Teaches Plants to Learn Faster and Forget Slower in Environments Where It Matters." *Oecologia* 175, no. 1 (2014): 63–72.

Gagliano, Monica, Vladyslav V. Vyazovskiy, Alexander A. Borbély, et al. "Learning by Association in Plants." *Scientific Reports* 6, no. 1 (2016): 38427.

Gardner, Beatrix T., and R. Allen Gardner. "Development of Phrases in the Early Utterances of Children and Cross-fostered Chimpanzees." *Evolution* 13, nos. 3–4 (1998): 161–88.

Gardner, Martin. *Science: Good, Bad and Bogus*. Prometheus Books, 1981.

Gardner, R. Allen, and Beatrix T. Gardner. "Teaching Sign Language to a Chimpanzee." *Science* 165, no. 3894 (1969): 664–72.

Gardner, R. Allen, Beatrix T. Gardner, and Thomas E. Van Cantfort, eds. *Teaching Sign Language to Chimpanzees*. State University of New York Press, 1989.

Gardner, R. Allen, and Beatrix Gardner. *The Structure of Learning: From Sign Stimuli to Sign Language*. Lawrence Erlbaum Associates, 1998.

Gaudiano, Paolo, and C. Chang. "Adaptive Obstacle Avoidance with a Neural Network for Operant Conditioning: Experiments with Real Robots." *Proceedings 1997 IEEE International Symposium on Computational Intelligence in Robotics and Automation CIRA '97: Towards New Computational Principles for Robotics and Automation*: 13–18. doi:10.1109/CIRA.1997.613832.

George, Marie I. "Mind Forming and Manuductio in Aquinas." *The Thomist* 57, no. 2 (1993): 201–13.

George, Marie I. "Descartes's Language Test for Rationality: A Response to Miller." *American Catholic Philosophical Quarterly* 83, no. 1 (2009): 107–25.

George, Marie I. "On the Occasion of Darwin's Bicentennial: Finally Time to Retire the Fifth Way?," *Proceedings of the American Catholic Philosophical Association* 83 (2009): 209–26.

George, Marie I. "On the Meaning of 'Immanent Activity' According to Aquinas." *The Thomist* 78, no. 3 (2014): 537–55.

George, Marie I. "A Defense of the Distinction Between Plants and Animals." *Proceedings of the American Catholic Philosophical Association* 93 (2019): 349–66.

George, Marie I. "Aquinas's Teachings on Concepts and Words in His Commentary on John Contra Nicanor Austriaco, OP" *American Catholic Philosophical Quarterly* 94, no. 3 (2020): 357–78.

George, Marie I. "Does Knowing What Things Are Require Language (As a System of Physical or Imaginable Signs)?," *American Catholic Philosophical Quarterly* 95, no. 1 (2021): 357–78.

George, Marie I. "A Rambutan by Any Other Name Would Taste as Sweet: Response to Professor Nicanor Pier Giorgio Austriaco, OP." *American Catholic Philosophical Quarterly* 95, no. 1 (2021): 149–53.

George, Marie I. "A Defense of the Distinction Between Plants and Animals." *The Aquinas Review* 26, 2 (2023): 69–108.

George, Marie I. "Philosophers of Mind Would Do Well to Keep Aquinas's Teachings in Mind." *Proceedings of the American Catholic Philosophical Association* (2024), forthcoming.

Gianoli, Ernesto, Marcia González-Teuber, Claudia Vilo, et al. "Endophytic Bacterial Communities Are Associated with Leaf Mimicry in the Vine *Boquila trifoliolata*." *Science Reports* 11, no. 22673 (2021), https://doi.org/10.1038/s41598-021-02229-8.

Gillan, Douglas, David Premack, and Guy Woodruff. "Reasoning in the Chimpanzee: I. Analogical Reasoning." *Journal of Experimental Psychology: Animal Behavior Processes* 7, no. 1 (1981): 1–17.

Gleiser, Marcelo. "Is Neuroscience Rediscovering the Soul?," NPR, April 5, 2017. https://www.npr.org/sections/13.7/2017/04/05/522738015/is-neuroscience-rediscovering-the-soul.

Glorioso, Gabrielle C., Shannon L. Kuzmanr, Mateja Pavlic, et al. "Still No Solution to Non-Verbal Measures of Analogical Reasoning: Reply to Walker and Gopnik (2017)." *Cognition* 214: 104288.

Glurfa, Martin, Shaowu Zhang, Armin Jenett, et al. "The Concepts of 'Sameness' and 'Difference' in an Insect." *Nature* 410, no. 6831 (2001): 930–33.

Goldin-Meadow, Susan. "Meeting Other Minds Through Gesture." In *Roots of Human Sociality: Culture, Cognition and Interaction*, edited by N. J. Enfield and Stephen C. Levinson. Berg, 2006.

Goldmann, Wolfgang H. "Mechanosensation: A Basic Cellular Process." *Progress in Molecular Biology and Translational Science* 126 (2014): 75–102.

Gómez, Juan Carlos. *Apes, Monkeys, Children, and the Growth of Mind*. Harvard University Press, 2004.

Goodsell, David. "*Molecule of the Month, Phototropin*." *PDB-101* (Training and Outreach Portal of Protein Data Bank), March 2015. http://pdb101.rcsb.org/motm/183.

Gould, James L. *Ethology: The Mechanism and Evolution of Behavior*. W. W. Norton & Company, 1982.

Gould, Stephen Jay. *Ever Since Darwin: Reflections in Natural History*. Norton, 1977.

Gould, Stephen Jay. "The Evolution of Life on Earth." *Scientific American* 271, no. 4 (1994): 85–91.

Gould, Stephen Jay. *Wonderful Life: The Burgess Shale and the Nature of History*. Norton, 1989.

Goyette, John. "St. Thomas and the Unity of Substantial Form." *Nova et Vetera* 7, no. 4 (2009): 781–90.

Grainger, Jonathan, Stéphanie Dufau, Marie Montant, et al. "Orthographic Processing in Baboons (Papio papio)." *Science* 336 (2012): 245–48.

Grandin, Temple. *Thinking in Pictures*. Vintage Books, 2016.

Gredt, Joseph. *Elementa Philosophiae Aristotelico-Thomisticae*. Herder, 1958.

Gregory, J. K., D. C. Clary, K. Lius, et al. "The Water Dipole Moment in Water Clusters." *Science* 275 (1997): 814–17.

Griffin, Donald R. *Animal Minds*. University of Chicago Press, 1992.

Grimes, John. "On the Failure to Detect Changes in Scenes Across Saccades." In *Perception*, edited by K. A. Akins. Oxford University Press, 1996.

Guo, Hongwei, and Joseph R. Ecker. "Plant Responses to Ethylene Gas Are Mediated by SCFEBF1/EBF2-Dependent Proteolysis of EIN3 Transcription Factor." *Cell* 115, no. 6 (2003): 667–77.

Guzei, Ilia. "How Are Crystals Formed?," https://morgridge.org/blue-sky/how-are-crystals-formed/.

Halina, Marta, Katja Liebal, and Michael Tomasello. "The Goal of Ape Pointing." *PLoS ONE* 13, no. 4 (2018): e0195182.

Halvorson, Todd, and Robyn Suriano. "Finding Other Life Wouldn't Shake Most Faiths." *Florida Today*, November 19, 1999.

Hare, Brian, Josep Call, and Michael Tomasello. "Do Chimpanzees Know What Conspecifics Know?," *Animal Behaviour* 61 (2001): 139–51.

Harris, Errol. *Cosmos and Anthropos: A Philosophical Interpretation of the Anthropic Cosmological Principle*. Humanity Press International, 1991.

Harrison, Peter. "Do Animals Feel Pain?," *Philosophy* 66, no. 255 (1991): 25–40.

Hartmann, J. Quentin. "Timing of Turn Initiations in Signed Conversations with Cross-Fostered Chimpanzees (*Pan troglodytes*)." *International Journal of Comparative Psychology* 24 (2011): 177–209.

Hatfield, Elaine, John T. Cacioppo, and Richard L. Rapson. "Primitive Emotional Contagion." In *Emotion and Social Behavior,* edited by M. S. Clark. Sage Publications, 1992.

Hauser, Marc D. *Wild Minds: What Animals Really Think*. Henry Holt, 2000.

Hauser, Marc D., and Victor Juhasz. "Morals, Apes, and Us: Can Animals Learn to Share, Cooperate, Punish, and Show Empathy?," *Discover* 21, no. 2 (2000). https://www.discovermagazine.com/mind/morals-apes-and-us.

Henley, Ty, and Daniel J. Povinelli. "Seeing Through <seeing through>: An Analysis of Kano et al. (2019)." *Animal Behavior and Cognition* 7, no. 4 (2020): 658–60.

Herman, Louis M., and Robert K. Uyeyama. "The Dolphin's Grammatical Competency: Comments on Kako (1990)." *Animal Learning & Behavior* 27, no. 1 (1999): 18–23.

Herman, Louis M. "Cognition and Language Competencies of Bottlenosed Dolphins." In *Dolphin Cognition and Behavior: A Comparative Approach*, edited by R. J. Schusterman, J. Thomas, and F. G. Woods. Psychology Press, 1986.

Hespos, Susan J., and Elizabeth S. Spelke. "Conceptual Precursors to Language." *Nature* 430 (2004): 453–56.

Heyes, Cecilia. "Animal Mindreading: What's the Problem." *Psychonomic Bulletin & Review* 22, no. 2 (2015): 313–27.

Heyes, Cecilia M. "Theory of Mind in Nonhuman Primates." *Behavioral and Brain Sciences* 21, no. 1 (1998): 101–48.

Hill, Jane H. "Apes and Language." In Sebeok and Umiker-Sebeok, *Speaking of Apes*.

Hippler, Arthur Martin. "Impediments to Aristotle's Life-Sciences." PhD diss., Boston College, 1993.

Hixson, Michael D. "Ape Language Research: A Review and Behavioral Perspective." *The Analysis of Verbal Behavior* 15 (1998): 17–39.

Hochschild, Joshua P. "Mental Language in Aquinas?," In *Intentionality, Cognition, and Mental Representation in Medieval Philosophy*, edited by Gyula Klima. Fordham University, 2015.

Hohm, Tim, Tobias Preuten, and Christian Fankhauser. "Phototropism: Translating Light into Directional Growth." *American Journal of Botany* 100, no. 1: 47–59.

Horgan, Terence. "From Supervenience to Superdupervenience." In *Philosophy of Mind*, edited by David J. Chalmers. Oxford University Press, 2002.

Holmes, Eric, and Gail Gruenberg, "Learning in Plants," *Worm Runner's Digest* 7, no. 1 (1965): 9–12.

Horikawa T., M. Tamaki, Y. Miyawaki, and Y. Kamitani. "Neural Decoding of Visual Imagery During Sleep." *Science* 3 (May 2013): 639–42.

Hu, Jane C. "What Do Talking Apes Really Tell Us? The Strange, Disturbing world of Koko the Gorilla and Kanzi the Bonobo" *Slate*, August 20, 2014. https://slate.com/technology/2014/08/koko-kanzi-and-ape-language-research-criticism-of-working-conditions-and-animal-care.html.

Hurley, Susan and Matthew Nudds, eds. *Rational Animals?* Oxford University Press, 2006.

Huth, Alexander G., Wendy A. de Heer, Thomas L. Griffiths, et al. "Natural Speech Reveals the Semantic Maps That Tile Human Cerebral Cortex." *Nature* 532 (2016): 453–58.

Inoue, Shin-ichiro, Atsushi Takemiya, and Ken-ichiro Shimazaki. "Phototropin Signaling and Stomatal Opening as a Model Case." *Current Opinions in Plant Biology* 13, no. 5 (2010): 587–93.

Isern-Mas, Carme, and Antoni Sureda Gomila. "Making Sense of Emotional Contagion." *Humana.Mente Journal of Philosophical Studies* 12 (2019): 71–100.

Jackendoff, Ray. *Patterns in the Mind.* Basic Books, 1994.

Jackson, Stephen D. "Plant Responses to Photoperiod." *New Phytologist* 181 (2008): 517–31.

Jakosky, Bruce. *The Search for Life on Other Planets.* Cambridge University Press, 1998.

Jensen, Keith, Josep Call, and Michael Tomasello. "Chimpanzees Are Vengeful but Not Spiteful." *Proceedings of the National Academy of Science* 104, no. 32 (2007): 13046–13050.

John, R, N. A. Anjum, S. K. Sopory, N. A. Akram, et al. "Some Key Physiological and Molecular Processes of Cold Acclimation." *Biologia Plantarum* 60, no. 4 (2016): 603–18.

John of Damascus. *On the Orthodox Faith.* Translated by Norman Russell. St Vladimir's Seminary Press, 2022.

John of St. Thomas. *Cursus Philosophicus Thomisticus.* Marietti, 1937.

Johnson, George. "Chimp Talk Debate: Is It Really Language?," *New York Times*, June 6, 1995.

Jones, Eric M. "Where Is Everybody?," *Physics Today* 38, no. 8 (1985): 11–13.

Jonsson, Carl-Otto, David Clinton, Monica Fahrman, et al. "How Do Mothers Signal Shared Feeling-States to Their Infants? An Investigation of Affect Attunement and Imitation During the First Year of Life." *Scandinavian Journal of Psychology* 42, no. 4 (September 2001): 377–81.

Jordania, Joseph. *Who Asked the First Question? The Origin of Human Choral Singing, Intelligence, Language and Speech.* Logos, 2006.

Kaiser, Christopher B. "Extraterrestrial Life and Extraterrestrial Intelligence." *Reformed Review* 51 (Winter 1997–98): 77–91.

Kaminski, Juliane, Josep Call, and Julia Fischer. "Word Learning in a Domestic Dog: Evidence for 'Fast Mapping.'" *Science* 306, no. 5677 (2004): 1682–83.

Kano, Fumihiro, Christopher Krupenye, Satoshi Hirata, et al. "Great Apes Use Self-Experience to Anticipate an Agent's Action in a False-Belief Test." *PNAS* 116, no. 42 (2019): 20904–9.

Karin-D'Arcy, M. Rosalyn, and Daniel J. Povinelli. "Do Chimpanzees Know What Each Other See? A Closer Look." *International Journal of Comparative Psychology* 15, no. 1 (2002): 21–54.

Keller, Helen. *The Story of My Life*. https://www.holloway.com/g/helen-keller-the-story-of-my-life/sections/chapter-vi.

Kevles, Bettyann. *Thinking Gorillas: Testing and Teaching the Great Ape*. E. P. Dutton, 1980.

Keysers, Christian. "Inside the Mind of a Psychopath—Empathic, But Not Always." *Psychology Today*, July 24, 2013. https://www.psychologytoday.com/us/blog/the-empathic-brain/201307/inside-the-mind-psychopath-empathic-not-always.

Kim, Yena, and Mariska Kret. "The Emotional Expressions and Emotion Perception in Nonhuman Primates." In Dukes, *Oxford Handbook of Emotional Development*.

Kirkpatrick, Casey. "Tactical Deception and the Great Apes: Insight into the Question of Theory of Mind." *Totem* 15, no. 1 (2006–2007): 31–37.

Kitazawa, Daisuke, Yasuko Hatakeda, Motoshi Kamada, et al. "Shoot Circumnutation and Winding Movements Require Gravisensing Cells." *PNAS* 102, no. 51 (2005): 18742–47.

Köhler, Wolfgang. *The Mentality of Apes*. Translated by Ella Winter. Routledge & Kegan Paul, 1973. Rept. of 1925 edition.

Koren, Henry J. *An Introduction to the Philosophy of Animate Nature*. B. Herder Book Co., 1955.

Koren, Henry J. *An Introduction to the Philosophy of Animate Nature*. Pearson Custom Publishing, n.d. Originally published in 1955 by Herder.

Kornell, Nate, Lisa K. Son, and Herbert S. Terrace. "Transfer of Metacognitive Skills and Hint Seeking in Monkeys." *Psychological Science* 18, no. 1 (2007): 64–71.

Koski, Sonja E., and Elisabeth H. M. Sterck. "Triadic Postconflict Affiliation in Captive Chimpanzees: Does Consolation Console?," *Animal Behaviour* 73, no. 1 (2007): 133–42.

Kowade, Yoshimi. "On the Nature and Subjectivity of Living Things." *Biosemiotics* 2 (2009): 205–20.

Krachun, Carla, Robert Lurz, Lindsay M. Mahovetz, et al. "Mirror Self-Recognition and Its Relationship to Social Cognition in Chimpanzees." *Animal Cognition* 22 (2019): 1171–83.

Krause, Mark A., and Michael J. Beran. "Words Matter: Reflections on Language Projects with Chimpanzees and Their Implications." *American Journal of Primatology* 82, no. 10 (2020): e23187.

Kret, Mariska E., Eliska Prochazkova, Elizabeth H. M. Sterck, et al. "Emotional Expressions in Human and Non-Human Great Apes." *Neuroscience & Behavioral Reviews* 115 (2020): 378–95.

Kröse, Ben, and Joris van Dam. "Neural Vehicles." In Omidvar, *Neural Systems for Robotics*.

Kupczak, Rafał. "Selected Aspects of Biophilosophical Controversies in Complex Plant Behaviour Research." *Studia Philosophiae Christianae* 53, no. 2 (2017): 123–44.

Lavery, J. J., and P. J. Foley. "Altruism or Arousal in the Rat?," *Science* 140, no. 3563 (1963): 172–73.

Lazzari, Edmund Michael. "Would St. Thomas Aquinas Baptize an Extraterrestrial?," *New Blackfriars* 99, no. 1082 (2018): 440–57.

Leavens, David A., William D. Hopkins, and Kim A. Bard. "Understanding the Point of Chimpanzee Pointing: Epigenesis and Ecological Validity." *Current Directions in Psychological Science* 14, no. 4 (2005): 185–89.

Lee, M. H., Q. Meng, and F. Chao. "Developmental Learning for Autonomous Robots." *Robotics and Autonomous Systems* 55, no. 9 (2007): 750–59.

Leeds, Charles Austin, and Mary Lee Jensvold. "The Communicative Functions of Five Signing Chimpanzees (*Pan troglodytes*)." *Pragmatics and Cognition* 21, no. 1 (2013): 224–47.

Lewis, C. S. "Religion and Rocketry." In *Fern-Seed and Elephants*, edited by Walter Hooper. Fontana, 1975.

Lindegaard, Marie R., Lasse S. Liebst, Wim Bernasco, et al. "Consolation in the Aftermath of Robberies Resembles Post-Aggression Consolation in Chimpanzees." *PLoS One* 12, no. 5 (May): e0177725.

Logan, Darren W. "Hot to Touch: The Story of the 2021 Nobel Prize in Physiology or Medicine." *Disease Models and Mechanisms* 14, no. 10 (2021): dmm049352.

Lonergan, Bernard. *Verbum: Word and Idea in Aquinas*. Vol. 2 of *The Collected Works of Bernard Lonergan*. Edited by Frederick Crowe, SJ, and Robert Doran, SJ. University of Toronto Press, 1997.

Lurz, Robert. "If Chimpanzees Are Mindreaders, Could Behavioral Science Tell? Toward a Solution of a Logical Problem." *Philosophical Psychology*, 22, no. 3 (2009): 305–28.

Lurz, Robert, Carla Krachun, Lindsay Mahovetz, et al. "Chimpanzees Gesture to Humans in Mirrors: Using Reflection to Dissociate Seeing from Line of Gaze." *Animal Behaviour* 135 (2018): 239–49.

Lyn, Heidi, Patricia M. Greenfield, E. Sue Savage-Rumbaugh, et al. "Nonhuman Primates Do Declare! A Comparison of Declarative Symbol and Gesture Use in Two Children, Two Bonobos, and a Chimpanzee." *Language and Communication* 31, no. 1 (2011): 63–74.

MacIntyre, Alasdair. *Dependent Rational Animals: Why Human Beings Need the Virtues*. Open Court, 1999.

Maffei, Massimo E., and Wilhelm Boland. "The Silent Scream of the Lima Bean." June 2007. DOI:10.13140/2.1.4887.6806.

Maffei, Massimo E., Gen-Ichiru Arimura, and Axel Mithöfer. "Natural Elicitors, Effectors and Modulators of Plant Responses." *National Products Report* 29 (2012): 1288–1303.

Mallett, Jon, Michael R. Blatt, Andreas Draguhn, et al. "Debunking a Myth: Plant Consciousness." *Protoplasma* 258 (2021): 459–76.

Mandler, Jean M. "Thought Before Language." *TRENDS in Cognitive Sciences* 8, no. 11 (2004): 508–13.

Manning, Heidi. "Yes, We Will Meet Them: The Drake Equation Tells Me So." In *Astrotheology*, edited by Ted Peters. Cascade Books, 2018.

Markel, Kasey. "Lack of Evidence for Associative Learning in Pea Plants." eLife 9 (2020): e57614. https://doi.org/10.7554/eLife.57614.

Martin, Stéphanie, Peter Brunner, Chris Holdgraf, et al. "Decoding Spectrotemporal Features of Overt and Covert Speech from the Human Cortex." *Frontiers in Neuroengineering* 7 (2014). https://doi.org/10.3389/fneng.2014.00014.

Masserman, J. H., S. Wechkin, and W. Terris. "'Altruistic' Behavior in Rhesus Monkeys." *American Journal of Psychiatry* 121 (1964): 584–85.

Masson, Jeffrey. *When Elephants Weep*. Delta, 1996.

Mayr, Ernst. *Towards a New Philosophy of Biology*. Harvard University Press, 1988.

McCrone, John. "A Bifold Model of Freewill." *Journal of Consciousness Studies* 6, nos. 8–9 (1999): 241–59.

McMullin, Ernan. "Persons in the Universe." *Zygon* 15, no. 1 (1980): 69–89.

McMullin, Ernan. "Life and Intelligence Far from Earth: Formulating Theological Issues." In *Many Worlds*, edited by Steven J. Dick. Templeton Foundation Press, 2000.

Mele, Alfred R. *Why Science Hasn't Disproved Free Will*. Oxford University Press, 2014.

Merola, Isabella, Emanuela Prato-Previde, and Sarah Marchall-Pescini. "Dogs' Social Referencing Towards Owners and Strangers." *PLoS One* 7, no. 10 (2012): e47653.

Mescher, Mark C., Justin B. Runyon, and Consuelo M. De Moraes. "Plant Host Finding by Parasitic Plants: A New Perspective on Plant to Plant Communication." *Plant Signaling & Behavior* 1, no. 6 (2006): 284–86.

Miles, H. Lyn White. "The Cognitive Foundations for Reference in a Signing Orangutan." In *'Language' and Intelligence in Monkeys and Apes*, edited by Sue Taylor Parker and Kathleen Rita Gibson. Cambridge University Press, 1990.

Miller, J. F., and R. S. Chapman. "The Relation Between Age and Mean Length of Utterance in Morphemes." *Journal of Speech and Hearing Research* 24, no. 2 (1981): 154–61.

Mithen, Steven. *The Singing Neanderthals: The Origins of Music, Language, Mind and Body*. Harvard University Press, 2007.

Mithöfer, Axel, and Wilhelm Boland. "Recognition of Herbivory-Associated Molecular Patterns." *Plant Physiology* 146 (March 2008): 825–31.

Molloy, Antonia. "Free Will Could Be the Result of Background Noise in the Brain Study Suggests." *Independent*, June 21, 2014. https://www.independent.co.uk/news/science/free-will-could-be-the-result-of-background-noise-in-the-brain-study-suggests-9553678.html.

Monod, Jacques. *Chance and Necessity*. Translated by Austryn Wainhouse. Vintage Books, 1970.

Monroe, J. Grey, Thanvi Srikant, Pablo Carbonell-Bejerano et al. "Mutation Bias Reflects Natural Selection in *Arabidopsis thaliana*." *Nature* 602, no. 7895 (2022): 101–5.

Morse, Stephen J. "Neuroscience, Free Will, and Criminal Responsibility." In *Free Will and the Brain: Neuroscientific, Philosophical, and Legal Perspectives*, edited by Walter Glannon. Cambridge University Press, 2015.

Moses, David A., Sean L. Metzger, Jessie R. Liu et al. "Neuroprosthesis for Decoding Speech in a Paralyzed Person with Anarthria." *New England Journal of Medicine* 385 (2021): 217–27.

Mundinger, Paul C. "Animal Cultures and a General Theory of Cultural Evolution." *Ethology and Sociobiology* 1, no. 3 (1980): 183–223.

Mundinger, Paul C. "Behaviour-Genetic Analysis of Canary Song; Inter-Strain Differences in Sensory Learning, and Epigenetic Rules." *Animal Behaviour* 50, no. 6 (1995): 1491–1511.

Murphy, Nancey. "Physicalism Without Reductionism: Toward A Scientifically, Philosophically, and Theologically Sound Portrait of Human Nature." *Zygon* 34, no. 4 (January 2003): 551–71.

Murray, Jean-Philippe. "Qu'est-ce que l'âme? Examen de la conception Aristotélicienne de cette notion." *Peripatetikos* 12 (2017): 79–98.

Murray, Warren. "If T'were a Substance." *Philosophia Perennis* 1, no. 1 (1994): 113–32.

Musgrave, Stephanie, Elizabeth Lonsdorf, David Morgan, et al. "The Ontogeny of Termite Gathering Among Chimpanzees in the Goualougo Triangle, Republic of Congo." *American Journal Physical Anthropology* 174, no. 2 (2021): 187–200.

Naeye, Robert. "Are We Alone in the Universe?," *Astronomy* 24, no. 7 (1996): 36–43.

National Oceanic and Atmospheric Administration. "What Are Corals." https://oceanservice.noaa.gov/education/tutorial_corals/coral01_intro.html.

Newsome, Bill. "Neuroscience, Faith & Free Will." *Biologos*, https://biologos.org/podcast-episodes/bill-newsome-neuroscience-faith-free-will.

Oba, Yasuhiro, Yoshinori Takano, Hiroshi Naraoka, et al. "Extraterrestrial Hexamethylenetetramine in Meteorites—A Precursor of Prebiotic Chemistry in the Inner Solar System." *Nature Communications* 11, no. 1 (2020): 6243.

O'Callaghan, John. *Thomist Realism and the Linguistic Turn: Toward a More Perfect Form of Existence*. University of Notre Dame Press, 2016.

Oderberg, David S. *Real Essentialism*. Routledge, 2007.

Oderberg, David. "Synthetic Life and the Bruteness of Immanent Causation." In *Aristotle on Method and Metaphysics*, edited by Edward Feser. Palgrave MacMillan, 2013.

Olendorf, Robert, Thomas Getty, and Kim Scribner. "Cooperative Nest Defence in Red-Winged Blackbirds: Reciprocal Altruism, Kinship or By-Product Mutualism?," *Proceedings of the Royal Society B: Biological Sciences* 271, no. 1535 (2004): 177–82.

Omidvar, Omid and Patrick van der Smagt, eds. *Neural Systems for Robotics*. Academic Press, 1997.

O'Neil, Dennis. "Human Biological Adaptivity: An Introduction to Human Responses to Common Environmental Stresses." On-line tutorial. https://www2.palomar.edu/anthro/adapt/adapt_3.htm.

Oostenbroek, Janine, Thomas Suddendorf, Mark Nielson, et al. "Comprehensive Longitudinal Study Challenges the Existence of Neonatal Imitation in Humans." *Current Biology* 26, no. 10 (2016):1334–8.

Osvath, Mathias. "Spontaneous Planning for Future Stone Throwing by a Male Chimpanzee." *Current Biology* 19, no. 5 (2009): R190–91.

Pacherie, Élisabeth. "L'empathie et ses degrés." In *L'empathie*, edited by Alain Berthoz and Gérard Jorland. Editions Odile Jacob, 2004.

Pack, Adam A. "Language Research: Dolphins." In *Encyclopedia of Animal Cognition and Behavior*, edited by Jennifer Vonk and Todd K. Shackelford. https://doi.org/10.1007/978-3-319-47829-6_1628-1.

Pagel, Mark, Ciara O' Donovan, and Andrew Meade. "General Statistical Model Shows That Macroevolutionary Patterns and Process Are Consistent with Darwinian Gradualism." *Nature Communications* 13, no. 1113 (2022): https://doi.org/10.1038/s41467-022-28595-z.

Paine, Thomas. *The Age of Reason*. Prometheus Books, 1984.

Pallante, Virginia, Roscoe Stanyon, and Elisabetta Palagi. "Calming an Aggressor Through Spontaneous Post-Conflict Triadic Contacts: Appeasement in *Macaca tonkeana*." *Aggressive Behavior* 44, no. 4 (2018): 406–15.

Parr, Lisa A. "Cognitive and Physiological Markers of Emotional Awareness in Chimpanzees (*Pan troglodytes*)." *Animal Cognition* 4, nos. 3–4 (2001): 223–29.

Parr, Lisa A., and Bridget M. Waller. "Understanding Chimpanzee Facial Expression: Insights into the Evolution of Communication." *Social Cognitive and Affective Neuroscience* 1, no. 3 (2006): 221–28.

Patterson, Penny, and Eugene Linden. *The Education of Koko*. Henry Holt, 1988.

Pawl, Timothy. "Brian Hebblethwaite's Arguments Against Multiple Incarnations." *Religious Studies* 52 (2016): 117–30.

Pawl, Timothy. "Thomistic Multiple Incarnations." *The Heythrop Journal* 57 (2016): 359–70.

Paxinos, George. "Why Psychology Lost Its Soul: Everything Comes from the Brain." The Conversation, September 22, 2016. https://theconversation.com/why-psychology-lost-its-soul-everything-comes-from-the-brain-54828.

Penn, Derek C., Keith J. Holyoak, and Daniel J. Povinelli. "Darwin's Mistake: Explaining the Discontinuity Between Human and Nonhuman Minds." *Behavioral and Brain Sciences* 31, no. 2 (2008): 109–30.

Pepperberg, Irene M. "Cognitive and Communicative Abilities of Grey Parrots." *Applied Animal Behaviour Science* 100, nos. 1–2 (2006): 77–86.

Pepperberg, Irene M. "Animal Language Studies: What Happened?," *Psychonomic Bulletin Review* 24 (2017): 181–85.

Pepperberg, Irene M., Suzanne Gray, Shilpa Mody, et al. "Logical Reasoning by a Grey Parrot (*Psittacus erithacus*)? A Case Study of the Disjunctive Syllogism." *Behaviour* 156, no. 5 (2018): 1–37.

Pérez-Manrique, Ana, and Antoni Gomila. "The Comparative Study of Empathy: Sympathetic Concern and Empathic Perspective-Taking in Non-Human Animals." *Biological Review, Cambridge Philosophical Society* 93, no. 1 (2018): 248–69.

Pérez-Manrique, Ana, and Antoni Gomila. "Emotional Contagion in Non-Human Animals: A Review." *WIREs Cognitive Science*, 13 (2021): e1560.

Persson, Tomas, Gabriela-A. Sauciuc, and Elainie A. Madsen. "Spontaneous Cross-species Imitation in Interactions Between Chimpanzees and Zoo Visitors." *Primates* 59, no. 1 (2018): 19–29.

Peterson, Dale. "Those Lying Apes." *Psychology Today*, December 13, 2011. https://www.psychologytoday.com/us/blog/the-moral-lives-animals/201112/those-lying-apes.

Pfeffer, Wilhelm. *Physiologische Untersuchungen*. Leipzig: W. Engelmann, 1873. English: *The Physiology of Plants*, trans. Alfred J. Ewart. Clarendon, 1906.

Pinker, Steven. *The Language Instinct*. Harper Perennial, 2007.

Plato. *Timaeus*. In *The Collected Dialogues of Plato*, edited by Edith Hamilton and Huntington Cairns, and translated by Benjamin Jowett, 1151–1211. Pantheon Books, 1961.

Plotnik, Joshua M., and Frans B. M. de Waal. "Asian Elephants (*Elephas maximus*) Reassure Others in Distress." *PeerJ* 2 (2014): e278.

Povinelli, Daniel J., and Christopher G. Prince. "When Self Met Other." In *Self-Awareness: Its Nature and Development*, edited by Michel Ferrari and Robert J. Sternberg. Guilford Press, 1998.

Povinelli, Daniel J. *Folk Physics for Apes: The Chimpanzee's Theory of How the World Works*. Oxford University Press, 2000.

Povinelli, Daniel J., and Christopher G. Prince. "Can Comparative Psychology Crack Its Toughest Nut?" *Animal Behavior and Cognition* 7, no. 4 (2020): 589–652.

Povinelli, Daniel J., and Jennifer Vonk. "Chimpanzee?," *Trends in Cognitive Sciences* 7, no. 4 (2003): 157–60.

Povinelli, Daniel, and Jennifer Vonk. "We Don't Need a Microscope to Explore the Chimpanzee's Mind." In Hurley, *Rational Animals?*

Premack, Ann J. *Why Chimps Can Read*. Harper & Row, 1976.

Premack, David. *Gavagai: Or the Future History of the Animal Language Controversy*. The MIT Press, 1986.

Premack, David, and Guy Woodruff, "Does the Chimpanzee Have a Theory of Mind?," *Behavioral and Brain Sciences* 1, no. 4 (1978): 515–26.

Preston, Stephanie D., and Frans B. M. de Waal. "Empathy: Its Ultimate and Proximate Bases." *Behavioral and Brain Sciences* 25, no. 1 (2002): 1–71.

Provine, William. "Evolution and the Foundation of Ethics." *MBL Science* 3, no. 1 (1998): 25–29.

Pullum, Geoffrey K. "Koko Is Dead, But the Myth of Her Linguistic Skills Lives On." *The Chronicle of Higher Education*, June 27, 2018.

Purves, William K., Gordon H. Orians, and H. Craig Heller. *Life: The Science of Biology*. 5th ed. Sinauer, 1998.

Quine, Willard V. O. *Word and Object*. Massachusetts Institute of Technology, 1960.

Ramelow, Tilman Anselm. "Language Without Reduction: Aquinas and the Linguistic Turn." *Angelicum* 85, no. 2 (2008): 497–517.

Ramelow, Tilman Anselm. *Beyond Modernism? George Lindbeck and the Linguistic Turn in Theology*. Ars Una, 2005.

Ramilowski, Jordan A., Tatyana Goldberg, Jayson Harshbarger, et al. "A Draft Network of Ligand-Receptor-Mediated Multicellular Signalling in Human." *Nature Communications* 6, no. 7866 (2015), DOI: 10.1038/ncomms8866.

Raymann, Kasie, Céline Brochier-Armanet, and Simonetta Gribaldo. "The Two-Domain Tree of Life Is Linked to a New Root for the Archaea." *Proceedings of the National Academy of Sciences, USA* 112, no. 21 (2015): 6670–75.

Reber, Arthur S. "Sentient Plants? Nervous Minds?," *Animal Sentience* 11, no. 17 (2018), DOI: 10.51291/2377-7478.1307.

Remer, Vincentio. *Summa Philosophiae Scholasticae: Psychologia*. Gregorian University, 1956.

Renard, Henri. *Philosophy of Man*. Bruce Publishing Co., 1948.

Rilling, James K., Jan Scholz, Todd M. Preuss, et al. "Differences Between Chimpanzees and Bonobos in Neural Systems Supporting Social Cognition." *Social Cognitive Affective Neuroscience* 7, no. 4 (2012): 369–79.

Rimpau, James B., R. Allen Gardner, and Beatrix T. Gardner. "Expression of Person, Place, and Instrument in ASL Utterance of Children and Chimpanzees." In Gardner, *Teaching Sign Language to Chimpanzees*.

Rivas, Esteban. "Recent Use of Signs by Chimpanzees (*Pan Troglodytes*) in Interactions with Humans." *Journal of Comparative Psychology* 119, no. 4 (2005): 404–17.

Roma, Peter G., Alan Silberberg, Angela M. Ruggiero, et al. "Capuchin Monkeys, Inequity Aversion, and the Frustration Effect." *Journal of Comparative Psychology* 120, no. 1 (2006): 67–73.

Romero, Teresa, Miguel A. Castellanos, and Frans B. M. de Waal. "Consolation as Possible Expression of Sympathetic Concern Among Chimpanzees." *PNAS* 107, no. 27 (2010): 12110–15.

Romero, Teresa, Miguel A. Castellanos, and Frans B. M. de Waal. "Post-Conflict Affiliation by Chimpanzees with Aggressors: Other-Oriented Versus Selfish Political Strategy." *PLoS ONE* 6, no. 7 (2011): e22173.

Ross, Hugh. "Interstellar Space Travel." In Hugh Ross, Kenneth Samples, and Mark Clark, *Lights in the Sky & Little Green Men*. NAVPRESS, 2002.

Roth-Hananiaa, Ronit, Maayan Davidovb, and Carolyn Zahn-Waxler. "Empathy Development from 8 to 16 Months: Early Signs of Concern for Others." *Infant Behavior & Development* 34, no. 3 (2011): 447–58.

Rumbaugh, Duane M., ed. *Language Learning by a Chimpanzee: The Lana Project*. Academic Press, 1977.

Rumbaugh, Duane. "Reasoning and Language in Chimpanzees." In *Animal Intelligence: Insight into the Animal Mind*, edited by R. J. Hoage and Larry Goldman. Smithsonian Press, 1986.

Rumbaugh, Duane. "Language Behavior of Apes." In Sebeok and Umiker-Sebeok, *Speaking of Apes*.

Rumbaugh, Duane M., and E. Sue Savage-Rumbaugh. "Language in Comparative Perspective." In *Animal Learning and Cognition*, edited by N. J. Mackintosh. Academic Press, 1994.

Rumbaugh, Duane M., Harold Warner, and Ernst von Glasersfeld. "The LANA Project: Origin and Tactics." In Rumbaugh, *Language Learning by a Chimpanzee*.

Rumbaugh, Duane M., and Timothy V. Gill. "Lana's Acquisition of Language Skills." In Rumbaugh, *Language Learning by a Chimpanzee*.

Runyon, Justin B., Mark C. Mescher, and Consuelo M. De Morales. "Volatile Chemical Cues Guide Host Locations and Host Selection by Parasitic Plants." *Science* 313, no. 5795 (2006): 1965–76.

Russell, Connie L., Kim A. Bard, and Lauren B. Adamson. "Social Referencing by Young Chimpanzees (*Pan troglodytes*)." *Journal of Comparative Psychology* 111, no. 2 (1997): 185–93.

Sacks, Oliver. "An Anthropologist on Mars." *The New Yorker*, December 27, 1993.

Saijo, Yusuke, Eliza Po-iian Loo, and Shigetaka Yasuda. "Pattern Recognition Receptors and Signaling in Plant-Microbe Interactions." *The Plant Journal* 93, no. 4 (2018): 592–613.

Salay, Nancy A. "Accepting the Povinelli-Henley Challenge." *Animal Behavior and Cognition* 9, no. 2 (2022): 239–56.

Sanford, Emily M., Emma R. Burt, and Julia E. Meyers-Manor. "Timmy's in the Well: Empathy and Prosocial Helping in Dogs." *Learning & Behavior* 46 (2018): 374–86.

Santamaria, M. Estrella, Ana Arnaiz, Pablo Gonzalez-Melendi, et al. "Plant Perception and Short-Term Responses to Phytophagous Insects and Mites." *International Journal of Molecular Science* 19, no. 5 (2018): 1356.

Savage-Rumbaugh, E. Sue. *Ape Language: From Conditioned Response to Symbol*. Columbia University Press, 1988.

Savage-Rumbaugh, E. Sue. *Kanzi: The Ape at the Brink of the Human Mind*. John Wiley & Sons, 1994.

Savage-Rumbaugh, E. Sue, Duane M. Rumbaugh, and William M. Field. "Language as a Window on Rationality." In Hurley, *Rational Animals?*.

Savage-Rumbaugh, Sue, M. McDonald, R. A. Sevcik, et al. "Spontaneous Symbol Acquisition and Communicative Use by Pygmy Chimpanzees." *Journal of Experimental Psychology: General* 115, no. 3 (1986): 211–35.

Savage-Rumbaugh, Sue, Stuart Shanker, and Talbot J. Taylor. "Apes with Language." *Critical Quarterly* 38, no. 3 (1996): 45–57.

Savage-Rumbaugh, E, Sue, Stuart G. Shanker, and Talbot J. Taylor. *Apes, Language, and the Human Mind*. Oxford University Press, 1998.

Schaller, Susan. *A Man Without Words*. Summit Books, 1991.

Schönborn, Christoph. "Finding Design in Nature." *The New York Times*, July 7, 2005.

Schrödinger, Erwin. *What Is Life? With Mind and Matter and Autobiographical Sketches*. Cambridge University Press, 1992.

Sebeok, Thomas A. "Looking in the Destination for What Should Have Been Sought in the Sources." In Sebeok and Umiker-Sebeok, *Speaking of Apes*.

Sebeok, Thomas A. and Jean Umiker-Sebeok, eds. *Speaking of Apes.* Plenum Press, 1980.

Sebeok Thomas A., and Robert Rosenthal, eds. *The Clever Hans Phenomenon: Communication with Horses, Whales, Apes, and People.* New York Academy of Sciences, 1981.

Seyfarth, Robert M., and Dorothy L. Cheney. "The Evolutionary Origins of Friendship." *Annual Review of Psychology* 63 (2012): 153–77.

"Skin 'Sees' UV Light, Starts Producing Pigment." *News from Brown,* Nov. 3, 2011. https://news.brown.edu/articles/2011/11/melanin.

Song, Young Hun, Jae Sung Shim, Hannah A. Kinmonth-Schultz, et al. "Photoperiodic Flowering: Time Measurement Mechanisms in Leaves." *Annual Review of Plant Biology* 66 (2015): 441–64.

Stock, Michael. "Sense Consciousness According to St. Thomas." *The Thomist* 21, no. 4 (1958): 415–86.

Swartz, Anna. "Orphaned Animals Who Were Adopted by a Different Species." *Dodo,* Jan. 28, 2015. https://www.thedodo.com/inspiring-animal-families-958705512.html.

Swenson, Jr. George W. "Intragalactically Speaking." *Scientific American* 283, no. 1 (2000): 44–47.

Tabaczek, Mariusz. *Emergence: Towards a New Metaphysics and Philosophy of Science.* Notre Dame University Press, 2019.

Taiz, Lincoln, and Eduardo Zeiger. *Plant Physiology.* 2nd ed. Sinauer Associates, Inc., 1998.

Taiz, Lincoln, Daniel Alkon, Adreas Draguhn, et al. "Plants Neither Possess Nor Require Consciousness." *Trends in Plant Science* 24, no. 8 (2019): 677-87.

Taiz, Lincoln, Daniel Alkon, Adreas Draguhn, et al. "Reply to Trewavas et al. and Calvo and Trewavas." *Trends in Plant Science* 25, no. 3 (2020): 218–20.

Tanaka, Masayuki. "Discrimination and Categorization of Photographs of Natural Objects by Chimpanzees (*Pan troglodytes*)." *Animal Cognition* 4 (2001): 201–11.

Telegraph Staff and Agencies. "Mothers Asked Nearly 300 Questions a Day, Study Finds." *The Telegraph,* March 28, 2013. http://www.telegraph.co.uk/news/uknews/9959026/Mothers-asked-nearly-300-questions-a-day-study-finds.html //.

ten Cate, Carel. "Acoustic Communication in Plants: Do the Woods Really Sing?," *Behavioral Ecology* 4, no. 1 (2013): 799–800.

Terrace, H. S., L. A. Petito, R. J. Sanders, et al. "Response: Ape Language." *Science* 211 (1981): 87–88.

Terrace, Herbert S. "Is Problem Solving Language?," In Sebeok and Umiker-Sebeok, *Speaking of Apes.*

Terrace, Herbert S. *Nim.* Columbia University Press, 1987.

Thakur, Ankita, Shalini Verma, Vedukola P. Reddy, et al. "Hypersensitive Responses in Plants." *Agricultural Review* 40, no. 2 (2019): 113–20.

THEFAMOUSPEOPLE. "83 Notable Quotes by Dorothy Day, The Founder of Catholic Worker Movement." https://quotes.thefamouspeople.com/dorothy-day-1255.php.

Theophrastus. *De Causis Plantarum*. Edited and translated by Benedict Einarson and George K. K. Link. Harvard University Press, 1990

Thompson, R. "Habituation." In *International Encyclopedia of the Social and Behavioral Sciences*, edited by Neil J. Smelser and Paul B. Bates, 6458–62. Elsevier Ltd., 2001.

Thompson, Roger K. R., David L. Oden, and Sarah T. Boysen. "Language-Naive Chimpanzees (*Pan troglodytes*) Judge Relations Between Relations in a Conceptual Matching-to-Sample Task." *Journal of Experimental Psychology: Animal Behavior Processes* 23, no. 1 (1997): 31–43.

Tomasello, Michael. "Cultural Transmission in Chimpanzee Tool Use and Signaling?," In "*Language" and Intelligence in Monkeys and Apes*, edited by Sue Taylor Parker and Kathleen Rita Gibson, 27–311. Cambridge University Press, 1990.

Torley, Vincent. "Excursus Plants." http://www.angelfire.com/linux/vjtorley/plants.html.

Twewavas, Anthony. "Aspects of Plant Intelligence: An Answer to Firn." *Annals of Botany* 93, no. 4 (2004): 353–57.

Twewavas, Anthony. "What Is Plant Behaviour?" *Plant, Cell & Environment* 32, no. 6 (2009): 606–16.

van der Vaart, Elske, and Charlotte K. Hemelrijk. "'Theory of Mind' in Animals: Ways to Make Progress." *Synthese* 191 (2014): 335–54.

Vass, Beck. "Mummy, Why Is Your Tummy Fat?," *The New Zealand Herald*, June 5, 2017. http://www.nzherald.co.nz/lifestyle/news/article.cfm?c_id=6&objectid=11870317.

Vestergaard, M., M. Carta, G. Güney, et al. "The Cellular Coding of Temperature in the Mammalian Cortex." *Nature* 614 (2023): 725–31.

Volkov, Alexander G., Tejumade Adesina, Vladislav S. Markin, et al. "Kinetics and Mechanism of *Dionaea muscipula* Trap Closing." *Plant Physiology* 146, no. 2 (2008): 694–702.

von Glasersfeld, Ernst. "The Yerkish Language and Its Automatic Parser." In Rumbaugh, *Language Learning by a Chimpanzee.*

Vonk, Jennifer. "Gorilla (*Gorilla gorilla gorilla*) and Orangutan (*Pongo abelii*) Understanding of First- and Second- Order Relations." *Animal Cognition* 6, no. 2 (2003): 77–86.

Vonk, Jennifer. "Matching Based on Biological Categories in Orangutans (*Pongo abelii*) and a Gorilla (*Gorilla gorilla gorilla*)." *PeerJ* 1, no. 1 (2013): e158.

Ward, Peter D., and Donald Brownlee. *Rare Earth*. Copernicus Books, 2000.

Warneken, Felix, and Michael Tomasello. "Altruistic Helping in Human Infants and Young Chimpanzees." *Science* 311, no. 5765 (2006): 1301–3.

Watson, James B. *Behaviorism*. W. W. Norton & Company, 1970.

Webb, Stephen. *If the Universe Is Teeming with Aliens, Where Is Everybody? Fifty Solutions to Fermi's Paradox and the Problem of Extraterrestrial Life*. Copernicus Books, 2002.

Wellman, Henry M., David Cross, and Julanne Watson. "Meta-Analysis of Theory-of-Mind Development: The Truth About False Belief." *Child Development* 72, no. 3 (2001): 655–84.

Whewell, William. *Of the Plurality of Worlds*. Revised ed. Edited by Michael Ruse. The University of Chicago Press, 2001.

Whitbourne, Susan Krauss. "Psychopaths Don't Care If They Hurt You. This Is Why." *Psychology Today*, June 3, 2017. https://www.psychologytoday.com/us/blog/fulfillment-any-age/201706/psychopaths-dont-care-if-they-hurt-you-is-why.

White, Jacob, and Felipe Yamashita. "*Boquila trifoliolata* Mimics Leaves of an Artificial Plastic Host Plant." *Plant Signaling & Behavior* 17, no. 1 (2022): e1977530.

Whiten, Andrew, and W. R. Byrne. "Tactical Deception in Primates." *Behavioral and Brain Sciences* 11, no. 2 (1988): 233–44.

Wicks, Nadine L., Jason W. Chan, Julia A. Najera, et al. "UVA Phototransduction Drives Early Melanin Synthesis in Human Melanocytes." *Current Biology* 21, no. 22 (November 2011): 1906–11.

Wilcox, Christie. "Can Plants See? In the Wake of a Controversial Study, the Answer's Still Unclear." *New Scientist*, November 30, 2022. https://www.the-scientist.com/news-opinion/can-plants-see-in-the-wake-of-a-controversial-study-the-answer-is-still-unclear-70796.

Wiltschko, Roswitha, and Wolfgang Wiltschko. "The Discovery of the Use of Magnetic Navigational Information." *Journal of Comparative Physiology A: Neuroethology, Sensory, Neural, and Behavioral Physiology* 208, no. 1 (2022): 9–18.

Wimmer, Heinz, and Josef Perner. "Beliefs About Beliefs: Representation and Constraining Function of Wrong Beliefs in Young Children's Understanding of Deception." *Cognition* 13 (1983): 103–28.

Wise, Steven M. *Drawing the Line: Science and the Case for Animal Rights*. Perseus Books, 2002.

Wittgenstein, Ludwig. *Philosophical Investigations*. Translated by G. E. M. Anscombe. MacMillan Publishing Company, 1953.

Woese, Carl R., Otto Kandler, and Mark L. Wheelis. "Towards a Natural System of Organisms: Proposal for the Domains of Archaea, Bacteria, and Eucarya." *Proceedings of the National Academy of Sciences, USA* 87 (1990): 4576–79.

Woese, Carl R. "A New Biology for a New Century." *Microbiology and Molecular Biology Reviews* 68, no. 2 (2004): 173–86.

Wood, James. "Machine That Can Read Your Mind and Convert THOUGHTS into Speech Is Developed by Scientists and Gives Fresh Hope to Stroke Victims." Daily Mail.com, January 29, 2019.

Wynne, Clive D. L. *Do Animals Think?* Princeton University Press, 2004.

Zhang, Xiaoping, Xiaogang Ruan, Yao Xiao, et al. "A Self-Learning Sensorimotor Model Based on Operant Conditioning Theory." 2015 IEEE Advanced Information Technology, Electronic and Automation Control Conference (IAEAC), Chongqing, China (2015): 572–76. DOI: 10.1109/IAEAC.2015.7428618.

Index

D

F

G

H

I

J

K

L

M

N

O

P

Q

R

S

T

U

V

W